# Spitfire Over Everest

# Spitfire Over Everest

## KENNETH D. NEAME

HAYLOFT PUBLISHING

First published by Hayloft Publishing Ltd., 2018

(The first edition of this book was privately printed in 1992 for the author's family)

Text and photographs © the Estate of Kenneth D. Neame, 2018

The right of Kenneth D. Neame to be identified as the Author of the Work has been asserted by him in accordance with the Copyright, Designs and Patents Act 1988

All rights reserved. Apart from any use permitted under UK copyright law no part of this publication may be reproduced, stored in a retrieval system, or transmitted, in any form or by any means without the prior written permission of the publisher, not be otherwise circulated in any form of binding or cover other than that in which it is published and without a similar condition being imposed on the subsequent purchaser.

A CIP catalogue record for this book is available from the British Library

ISBN 978-1-910237-39-7

Designed, printed and bound in the EU

Hayloft policy is to use papers that are natural, renewable and recyclable products and made from wood grown in sustainable forests. The logging and manufacturing processes are expected to conform to the environmental regulations of the country of origin.

Hayloft Publishing Ltd,
a company registered in England number 4802586
2 Staveley Mill Yard, Staveley, Kendal, LA8 9LR (registered office)
L'Ancien Presbytère, 21460 Corsaint, France (editorial office)

Email: books@hayloft.eu
Tel: 07971 352473
www.hayloft.eu

Frontispiece image: Kenneth D. Neame, shortly after gaining his wings.

This book was printed with the offset of carbon emissions and support for Forest Protection in Pará, Brazil.

*To Marion and the family*

# Contents

| | |
|---|---:|
| *Tables* | *ix* |
| *Figures* | *x* |
| *Plates* | *xi* |
| *Preface* | *xiii* |
| *Foreword* | *xiv* |

| | | |
|---|---|---:|
| 1 | How It All Started | 1 |
| 2 | Early Days in the Royal Air Force | 9 |
| 3 | Learning to Fly – The Tiger Moth | 16 |
| 4 | Advanced Flying – The Harvard | 29 |
| 5 | Photo Recce Training – The Spitfire | 39 |
| | Technique of photographic reconnaissance in the Spitfire | |
| | The Course at RAF Benson | |
| 6 | Germany | 54 |
| 7 | India | 73 |
| | The Climate | |
| | The people of India | |
| | Servants and living conditions | |
| | Health | |
| | More of life at Mauripur | |
| 8 | Getting Settled In | 88 |
| | Number 34 Photographic Reconnaissance Squadron | |
| | Round and about Palam | |
| 9 | First Sortie in India | 108 |
| | Sortie to Shahjahanpur | |
| 10 | Further Afield | 119 |
| | Sortie to Indore, Hoshangabad and Lalitpur | |
| | Sorties to Fyzabad and Cawnpore | |
| | To the south of India | |
| | Other sorties | |
| 11 | Low-level Sortie and the Bombay Bibbies | 130 |
| | The smallest of sorties | |
| 12 | Lost! | 141 |
| 13 | Kangchenjunga and Everest | 148 |
| 14 | Everest – The Aftermath | 162 |
| | Mount Everest: Other Flights: | |
| | The Westland-Houston Expedition, 1933 | |
| | Mosquito flight, 1945 | |
| | Indian Air Force flight, 1953 | |
| | Photographic survey, 1984 | |
| | Flights directly over the summit of Mt Everest | |

| | | |
|---|---|---|
| 15 | Wild Hill Country | 169 |
| 16 | Holiday in Kashmir | 180 |
| 17 | The Search (Air-Land Rescue Exercise) | 188 |
| 18 | Farewell to a Spitfire – and to India | 199 |
| | Ferry to Drigh Road; What of the future? Farewell, India! | |
| 19 | Germany again | 212 |

*Postscript* — *221*
*Appendices:* — *223*
*Dates of major postings*
*My medical records*
*Size of units to which I was attached*
*My flying record*
*Analysis of flights during training*
*Flying record in terms of flights*
*Flying record in terms of aircraft*
*Details of aircraft in which I flew*
*General details*
*Technical data of Spitfires*
*Normal maximum weight; Engine; Fuel capacity;*
*Rate of fuel consumption; Range; Flying speeds;*
*Spitfire XIX, my own records*
*Fatal flying accidents of colleagues*

*Glossary* — *235*
*Bibliography* — *248*
*Index* — *252*

# Tables

| | | |
|---|---|---|
| 1 | Training exercises from RAF Benson | 52 |
| 2 | Details of my flights on the Salzgitter Gliding Course | 68 |
| 3 | The journey to Yelahanka and back | 127 |
| 4 | Publication details of text and photographs of Everest flight | 164 |
| 5 | Number of glider flights on each flying day | 215 |
| 6 | Major postings | 223 |
| 7 | Medical records | 224 |
| 8 | Details of personnel of various groups | 225 |
| 9 | Flying time, number of flight in various aircraft during training | 226 |
| 10 | Frequency and duration of flights | 227 |
| 11 | The number of flights and total flying time in various aircraft | 228 |
| 12 | Technical details of aircraft mentioned in the text | 229 |
| 13 | The engines of the various Spitfires | 230 |
| 14 | Fuel capacities of Spitfires XIV and XIX | 231 |
| 15 | Fuel consumption of Spitfires XIV and XIX | 231 |
| 16 | Estimate of range of unpressurized Spitfire XIX | 232 |
| 17 | Flying speeds of Spitfires XIV and XIX | 232 |
| 18 | Relationships between Indicated Airspeed and True Airspeed | 233 |
| 19 | Data from my own flights | 233 |
| 20 | Fatal flying accidents of colleagues | 234 |

## Figures

| | | |
|---|---|---|
| 1 | Runs flown over a target for vertical photography | 42 |
| 2 | Sorties and cross-country flights from RAF Benson | 50 |
| 3 | Practice sorties carried out from Celle | 56 |
| 4 | Map of north India | 74 |
| 5 | Map of Palam airfield | 88 |
| 6 | Jantar Mantar, the ancient observatory in Delhi | 105 |
| 7 | Photographic sorties in India | 109 |
| 8 | First three photo recce sorties in India | 115 |
| 9 | Airfields in India | 121 |
| 10 | Long-distance sortie to the south of India | 126 |
| 11 | Flight in Spitfire XI | 145 |
| 12 | Flights to Kangchenjunga and Everest | 151 |
| 13 | Flights to RAF Samungli | 171 |
| 14 | Areas photographed from RAF Samungli | 173 |
| 15 | Northern hill country | 181 |
| 16 | Search area | 191 |
| 17 | Flights from RAF Wunstorf | 213 |

Additional figures:

| | |
|---|---|
| Oxford | 6 |
| Anson | 7 |
| Hotspur (glider) | 8 |
| Tiger Moth | 18 |
| Harvard II | 30 |
| Master II | 45 |
| Spitfire IX | 47 |
| Spitfire XI | 48 |
| Spitfire VII | 53 |
| Spitfire XIV | 57 |
| Spitfire XIX | 59 |
| Auster | 61 |
| Dakota | 65 |
| SG 38 (glider) | 66 |
| Grunau (glider) | 66 |
| York | 71 |

# Plates

| | | |
|---|---|---|
| 1 | Model of a Tiger Moth | 17 |
| 2 | Author shortly after joining the Royal Air Force as a Cadet, 1944 | 27 |
| 3 | A Harvard in flight | 31 |
| 4 | Bringing a Harvard out on to the airfield | 32 |
| 5 | The crew-room at Cranwell | 33 |
| 6 | The Passing-out Parade at Cranwell | 37 |
| 7 | Number 16 SPR Course at Benson | 41 |
| 8 | The cockpit of the (fighter) Spitfire XIV | 49 |
| 9 | The main street of Celle | 54 |
| 10 | Number 2 Squadron Dispersal at RAF Celle | 55 |
| 11 | Celle Control Tower | 58 |
| 12 | A Spitfire XIX | 60 |
| 13 | A Spitfire XIV | 60 |
| 14 | Daily Inspection on a Spitfire XIV | 62 |
| 15 | Spitfire XIX | 62 |
| 16 | Author with a Spitfire XIV at Celle | 63 |
| 17 | Spitfire XIV taxiing out at Celle | 64 |
| 18 | An SG 38 glider at Salzgitter | 67 |
| 19 | Ruins of Brunswick | 69 |
| 20 | A mad Belgian in a Spitfire XVI | 69 |
| 21 | A colleague at the border | 70 |
| 22 | A street grain-seller in Karachi | 77 |
| 23 | The barber's shop in the street in Karachi | 78 |
| 24 | A goatherd in Karachi | 81 |
| 25 | A street in Karachi | 82 |
| 26 | A scribe on the pavement in Karachi | 85 |
| 27 | Photo reconnaissance picture of Palam airfield | 89 |
| 28 | Flying Control and one of the residential blocks | 90 |
| 29 | Field-Marshal Auchinleck and Lord Louis Mountbatten | 91 |
| 30 | Colleagues off duty | 92 |
| 31 | The Officers' Mess at Palam | 92 |
| 32 | T.-E., Robbie and Johnny Rees | 93 |
| 33 | Johnnie Shukla and Blackie | 94 |
| 34 | Number 34 Squadron | 95 |
| 35 | The squadron char-wallah | 96 |
| 36 | Wheeling out a Spitfire XIX | 97 |

| | | |
|---|---|---|
| 37 | Two Spitfire XIXs at the Dispersal | 98 |
| 38 | Two Spitfire XIXs taking off together | 99 |
| 39 | The remains of Arthur Chin's crash | 99 |
| 40 | Gerry Fray's Spitfire after landing with a burst tyre | 100 |
| 41 | The burst tyre | 100 |
| 42 | Ruins near Palam | 102 |
| 43 | The Viceroy's Palace in New Delhi | 104 |
| 44 | The Taj Mahal, Agra | 107 |
| 45 | Information pamphlet on Palam airfield (side one) | 112 |
| 46 | Information pamphlet on Palam airfield (side two) | 113 |
| 47 | Adapted RAF Navigational Computer: compass ring | 116 |
| 47a | Adapted RAF Navigational Computer: circular slide rule | 117 |
| 48 | The author with a photo reconnaisance friend | 131 |
| 49 | Plot of the reconnaissance photographs of Agricultural Institute | 139 |
| 50 | The flat-topped Gari Parbat and Hathi Parbat | 143 |
| 51 | The Nanda Devi group | 146 |
| 52 | View eastward during the approach to Kangchenjunga | 152 |
| 53 | Looking north over Tibet | 153 |
| 54 | The Kangchenjunga massif, looking west | 155 |
| 55 | Looking down on Kangchenjunga from the north | 156 |
| 56 | Everest from the west | 157 |
| 57 | Everest from the south | 159 |
| 58 | Two of my Everest photographs combined by *The Times* | 163 |
| 59 | Title page of an account of my flight published in Lilliput | 163 |
| 60 | Photograph from *First over Everest* | 168 |
| 61 | The desolation that was Samungli | 175 |
| 62 | Author's Spitfire being refuelled at Samungli | 177 |
| 63 | The Nagin Bagh | 185 |
| 64 | On the way to the Nagin Bagh | 187 |
| 65 | An Indian village photographed from the Auster | 188 |
| 66 | Country railway station photographed from the Auster | 189 |
| 67 | Portion of 16 inches to mile flying map showing Palam & Delhi | 207 |
| 68 | The stern deck of the m.v. *Georgic* | 209 |
| 69 | Going through the Suez Canal | 211 |
| 70 | A weekend stint in the Control Tower at Wunstorf | 214 |
| 71 | An evening on the bottle | 217 |

# *Preface*

In spite of the title, this is not a book about flying over Mount Everest. It is an account of nearly three and a half years when I was in the Royal Air Force during and just after the Second World War. It describes my introduction to the RAF, my entry into it, then my selection as a pilot, the actual training of how to fly an aircraft, and my ending up as a photographic reconnaissance pilot flying Spitfires. The account of the flight to Everest (over whose suimmit I did not actually fly!) is just one of several chapters.

The title arose from a time when I thought that it might be possible to publish these memoirs, but the few publishers I approached were not interested; they didn't even want to look at the text, and I think that this was partly a result of the recession in 1991 which hit publishers rather badly. Anyway, just for fun I have left the title as it was.

The account of my flying days was originally going to be part of a general memoir of my early life, but when I started writing, the RAF part began to get out of hand, and it was clear that it would have to comprise a separate volume in its own right.

Parts of that period are now too hazy in my memory to be able to say anything about them, and many others have so completely disappeared that they might never even have existed, such as practice photographic sorties from RAF Benson (near Oxford) which I know I did only because they are shown in my Flying Log Book, but of most of which I have no memory whatsoever!

However, all was not lost. Not long after the main events described in this book I wrote down detailed accounts of them because the events stood out in my mind as particularly interesting, and I thought it worth keeping a permanent record. Indeed, I must at the time, have considered the possibility of publishing the text since shortly after being demobbed I sent the typescript to the Air Ministry asking for permission to publish it, a request which was granted. But it went no further than that, and those accounts, which comprise the main bulk of Chapters 1-15 and 17-8, have not seen the light of day again until now. It is from them, written long ago, that the detailed descriptions of navigation, of landmarks and of happenings of various kinds are derived, not from memory. I have had to edit them for readability and have removed much of the current RAF slang which was included, but which now appears stilted; otherwise they are still much as I wrote them.

Further detail comes from my Flying Log Book and from numerous photographs taken with my own camera which brought back other memories. The technical data in the appendices come from manuals and books as well as from my own records.

Kenneth Neame, 1992

# *Foreword*

A few years ago I became aware of a slender, elderly gentleman walking slowly and quietly through our little village of Hartley and crossing the field to Kirkby Stephen, shopping bag in hand. He replied courteously if greeted but did not engage in casual conversation. It soon became clear that he was the new occupant of the annexe that Mike Sunderland and Jill Neame had constructed in their house. A notice by the door announced his name 'Dr K D Neame'. He was Jill's father. Shortly afterwards the 'Dr' was removed. Clearly he did not want casual patients.

Then I found myself reading Michael Ward's book *Everest: A Thousand Years of Exploration* – the most comprehensive and informative book ever written about the exploration of the world's highest mountain. My eye was caught by a short paragraph on page 185. It tells how, in 1947, a young Flight Lieutenant K D Neame took photographs of the South Ridge and South Col of the mountain while on 'an unofficial flight' over Everest.

Neame is a relatively uncommon name, and the match of initials was striking. Could it be…? I asked Jill. Yes – and her father had written a book about his experiences in the Royal Air Force at the end of the Second World War. It had never been published, but the family had had it printed in 1992. She had a copy. Would I like to see it?

So the family volume came into my hands, and I was fascinated. It told a story of happenstance and coincidence, of skill and improvisation, and of routine and seized opportunity. Anyone who has been on expeditions or served in the armed forces will probably say that this is indeed the flavour of such a life. But the thread runs through this book. Consider.

Kenneth Neame was coming to the end of his schooldays in 1943, and would shortly need to join the Services. He opted for the Royal Air Force, but by the time his flying training (first in Tiger Moths and then in Harvards) was coming to completion the war was over. Was it all for nothing?

Fortunately the answer was a resounding negative. Pilot Officer Neame found himself training to fly Spitfires for photographic reconnaissance. This, in itself, was nothing new – indeed a chief value of aircraft in the First World War had been for airborne reconnaissance and in the Second World War aerial photography had proved its worth. It was clear that it would be an equally valuable tool in the time of peace, as a guide to reconstruction and development. But – as the account in this book shows – today's sophisticated, computer-controlled, techniques lay far in the future and a lot hinged on the pilot's judgement and skill. The value of a quick wit and improvisation stand out in these pages – especially when Ken Neame, after a short spell in Germany, found himself in pre-partition India in 1946 in the only photo-reconnaissance squadron in the whole sub-continent.

Much of this book is concerned with the time that followed. As you will discover as you read, it was a time of excitement – and also of what those experiencing it probably termed 'hairy moments'. Ken Neame's service nickname was 'Nemesis' – doubtless a play on his surname – but it is also clear that the Fates were kind to him. Getting lost and reaching home with just enough fuel for another 7½ minutes? Flying blind with an unserviceable radio through a monsoon storm? Making an unauthorised sortie into another country to come home with outstanding pictures of the world's greatest mountains – taken one-handed with the Leica jammed against the hood while the other hand grasped the stick and kept the Spitfire level!

The Everest sortie was a splendid example of opportunism. Ken Neame was sent to photograph snowfields on the southern flanks of the Himalayas, because scientists wanted to assess their potential as sources of water for irrigation. How, then, did he find himself over the southern flanks of Everest? Well, the snowfields were partly clouded out – but the high peaks were clear… and 'with Everest only 100 miles away, plenty of petrol and my own camera, could I go back?' The fact that he had no authorisation to fly deep into Nepal clearly did not trouble him. Instead he swung north over Kangchenjunga and west over Makalu (both duly snapped) to take the first ever clear photographs of the South Col and the South Ridge by which Hillary and Tensing were eventually to reach the summit of Everest. Next day the weather over the snowfields was clear, so the 'official' mission was duly accomplished – and nothing, of course, was said about the unofficial one until Neame had left the RAF!

Officialdom was unhelpful when he did tell the Air Ministry the story in 1948. Permission to publish the photographs was refused until 1951 when they were among those used by the Royal Geographical Society to compile a new and accurate map of the Everest group. They were pored over by Eric Shipton, about to explore the southern side of the mountain, and appeared as a spread across the back page of *The Times*. The photographer was un-named, although by then Ken Neame had left the RAF and was a medical student in London.

This book is about far more than this single exploit. It records what it was like to undertake aerial photography all over India using what we would now consider highly primitive equipment, mounted in aircraft designed as fighters rather than camera platforms. Yet it is clear that Ken Neame loved Spitfires, awkward beasts though they could be, and this book gives a clear insight into their versatility in tasks for which they were certainly never intended.

And afterwards? You would never guess it from these pages, but Ken Neame went on to have a distinguished career as a physiologist, specialising in the transport of amino acids across membranes! But that, as he would have asserted, is another story…

Martin Holdgate
Hartley, Cumbria, October 2017

*The aeroplane has unveiled for us the true face of the earth*

Antoine de Saint Exupery (1900-44)

# 1

## How It All Started

*Conscription, which had been used in the First World War, was restarted in 1939. By 1942, all males, with some exceptions, between 18 and 51 years of age were liable to be called up for military duty. The age range was reduced in 1948 to 17-21 year old males, who were expected to serve in the armed forces for 18 months (National Service). This ended in 1960.*

The Second World War had been going for four years, and I was at school with a year still to run. The time was coming when I would have to think about joining one of the Services. If I did nothing about it I would be conscripted and be told where to go and what to do – the Army, perhaps, or even down the coal-mines with the Bevin Boys if my luck was down. On the other hand, volunteering before they got your hands on you often gave you a better choice.

I had decided which arm of the Services I preferred: the Royal Air Force. I looked upon them as being more civilized than the Army; they wore shoes, and not boots, or so I thought, and I did not like wearing boots – horrible clumpy things, but I found out later to my disgust that they did wear boots. The Navy didn't get a look in. To add to my chances and because it was the obvious thing to do I joined the school Air Training Corps which instructed would-be candidates for RAF aircrew in the elements of flight, aircraft recognition and so on.

At that time the RAF had a scheme whereby aircrew candidates with suitable academic qualifications could, before joining the Air Force proper, spend six months studying a University Short Course. This consisted of a mixture of Air Training Corps training, and university work which covered the first year of the academic syllabus. It was a kind of sideways entry with a view to getting a commission in the RAF, and required a special RAF interview before you could be accepted. To qualify you had to have five credits in the School Certificate examination (somewhat similar to GCSEs) and luckily I had these. It sounded like a good idea, so I applied – it was all part of the concept of volunteering.

A squadron leader came to the school to interview those wanting to go into the RAF. He asked questions concerning my school life and also what type of aircrew I wanted to be. In common with everyone else I wanted to be a pilot, but I believed that a pilot had not only got to be a good all-rounder, but more particularly he had to be good at sports – a belief which was the result of the general brainwashing at the school that it was team games that mattered, and to hell with academic work; if you were good at games you were 'made', but if you were not you were 'out', however bright you might be. I was definitely 'out' and so I concluded that I was not the stuff of which pilots are made. I therefore decided that I had better aim at something for which I did have a chance and which would also be interesting, so I told the squadron leader that I wanted to be a navigator. To my delight I passed the interview.

The next thing was to go up to London for an aircrew medical examination at Euston House, a building taken over by the Air Ministry. I did not think that I had much chance of passing since I knew that the medical was stiff. I set off, rather apprehensive about what kind of an ordeal I would be put through, but there were two others from the school going as well, so at least I didn't feel lonely.

At Euston House they put us through numerous examinations which I had never come across, such as testing reflexes, checking for colour blindness, making us blow into a tube to support a column of mercury as long as possible – I managed to do this for about a minute – as well as carrying out standard medical tests. This was the first really comprehensive medical that I had ever had, and it was quite formidable. Somewhere in the middle of it I was rather scared when I caught sight, through an open door, of one candidate having a long needle being pushed up his nose; to this day I still do not know what that was all about, but at least it turned out not to be part of the routine examination. The whole thing took two or three days, but all three of us passed, to the amazement of everybody back at school. The results of the examination classed me as fit for any category of aircrew (see Table 7 in the Appendices).

Finally I had to go for a special interview for the University Short Course at Adastral House in London, the main Air Ministry building. When I went in for the interview I was given a hard chair to sit on and found myself facing three RAF officers across a wide table. They seemed to me at the time to be of very high rank, but I suspect that they were probably no more than squadron leaders. Unfortunately I had never been briefed at school on what to expect at such an interview, so the whole thing was rather daunting. Luckily most of the questions were fairly straightforward, but the one that seemed to matter most to the examiners floored me. This was 'What are the important qualities of a leader?' The word leader had hardly entered my vocabulary at that time, and I just had no idea. I hummed and hawed and made various guesses, such as 'He must be good at his job', but this was clearly not what they were looking for. It was only after a great deal of priming and hinting and almost being told the answer that I eventually got somewhere near it, which in essence was 'He must always put the welfare of his men first.' Somehow I passed.

I had passed both medical examination and interview, but I felt that I had barely scraped through. I was now sworn in, to the effect that I would be loyal to King and Country and not divulge State Secrets, etc. So it was that on 15 November 1943, I officially became a member of the RAFVR (Royal Air Force Volunteer Reserve), a branch of the RAF which in peacetime consisted of those who served only part-time at weekends. In this case it was because we had volunteered instead of being drafted, but by the time I had finished my flying training the use of the term RAFVR seemed to have disappeared and we all considered ourselves RAF.

Before leaving Adastral House I once again had to put down what type of aircrew I wanted to be. I still believed that I fell short of the requirements for being a pilot, so again I put down navigator. A pilot to me was still some kind of superman; little did I know that learning actually to fly an aeroplane is really not much more difficult than learning to drive a car.

I had one term left at school and during this I learned that I would be going to the University Short Course at Durham University; this would last from April to September of the following year. With my experience of England mostly limited to the southern counties I looked upon Durham as being at the back of beyond, but I was in for a pleasant surprise.

## Durham – The RAF University Short Course

That final school term came to an end almost before I was ready for it. It was followed by ten days' holiday at my home in Kent before starting on the lonesome journey to Durham with a queer feeling in the pit of my stomach. My father came all the way to St Pancras Station in London to see me off into the wide world.[1] Almost his last words were to warn me about the dangers of cocktails, but this was rather lost on me since in my sheltered innocence I hardly knew what a cocktail was!

The journey north, like so many which were to follow in the next few years, broke new ground. On the western side of England I had once been as far north as the Lake District, but on the eastern side no further north than Suffolk. I was expecting to see the Durham countryside to be flat and dull, but I was surprised to find that it was quite hilly and attractive and with little sign of the coal mines that I was expecting.

If you arrive by train, Durham can be spellbinding, and I was enchanted with the place from the start. The station itself is high on a hillside with a vista overlooking the town. The sight is dramatic. The ground falls steeply away to the town below and your gaze is immediately arrested by the sight of the splendour of the cathedral and castle standing on the high ground beyond.

After I had got off the train I found that there were one or two others also going to the university, all of us having been told to report to its administrative centre at Durham Castle. So we all set off together on foot down the steep road into the town – a place of steep hills and cobbled streets – with my bicycle, which I had brought with me, bumping about on the cobbles. We walked over the bridge which spans the River Wear and then up the hill on the other side along the main street which became narrower and more twisting until it eventually opened out into the main square of the city. In a little stone kiosk in the middle of this square was a policeman directing the traffic with the help of mirrors; these enabled him to see any traffic out of sight round the narrow corners leading into the square.

Round to the right we went up another cobbled hill hemmed in with old shops, until we came out on to a large flat green surrounded by university buildings. These were dominated by Durham Cathedral, tall and majestic, on the left and the castle, chunky and mediaeval, on the right. Thirty-five years later when I next visited Durham I found that although the castle and cathedral were still as I remembered them, the city itself had lost much of its charm through so-called development, with chain stores and ugly

---

1 Dates of the various periods connected with the RAF are given in Table 6 in the Appendices.

modern buildings replacing many of the old attractive ones.

We had to report to the castle office to sign in. We were issued with black academic gowns and sent, now as genuine undergraduates, to our two respective colleges, those for University College being accommodated in the castle itself, and those for Hatfield College in residential buildings around the green or in neighbouring streets.

I was sent with Claude Mason, another cadet (as we were to be called) to Cosins Hall, a house looking directly on to the green. We each had separate rooms; Claude was half-way up the building with a bedroom and sitting-room, and I was right at the top with the same. I have never discovered whether this palatial accommodation was normal for Durham students or whether it was because most were now in the Forces.

There were sixty of us on the course and we were divided up into arts and science groups. We did Air Squadron work for two whole days each week, the remaining three and a half being occupied with university studies. We were kept at it for the whole six months; not a moment did we have to ourselves during working hours, nor was there a vacation, but it was so enjoyable that we never felt overworked.

The academic subjects were limited to a set curriculum for each group, and probably depended on which of the university staff remained after many had gone into the Forces. I chose science, which consisted of mathematics, physics and geology; English must also have been included since I still have some English essays which I wrote. In view of the School Certificate requirements for getting on to the course, we were all at more or less the same standard. The mathematics and physics therefore started at a fairly advanced level, the mathematics taking us through calculus – which I never managed to get to grips with – and the physics taking us up to atomic theory, including ionic discharge and X-rays. The geology, though, started at a basic level and was taught exceedingly well and entertainingly by two lecturers. One was L. R. Wager, who was among those to climb highest in the 1933 Mt Everest expedition and was a delightful and approachable person; the name of the other I forget, but he talked so often of the delights of the limestone area of Ingleborough (near Ingleton in Yorkshire) that we gave him the name Ingleborough Jack.

The Air Training Corps part of the course was excellent, and took place in one of the newer university buildings in the countryside beyond the River Wear.[2] It consisted of detailed instruction in theory of flight, navigation, aircraft recognition, and the mechanism of the piston engine. One memorable demonstration was designed to show that a petrol/air mixture in the cylinder of a combustion engine does not explode, as is a common belief, but rather burns rapidly from the point of ignition across the whole mixture. A long glass tube was filled with a suitable mixture which was then ignited at one end; the flame simply travelled smoothly but rapidly from one end to the other.

For this part of the course we had to wear RAF uniform, consisting of RAF blue battledress and fore-and-aft caps with a white flash in the front which signified aircrew under training. We had to march everywhere in columns, and while we did so we sang,

---

2 Details of the personnel involved in the Air Squadron and in organisations to which I later belonged are given in Table 8 in the Appendices.

at the tops of our voices, the typical bawdy songs of the time. Although I have always looked upon them as Service songs, none of us could have picked them up in the Services since we had all come straight from school. I still remember parts of the particularly catchy ones. To make the picture complete here are the first verses of two of them.

Song 1:   *Cats on the rooftops, cats on the tiles,*
          *Cats with syphilis, cats with piles,*
          *Cats with their arseholes wreathed in smiles,*
          *As they revel in the joys of copulation…*

Song 2    *The village magician he was there,*
          *He made a magic pass,*
          *He pulled his foreskin over his head,*
          *And vanished up his arse…*

They were all sung to well-known tunes, that of *D'ye ken John Peel* accompanying the first one. Another favourite was the ballad *Eskimo Nell*, but because of its length it was seldom heard and could only be recited by those with a sufficiently retentive memory. These songs were repeated on and off mostly during my early flying training and then seemed to disappear; I do not recall ever hearing them later on in Squadron life. It must be that initially they were something novel, and then they eventually became old hat and rather mundane.

As part of the Air Training Course we sometimes went to RAF Ouston, an airfield to the west of Newcastle-upon-Tyne, to get some practical flying experience. The airfield must have been a Communications and Training Centre, since the aircraft in which we flew were Ansons, Oxfords and Hotspur gliders. The first two were twin-engined communications 'planes which could carry passengers, but the Hotspur was a glider for training Army pilots who would later be flying the much larger Horsa troop-carrying gliders. It was all very exciting since as far as we were concerned this was what life was really all about.

The flights in the Anson and Oxford were aimed at teaching us to map-read from the air. This was far from straightforward, since from above everything suddenly appeared in much more detail than when seen from the ground, so that at first it was difficult to match ground and map, but we eventually began to pick out what was important and what to ignore. The flights were too few, though, to be able to learn much that was really useful.

There was a great difference between the Oxford and the Anson, the Oxford being more like a race-horse, fairly fast but with a few unpleasant tricks up its sleeve, whereas the Anson was much more like a cart-horse, rather lumbering, but it was lovely to be in and safe as houses. Pilots who flew both always preferred the Anson.

I learned that a cousin of mine, Geoffrey Neame, a pilot in the RAF, was stationed at RAF Ouston flying Ansons and Oxfords. After some persuasion I managed to get him to take us up in an Oxford. He too thought little of flying it compared with the more docile Anson. As he remarked: 'The snag about flying an Oxford after an Anson is that the wheel and flap levers are the opposite way round, and I might whip the wheels up after landing in mistake for the flaps!'

On that flight Geoffrey was second pilot to Flight Lieutenant Uberoi, one of our regular pilots, who flew us across to Carlisle. He gave us each a ¼ inch map and told us to map-read. With our lack of experience none of us had a clue. I now remembered the words of a pilot instructor back in the Air Training Corps: 'Too many people map-read by looking over the side all the time and wondering where they are. The correct way is to find out when various pinpoints are going to turn up, and then put the map away until they are just about due – only then do you need to get the map out.' Very true – provided that you yourself have arranged the flight plan and know what is coming up and when. But it

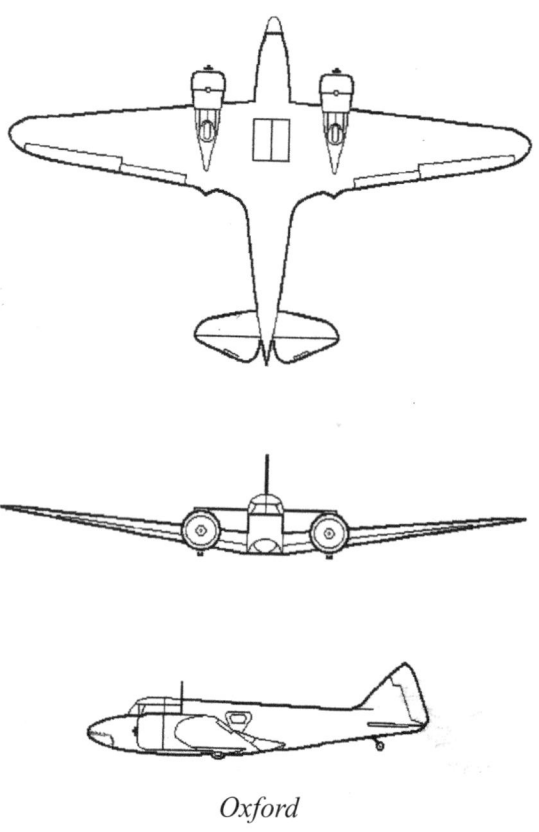

*Oxford*

is not much use if you are a mere passenger and have no idea of the details of the route. I certainly got hopelessly muddled until I could eventually identify Carlisle ahead.

On that particular trip one of us had had rather a large lunch which resulted in his being airsick. That made all of us feel a bit peculiar as well, and after we had landed even Uberoi remarked that he didn't feel too good, although that may have been more to console us than anything else.

The gliding trips were great fun. The Hotspur was towed by a Dakota to about one or two thousand feet and then released to glide down and land again on the airfield. These flights were made more intriguing by the lack of engine noise; there was just the rush of the slipstream over the wings and fuselage followed by a bump, bump, rumble on landing.

The officer officially in charge of the Air Squadron at Durham was a rather bumbly sort of person, but the one who really ran the squadron was the adjutant, Flight Lieutenant Watson, a formidable looking officer of the old school with greying hair and a clipped moustache. My first impression was of a fearsome and distant person, but he turned out to be one of the kindest and most considerate of men and could not do too much for us. He arranged some unorthodox trips, one being down a working coal mine at Easington, and another to watch a ship being launched at one of the shipyards in

Sunderland. His great aim in life seemed to be to get us to see as much of the world as possible 'for the furtherance of your education', as he would say. A great man.

The visit to Easington Colliery was fascinating, since of course none of us had ever been down a coal mine, and few people other than miners ever get the chance. It was quite an experience to descend in the fast-moving lift, and then walk along the electrically-lit tunnels right up to the coal face.

The ship launch was intriguing. There were neither the crowds nor the pomp normally associated with launchings, since this was just an ordinary cargo ship, and potential audiences would be serving elsewhere in various capacities in the war. So it was only the local dockyard workers whom we joined to watch the great hull slide majestically, funnel-less, down the slipway after all the props had been knocked away, eventually to float quietly out in the River Wear.

Flight Lieutenant Watson also encouraged us to get out into the world on our own, so one Bank Holiday weekend Claude Mason and I decided to pay a visit, our first ever, to Scotland. We took our bicycles by train to Edinburgh and then on to Perth; from there we cycled to Dunkeld, along Loch Tay, and back to Perth again by way of Loch Earn. The weather was superb the whole time. Before we left Perth we bought some freshly baked bread, and tied it to the carrier of one of the bicycles. It was so good that we simply tore hunks from the loaf as we cycled along, satisfying our greed with this delicious food. We stopped for the night at a Youth Hostel on the road running along Loch Tay; it was not very comfortable, since for mattresses we had crunchy crinkly straw palliasses. That evening we walked up the hill behind the hostel in the warm still air, only to discover the menace of the midges which plague Scotland; but the beauty of the countryside certainly made me want to go back there.

Sometimes at weekends I would cycle off on my own and explore the surrounding countryside, going through the mining villages and past the collieries, occasionally getting as far as the Pennine dales, with their beautiful valleys, streams and high moorland.

Durham had, and still had when I last visited it, an ice skating rink, and it was here that I spent much of my spare time. I did not know the first

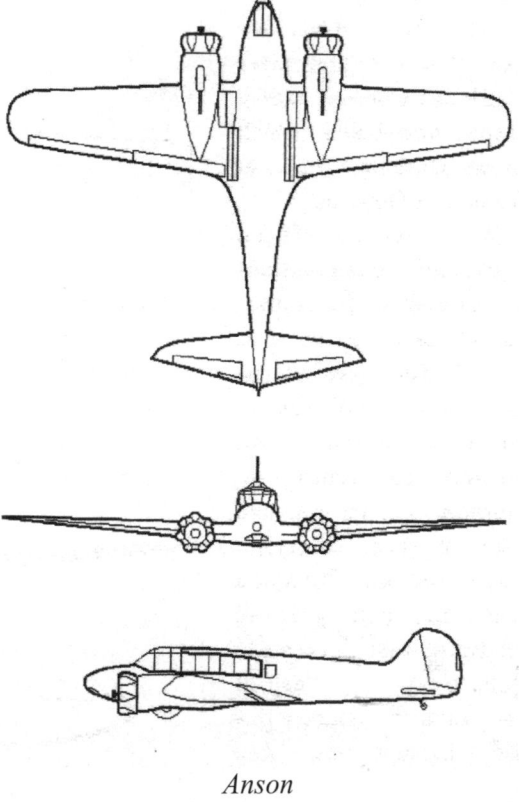

*Anson*

thing about skating, but on only our second evening at Durham, Claude and I went there to try our hand at it. The rink was under a huge marquee, and we could hire skates and boots for about a shilling a time, but they were terrible and flopped all over the place. I managed to get unsteadily on to the ice, slipping and slithering, holding on to the wooden barrier to stop myself from falling over and eventually decided that I was not much good at it.

However, I discovered that my father possessed some old skates with boots attached, so I asked if he would send them to me – and what a difference they made! From then on I progressed by leaps and bounds, particularly when I could get some sense of balance and eventually venture on to the ice unsupported. I made no attempt to acquire anything like a good standard, but simply enjoyed going round and round the rink at high speed.

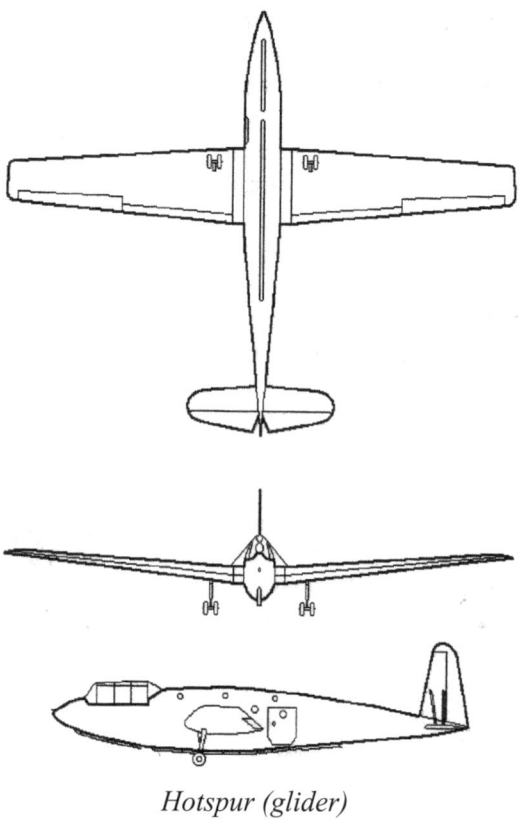

*Hotspur (glider)*

Those were happy, carefree days, but eventually the course came to an end with a formal Passing-out Parade. An Air Commodore, no less, came to inspect us, and made a speech after we had first marched round the university green. Then we had to cheer him after which a course photograph was taken which shows Durham Cathedral rising up behind us.

We took the official university examinations at the end of the course, and all, or almost all of us passed. This gave us the Inter-BSc qualification, which meant that if we wanted to return to Durham after the war and take a full university course, we were exempted from the first year of study. It was never made quite clear from which of the university courses this did exempt us, and although I had passed physics and maths, I doubt whether I could have coped with a second year university level in these subjects later on. In fact, I doubt whether anybody took the qualification seriously; it just provided a satisfactory ending to an enjoyable time.

The next stage in our lives, after first going home for a fortnight's leave, was to report to what was known as the Aircrew Receiving Centre, in Torquay, where we were to join the RAF proper. The task of arranging the details of how we were to get there had been given to the Senior Cadet, Ian Sutherland, to work out after we had left, and he would later contact us at our various homes.

# 2

## Early Days in the Royal Air Force

Ian sent each of us a postcard giving a date and time to meet again so that we could all report together at the Aircrew Receiving Centre (ACRC). The final part of the journey to Torquay by train was beautiful, the line wandering along the coastline much of the way and passing through lovely scenery, the engine occasionally puffing its way through short tunnels cut through the coastal cliffs.

We had to make our way to an address in Babbacombe, a suburb of Torquay, which was the headquarters of Number 7 Aircrew Receiving Centre. There we joined others like us, all in civilian clothes, and filled in form after form with personal details. We were then split into small groups called flights, and each flight given an intake number. I was one of eight in a flight called B whose full title was Number 2B/30/30, where 2 represented the Squadron, B the Flight, the first 30 the number of the intake as a whole, and the second 30 the Wing, where Wing, Squadron and Flight represent progressively smaller subdivisions. These names had nothing to do with flying; they were just the standard titles of RAF subdivisions.

We of B Flight were then marched to our billet, Widdecombe Cot, a two-storey detached house with four rooms on each floor, presumably commandeered from some unfortunate owner. There we met up with several other flights, all from short courses at either Durham, Oxford or Cambridge. Those of us from Durham kept together in a couple of rooms upstairs. Several other houses in the area had also been commandeered by the RAF, our food and mail being supplied at a building further up the hill called Heywood Tower, while beyond were two or three more billets.

We were referred to as cadets, i.e. aircrew in training, but our rank was Aircraftman Second Class (AC2), the lowest possible. As potential aircrew we were distinguished by a white flash tucked into the front of our forage caps.

This period at Torquay, which would last eight weeks, was both an initiation period to prepare us for life in the RAF and a selection period to sort out the sheep from the goats, but we also had our quota of parades, with routine drilling or square-bashing, and a great deal of marching from one place to another and back again. During one of these marches along the sea front we were surprised to see a man swimming in the rather rough water – and this in November!

Every morning we got up at a quarter to six, marched up the hill to breakfast, and then back again to make up our beds in the age-old fashion of the lowest of the low in the Services, dismantling the bedding and then piling the biscuits – square mattress pieces – on top of each other, surrounding them with blankets, and shoving a bolster, tin hat and a few more oddments on top. We would then give a last vain polish to the brass buttons with the RAF eagle on them which never seemed to come up shiny enough, before marching off again up the hill – with Dartmoor showing faintly in the distance through the pine trees – ready to start the day's duties. Those early morning marches were enhanced by the most glorious sunrises over the sea, better than any sunset.

Shortly after our arrival we were kitted out with all the uniform and other clothing that we needed, together with a kitbag, on which we had to paint our name and number in large letters, and irons, consisting of knife, spoon, fork and cup, which we used at all meals as long as we remained in the lowest rank. We washed these irons in a huge communal tub of scalding water after each meal.

The food was mediocre institutional stuff, so we were always glad to get off duty in the evenings for a good tuck-in in the town. The official centre for entertainment and food was the Navy, Army and Air Force Institutes Club (NAAFI), a massive place used also occasionally as a theatre, but it had a depressing atmosphere, and so we seldom went there. Our favourite place for food was the Toc H (see Glossary) up a side alley, where they served superb mixed grills of scrambled eggs, tomatoes, bacon, fried bread and so on, so that I have always since had a soft spot for that organization.

As part of the initiation routine we were given jabs, or injections, against tetanus and typhoid, vaccination against smallpox, and a blood test to determine our blood groups (see Table 7 in the Appendix). Shortly afterwards we were issued with identity discs for wearing round our necks at all times – a flat hexagonal piece of what looked like pressed fibre, with name and number on one side and blood group on the other. There were also some signals and anti-gas training, with rifle shooting and physical training (PT) thrown in for good measure, but these were not taken seriously, since we were there mainly for being sorted out rather than for training.

The corporal in charge of our Flight, whom we called Robbie, was one of those cockneys who understand what makes people tick, since he was always friendly, yet knew just where to draw the line between firmness and leniency. He was not a confirmed disciplinarian, and always made us feel that he was on our side, yet he never abused his position. He told us that he had been pushed into the job by force of circumstances – whatever that might mean. He would do anything he could for us, as well as turning a blind eye on our misdemeanours, and quite often managed to get us off PT classes, which were our pet hate. The commanding officer (CO), on the other hand, was the opposite; he never turned a blind eye on anything, and frequently gave us short lectures on discipline, morals and bad language, which never had any effect on anybody.

Towards the end of our time at Torquay we all had to go to the Grand Hotel on the sea front – also commandeered by the RAF – to take 'aptitude tests', which to us were the most important part. These were the so-called intelligence tests together with special tests for co-ordination and manual dexterity. It was these tests which would decide our future.

The various categories for which we were being tested were pilot, navigator, flight engineer, radio operator and air gunner, and the aptitude tests were supposed to show into which category we best fitted. Although there is much scepticism these days about 'intelligence tests' the ones which we took were quite comprehensive and for want of anything better were probably the best that could be done in the time available. Initially we had to fill in a form to say what type of aircrew we wanted to be. This time I switched from my erstwhile choice of navigator, and thought that, since there was no longer anything to lose, I would put down 'pilot'.

The written tests consisted of many pages of mathematical, word and figure problems, as well as problems on shapes and patterns, which became harder as you went through the pages. The tests for co-ordination involved mostly an oscilloscope with a moving bright spot on it; using levers worked by hands and feet you had to keep the spot as near as possible to a cross in the centre of the screen. Eventually the results of these tests were announced, and I found to my delight that I had been selected for training as a pilot.

Before leaving Torquay we went to hear a speech by some high-up person from the Air Ministry: 'You are the cream of Britain's youth and after the war some of you will want to stay on in the RAF with permanent commissions. So it has been decided that certain of those who apply will be selected for a special accelerated course for training in the UK [most training was at that time being carried out overseas in Canada, the USA and Africa]. This will only apply, however, to those who have been selected for pilot training. Interviews for the course will take place at RAF Bridgnorth, where you will be going after some leave… etc., etc.'

At that time there was a glaring anomaly over commissions which was never resolved during the war, not all aircrew in highly responsible positions were commissioned officers; some pilots, for example, were sergeants. This could produce the embarrassing situation in which the pilot of, say, a Lancaster bomber, who was in charge of the aircraft, might be a sergeant, while the flight engineer under him might be a commissioned officer, i.e. of superior rank. It also meant that colleagues on operations might not be able to meet afterwards in the Mess, the Officers' Mess and the Sergeants' Mess being quite separate.

When the results of the aptitude tests had been announced we went home for Christmas, having to report back on 1st January 1945 to RAF Bridgnorth, a transit camp, to be interviewed for the accelerated course. Eventually we arrived as a group at Bridgnorth Railway Station where we had to form up as if on parade and then wait for a good half hour wearing full packs and equipment before moving off on a march of about three miles in the dark, including a stiff climb up the hill opposite the town, to the RAF camp on the top.

Next morning we woke up to find ourselves in the most miserable camp I ever encountered; it was not only desolate, but being on top of a hill it was very windy, and in January that was not pleasant. It was composed entirely of temporary huts and looked like a concentration camp. Luckily we only had to stay there for two weeks, so we decided that we could put up with anything for that short time. I paid a visit to the site many years later to see what had eventually become of it. It had been turned into an industrial estate of the most tawdry-looking kind, and I decided that there must be a jinx on the place.

The atmosphere of the camp was not helped by an unpleasant commanding officer who hated us as much as we hated him. Into the bargain we had to do night sentry duty, sleeping in an isolated hut with two 2-hour spells of duty shared alternately with a colleague – cold and depressing in midwinter. But one evening we saw a fire somewhere in the camp, so wandered over to have a look, to find the Officers' Mess blazing away merrily. That cheered us up no end in that depressing place, since we hated officers on principle.

It was at Bridgnorth that I first encountered the belief in the Services that bromide was put into the drinking water to reduce sexual drive. How this idea arose I cannot imagine, but it seemed to be universal, and it would not surprise me if it was a carry-over from the First World War when some peculiar ideas existed.

We eventually had our interviews, and it turned out that there was to be an understanding, which they called a 'gentleman's agreement', that if we got on to the accelerated course and were then commissioned we were put on our honour to stay in the RAF on a Short Service Commission for four years, at the end of which the appointment might be made permanent. It was at this time that I had second thoughts about my original choice of career which I had been working towards while at school. This was farming, and I suddenly realized that I was really not keen on it after all. The RAF seemed to provide the perfect alternative if I could make the grade, so I said that I would be glad to stay in, and that I would take the risk that I might not be given a permanent commission. The rest of the interview consisted of a few more leadership-type questions, but by now I had begun to know the kind of answers required and had no further difficulty.

At the time of the interview at Bridgnorth I genuinely intended to stay in the RAF after the war. However, since I had only been in the Service for about two months in wartime, I knew little about its peacetime guise, and several months later on after the war had ended I began to see how things might change as peacetime conditions took over. It was clear that the amount of flying would decrease and the amount of bullshit and discipline would increase. In addition, as I myself climbed the ladder of promotion there would be more and more administrative duties and less and less flying. I eventually came to the conclusion that such a life was really, after all, not for me.

In addition, if I was not in the end given a permanent commission it would mean leaving the RAF after the four years with nothing at all to fall back on – which seemed rather a one-sided bargain. This decision was later vindicated in several ways. Firstly, I began to experience peacetime bull just before getting demobbed, and did not like it one bit. Secondly, the amount of flying was by then beginning to be reduced and thirdly, there were financial cuts several years after the end of the war, and a number of officers on permanent commissions were thrown out. I have also discovered that the social life in the peacetime Air Force, particularly of married personnel, is unpleasantly hidebound with extremes of class distinction, as I believe it is in all the Services; for example, wives whose husbands are on one level of rank cannot fraternize with those on another level. In the wartime Air Force this hardly existed.

There is one other point which can only be seen in retrospect. If I had stayed on for a short service commission and had then had to leave the Service I would not have been able to get an education grant of the type which I was later given for my further education; indeed, the chances of admission to higher education itself would also then have not been so good. At the time when I left the RAF, preference for entry into universities was given to those who had entered the Services from school and who were demobbed at the normal time; that advantage would probably have disappeared after I had served for a further four years.

Three or four days after the interviews we heard the results. I had got through, but those who had either failed the interview or were unwilling to accept the terms would be departing in the near future for normal flying training overseas, most of them going to Canada. We heard later that their training was stopped just before they got their Wings when the war in the Far East ended, which we all thought rather a shabby trick. Those of us who had passed the interview and accepted the conditions were able to complete our training and eventually entered Squadron service in the early peacetime Air Force.

I now had to say goodbye to many friends from the days at Durham. Those of us who had passed the interview were sent for a month's course at Aircrew Officers School, a part of RAF Credenhill about four miles north-west of Hereford. This school normally ran courses for toughening up commissioned aircrew of some standing who might have lost touch with RAF discipline on the ground. We ourselves were unusual in being put through the school before we had even flown, let alone been commissioned. The course we entered was a concentrated but enjoyable slog which covered RAF law and other facets of administration together with a lot of hard physical work of various kinds.

We now wore yellow and white shoulder flashes to show that we were officers under training, in addition to the white flash in our caps showing that we were aircrew under training. We were the first cadets to attend the Aircrew Officers School, and were wholeheartedly disapproved of by the aircrew officers who were on their own separate courses. Apart from the fact that we were an innovation we were much too keen for their liking. We were too smart, and our marching was too disciplined. What they also disliked was that we, although no more than embryo officers, were treated as if we were already fully-fledged, even to the extent of eating in the Officers' Mess; that really rankled! Indeed, we never again inhabited an Airmen's or Other Ranks Mess. In our turn we disapproved of the scruffiness of those officers – we felt that they could all do with a bit of smartening up.

We were split up into Flights and Squadrons, and each of us in turn took charge of our own flight and also of the whole squadron, acting as our own non-commissioned officers (NCOs). There were three squadrons: two of these consisted of those from the university air squadrons of the summer of 1944, while the third was composed of some from the year before who had up to now been relegated to mundane jobs like motor transport (MT) driving.

Our squadron commanding officer was probably a misfit for the kind of course that we were on. He was of the sympathetic and fatherly sort, but really didn't do much. In contrast, his superior – in charge of the Wing (all three squadrons) – was keen as mustard and tried to make us the same. He had short, sharp staccato speech and looked as if he had been made for the Navy. Although a slave-driver, he earned our respect since it was clear that he had our interests at heart.

The NCO in charge of our squadron was a remarkable corporal by the name of Holt. He was an ex-sergeant of the Guards, and was the most well-turned-out and efficient man I ever came across. Unlike the stereotyped disciplinarian he was admired and respected by all of us. He knew all the secrets of bull from A to Z and would go out of his way to help us whenever he could.

Lastly, but by no means the least, was our RAF Regiment officer who was with us at all times and went by the name of MacFee. Unlike the others he was really unpleasant. He was short in stature – so that he was given the nickname of the Wee MacFee – and he was always pushing us around, telling us off for this, telling us off for that, telling us that this was wrong and that was wrong. His motto was 'Now, gentlemen [they all called us 'gentlemen'] it's the little things that count' and off he would go with his quick short step to the head of the marching column to tell off somebody who was not holding his rifle properly. We got a lot of amusement from watching his antics.

We learned a great deal at Aircrew Officers School, and enjoyed most of what we did there. There was of course the routine marching and rifle drill, an assault course and physical training. We also did a lot of fieldcraft, much of it to do with rope: splicing it, coiling it, plaiting it, knotting it, and finally using it along with wooden poles to make cranes. We finally hauled a lorry out of a ditch using nothing more than poles, ropes and pulleys. We also used live hand grenades – a rather frightening experience – and various types of gun. At other times we went out into the country for a whole day at a time on map-reading exercises (now called by the peculiar name of orienteering), usually divided into two groups, one representing the defenders of the home territory, the other the invading enemy. There were even occasional exercises at night, which for some peculiar reason we enjoyed most.

We were also taught how to survive off the land both in Europe and the Far East – the war in the Far East still showed no signs of ending – in case we should crash or bale out over enemy territory. But this was only theoretical; we made no attempt to put it into practice.

Although Credenhill was not an airfield, it possessed a large hangar; the RAF have a predilection for putting up hangars, perhaps to make it seem like home from home. In it we were taught parachute jumping, although there were no parachutes; instead there was a rope and pulley system attached to a parachute harness. After putting on the harness we would launch ourselves from a great height to the floor, the pulley system reducing our rate of fall to something like that which we might experience in a genuine jump. The purpose was simply to teach us how to land on the ground when coming down fast by bending our knees and rolling sideways. At no time did we ever carry out real parachute jumps from an aeroplane; the only people who did that in those days were the airborne parachute troops.

There was a fair amount of book learning to be done as well: we learned all about the responsibilities and duties of commissioned officers, as well as about RAF law and administration, and what was required at a court martial. For the first time we became acquainted with the formidable RAF legal book, *King's Regulations*, and discovered that, like other similar publications, it provided a legal let-out for when you cannot think of a basis on which to charge somebody: 'Behaviour prejudicial to good order and Air Force discipline' covers a multitude of sins.

Halfway through the course those who had come from the university air squadrons of 1943, the year before us, were suddenly called away prematurely to start their flying training. Were we jealous! But the tables were turned when they had to return later on to complete their course at Aircrew Officers School.

We lived in dormitory-style huts, each with a black coke stove in the middle, and about a week before the end of the course the group I was with somehow got keen on bulling ours. We painted the porches, polished the linoleum, and dusted the shelves, not to mention painting the external cowls on top of the stove chimneys. This last brought howls of ridicule from the other huts whose inmates did not take things quite so seriously.

This enthusiasm, however, was rather premature for some of us. After the exams and general assessments at the end of the course, we were divided into two groups, depending on our results. The top half would go straight on to flying training, but the lower half would remain attached to the Aircrew Officers School for another four weeks, camping on the River Wye. I was in the top half, which was just as well, since we heard later that the others had had a terrible time with poor conditions, including outbreaks of dysentery.

We lucky ones would now at last be on our way to flying!

# 3

# Learning to Fly – The Tiger Moth

*VE (Victory in Europe) day was 8 May 1945, one month after soloing*

After a week's leave we were sent to Number 11 Elementary Flying Training School, RAF Perth. The RAF Station was at what had previously been the civilian airfield of Scone (pronounced 'skoon') about four miles to the north east of Perth. It was an all-grass airfield and was to be our base for the next three months. The region was excellent for early flying training in wartime, since it was well away from regions prone to air raids.

We were collected from Perth Railway Station by 15-cwt trucks and taken direct to the airfield; as we went through its gates a Tiger Moth took off and roared over our heads. A cheer went up, and an excited chatter broke out. These were the kites that we had come to fly. We never considered that after our training we would be fighting against an enemy who might kill us; all that mattered was to get into the air.

When we piled out of the trucks there was a shout of 'Get yerselves fell in!' from the sergeant accompanying us, who took us to our billets – huts a few hundred yards from the main building. Then we went straight off to collect our flying kit in one of the hangars, where we walked admiringly past several Tiger Moths (formally the De Havilland 82A) parked there.

Before I go any further this would be a good place to say something about the Tiger Moth itself, an aircraft which throughout the war was the basic trainer for the RAF. It was an aeroplane which has always been loved by anyone who has ever flown it, and sad was the day when it was eventually replaced by something faster and more sophisticated. It was fabric-covered, and so there was always a smell of dope[1] about the place, a nostalgic smell which has ever afterwards brought to my mind a memory of hangars and aeroplanes.

The Tiger Moth was a biplane whose wings were braced with struts and wires; in the central part of the upper wing was the petrol tank. It had two open cockpits, the rear one for the pupil, or for the pilot when on his own, and the front one for the instructor. The front cockpit was at the centre of gravity, so it did not matter from the point of view of flying stability whether it was occupied or not, but any change in weight in the rear cockpit would alter the aircraft's balance.

There was a duplicated set of basic instruments and controls in the cockpits, while just behind the rear cockpit there was a fabric hood which could be pulled forward to

---

1  Dope was a thin liquid (i.e. not like paint) that was applied to the fabric that covered the wings and fuselage of planes like the Tiger Moth. It shrank the fabric, and therefore made the structure stronger, and also made it waterproof and airproof.

*Plate 1, Model of a Tiger Moth.*

enclose the pupil for training in instrument flying. The flying controls were the usual stick – or control column – and rudder pedals, while the engine controls consisted of throttle and mixture levers together with two magneto switches. The cables to rudder and elevators emerged through the side of the fuselage and were attached to the control surfaces externally, making it simple to check their integrity.

Communication between the cockpits was by means of a voice tube called a 'gosport', a flexible hollow tube which passed from an open mouthpiece in one cockpit, through the framework between the cockpits and into the hollow-tubed earphones in the flying helmet of the person in the other cockpit. Each cockpit had mouthpiece and earphone socket so that pilot and instructor could speak to each other. The system worked extremely well, and since the Tiger Moth had no radio, there was no need for anything more sophisticated.

Attached to one of the outer wing-struts was a simple but foolproof airspeed indicator (in addition to the standard instrument in the cockpit) – a spring-loaded vane with an indicator which moved across a scale. As the airflow increased, so the vane was pushed back and the indicator was moved. I have always admired the genius of the person who designed such a simple yet reliable piece of equipment.

To return to the hangar where we were being kitted out; the flying kit which we collected consisted of overalls of a thick, almost canvas-like material, leather helmet, goggles and gloves. The gloves were of three types worn over each other: silk undergloves, woollen mittens and leather gauntlets on top. Surprisingly they were not clumsy in use, probably because of the softness of the leather. This was real flying clothing! It had of necessity to be warm, since the slipstream in an open cockpit would be particularly cold in March.

We were also each issued with a parachute and taught how to put it on: one strap over each shoulder and one strap round each thigh, all meeting together in a circular quick-release box over the stomach. As I have said earlier we never practised real jumps; the parachute would only be needed in an emergency, and all that mattered was to know where the handle of the ripcord was. The wearing of a parachute would be routine on all flights in operational and training single-engined aircraft (other than pure passenger aircraft). In fact, it would have been impossible to fly without one in such an aircraft, since in the cockpit you sat on the parachute which fitted into a deep depression in the 'bucket' seat; without the parachute you could not have seen out of the cockpit properly. The only single-engined aircraft in which I did not later wear a parachute was the Auster, whose seats were not designed to accommodate them. Even though I accepted this in the Auster, I always felt a little uncomfortable without one in other types of passenger aircraft.

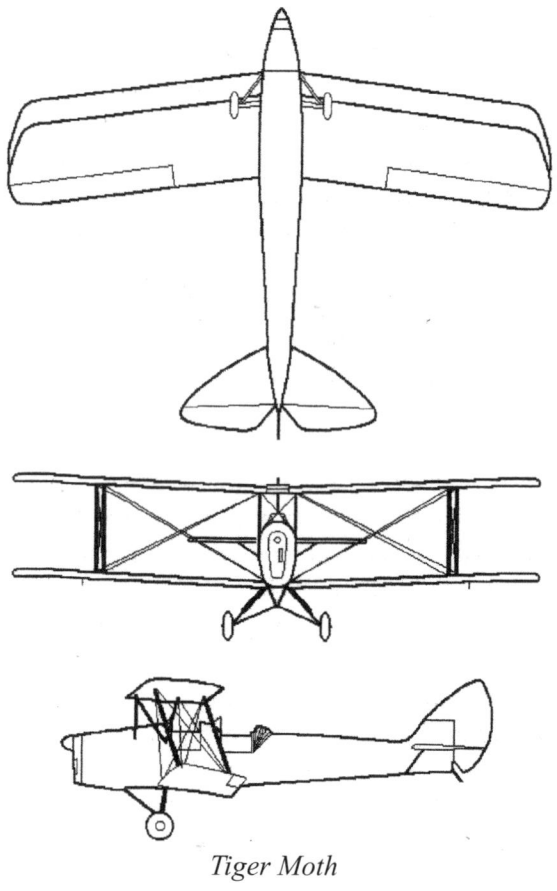

*Tiger Moth*

There was a similar sort of arrangement, as with the parachute, for strapping yourself into the aircraft – again four straps meeting in a quick-release mechanism. As soon as you were seated in a 'plane with your parachute on the first thing you did was to do up the restraining straps, and for take-off and landing you always made them as tight as possible. They never hampered your activity, since everything was within easy reach, and they could easily be loosened or tightened.

We were to be called Number 2 Course, Number 1 Course being those who had left Aircrew Officers School prematurely. We were split up into two groups, half of us flying in the morning while the other half studied theory, then changing round in the afternoon. The group that I was with would not be flying from Perth airfield itself, but from a large grass field called Whitefield about four miles to the north surrounded by fields and woods and obviously commandeered from some farmer. It had been made into a temporary airfield by the simple expedient of building blister hangars and a crew-room in one corner, known collectively as the Dispersal.

Whitefield had the advantage of being better drained than the main airfield which often had large patches made unserviceable when it rained. When we arrived for the first time we found several Tiger Moths sitting out on the grass waiting for us. We were split up among the various instructors, mine being Flight Sergeant Pow, who immediately took a few of us over to one of the Tiger Moths to demonstrate the various controls and instruments.

He climbed in and seated himself in the rear cockpit while we leaned enthusiastically over the side as he described the various controls: 'This is the stick. If I move it back the elevators go up, and if I move it forwards they go down. I move it to the left, the left aileron rises and the right one drops; move it the right, the left aileron drops and the right one rises. I push the left rudder forward and the rudder swings to the left; push on the right one and it swings to the right.

'This lever on my left is the throttle; to open it push it forward, and to close it pull it back. The small lever beside it is the mixture control, but you don't have to worry about that. Down below it is the tail trimmer, but I'll show you what that does when we get into the air. On top of the centre section [of the wing] you can see the fuel gauge sticking up out of the petrol tank. All OK?' We knew what he was talking about as a result of the many lessons which we had had in the past on the theory of flight, but practice is always different from theory, and we needed to use the controls in the air really to get the hang of them.

Then we went on to the next stage, which was learning how to 'swing' the 'prop' or propeller. The Tiger Moth did not have a self-starter, but, like most small aircraft of the period, could only be started on the ground by one person sitting in the cockpit at the controls and another standing in front of the aircraft turning the prop by hand; the principle was similar to that of starting a car with a starting handle. But there was a ritual that had to be gone through meticulously. Although to the outsider it might have looked rather pedantic, it was important if accidents were to be avoided. It would be all too easy for the ignition of the engine to be on when the person swinging the propeller thought that it was off; if the engine then fired unexpectedly he could be killed or severely injured by the propeller. We were in fact remarkably free of such accidents, although at another airfield I once saw somebody get a nasty blow across the back of the hand in this way, not through any fault in procedure, but because of what was probably a hot spot in a cylinder, causing the engine to fire.

Chocks first had to be wedged in front of the wheels to stop the aircraft from rolling forward. When the propeller swinger was ready he would call out 'Switches off, petrol on, throttle closed, suck in' and this would be repeated by the pilot who would check the various items, at the same time repeating the words. The propeller swinger would then pull the propeller down several times to draw petrol into the engine, or 'prime' it. He would then shout 'Switches on!' The pilot would turn the ignition switches on and shout back 'Switches on!' The final shout, also repeated in the cockpit, would be 'Contact!' the propeller would be pulled down sharply and with luck the engine would fire. If it did not fire first time the propeller had to be swung again.

If after several attempts the engine would not fire it would by now have become flooded with petrol which had to be cleared out. There would then be the cry, 'Switches off, throttle open, blow out', and round the prop would have to go for several turns but in the opposite direction. The whole starting ritual would now have to be repeated.

Swinging the propeller was easiest for those who were tall, but the smallest of our bunch, 'Hutch' Hutchinson, found it difficult because he could only just reach it, and almost had to be lifted up to it; but he had a stout heart and somehow managed to cope.

Because of the inherent danger in swinging a propeller we had to sign a certification in our logbooks that we had had the appropriate instruction. In my case this appears as: 'Certified that I, K. D. Neame, have been instructed in Airscrew [sic] Swinging in accordance with the Standard Procedure, as laid down in… We also had to sign a more general statement: …understood the methods of operation of the DH 82A and the Petrol, Oil and Ignition Systems of this type.'

By the time we had done all this the afternoon was over and the Tiger Moths had to be flown back to Scone airfield to be bedded down for the night. This would give some of us the chance of our first flight. One of the instructors took me over to one and got me strapped into the rear cockpit with my parachute. He then climbed into the front cockpit, started up, taxied to the downwind end of the field, opened the throttle and off we went. Bump, bump, bump, faster and faster over the grass, until suddenly there was a wonderful calm smoothness and we had left the ground. I have never forgotten the exhilaration on that first flight of the transition from being on the ground to the tranquillity of being airborne; it was quite something. Even when I got used to it I never really lost the thrill of that marvellous sensation when taking off from a grass airfield which is missing when taking off from a concrete runway. Up we went, a quick circle over the field, then headed for the main airfield and down again to land. A short trip of only a quarter of an hour – entered in my Flying Log Book as Air Experience – but exciting enough!

Next day Pow took me up after first instilling the ritual of communication between the front and rear cockpits using the gosports. It was important that there should be no confusion as to who had control of the aircraft, since, being one behind the other, neither pilot could see what the other was doing. Any misunderstanding could of course end in disaster. So before the first flying lesson he told me, 'When I say, You've got her, you take over the controls, and when you're ready you reply I've got her. And when you want me to take over the controls you say You've got her but it's important that you don't let go until I've answered I've got her.' It all seemed a bit silly at first, but I soon realized how important it was.

Pow took off and up we went. When we were at a reasonable height he said, 'Now if I put the stick forward the nose goes down, if I pull it back the nose goes up; if I move it to the left the left wing goes down, and if I move it to the right the right wing goes down. Give left rudder and she yaws to the left, right rudder and she yaws to the right.'

Then over the gosport I heard his voice 'You've got her' – 'I've got her, sir' I answered. He added 'Just hold her level, with the nose on the horizon, and see what you can make of it.' He gave me a running commentary as I fumbled with the controls. 'Hold the stick lightly, don't grip it.' 'You only need quite small movements of the stick.' And so on. After a flight of 25 minutes I could even manage to fly straight and level – after a fashion.

Back on the ground he impressed on me the importance of careful taxying and of going slowly when moving around on the ground; this was particularly important with the Tiger Moth since it had no brakes. Turning was then solely by the action of the slipstream on the rudder, and it would often require a burst of throttle to turn the tail and alter direction. Yet you had to go slowly enough so that the aircraft came to a halt fairly quickly when the throttle was closed; it was all too easy to lose control and hit something by going a little too fast.

I had another flight that day, this time of 45 minutes, when Pow showed me how to climb, descend and stall the machine. I thought that stalling was going to give me a horrible feeling in the stomach, but I was surprised how remarkably gentle it was.

The next day I had three flights altogether, learning how to glide, turn and take off. Taking off seemed remarkably difficult at first, although later on I found it one of the easiest of manoeuvres. To start with I had control of the rudder while Pow did all the rest, and even with nothing else to think about I found it quite a problem just to keep her straight. Then it was the stick alone, gently raising her off the ground; finally it was the two together. I also had my first instruction on landing, and as we came in Pow helped me with a running commentary: 'Check…, throttle off…, level off…, stick back…, back…, OK, you're down!' Landings were not all quite as easy as that. Sometimes I would hold off too high, and had to give some throttle to ease her down without stalling. Sometimes I would overshoot and have to go round again – or else would bounce and either go round again or give a small burst of throttle and sink gently to the ground.

Then one day we did spinning. Pow took us up through a hole in the cloud, and over that hole we spun. A spin is rather horrible the first time you do it, since the aircraft is effectively out of control and the ground is whirling round in front of you. In the early stages of the First World War nobody knew how to get out of a spin, so it was never done as a practice exercise, but spinning had now become an important part of flying training. An aircraft in a spin is an aircraft out of control and it was essential to know how to get it under control again.

To get into a spin, you shut off the engine, pulled gradually back on the stick, with the nose going up, up, up, and just as she stalled, hard over with the rudder and over on one side down you went while the fields below started to go round and round the nose, faster and faster. Once in the spin, no controls appeared to work, and you sat there with extra G (force of gravity) pushing you into your seat, and with the nose pointing towards the ground. To get out of a spin in a Tiger Moth, you pulled back on the stick to bring the elevators up so as to reduce their shielding effect on the rudder, and then pushed the rudder hard in the direction opposite to that of the spin. This straightened the aircraft out, the spinning stopped, you centralized the rudder, and you were now simply in a gliding dive from which it was easy to recover.

At first I hated spinning, which made me feel faintly sick, but later I got so used to it that I quite often did it just for fun. The one risk in spinning that we were warned about was not to let the spin flatten. As a spin continues, the diving attitude of the aircraft gradually becomes shallower and the rudder becomes less effective, so that it becomes much more difficult, perhaps impossible, to recover from the spin.

The other type of spin that I did just once, but never a second time, was the inverted spin. Here the spin is upside down and the G forces are negative so that everything is pushed outwards away from the floor of the cockpit. The pilot is pulled upwards against his straps, and his blood, instead of being pushed towards the legs by normal positive G forces, is being pushed towards his head, so that the eyes bulge and the head feels swollen – a most unpleasant experience.

Then one day my instructor was changed. Flight Sergeant Pow went to teach somebody else, and was replaced by Flying Officer Shaw, for what reason I never discovered. Shaw was a delightful person to be instructed by – kind, never got into tantrums, taking the rough very much with the smooth. (In contrast there were a few instructors who would shout at their pupils, probably because of their own worry about the safety of the aircraft, but Shaw never did.)

So under my new instructor I went on learning how to fly: taking off and landing – always referred to as circuits and bumps – gliding, climbing, turning, spinning. Then one day after I had got eight and a half flying hours to my credit, I was sent up with another instructor, Flying Officer Barrow, for a final check before going solo. Up we went round the circuit and in to land. There was a bit of a cross-wind if you landed, as you should, according to the T (landing direction indicator on the ground) and I bounced a bit. So round we went again, this time ignoring the T and landing instead directly into wind. That was much better. Up, and round again for another trial, which was not much worse. Then we taxied back to the starting place and Barrow climbed out.

'OK take her off, remember what I've told you, and don't bother about the T – just land into wind according to the windsock' he shouted to me above the roar of the engine, and walked away to the hedge to stand biting his nails as I got airborne. So off I went on my own for the first time. It was rather unnerving knowing that there was now no one in the front cockpit to help me if I got into trouble. Round the circuit I went as before, then turn in to land, throttle back, now watch the hedge, just a bit of throttle, cut, back with the stick, back, back, and that was the best landing to date – and the best landing for weeks to come. Barrow walked over when I taxied back, shook me by the hand, and yelled above the noise of the engine, 'Congratulations! Nice landing!' He then climbed into the front cockpit and we taxied back to the tea-room. After a few minutes Shaw came in from instructing somebody else, and – as if he had not known anything about it – said that he had heard that I had gone solo which was a good show. That day was my nineteenth birthday, 4 April 1945.

Now I could practise straightforward flying on my own, and only have an instructor when having to learn new techniques or to polish up old ones. But there was a great deal still to learn: side-slipping, low flying, landing and taking off across wind, forced landings, restarting the engine in flight, aerobatics, formation flying, and cross-country navigation.

Solo flights would last anything from ten minutes to over an hour depending on the exercise being practised. You were in complete charge of the aircraft, and had to watch out all the time for other aircraft in the neighbourhood. A good look-out was particularly important in view of the large number of Tiger Moths in the region. There was no radio, no communication with the ground or with a control tower; you just took off, flew in your chosen direction, entered the circuit and landed entirely on your own initiative. There was a Very Light available at Dispersal to send up a red flare in an emergency for telling a pilot on the approach to landing that he was not to land, but I never saw one used at Whitefield.

All these flights had to be entered up meticulously in the Pilot's Flying Log Book (Form 414) with which we were provided, showing date, type of aircraft, its number, the name of the pilot and second pilot, the duration and nature of the flight, and whether it was dual or solo. Entries for practices of possible emergencies had to be underlined in red ink: spinning, low flying, and restarting the engine in flight. Night flying details were also entered in red. Jeffrey Quill, the test pilot, in his book *Spitfire,* says that when he was learning to fly in the RAF in 1931 'regulations required that no pupil could do more than two and a half hours of consecutive solo flying without a period of dual from his instructor. This was to guard against the accumulation of bad or potentially dangerous habits or over-confidence.' I had never realized that there might be such a regulation, but after reading his book for the first time recently I looked up my own flying log book and found a similar relationship between solo and dual all through my own training.

Flying the Tiger Moth was really enjoyable. It was an aircraft that was extremely safe, yet had to be flown accurately with ailerons, rudder and elevators at all times if it was to fly at its best. Faster, more advanced aircraft can be flown virtually with stick alone and if you bank to the left they will automatically turn to the left. But not the Tiger Moth; to turn to the left you had to bank it and also give just the right amount of left rudder and of elevator, otherwise you would slip or skid. It was also extremely sensitive to the controls. If the aircraft was well trimmed you could take your hand off the stick and it would still fly straight and level. If you then put your hands out into the slipstream palms down but with the fingers higher or lower than the wrist it would climb or descend; if you lowered your left arm and raised your right arm it would turn to the left, and so on.

I loved doing aerobatics. Although they look dramatic at an air show, most of them are remarkably easy, although to do them really well is difficult. In a Tiger Moth, unlike in a fighter aircraft, every part of the manoeuvre had to be flown. With a fighter a slow roll, for example, requires no more than a movement of the stick to the side, together with a slight forward pressure when you are upside down to stop the nose from falling. But with a Tiger Moth if you wanted to roll to the left, you had to move the stick to the left, at the same time giving right rudder to stop the nose from falling, and then as you became inverted the rudder had to be centralized and the stick pushed forward to keep the nose up, and so on. It all had to be carefully coordinated if the roll was to be a good one. And as you came out the other side of the roll you had to reverse it all. It was always wise to make sure that your straps were tight, since when upside down there was nothing between you and the ground!

There was one amusing mishap while doing aerobatics. I was at a few thousand feet upside down in the middle of a slow roll when something from the front cockpit suddenly flashed past in front of me and disappeared upwards towards an area of marshland beneath. 'Oh, dear,' thought I, 'I hope it's not something that matters.' It is a bit worrying when the 'plane you are in starts falling to bits. When I had landed I looked into the front cockpit to see what was missing. It was the magnetic compass, obviously not properly secured by the groundcrew. Somewhere in the middle of Perthshire, probably a foot or two under the ground by now, there still lies a beautiful RAF compass.

For some reason I developed a passion for height, and now and again I would go up and see how high I could get. The Tiger Moth was not designed for flying at more than about 10,000 feet, above which it was sluggish and sloppy on the controls. But I managed to get to 11,000 feet first of all, and then the next time to 12,000 feet, from where I could see Ben Nevis and miles of country round about – even the Firth of Forth 60 miles away to the south. Finally I made it to 13,000 feet, quite a height for a Tiger Moth! While up there I suddenly realized what a beautiful country Scotland was, and how particularly lovely was the county of Perth with its woodlands and rivers. I did no more height climbs after that, since it was time-consuming and there were more important things to do. I also felt that I might get frostbite in the open cockpit; the cold came through my helmet, and my nose felt as if it was going to fall off, so I decided that enough was enough.

On the whole the weather was good and the air was beautifully clear with none of the hazes of industrial England. It was also cold and there were occasional snow showers and rain squalls, but it was good to be up in them. On one occasion when it had been raining and the sun had broken through again I looked down to see a rainbow as a complete circle below me.

Being April the weather was liable to change quickly, or rain on the ground might turn to snow at a higher altitude. Once, immediately after take-off, I flew straight into a snowstorm even though it was clear when I took off. I could still just see the airfield from a thousand feet up so I circled a bit to wait for it to clear. Then I saw another Tiger Moth coming up behind me, and thought that it might be one of the instructors who had taken off to lead me in. I landed as soon as the storm was over, and discovered that my companion in the air had been none other than Hutch, clearly also getting some snow-flying time in. We had a good laugh about it when I told him that I had thought he was an instructor.

There was often a lot of cumulus cloud around, and it was glorious to dive and swoop around it, twisting and turning through the valleys and mountains of the cloud formations. It never ceased to amaze me that whereas from the ground a cloud might look sharp and well-defined, when you got close to it the edge was fuzzy, turning into no more than an ill-defined haze.

I now began to do some cross-country flights – all over the Perth-Stirling valley, seeing from the air sights like Drummond Castle, Crieff (where Shaw had a girl friend) and Dunkeld and all the places of Macbeth. And then a new and exciting experience: landing somewhere else for the first time. This was to be Stracathro Airfield about twelve miles to the east near Montrose. To get there my instructor and I first flew south to Kinross as an exercise in navigation and then north east to Dundee and beyond it, finally landing at Stracathro itself. A quick refuel, then airborne again and back to Perth where, as we joined the circuit, I had the unnerving experience of seeing another Tiger Moth lying on its back just inside the airfield boundary hedge, apparently otherwise undamaged. It turned out that somebody had come in too low, caught his wheels on the hedge and tipped over on to his back; luckily nobody was hurt.

That was the first accident I had seen, but mishaps were anyway rare. Once there was an engine failure in a Tiger Moth flown solo by one of our number, 'Jeep' Jelpke. He was doing a slow roll at about 4,000 feet when his engine cut while he was upside down, so, scouting around for somewhere to land he saw an airfield with concrete runways, but at the end of each runway a white cross had been painted to indicate that they were not to be used even in an emergency. Jeep, however, pressing on regardless, decided that that was the place for him, and down he went. He made a good landing on the grass beside one of the runways – forced landing practice was high on our list of frequent exercises – and was immediately surrounded by hordes of Poles who apparently lived there. They could speak no word of English, and of course he could speak no Polish. Somehow he managed to find a telephone, rang up Perth, and one of the instructors soon arrived to fly him out.

A little later I flew to Stracathro solo, which gave me a great thrill: the whole cross-country there and back, together with the landing and refuelling, all on my own. While they were refuelling the machine at Stracathro the mechanics told me that I had got a petrol leak in the induction manifold pipe; they made a temporary repair and said that it ought to be seen to at Perth. Not being very good at the anatomy of engines, I got the wording back to front and reported back at Perth that there was a leak in the manifold induction pipe, which made me look somewhat foolish.

Living quarters were on the whole comfortable, but we moved billets a couple of times, first of all to an ex-Institute of sorts at New Scone, an attractive stone building looking something like an almshouse, and then to a large private house within the boundary of Perth itself where the garden sloped down to the River Tay. That house was a marvellous place, really spacious, and we were allowed to some extent the run of the kitchen. My main memory of it is of making toast on the gas stove, slapping stacks of margarine on, cheese on top of that, grilling it, and putting jam on top of the lot. It was delectable, although I regret that it is the Americans who have to be given credit for inventing the concoction. The other food that impressed me there was the porridge; never since those days have I tasted porridge so good. Sadly, I never discovered the secret.

The keenest on our course was one Aubrey Parke. He would go off on his own every weekend to nearby airfields to try and get free flights. One day he asked me if I would like to join him, so I agreed, since it would be interesting to find out exactly what he did get up to. First of all we hitch-hiked to RAF Errol, between Perth and Dundee, but found that nobody wanted to know about us. We then hitched to Dundee, took a train across the Tay Bridge and got off at Leuchars, where the RAF had a large transport airfield. The guard at the gate would not let us in, so we had to retrace our steps. By this time it was getting dark, and although Aubrey tried to persuade me to continue I was by now so fed up that I took a bus straight back to Perth, while he followed later. The irony of it was that in spite of his keenness he never finished the course.

Another to be thrown off the course was, to our great surprise, Ian Sutherland who had been Cadet Leader back at Durham and had organized our journey to Aircrew Receiving Centre at Torquay. He was well liked by all and was a thoroughly conscientious person. It appeared to worry him not in the least, and later we were amused to learn that he had ended up as a corporal in the Service Police.

Eventually the day for my first night flying arrived. It was chilly, so I wrapped myself up well. My instructor and I got into a Tiger Moth, and he taxied it out, weaving skilfully among all the white, amber, red and green lights that appeared around us. Then roaring down the flare path we got airborne. Looking behind me I could see the grass landing strip as a single line of flares, but nothing of Perth beyond, since at that time blackout restrictions were still in force; on later flights when the war in Europe had ended I would see them twinkling below. We turned downwind, then turned in to land, just as for daylight flying except that there was a coloured glide path indicator to one side of the runway to help; you had to judge your height partly by that, depending on whether you saw a red or a green light, and partly by the angle of the flares. It was enjoyable but chilly. I had been scheduled for an hour's flying, so we continued to do circuits and bumps before finishing for the night.

Then came the great moment of going off solo at night, although surprisingly I cannot remember much about it, so perhaps I had got rather used to new experiences and another one simply joined the collection. I had certainly developed more confidence in flying, and certainly felt rather more capable than when I did my first solo in daylight!

When the war in Europe ended, with VE day on the 8 May 1945, we all went into Perth in the evening to celebrate. That normally sleepy town had suddenly woken up for a brief moment. Dancing and reels continued well into the night, with fireworks overhead. Even so, everything had once again all closed down by one o'clock in the morning which we all thought was rather early for the occasion.

In spite of this there was no let-up in the flying; the war in the Far East was still being fought, and to judge from how it was going, it looked as if it would continue for quite a long time. Although the Japanese were on the run, they were putting up a stiff fight, and would most likely do what the Germans had done: fight to the bitter end with no thought of surrender until Japan had been entirely overrun.

At last in June came the end of the Elementary Flying Training Course, with exams

*Plate 2, Kenneth D. Neame, shortly after joining the Royal Air Force as a Cadet in 1944.*

and tests in which I think everyone who had not already been thrown off the course passed. These consisted of written work and a 50 minute assessment in the air. I was classed as proficient, with the following qualifications: forced landings weak; needs to improve lookout. (The grades given on the official form – exceptional, above the average, and average – were apparently not used at Perth; it seems that we were either proficient or not proficient.)

When it was all over we had a celebration with our instructors in a small country pub at Balbeggie, a tiny hamlet about a mile up the road outside the camp. It was a bit squashed, but we somehow piled into the place, and set to work swilling down the beer. Bawdy songs started up, each of us having to sing one solo. My choice was *The Village Magician…*, a favourite of mine from the Durham days and one of the few that I could remember.

We had found the instructors a good crowd and we had got on well with them, but they must sometimes have got a bit tired of instructing day in day out. My own instructor, Shaw, would amuse us by saying that when he was demobbed he would build a little model airfield complete with hangars, Tiger Moths, control tower and flagstaff for flying signals. At the top of the flagstaff he would have a permanent black flag (which indicates No Flying). He was going to keep this in his bedroom so that every morning when he woke up he would see the little black flag, and could then turn over and go to sleep again.

The instructors occasionally had their own parties, followed by the usual hangovers. One morning after such a party our flight commander had come in feeling a bit under the weather, so on the ferrying flight over to Whitefield with me in the rear cockpit he went through all the aerobatics that he could think of, which were quite a few – 'to get rid of the hangover' as he said afterwards! If ever I went through that lot after a party, I would have been as sick as a dog.

One often hears about airsickness in connection with flying, although much less these days when most passenger jets fly above turbulent weather. It is seldom the pilot who is airsick, more usually the passenger. But there was one of us who did suffer from it, the small 'Hutch' Hutchinson. Poor Hutch did have his problems. He was the one who had difficulty in reaching the propeller, and he always had to have a cushion to sit on if he was to see out of the cockpit properly. We liked him immensely, and some time later he got married to a wife who matched him both in size and pleasantness. This airsickness dogged him through all his training but eventually he got his Wings, but I lost touch with him after that.

I must also mention Hippo, our chief flying instructor. He was a real character, mainly because of the size of his stomach. He was fat and big, and it was always a mystery to everyone how he ever got into a Tiger Moth, let alone how it managed to get him off the ground. At our final flying tests he himself examined half the course and one of the pupils did rather a bad landing. The controls of the Tiger Moth, as I have said, were duplicated in the front and rear cockpits and when landing, the stick had to be pulled gradually back and back until it should be right back in your stomach when you touched the ground. This pupil swore that he did the bad landing because Hippo's stomach in the other cockpit had got in the way and he could not get the stick far enough back.

We had now finished the elementary training in the Tiger Moth, and it was time to move on.[2] After a spell of leave we would be starting the next stage at RAF Cranwell in Lincolnshire.

---

2  Analysis of flights and flying times during training and squadron service are shown in Tables 9-11 in the Appendix.

# 4

# Advanced Flying – The Harvard

*The 15 August 1945 was the official VJ (Victory in Japan) Day for the UK, while the official US commemoration is 2 September*

We had spent three months at Perth, but there would still be another six months of advanced training at Number 19 [Advanced] Flying Training School, RAF Cranwell, before we could qualify for our Wings. We would be housed in the RAF College there which was equivalent to Sandhurst and had been founded in 1920 for training selected recruits for a lifetime career in the RAF as commissioned aircrew officers. During the war its original purpose had gone by the board but it was now being disinterred and used once again for its original purpose. (The Flying School and airfield were only a small part of the station, which covered a large area and included numerous Apprenticing Schools and a small Signals School.)

We were the second of the new courses for potential officers, and so were officially referred to as Number 2 Course, but we would be the first of these actually to inhabit the college building, which had been opened in 1934.

These courses were composed solely of those who had agreed by the original 'gentlemen's agreement' to stay on in the RAF and had passed the appropriate selection interview. The war in the Far East finally came to an end on what was known as V-J Day, three months after we had arrived at Cranwell, and we were then asked to make a definite decision about staying on in the RAF. It was rather a mug's game on both sides, since there was still nothing in writing, but we knew that if we said 'No' our flying training would stop immediately, as did that of our friends training overseas. I think that everyone must have said 'Yes' regardless of their intentions. After all, who wouldn't, with the sword of Damocles hanging over his head.

The college was like no other RAF establishment that I had seen. Most of the peacetime RAF stations were much of a muchness, with housing blocks of a uniform type set slightly apart from the hangars and administrative offices. Cranwell RAF Station also had these, but the college itself was set in isolation away from the rest of the camp and on the opposite side of a through road. It was an imposing and attractive building set within its own grounds of lawns, shrubs and trees. It gave the impression of a scholastic edifice, with its broad two-storeyed frontage and central main entrance with pillared portico, above which was a domed clock tower.

Inside the college there was a feeling of opulence, with long broad corridors and much marble. We each had an individual bedroom instead of the communal dormitory or barracks that we had had up to now, and there was no doubt that we were really being given special treatment; although still officially having the rank of AC2, we were now treated to a large extent as officers.

The aircraft that we flew at Cranwell was an American one, the North American Harvard (plates 3 and 4). The British counterpart was the Miles Master, a somewhat outdated wood-and-fabric machine; although perfectly adequate and still widely used, it lacked the power and sophistication of the Harvard. The Harvard itself was a fast all-metal low-wing monoplane with retractable undercarriage, or undercart as it was always called, and variable-pitch propeller. It also had a radio, and an electrical intercom for communication between instructor and pupil. As with the Tiger Moth there were two cockpits, one behind the other, the instructor again sitting in the front one when flying dual. However, when flying solo the pilot now sat in the front cockpit instead of the rear one. Both cockpits were enclosed within a single perspex and metal canopy.

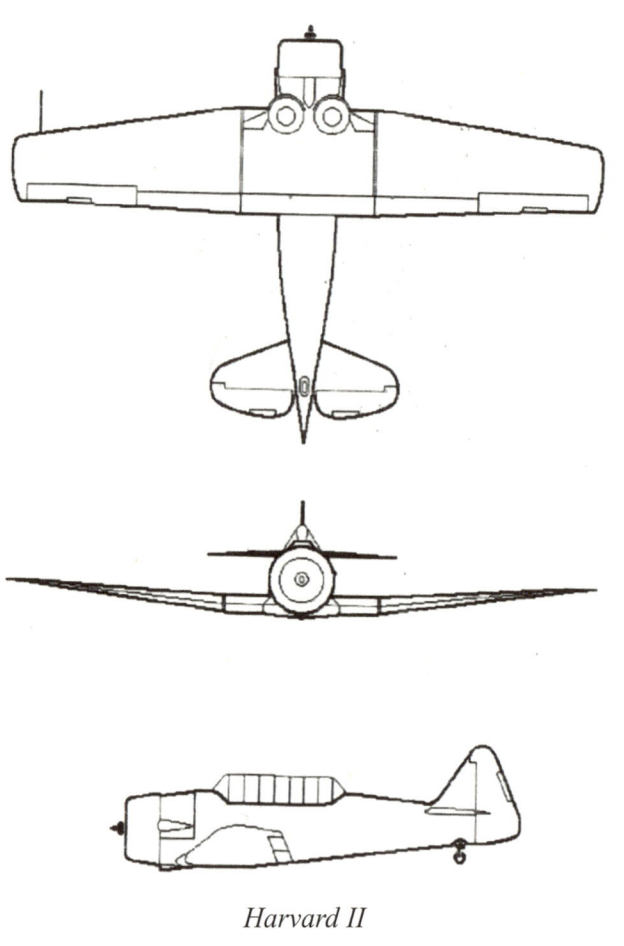

*Harvard II*

When the aircraft passed immediately overhead, one heard a cracking kind of noise, and for this reason it has always been easy to identify a Harvard from the noise alone. It was probably caused by the tips of the propeller blades approaching the speed of sound and causing something akin to a sonic boom.

There was a great deal more flying that we had to learn in the Harvard which was half-way to a fighter and so was much more sophisticated than the Tiger Moth. One new item, for example, was the ability to vary the pitch of the propeller, altering the angle at which the blades sliced into the airstream; this is comparable in function to the gear system in a car. The undercarriage was retractable, and so it was essential to develop a routine to avoid landing with the wheels up – I don't think anybody did, but he would probably have been out on his neck if he had. The radio was used for communication with the Control Tower, which regulated our movements in the vicinity of the airfield; no longer could we decide to land just when we felt like it.

Apart from being faster, the Harvard was trickier to fly than the Tiger Moth. For example, when you stalled, it did not just sag flatulently downwards, but would drop a wing and flick over to one side. This was a common fault with many high-powered low-wing aircraft.

*Plate 3, a Harvard in flight.*

There was the added complexity of learning how to cope with gadgets that we had never encountered before: not only the variable pitch propeller and retractable undercarriage, but also brakes, flaps and extra engine controls. It was important to check all these before every take-off and every landing. The propeller pitch had to be set at fine to give better speed control at landing or take-off but was set at coarse for normal cruising. The flaps, which increased the lift and reduced the stalling speed, were lowered on landing; they were not used on take-off since they increased drag and thereby slowed the aircraft. And it was of course vital to make sure that the wheels were down before landing. As an *aide mémoire* for all these there was a simple mnemonic, which lasted me throughout all my later flying experience: BUMPF, standing for Brakes, Undercarriage, Mixture, Pitch, Flaps. Muttering this aloud and checking each item before landing prevented foolish and dangerous mistakes

The course was initially much the same as at Perth. We were allocated instructors, and once again had to work towards a first solo, practising circuits and bumps, climbing, descending, stalling, gliding and so on, but now in what seemed a much faster and more formidable machine. And there was the same independent check with another instructor before we were allowed to go solo – in my case after nine hours of dual. My instructor was Flight Sergeant Hayes – later on in the course he was promoted to Warrant Officer – and a more pleasant person it would be hard to find. Indeed, the instructors at Cranwell were just as good a bunch as those at Perth; they were cheerful, had a sense of humour, and were only sharp if you did something really silly.

After going solo it was initially a question of polishing up flying technique, doing the same things as at Perth such as aerobatics, forced landings, spinning, instrument flying, and so on, together with an occasional cross-country flight following a triangular route to practice navigation by map reading. On one occasion Hayes thought that he would like to have a look at Nuneaton, his home town, just north of Coventry, so on that day we arranged a cross-country to include it, and when we got there he zoomed down to wave to his family.

*Plate 4, bringing a Harvard out onto the airfield.*

Night flying was now prominent, but since it depends on instruments we could only do it in the Harvard after acquiring reasonable competence at instrument flying. Although the Harvard, like the Tiger Moth, had a hood in the rear cockpit, this type of flying could be practised more cheaply and more safely on the ground in what was called the Link Trainer, the forerunner of the computer-based flight simulator. It was an elongated rectangular box to which had been added fixed wings and tailplane – solely for the look of the thing – with a cockpit containing the standard instruments, over which was a hinged lid to isolate you from the outside world. The pilot kept in contact with the instructor over an intercom. The illusion of an aircraft was helped by the fact that the machine was on a hinged pedestal and, according to the position of stick and rudder pedals in the cockpit, could rotate on its vertical axis, tilt upwards, downwards and to left and to right. It was all rather crude compared with the mock-ups of today, but was adequate for its purpose.

We had already used a Link Trainer at Perth on which we had practised mainly the simplest aspects of flying, such as following a course, keeping the aircraft in a satisfactory attitude when climbing, descending or turning, and also, since outside influences could be imposed on the trainer, in bumpy or turbulent air. But at Cranwell, after we had repeated many of the elementary procedures, we graduated to radio-controlled flying, following instructions of headings to follow, or using radio beacons to

*Plate 5, the crew room at Cranwell. The posters mentioned in the text can be seen on the far wall.*

guide us back to an imaginary airfield. Eventually we did the most difficult exercise of all, making use of a directional beacon with the compass out of action.

My log book shows that I did about thirteen hours of Link Trainer exercises at Perth and about fifteen at Cranwell, each practice varying from thirty minutes to an hour. The assessments of my own Link Trainer practices were 80% at Perth and 83% at Cranwell, though exactly what standard those figures represent I have no idea.

A new addition to the repertoire was air gunnery and bombing. For gunnery, cameras replaced guns so that pressing the gun button or tit caused photographs to be taken by a camera in the wing. The instructor then criticized the performance as shown on the resulting film. There was much guesswork in it, since you had to make a deflection shot on the aircraft that you were attacking and aim ahead of it. It was then up to the instructor to decide whether you had given enough deflection, but he too would only be guessing. Apparently fighter aces of both World Wars have considered deflection shooting to be too inaccurate to be reliable; it was better, they say, to get really close behind the enemy before firing the guns (see *Fighter Exploits* by E. H. Sims).

The bombing was fun, but tricky. Flying at low level we had to hit a target on the ground using smoke bombs, and it required considerable skill to be accurate. The difficulty was due to the fact that the aircraft was moving fast, while the bombs when released were moving initially at the aircraft's speed before following a curved trajectory under the influence of gravity. Three factors had to be taken into account – again by guesswork: the speed of the aircraft, the height of the aircraft and the speed of the wind. Speeds of aircraft and wind combined together to form groundspeed could be judged to some extent by the aircraft's track across the ground. But however the factors varied, the bomb had to be released well before the target in order to get anywhere near it. I found that once I had got into my head the amount to lay off, it then became not too difficult. It does not surprise me now, in the light of these exercises, what little damage our pilots caused to bridges during World War II in low level attacks.

As well as the flying there was classroom instruction on all kinds of subjects varying from engine function, theory of flight, radio, astronomy (for navigation), weapons and so on.

Along with the more advanced training at Cranwell we were also reminded of the dangers of not keeping our wits about us. In the crew-room, for example, where we waited between flights, there were various posters on the wall which warned us to be careful (see Plate 5). A couple said 'Could you cope if your artificial horizon packed up?' and 'Beware of the Hun in the Sun'. Another showed a cartoon of a pilot lolling in his cockpit dangling a camera over the side, under which was the caption 'Apathy and unconcern are symptoms of lack of oxygen'. At the same time we were provided with the superb semi-humorous magazine *Tee Emm* – short for Training Memorandum – which contained stringent warnings against clottishness. It was issued regularly to crew-rooms and was written for all air-crew. The main (fictional) character in it was a Pilot Officer Prune (resurrected in 1991 by HMSO in *The Life and Times of Pilot Officer Prune*), who was a real clot, always doing the silliest – but all too likely very real – things when flying; he was supported by his dog Binder, who accompanied him on these escapades. In the magazine there were also regular hypothetical awards of the Most Highly Derogatory Order of the Irremovable Finger for examples of really foolish behaviour taken from real life. It was all most entertaining and the magazine was widely read.

There was also training in various things unconnected with flying, such as rifle and pistol shooting. I managed all right with the rifle shooting since I had done this at school, but pistol shooting I found difficult, not being used to the upward kick which makes the bullet go high. We used the pistols one-handed, although nowadays it has become, sensibly, a two handed operation. After that experience I decided that anybody using a pistol one-handed against myself would not be all that dangerous unless really close.

In our spare time we sometimes went into Lincoln, about fifteen miles away, but since, like most RAF Stations, Cranwell is isolated, some form of transport was needed. As a result motorcycles were bought by several cadets who were often to be found in the yard at the back of the college tinkering with their machines or stripping down the engines. To enjoy life to the full I felt that I would have to have one, so I bought a 250cc Triumph which, for some obscure reason, came from a dealer in Thrapston, 50 miles away. The camaraderie of the RAF came in useful while I was riding it back to Cranwell since on the way it developed a blockage in the fuel line, and some mechanics in an Air Force Station near my route were happy to put it right for me.

That motorcycle gave me many hours of enjoyment, sometimes on a trip to Lincoln to the north, and once going down through Cambridge and across the ferry at Tilbury to my home in Kent for a weekend. Petrol rationing would of course have limited the amount of pleasure cruising on such a machine, but there was clearly enough to make it all worth while. It surprises me now that any petrol at all was allowed for such pleasure jaunts, since all petrol had to come into the country in tankers exposed to the ever-present threat from submarines.

Several of us also spent some of our spare time making models of aircraft. I set myself the task of making out of balsa wood a model of our old favourite, the Tiger Moth, shown in Plate 2 on page 17.

It was at this time that I bought my first really good camera, which took most of the illustrations in these memoirs. For many years I had been keen on photography; I had had my first camera at about the age of eleven and developed and printed my own films from my early teens onwards. I had to shelve all this when I entered the RAF, but now that the war had ended and there were less restrictions on photographing RAF premises and property I wanted to get it going again, and with the best I could afford. The quality cameras at the time and before the war were German, with names like Leica, Zeiss and Contax and used the relatively uncommon (at the time) 35mm film, but as the war progressed these cameras became less and less available and more and more expensive; nevertheless I felt that I had to have one of that type. So I answered an advertisement in a photographic magazine for a second-hand Leica II and bought it for £60.

The Leicas of the time ranged from the Leica I with no rangefinder and f3.5 lens to the Leica III with rangefinder and f2 lens; none of them had a built-in exposure meter. The Leica II was in the middle of the range and would do all I wanted. The lens, unlike that of cheaper cameras, was removable and could also be used as an enlarger lens, giving considerable economy in the cost of making enlarged prints from the 35mm film. Judging by the post-war Japanese cameras and allowing for inflation, £60 seems a high price to have paid for such a camera,[1] but at that time 35mm cameras were used only by the enthusiast who did his own processing, and considering the rarity of German cameras the price I paid would have been fair for the time.

That camera served me well for many years. It was made in the mid-1930s to a high standard and was remarkably robust, but it had one design fault; it was tricky to load. The back of the camera did not swing back in the conventional way; instead, the base came off and the film spool and take-up spool had to be slid in together from below. As a result I once missed what should have been a superb picture of a Spitfire taking off because I fumbled the loading of the film.

I often carried it with me in the air to the amusement of my colleagues, and I would take aerial shots of other Harvards, or even of the back of my instructor's head in front of me. I think that I was the only one among our lot who took photographs, and I sometimes feel that this enthusiasm must have contributed towards my being posted later to photographic reconnaissance.

Eventually the course approached its end and we were subjected to a mixture of

---

1 For comparing with more recent prices, the Retail Price Index was about 6.5 for 1945 and 126 for 1990.

written examinations and flying tests. If we passed them we would get our Wings, that coveted emblem above the left breast pocket of tunic or battledress which would show that we had successfully completed the RAF flying training course and were now qualified pilots. The written examinations, which covered the classroom course work, were straightforward and presented little problem if you had been reasonably conscientious. The great test was the final flying test. In fact, it was not just one test, but several, each lasting about an hour. There was a Handling Test, an Instrument Flying Test, a Navigation Test, an Assessment Test, and – according to my logbook – three Standard Beam Approach Tests, involving navigation by radio beam.

So it was with some trepidation that I climbed into the Harvard for my first test with one of the senior flying instructors. Luckily all the tests went well, although in one of them I did make one mistake which I was told cost me a grade, and that was when I had to do a steep turn. If you pull a Harvard round into too steep a turn it is liable to do what it does when it stalls, that is, it flicks over into what is almost the beginning of a spin. I was pulling it round as instructed but made the turn too tight so that the 'plane flicked over. We were not all that high, and by the time I had regained control we had lost quite a bit of height, which made it look bad. Nevertheless I still got an above average grade out of the four grades Exceptional, Above Average, Average and Below Average.

It was now December, and the end of six months of a very enjoyable course, but it did not quite end there. Normally we would have collected our travel warrants and bundled ourselves off to the station for the next stage in our lives, but this was the end of a special course which had to be celebrated in a big way. There was to be a Passing Out Parade, where each of us was to receive his Wings from a visiting Air Commodore.

We all lined up on the parade ground in front of the college building wearing white belts and with rifles at the slope, while the visitor took the parade and saluted the march past[2] (Plate 6). Then we trooped into the main hall of the college to have our Wings pinned on to our chests, and receive our commissions which turned us all suddenly into Pilot Officers. It was rather reminiscent of a school speech day even to the extent of being watched by fond parents who were invited for the occasion, quite unlike the normally self-contained RAF. My own parents came, staying the night at a small hotel in Sleaford, the neighbouring town. Looking back I now find it incredible that such a fuss was made. All during the war pilots had been trained and given Wings and commissions and everyone just got on with it, but in this case we were effectively being passed out as part of a new nucleus for the peace time Air Force, the college having returned to its original purpose.

I have still got the printed brochure of the final passing-out performance which makes interesting and to some extent curious reading. It is titled Graduation – No 2 Course and is dated 21 December 1945, but there is a note at the bottom stating effective date of commission and authority to wear wings – 6 January 1946, so that

---

2  It was all just the same 40 years later on television in a Channel 4 *Treasure Hunt* programme; Cranwell College and the parade both looked little different from when we paraded in 1945.

## ADVANCED FLYING – THE HARVARD

*Plate 6, the Passing Out Parade in front of Cranwell College*

we were not officially allowed to wear the Wings that had been pinned on to us for another two weeks or so. But nobody took any notice of that.

The brochure gives a list of all the members of the course in so-called Order of Merit, but it is far from clear what in fact determined the order. There were 42 of us and I was placed eighth. However, three are labelled Distinguished Pass, yet they come respectively sixth, ninth and sixteenth in the list, the cadet with the highest flying assessment came seventh, and two cadets labelled highest grounds subjects assessment came ninth and twenty-sixth respectively. There is only one consistency in the list, and that is the name at the top, Cadet Palmer, who is labelled as Senior Cadet and Best All Round Cadet. Another factor which might also have been taken into account is what is headed Brief Record of Achievement, which, on looking down the list, refers only to sport (I am down for shooting), but this is probably irrelevant in contributing to the order of names, since the third and fourth names on the list have nothing under the heading of sport. The Order of Merit is not broken down to show how it was produced, so perhaps our names were taken out of a hat!

For those who might believe, as I originally did, that there is some relationship between graduating as an RAF pilot and being 'sporty' I have laid out the numbers given in the brochure for the various types of sport:

| Soccer | 7 | Hockey | 4 | Rowing | 1 |
| Rugger | 9 | Squash | 1 | Shooting | 4 |
| Cricket | 4 | Swimming | 2 | Nothing | 13 |

It is clear that only about half took part in the standard types of team sport, and one third did no sport at all. So the myth of RAF pilots as a collection of athletes disintegrates. Nor, in contrast to the outlook of many schools, did you have to be at all interested in sport to do well in such circumstances. On the other hand this may be more a reflection of the Air Force in wartime. The pre-war selection interview, as described by S. J. Carr in *You are not Sparrows*, was apparently sport-orientated, and, in the post-war years, owing to the severely curtailed intake into Cranwell College (see *Per Ardua ad Astra* by P. Congdon), sport is once again probably one of the many things affecting the weeding-out process.

I was now a Pilot Officer, the lowest of the commissioned ranks, but proud of it at the age of just under 20. My airman's Service number 2235001 was replaced by an officer's number, 201750. Nevertheless it is always the first of these which comes readily to mind if I ever recall my Service number; the second I have to look up. It must be because when in the Ranks your number always had to be quoted along with your name, whether it was for collecting pay or reporting to an office, whereas for officers your name and rank alone were required.

The next thing was to get ourselves kitted out with officers' Best Blue uniforms. These were provided by Burberry Ltd, who came all the way from London to measure us up. And for the first time we were having to pay for our own clothes. Then it was home for a spot of leave.

# 5

## Photo Recce Training – The Spitfire

Basic flying training had now finished. The next step was to be trained to join a real squadron, out there where flying was serious. The war, both in Europe and the Far East, was over, and the country's flying strength would be reduced, but the RAF would still be around.

Before joining a squadron the newly fledged pilot had to go to an Operational Training Unit, where he would learn to fly operational as opposed to training aircraft, and obtain experience in the skills required for the type of squadron to which he would eventually be going. Since we who had just got our Wings at Cranwell were now effectively part of the permanent establishment of the RAF, all or most of us would continue to fly. Somebody in the Air Ministry would have decided where each of us was to be posted, depending presumably on the judgment by our instructors of our ability and temperament. Many of us, probably those with an inclination to sport and teamwork, would go to fighter squadrons. Few would go to bomber squadrons since these would now be reduced to a bare minimum.

I was selected for training in photographic reconnaissance, better known colloquially as photo recce, and I would be flying Spitfires. Whoever influenced that decision must have known more about each of us than we imagined, since for me it could not have been more suitable – everything fitted – I had always tended to be an individualist, disliked team games, flew with a camera whenever possible, had been assessed as above average for flying, and liked flying high (I had also repeated my high-flying escapades of Tiger Moth days in a Harvard, but since we were not supplied with oxygen, I could not get higher than about 15,000 feet). These would be great assets, since most photo recce of that time was a single-handed affair, although during the later years of the war the two-crew Mosquitos had done much of the low-level reconnaissance. Accurate flying was required while actually taking photographs, often at 20,000-30,000 feet, as was an ability to navigate over long distances; at the same time a knowledge of the technique of photography would be an asset.

I was delighted, and looking back I now realize how lucky I was, since photo reconnaissance was much more interesting than other types of flying, yet the pilots doing it were few. If I had been sent to a fighter or bomber squadron the flying would have consisted of no more than local exercises, while transport flying, a possible alternative, we all looked upon scornfully as bus driving. On the other hand the essence of photo recce, even when no more than for practice, meant cross-country navigation, tests of skill in photographing specific targets, and solitary flying at high altitude for several hours at a time.

After a long Christmas leave I went at the end of January 1946 to Number 8 Officer Training Unit at Benson, about ten miles south east of Oxford, to join Number 16 Spitfire Photo Reconnaissance Course. Compared with the previous courses containing sixty or so trainee pilots, this was tiny. There were just three of us, Flight Lieutenant James, Pilot Officer Bill Strachan, and myself, Pilot Officer Ken Neame. The number on the course was so small because few new pilots were needed; not only was the total number carrying out photo recce small, but on active service they survived better than fighter or bomber pilots.

RAF Benson had been the wartime centre for photographic reconnaissance, and worked in close cooperation with the Photographic Interpretation Unit at RAF Medmenham, a large pseudo-Tudor mansion a few miles away on the banks of the Thames, which was the centre for the processing and interpretation of aerial photographs, and whose work is described by Constance Babington Smith in her book *Evidence in Camera*. Benson was also a centre for high altitude flying generally, since it included, as well as a photo reconnaissance squadron, a meteorological flight to provide information for weather forecasting. In both cases the aircraft when I was there were Spitfires.

The photo recce Spitfire which we flew at Benson was the Mark XI with a Merlin engine and a four-bladed propeller (see Tables 12 and 13 in the appendix). The meteorological Spitfire was the Mark VII, fitted with extended wing tips for greater lift at high altitude.

**Technique of photographic reconnaissance in the Spitfire**
Before going further, I will describe the essentials of photo reconnaissance as carried out with the Spitfire, since it comes into the picture a great deal from now on. The photo recce Spitfires, of which several Marks were developed, had a greater range in terms of distance than the corresponding fighter versions. They were unarmed, the guns in the wings being replaced by fuel tanks so that a photo recce Spitfire might carry 217 gallons while the equivalent fighter version might carry only 111 gallons (see Table 14 in the Appendix). This extra fuel increased the range considerably, which was particularly important since the photo recce aircraft often had to go where the bombers went, which was further than most fighters could manage.

The range could be further increased by the addition of an expendable drop tank fixed under the belly of the aircraft, which might contain up to 90 gallons of petrol. A full 90-gallon drop-tank increased the overall weight of the aircraft at take-off so much that the full length of runway was needed to get airborne, and the take-off was remarkably lumbering and sluggish. The photo reconnaissance Spitfires relied on speed and height for evading the enemy; this was possible because not only did they not have the weight of guns and ammunition but as they used up the fuel in the wings their overall weight fell and their efficiency increased.

Two different types of photographs could be taken: vertical and oblique. Vertical

*Plate 7, Number 16 Spitfire Reconnaissance Course at Benson.*

photographs were taken usually from between 10,000 and 30,000 feet with two huge cameras of focal length 20 inches which pointed straight downwards through glass portholes in the floor of the aircraft behind the pilot, and which produced a negative – and contact print – measuring 8 x 6½ inches. They were fixed in the fuselage just behind the pilot, and diverged slightly so as to give a broad but overlapping coverage of the ground directly beneath (see Fig. 1, page 42). Each contained enough film for 500 exposures. Oblique photographs were mostly taken from a low altitude with a single camera of focal length 14 inches also just behind the pilot but which looked out sideways through a glass window on the port side; this camera contained enough film for 100 exposures and the size of the photograph was 5 x 5 inches. Both cameras were rigidly fixed in the aircraft and the whole aircraft had to be used for aiming the cameras.

Vertical photographs were the most common: in wartime for photographing enemy territory from high altitude and in peacetime for survey work. They were in the form of a continuous series of photographs, called a run, taken over a predetermined strip of ground while flying straight and level. The cameras were switched on and off by pressing a button on a control box in the cockpit; it could be set for repeated exposures at timed intervals or for single exposures. If, as was usually the case, the area or target to be photographed was greater than the field of view of the cameras, two or more parallel strips would have to be taken in order to photograph the whole target (see Fig. 1). Each picture on the film overlapped its neighbour by more than half so that the final prints could be examined stereoscopically, the slightly different angles of adjacent photographs producing the stereoscopic effect. When viewed through a stereoscope the ground could be seen in exaggerated relief, and trees and chimneys would appear to be thrusting up towards the viewer.

The cameras had to be aimed to some extent by guesswork since the ground directly

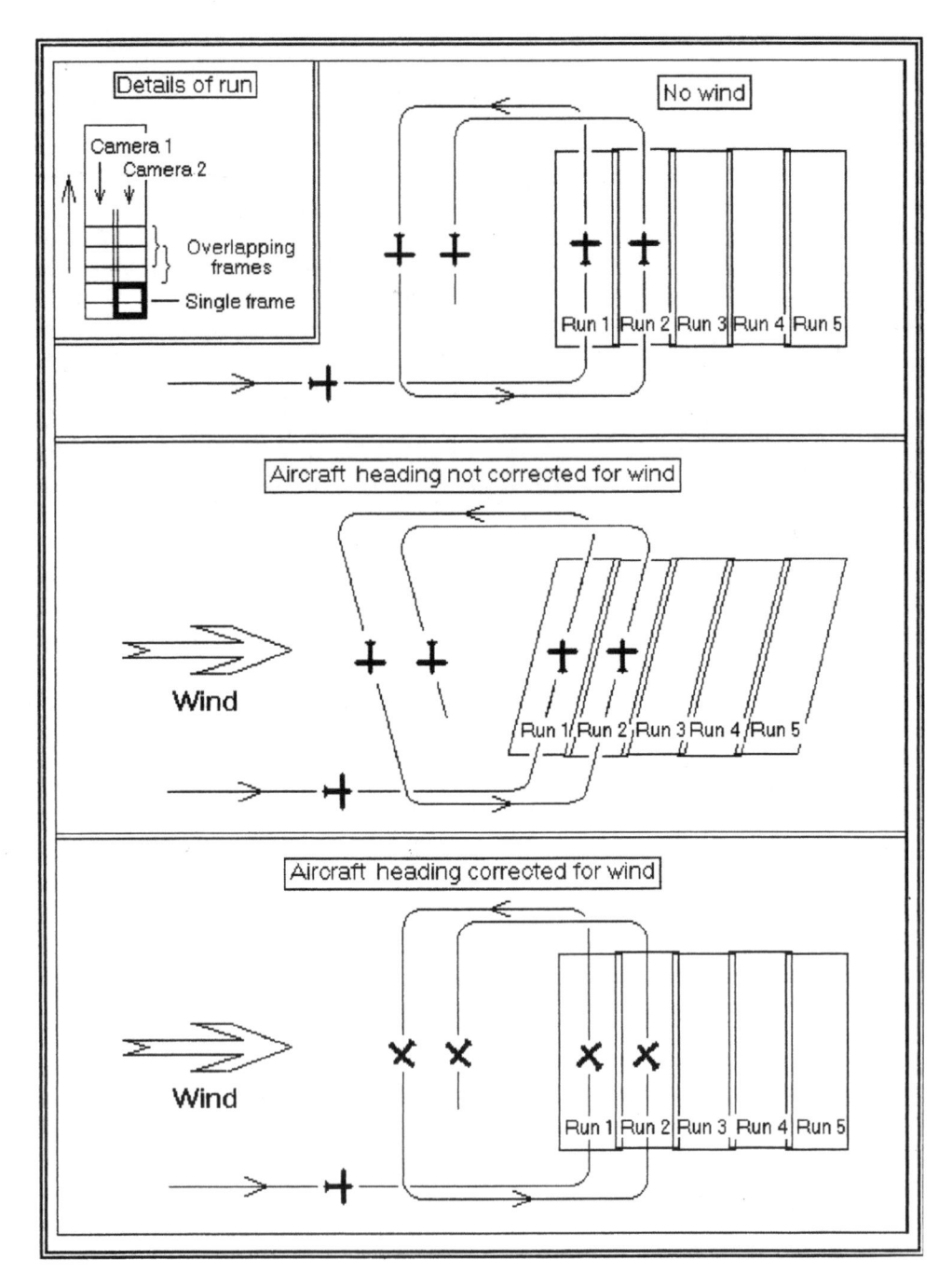

*Figure I: The runs flown over a target for vertical photography. Inset. Detail of a single run.*

below the aircraft could not be seen by the pilot while the pictures were actually being taken. The larger the area to be photographed at one time, the more the number of runs required and the more difficult it was to be sure that all parts were covered; it was all too easy to miss out a narrow strip between adjacent runs.

Before going on a photographic flight or sortie the pilot would have to make some calculations and measurements so that he knew exactly what to do when he arrived over the target. He would have to work out the best course to fly across it after allowing for both the speed of the aircraft and the velocity and direction of the wind predicted for the altitude at which he would fly. There might also be specific requirements laid down by the person requesting the photographs, such as direction of runs. Then, using a large scale map, he would divide the target into marked strips in such a way that each separate run which he made over the target would cover one strip and at the same time overlap the adjacent strip sufficiently to allow for error.

Because of his inability to see the ground while he was actually photographing, the pilot had to follow a particular technique (see Fig. 1, upper). He would approach the target at right angles to the beginning of the first strip to be photographed and far enough away to be able to see the target over the side of the cockpit. When virtually in line with the strip he would bank steeply, and, watching the ground, would position himself so that when he had finished the turn he would be directly over the beginning of the strip and heading along it. He would then steer the calculated course using the gyro compass (which did not oscillate like the magnetic compass; see Glossary) and at the same time press the button on the control box to start the cameras. He then had to hold that course accurately, flying straight and level for a specified time which he had calculated before leaving the ground. It was vital to fly absolutely straight and absolutely level; if not on the correct heading the aircraft would diverge from the strip to be photographed, and if not level the cameras would not be photographing the ground directly beneath.

At the end of the timed run he would press the button again to stop the cameras and immediately bank steeply to check whether he was still in line with the strip on the ground. This judgment itself was also to some extent guesswork, since it was not easy to determine precisely which bit of ground was vertically below the aircraft. If he was where he expected to be he would carry on with subsequent runs over adjacent strips in the same way, but if he was not, he would have to repeat the run after a correction to his heading. In practice a pilot would first make a dummy run – a test flight with the cameras switched off – since the calculated values for course and time were seldom accurate owing to the unpredictability of the wind. He would then measure on his map the angle between the actual track and the intended track, and alter the heading on the next run by this angle (see Fig 1, middle and lower).

He would also note the distance covered on the ground and if necessary alter the time between switching the cameras on and off. He would carry out these checks at the end of every run in order to give a continuous estimate of flying accuracy, and repeat any doubtful runs. This was important, since if one bit of a target was missed on an operational sortie the whole thing would have to be done again. In spite of all this it was still possible to leave gaps between strips, as I later found to my chagrin.

The wind could have a marked effect, particularly if it was a strong crosswind, and one episode (described in more detail in a later chapter) shows how vital it was to do a dummy run first. In this instance I knew that the wind was fairly strong, but for some reason the target had to be photographed in a certain direction which happened to be across wind. When I had finished the dummy run I found that I was quite a long way to one side of where I should be. So I made a second dummy run with a large correction and this time got it right by flying crabwise (as in Fig. 1, lower). When the pictures were developed and printed later, they were all set at about 45 degrees to the line of the run, and when I worked it out I calculated that the crosswind had been about 100 miles an hour – but at least I had covered the target.

Oblique photography was much simpler. Individual photographs were taken at an oblique angle of objects to one side of the aircraft; the pilot simply lined up the subject to be taken against a white strip painted on the trailing edge of the port wing, and then pressed the button on the control box, now set to take single exposures. This resulted in photographs of excellent definition and quality, although if taken too close to the subject, perhaps at too low an altitude, the picture might be blurred owing to the speed of the aircraft.

Neither type of camera could be adjusted in flight, the aperture being set and the film loaded by the groundcrew beforehand. After the flight the exposed film was sent to the local Air Headquarters Photographic Department where it was developed and printed, and the prints passed on to the interpreters and plotters. Only then could the pilot judge how accurate his flying had been.

To get to and from a target – or other location – a photo recce pilot needed to be able to navigate over long distances, and this seems a good place to describe in some detail the standard technique of navigation without radio aids, which is how we practised it; most of our navigation was by dead reckoning[1] and map-reading.

There were five facts that a pilot needed to know for his navigation before setting off: the direction and distance of the target, his airspeed, or speed through the air itself, and the direction and speed of the wind at the appropriate altitude. A side-wind would move him away from his intended route while a head- or tail-wind would slow him down or speed him up, and therefore it was vital to take the wind into account when working out beforehand the details of a flight. To follow the required track[2] or flight path across the ground he would have made an allowance for the direction and speed of the wind, the actual heading required being calculated beforehand using the simplest of trigonometry; knowing his airspeed – his speed within the mass of air in which he would be flying – this calculation would also provide him with his groundspeed, or speed over the ground. He could then determine from the map when he might expect

---

1 The expression 'dead reckoning' is derived from 'deduced reckoning', and usually refers to the assumed position of an aircraft based solely on previous navigational calculations.
2 The 'track' or flight path is the route or direction which an aircraft follows across the ground, whereas the 'course' is the direction steered by the pilot on his compass. The track is the course modified by the effect of the wind.

to pass over easily identifiable landmarks or pinpoints. On the flight he would look out for these shortly before he expected them to appear, and when he saw them would calculate how far to one side or the other of his intended track he was and whether he was ahead of or behind time. He would then make the necessary corrections to his flight as he went along.

He also had to correct for the two errors of the magnetic compass. One of these was Variation, the difference between the direction of the magnetic pole, to which his compass pointed, and the geographical pole, on which his map would be orientated; it is marked on aeronautical maps. The other was Deviation, which resulted from the effect on the compass of metal in the aircraft and was peculiar to each aircraft; every so often the aircraft had to be swung, that is, it would be turned in different directions on the ground while the readings on its compass would be compared with those of a prismatic compass some distance from the aircraft; from these readings a calibration scale was prepared, specific for that compass and aircraft.

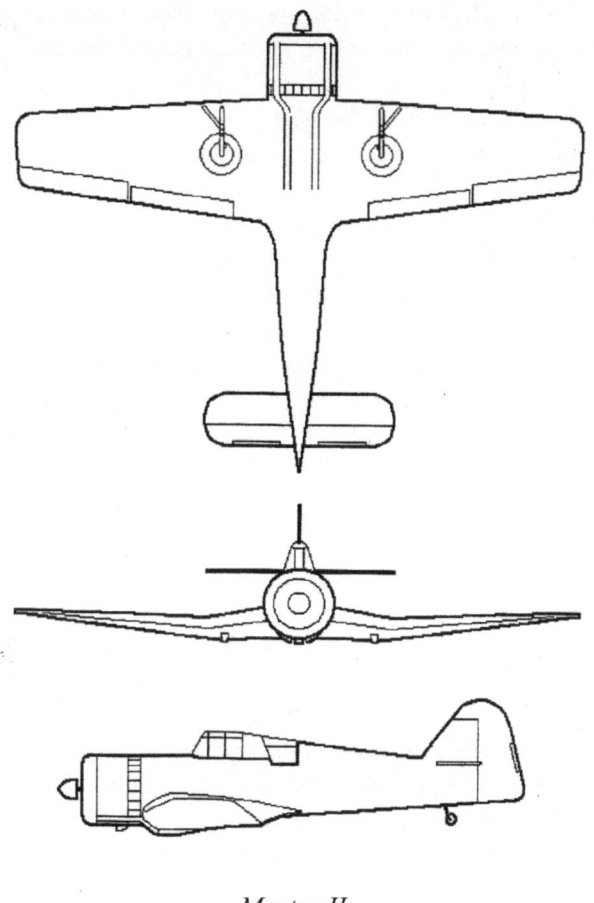

*Master II*

Sometimes when flying on cross-country journeys the ground was obscured by cloud. Navigation then had to be entirely by dead reckoning until the cloud eventually cleared and a pinpoint could at last be identified. The longer a pilot had to depend solely on dead reckoning the further he might be from where he expected to be and the greater the chance of his becoming lost.

During wartime a photo recce pilot had to be particularly competent at both navigation and photography, since it was vital that he succeed in photographing the target first time off. Photographs were often needed urgently, and enemy defences and weather did not make it easy to go back again for a repeat performance. The Spitfire pilot, always on his own, would have to navigate without any radio or external aids to what might be an obscure target over enemy territory. When he got there he had to be able to do the equivalent with cameras that a bomb aimer did with bombs. In other words he had to be pilot, navigator and bomb aimer all rolled into one while at the same time keeping an eye open for enemy fighters.

## The course at RAF Benson

Before any of us could actually start the course, we had to undergo a medical examination to check our suitability for high altitude flight. Most of it was routine stuff, but in addition we were given a check in a decompression chamber. This was a large strengthened cylinder in which the air could be progressively pumped out to simulate the fall in atmospheric pressure with increasing altitude. We entered this ominous-looking structure through an air lock, provided so that in a medical emergency a person could be taken out without altering the pressure in the main chamber. We sat ourselves on benches along each side and put on oxygen masks, after which the air was gradually pumped out to bring the pressure to the equivalent of 30,000 feet.

The object of the check was to see if anyone was particularly subject to the bends, a condition where nitrogen comes out of solution in the blood or nerve fibres. This is more familiar in deep sea diving where a too rapid ascent to the surface can be lethal. In our case the pressure difference between ground level and any height that we could reach would be too small to produce a lethal effect, but a slight attack could affect a pilot's ability to control his aircraft. Another effect that a fall in pressure of this sort can have is to cause any gas trapped in a tooth filling to expand and cause severe toothache.

There are also two temporary conditions which might arise as a result of flying at high altitude. A cold in the nose, particularly if the openings to the sinuses or to the middle ear are blocked, can cause severe pain on descending to a lower altitude owing to the expansion of trapped air, although there will seldom be symptoms while climbing. Excessive gas in the intestine, caused particularly, so it was said, by a meal of beans or peas, might produce pain while ascending.

All three of us on the course passed the medical and decompression tests, but before doing any photo reconnaissance we had of course to learn to fly the Spitfire. This aircraft had a British cockpit layout which was rather different from that in the Harvard whose layout was American. The American cockpit was neat and tidy, with switches in rows, while the British one was all over the place. You might think therefore that the American layout was the better one – not necessarily. When things are all in neat rows and all switches look alike it is all too easy to flip the wrong switch. When it is a case of life and death the haphazard layout may be the better one, since everything has its own special place with less risk of mistaking one for another.

Because of this difference in layout, and also because I had not flown for three months, I had to have some familiarization practice in a Miles Master II, a British trainer, a type which I mentioned briefly in the last chapter. I had three flights each of about half an hour with Flying Officer Kemp, one of the instructors, before being considered competent enough to be let loose on a Spitfire.

The jump from flying a training aircraft to flying a Spitfire was rather frightening. Firstly, the Spitfire, like any fighter, was far more powerful than any trainer; it had to be, since it was designed to compete in speed, height and manoeuvrability with the best that the Germans could put in the air. Secondly, and much more daunting, was the fact that you were on your own from the beginning. All Spitfires – and all fighters of the time, except for a few experimental ones – had no dual control, and so a pilot new to it had to fly this more powerful and different machine without any helpful instructor to get him out of trouble.

Before the first take-off in a Spitfire it was therefore important to become familiar not only with the cockpit layout (Plate 8, page 49 – although this is a photograph of the cockpit of a later version, only a few details are different), but also with the various settings required, such as engine revolutions (or revs), and boost, what the stalling speed, approach speed and landing speed were, and so on. There was no need to learn take-off speed, since take-off was purely by 'feel': the nose was pointed down the runway, the throttle opened wide, and the machine was eased into the air when it felt ready to go, quite different from the huge passenger jets of today which have little feel and have to be hauled off the ground at a specified textbook speed.

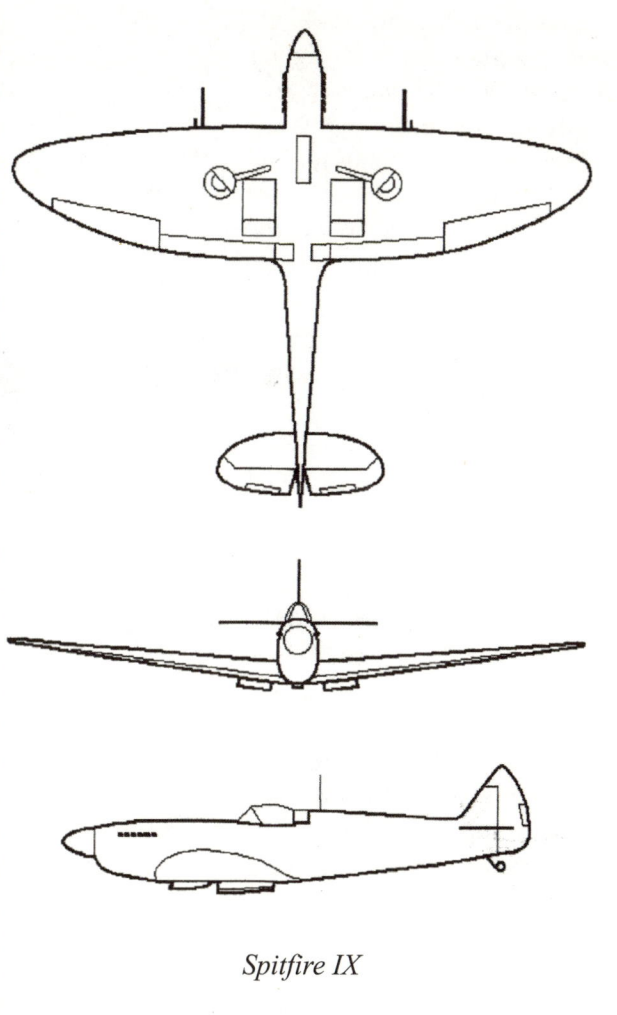

*Spitfire IX*

I do not remember being frightened of that first take-off; apprehensive, yes, but no more than that. Having done quite a bit of flying by now – 86 hours solo, 120 hours dual – this was just another staging post, formidable though it might be. One difficulty with the Spitfire which was a bit daunting at first, although one I soon got used to it, was that it had a particularly long nose stretching out ahead which severely restricted the forward view. But then the noses of the training aircraft that I had flown also blocked the view immediately ahead, so it was really only a question of degree. Luckily the Spitfire has always been a delightful aircraft to fly, having no vices, and the first flight was straightforward.

Kemp eventually took me out to a Spitfire IX – a fighter version – which was standing in front of the main hangar. I strapped my parachute on and climbed into the cockpit. He gave me a final check round the instruments, reminding me particularly of the approach speed for landing. After I had started up he walked back to the hangar to bite his nails. I waved the chocks away, got permission from the Control Tower, and taxied to the end of the runway.

The take-off was little trouble, although there was a tendency to swing to port owing to the torque of the propeller. Once airborne I went round the airfield circuit and, since it was my first flight, made a dummy landing, coming in at the approach speed of 110 mph to get the feel of it before opening the throttle and going round again for the landing proper. This itself went well, with a gentle touch-down at the Spitfire's landing speed of 75 mph and not too much bouncing. My first flight in a Spitfire had lasted 20 minutes and the date was 11 April 1946, a few days after my twentieth birthday.

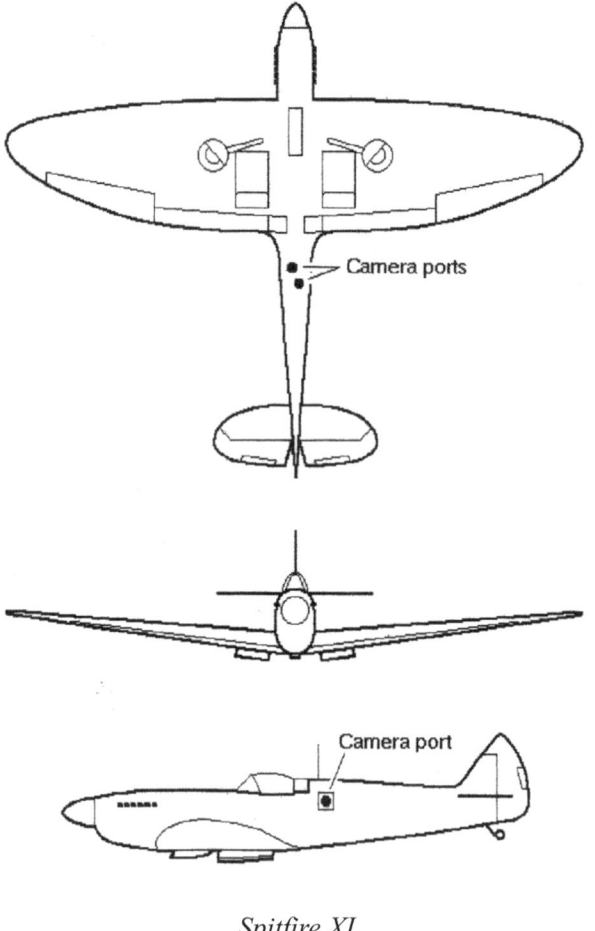

*Spitfire XI*

I realised later how lucky I was to be flying Spitfires and not some other type of fighter. It has always been said that the Spitfire was a favourite among pilots owing to its lack of vices and ease of flying, and although I never flew any fighters other than Spitfires I have no doubt that it was the best. I have watched numerous Tempests, for example, coming in to land, and they always looked, with their bulk and their high landing speed, like great lumps of concrete coming out of the sky. I was always thankful that I never had to fly such dangerous-looking machines!

That was enough for one day but on the next day I had two flights in a Spitfire VII to get used to the handling (the various Marks which we flew at Benson all handled the same) and to identify some of the local landmarks. Then I was given my first flight to a really high altitude, 30,000 feet, this time in a Spitfire XI, using oxygen for the

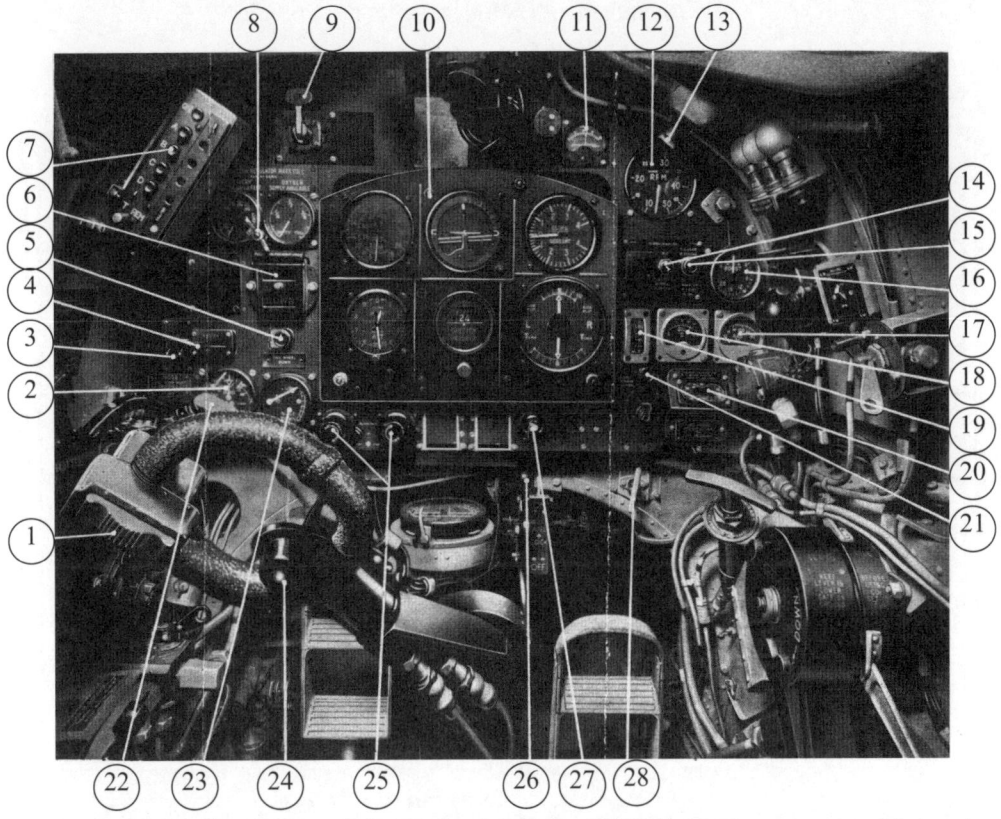

*Plate 8 (RAF). The cockpit of the (fighter) Spitfire XIV. The six instruments of the main central group comprise the instrument flying panel for guidance of the pilot in the air.*

| | |
|---|---|
| 1 Gun firing push-button | 15 Supercharger warning light |
| 2 Pneumatic pressure gauge | 16 Boost gauge |
| 3 Ignition switches | 17 Coolant temperature gauge |
| 4 Undercarriage indicator master switch | 18 Oil temperature gauge |
| 5 Tailwheel indicator | 19 Oil pressure gauge |
| 6 Undercarriage indicator | 20 Fuel contents gauge |
| 7 Radio push-button controller | 21 Fuel pressure warning light |
| 8 Oxygen regulator | 22 Starter breech reloading |
| 9 Flap control | 23 Engine starter bush-button |
| 10 Instrument flying panel | 24 Fuel cock control |
| 11 Voltmeter | 25 Cockpit floodlight switches |
| 12 Engine speed indicator | 26 Camera gun pushbutton |
| 13 Cockpit ventilator control | 27 Elevator tab indicator |
| 14 Supercharger override switch | 28 Brake lever |

**Not numbered in photograph**
In the Instrument Flying Panel (upper centre) reading from left to right:
Airspeed Indicator (mph), Artificial Horizon, Climb and Descent Indicator, Altimeter (feet), Gyro Compass, Turn and Bank Indicator
Directly below the Instrument Flying Panel, just in front of Control Column:
Magnetic Compass

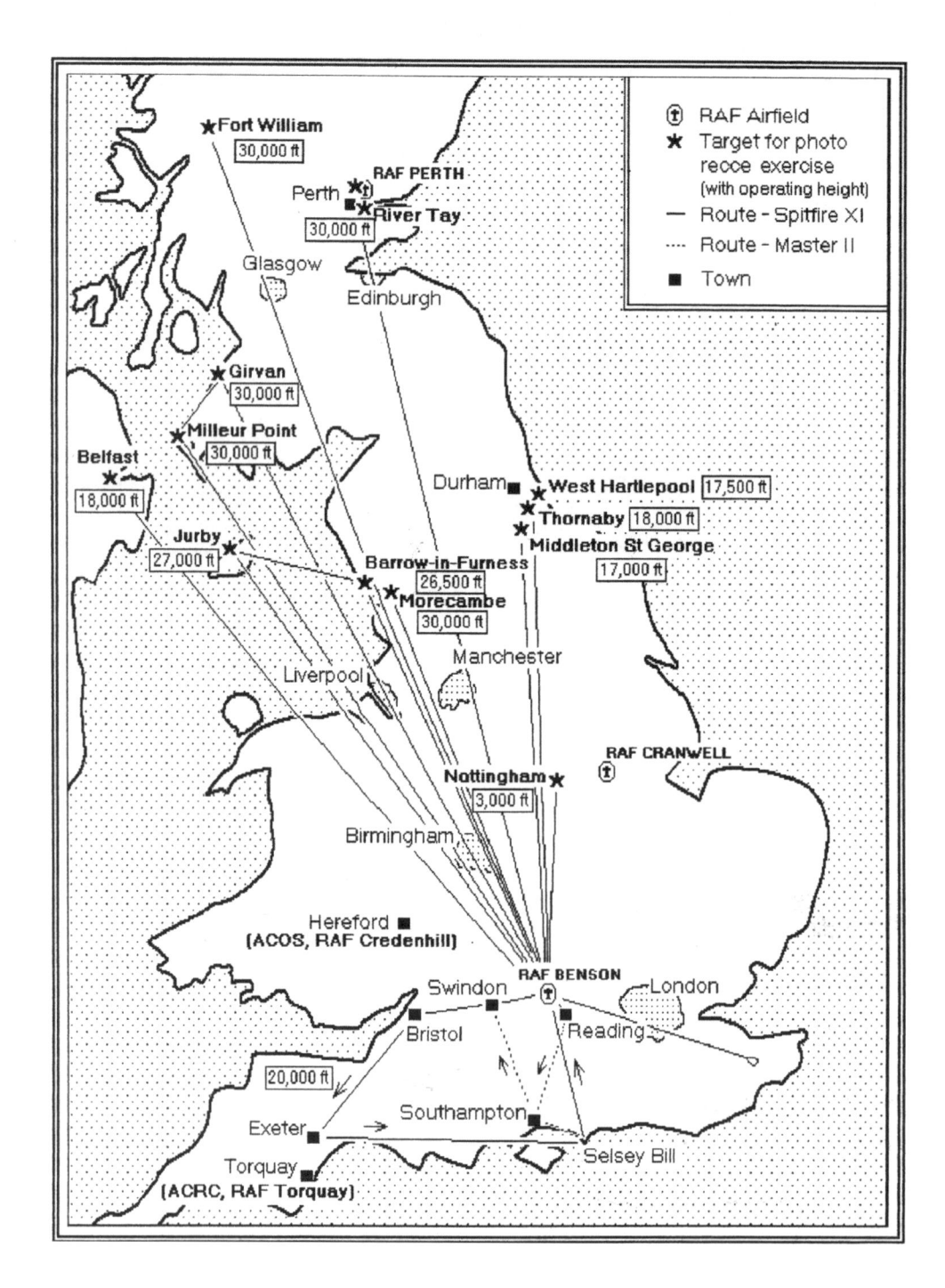

*Figure 2. Sorties and cross-country flights from RAF Benson.*

first time. I decided to fly over my home county of Kent. It was a lovely clear day, and when I reached the end of the long climb I could see the sea all round the coast, with France away in the distance. It might be thought that from that altitude the whole of Kent would have been laid out like a map, but that was not so. Only the ground directly below was at all map-like, while the coast of Kent was still quite a distance away on either side, and France was not much nearer than the horizon.

I thought that while I was over Kent I might as well go down and have a look at my home in the village of Selling not far from Canterbury. So I made a gentle descent to where I knew it lay, and when I had found the house I circled round it a few times at about 1,000 feet, the lowest height officially permitted when you were not authorized for low flying. My brother Roger tells me that he hasn't forgotten seeing the Spitfire circling, and, suddenly realizing who it was, immediately rushed indoors to tell our mother to come out and have a look – an exciting episode for all.

After a few more circlings it was time to return to Benson, so I climbed away and settled down for the return journey, landing back at Benson 1 hour 40 minutes after take-off.

From then on, most flights were longer than any that I had ever done before (see Fig. 2 and Table 1, page 52). I now had to learn not only how to take vertical photographs but also how to manage long-distance navigation, since the targets we were given could be anywhere in the United Kingdom. Previously I had never flown for more than two hours on any one flight but now it was to be anything up to three and a half hours. Since I really enjoyed flying, being in the air for such long periods was sheer bliss.

We had to take photographs with vertical cameras from any height up to 30,000 feet, mostly of towns and airfields. It might take an hour to reach the target, an hour to photograph it, and an hour to get back. The choice of target sometimes depended on local weather, and I might initially have to climb through several layers of cloud before reaching the required altitude over a target where the weather was miraculously clear. One trip I particularly remember was when I had to photograph Fort William on the shore of Loch Eil. The weather was perfect all the way, and I climbed to 30,000 feet, reaching a Scotland whose highlands, islands and surrounding sea looked really beautiful under a clear blue sky. But sometimes the cloud stayed with me all the way, and then I would have to return without any photographs.

Although most of the flights were for practising aerial photography, we also continued to carry out instrument and cross-country flying with an instructor in a Master to keep us up to scratch, as well as learning something about the use of radio beacons as an aid to navigation. It was vital to be able to navigate accurately on long-distance high altitude flights in a country such as the UK which is renowned for its cloud and bad weather.

One Spitfire flight which I made, a purely navigational exercise, involved both instrument flying and the use of the short-range direction-finding facility or Homer. The weather was overcast, with cloud base at about 1,500 feet so that I was in continuous

| Date (1946) | Target or turning point | Total time airborne | Altitude, feet |
|---|---|---|---|
| *Cross-country reconnaissance exercises – Spitfire XI* | | | |
| 15 April | Nottingham | 1.05 | 3,000 |
| 24 April | Middleton-St-George, West Hartlepool, Thornaby airfield | 2.10 | 18,000 |
| 4 May | Belfast | 3.00 | 18,000 |
| 5 May | Girvan, Milleur Point | 3.00 | 30,000 |
| 6 May | Morecambe | 2.25 | 30,000 |
| 7 May | Barrow-in-Furness railway, Jurby | 2.45 | 27,000 |
| 9 May | Perth airfield, River Tay | 3.30 | 30,000 |
| 10 May | Fort William | 3.15 | 30,000 |
| *Cross-country exercise – Spitfire VII* | | | |
| 30 April | Bristol, Exeter, Selsey Bill | 1.55 | 20,000 |
| *Cross-country instrument flying exercise – Master II (dual)* | | | |
| 1 May | Reading, Southampton, Selsey Bill | 1.00 | Low level |

*Table 1. Training exercises from RAF Benson. (Any disparities between distance and flying time are the result of variations in time over the target.)*

cloud shortly after take-off and had to fly entirely on instruments. I climbed higher and higher through the featureless whiteness, until at last at about 25,000 feet I broke out into a clear blue sky with the sun shining overhead and the cotton wool surface below stretching uninterrupted to the horizon. It made me realize that even when all is dark depressing on the ground on such a day, up there the sun is always shining. It was eventually time to descend, back on to the instruments, hoping that the cloud base had not got lower since I had left. I was relieved to be told over the radio that it was unchanged, and with the help of the Homer towards the end of the return flight landed after flying on instruments for the best part of an hour.

At that time of year, in the late spring, those high altitude flights were cold, since there was no heating in the cockpit, and what suffered most were my knees with the flying suit stretched tightly over them. My mother accordingly made me a couple of short cylindrical knee-muffs to wear under the flying suit, and these made all the difference.

While at Benson I had the dubious privilege of owning a half-share in an MG sports car. I got myself into the transaction because I felt that an MG would be a great thing to have. It was a crazy thing to do, since the training course would not last more than three months, and then I would be posted somewhere else; enthusiasm got the better of discretion, and I paid out the cash for a half-share in a four-seater open tourer MG. I loved driving it, particularly through London to Kent. In those days of petrol rationing London traffic was quite thin, and I enjoyed nipping in and out between cars and lorries; indeed I could never at that time understand why anybody would want to go to London by train when they could go by car. Somehow sharing the car worked, but the problem came at the end of the course when I was posted overseas and had to leave my half-share behind. A problem arose over recovery of the cash so I asked my father if he would sort it out for me after I had left; he kindly and long-sufferingly agreed and somehow managed to do so – such is the rashness of youth.

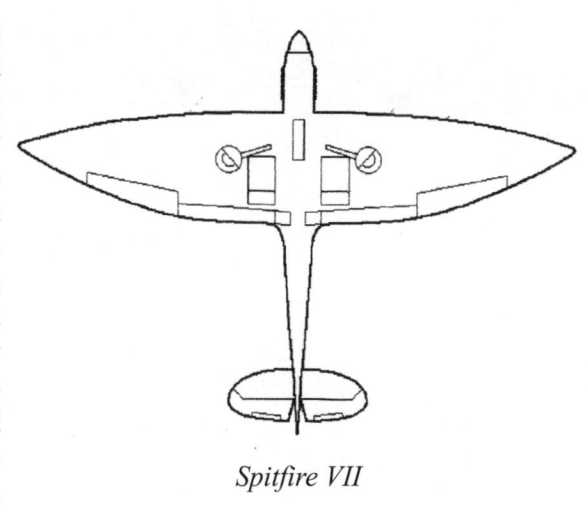

*Spitfire VII*

Of the other two on the course with me at Benson, James I heard no more of, but Bill Strachan later got killed in a Spitfire while flying in the UK when his oxygen supply became blocked by ice owing to contamination with water vapour.

Two completely unimportant episodes of my time at Benson stand out in stark contrast to the rest and show the tricks that selective memory can play. In one episode I remember standing on the main road outside the airfield, trying to hitch a lift. I got picked up not, as I expected, by a lorry or battered old car, but by a chauffeur-driven Rolls-Royce limousine with an aristocratic female in the back. The other episode was when I lent a WAAF officer one of the cheques out of my cheque book. I was ignorant at the time of the world of finance, and it was not until I had had a rather forceful letter from my bank telling me that I had broken a taboo and must not do it again that I realized that borrowing blank cheques was just not on. Why do I remember these two episodes so vividly when the detail of most of the flights from Benson have disappeared completely?

The course at Benson lasted three months and I was then posted to a Squadron in Germany. For those interested in the details of the training schedules of that time, my flying times in the various aircraft up to the end of my flying training are shown in Table 9 in the Appendix.

# 6

# Germany

For the first time in my life I was going abroad – to join Number 2 Squadron at an RAF airfield just outside Celle in Germany about 60 miles south of Hamburg, as part of British Air Force of Occupation within British Army on the Rhine. This Squadron was a mixed one of fighter and photo reconnaissance Spitfires.

To get to Celle I had to go by the roundabout way so beloved of the RAF when posting people from one place to another. The first stop was RAF Hornchurch in Essex which had been a fighter station during the Battle of Britain, but had now become no more than a transit camp for those on their way to RAF stations in Germany. Once again I was given injections against tetanus and typhoid, but typhus was now added to the list in view of the possible risk of this disease in devastated Germany. I then went by rail and sea ferry to the headquarters of Number 84 Group, British Air Force of Occupation, a group of imposing buildings not far from Celle, where I stayed for a couple of nights before going on to the airfield.

Soon after I arrived in Germany my promotion to Flying Officer – the lowest

*Plate 9, the main street of Celle in 1946.*

*Plate 10, Number 2 Squadron dispersal at RAF Celle. On the original photograph can be identified, reading clockwise, four Austers, a Tiger Moth, an Anson, a Harvard, four Spitfire XIVs and two Spitfire XIXs.*

commissioned rank but one – came through, which made me feel quite good, even though this first promotion was always given automatically six months after being commissioned.

It was now about a year since the Second World War in Europe had ended, and although the German cities were still in ruins from the bombing, the country was once again in some sort of order. Indeed, except in the big cities I saw little outward evidence of war; the countryside seemed hardly touched and the people that I came across who were employed by the RAF and other services appeared healthy enough. But then on any RAF station abroad we tended to be rather isolated from the general run of the population, and those Germans employed by the occupying troops were well provided for. In addition, the town of Celle itself had by some miracle remained virtually untouched; only the railway station had been bombed.

Celle is an attractive small town with steep-roofed half-timbered houses and cobbled streets, and with an attractive mediaeval air about it. In the suburbs there were rows of newer detached houses, each set in its little plot of land, also with the same steep roofs, and looking from the air like dolls' houses. Beyond was cultivated farmland, laid out rather after the fashion of the English mediaeval open field system, and interspersed with scattered patches of coniferous woodland. There seemed to be no evidence of the need for more *lebensraum* or living space, as expounded by Hitler in

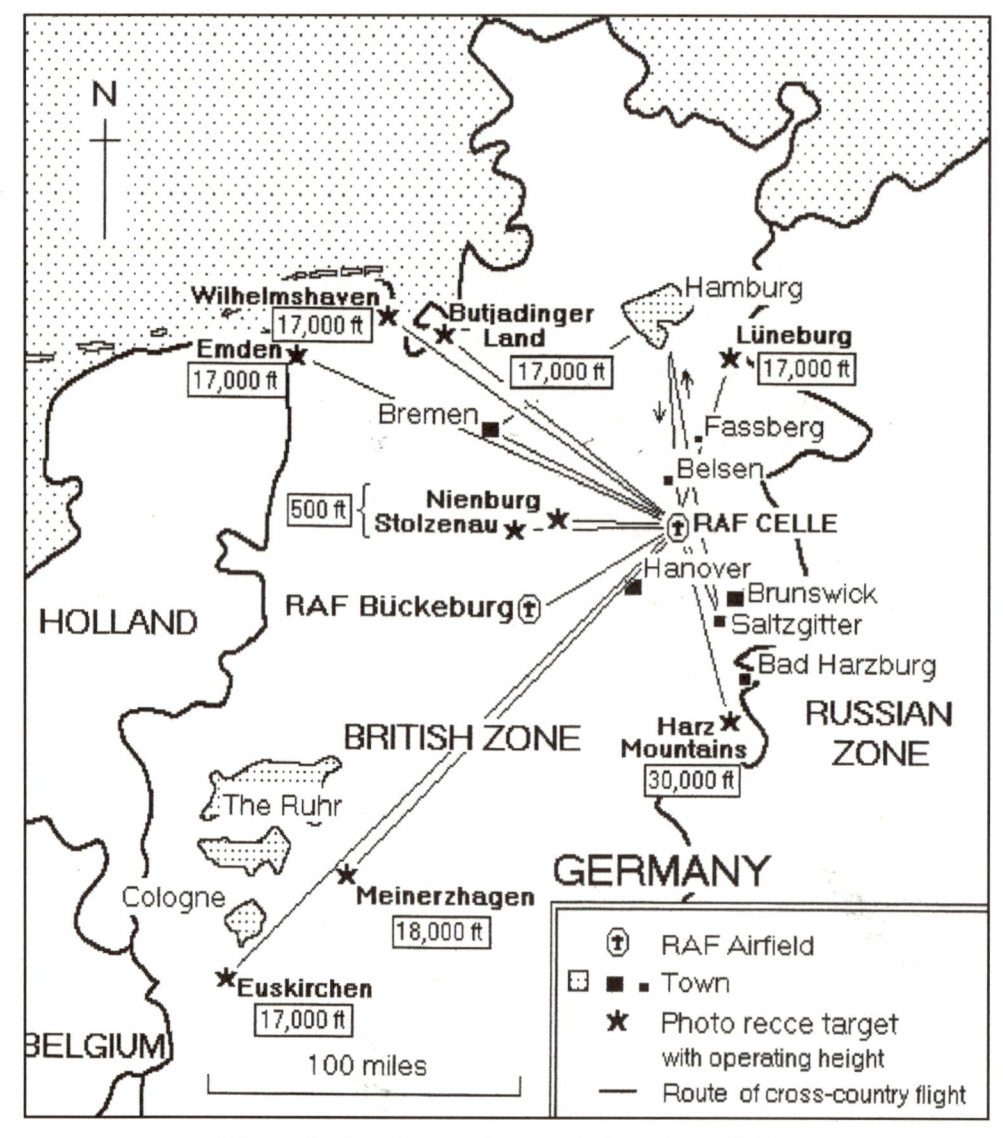

*Figure 3, Practice sorties, carried out from Celle.*

the pre-war years.

The airfield at Celle had been taken over from the Germans, and we were housed in the comfortable living quarters and Mess which had once been occupied by Luftwaffe officers. The Germans had fitted out their permanent quarters rather better than had the British in the UK; there was an excellent central heating system and all windows were double glazed. In our living quarters there was a pleasant fraülein called Gisela who came in every day, tidied our bedrooms, did the cleaning and arranged for our laundry.

The airfield was basically a grass one, but a temporary metal runway had been laid down using what was called perforated steel plating (see Glossary). This consisted of lengths of heavy steel plate perforated with holes perhaps six inches across, each plate being linked to the next to form a hard runway. Every time an aircraft landed on it the sound of clattering metal would carry across the airfield to where we might be relaxing in our crew room. There was no sign of bomb damage here, but scattered around in distant parts of the airfield were a few derelict aircraft of the German Air Force such as a Heinkel 111 and a three-engined Savoia-Machetti taken over from the Italians.

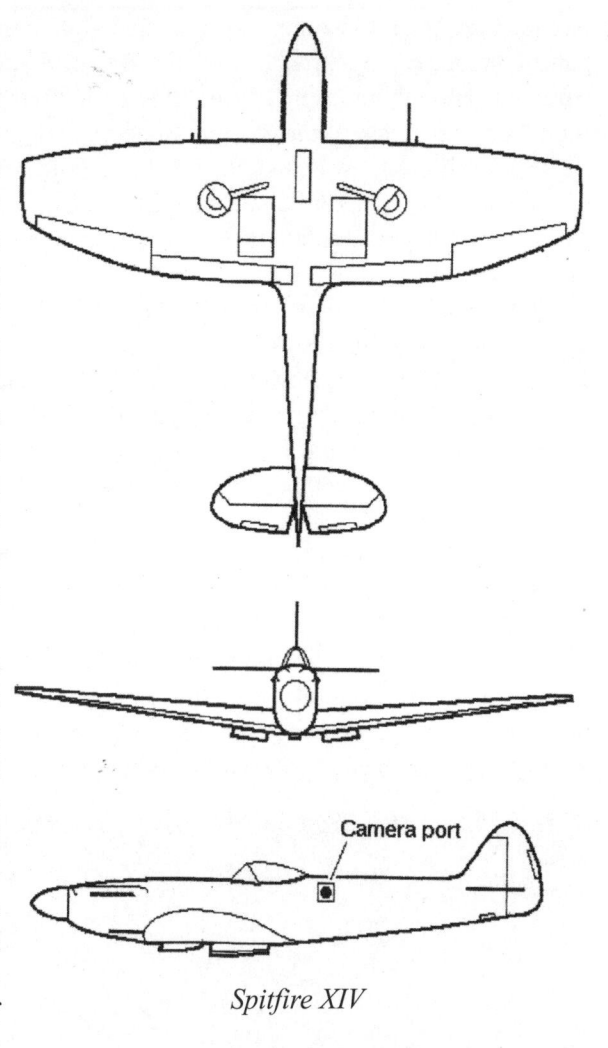

*Spitfire XIV*

The Squadron was equipped with Spitfire XIVs and XIXs, fighter and photo recce versions respectively of the same type of Spitfire; both were fitted with the Rolls-Royce Griffon engine which was more powerful than the Merlin engine in the Spitfires at Benson. In outward appearance the main differences between the XIV and XIX was that the XIVs that we flew had clipped wings for greater manoeuvrability, although at the expense of altitude, and the cockpit hood had a better all-round view. The cockpit instruments are shown in Plate 8 on page 49, and technical details of these Spitfires are given in Tables 12-19 in the Appendix.

The photo recce Spitfire XIXs had originally been built with a pressurized cockpit.

Because of this, unlike other Spitfires, they did not have a let-down flap at the side for getting in quickly. As a result we had to climb right over the high side of the cockpit, parachute and all, to get in. By the time I was flying them the pressurization was defunct because of deterioration in the rubber sealing edges.

The Spitfire XIX was, like the XI, fitted with two vertical photo recce cameras of twenty inch focal length behind the pilot. For oblique photography at Celle we used the Spitfire XIV, the fighter version, which had been modified to take the fourteen inch oblique camera.

There were also one or two other types of aircraft there, such as a Spitfire XI, an Anson, and a few Austers. A photograph which I took from the air shows that we also had a Harvard and a Tiger Moth. The Austers, which belonged to an Army Reconnaissance unit, were high-wing single-engined monoplanes with fixed undercarriage. They were similar in size to the Tiger Moth but had an enclosed cabin with space for one or two passengers, and were excellent for low-level reconnaissance or as a general runabout.

We were a happy crowd on the Squadron and spent our time doing quite a lot of photo recce (see Figure 3, page 56), although only for practice. As well as taking vertical photographs I was glad to be able to try my hand at oblique photography; for some reason this type of photography had been virtually ignored at Benson. I still have prints of one set of obliques which I took, some of Celle which show part of the impressive German *autobahn* system, motorway-type roads built as long ago as the 1930s, long before such roads had even been thought of elsewhere. Other pictures show the

*Plate 11, Celle Control Tower, with an Anson in the foreground.*

complete devastation of Hanover, with little but rubble and the skeletons of buildings. Yet others were of Celle, and it is interesting to compare these with photos which I took with my own camera from an Auster, which came out far better, simply because they were taken from a lower altitude so that there was less intervening haze. I found the Auster particularly good for taking photographs with my hand camera, since it was slow and could fly really low. I took several photos of the countryside in this way, and a few of the infamous concentration camp at Belsen which was now a site of mass graves.

Most of our flying was in Spitfire XIVs, since there were more XIVs than XIXs, and we did formation and cross-country exercises as well as photo recce. I once had a frightening experience on one of these flights. I was taking off as the third in a formation flight of three, and in order to catch up quickly with the other two I raised my wheels as soon as I could after taking off. The undercarriage control was a large lever on the right hand side of the cockpit and while operating it I looked down for a moment and must have inadvertently moved the control column because when I looked up again the aircraft was banked to the left with the nose pointing towards the ground. It was all too close for comfort, and just in time I pulled the stick back and once again managed to get myself on to an even keel. It certainly scared me, since for the next few minutes my right leg would not stop juddering up and down with the 'twitch'. When I landed I found that those who had been watching the take-off from the dispersal thought that I was trying to loop the loop!

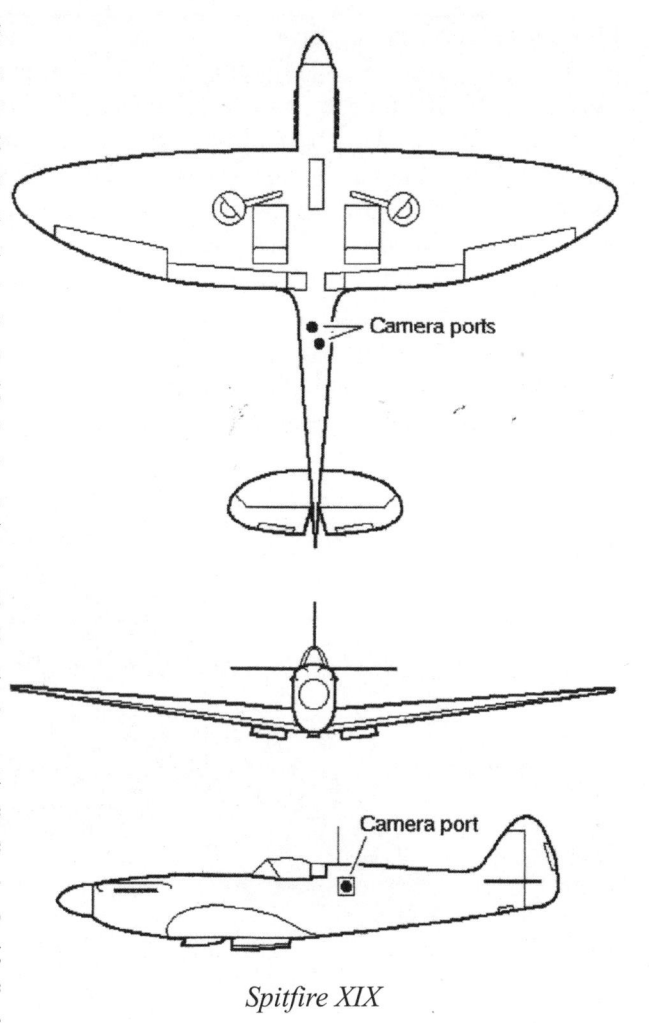

I enjoyed several flights in an Auster as passenger and then I was given the opportunity to fly it myself once I had been initiated into the mysteries of the cockpit and engine by another pilot, who then accompanied me as passenger – it had no dual control. It felt paper-light after the Spitfire, but did not have the fineness and precision of control of the Tiger Moth.

On only my second flight piloting an Auster, I was asked to fly a Flight Lieutenant Rylands to RAF Bückeburg, an airfield about 50 miles to the south-west of Celle. That may sound like throwing both of us in at the deep end, but the Auster was a simple machine to fly, and I had by now got more than 150 hours solo flying to my credit in various aircraft. The navigation was easy, since the weather was good and I had done enough local flying by this time to be familiar with the area. So we set off cheerfully and landed at Bückeburg forty minutes later. It felt most peculiar landing such a tiny and slow light aircraft on the huge concrete runway there, and after touching down I went along the rest of its length by taxying unduly fast – indeed almost fast enough to be flying – in order to get to the far end without delay before turning off towards the Control Tower. Rylands got out with a farewell wave and I taxied back to the runway

*Plate 12, a Spitfire XIX*

*Plate 13, a Spitfire XIV*

to take off and return on my own to Celle. This was a new experience – for the first time I had acted as a transport pilot!

My memories of Celle are largely of the social life. We quite often went into the town, among other things to visit a shop set up by the NAAFI for British Service personnel. This sold items from various European countries, particularly scents from France which were not available to the local Germans. The girls behind the counter were German and must have felt jealous at seeing what was available to the British troops.

In the evenings we would sometimes visit the local Ratskeller which had been taken over by the British – a rather élite version of the German beer cellar – untouched by war and probably looking much as it must have done in Hitler's day. There was no shortage of liquor, which was available in great variety and again came from all over Europe. It was here that I first encountered liqueurs and cocktails, some with, to me, fascinating names like White Lady and Bloody Mary. I set out to try a new one each time I went there just to see what they were all like. I eventually came to the conclusion that most liqueurs were overrated, many being rather oily, although some, particularly those with distinct flavours such as orange, coffee or chocolate, I quite liked. My favourite was Liqueur de Cassis, a blackcurrant liqueur which I have since found can be duplicated with almost as good a flavour as the original by mixing Ribena with vodka in suitable proportions.

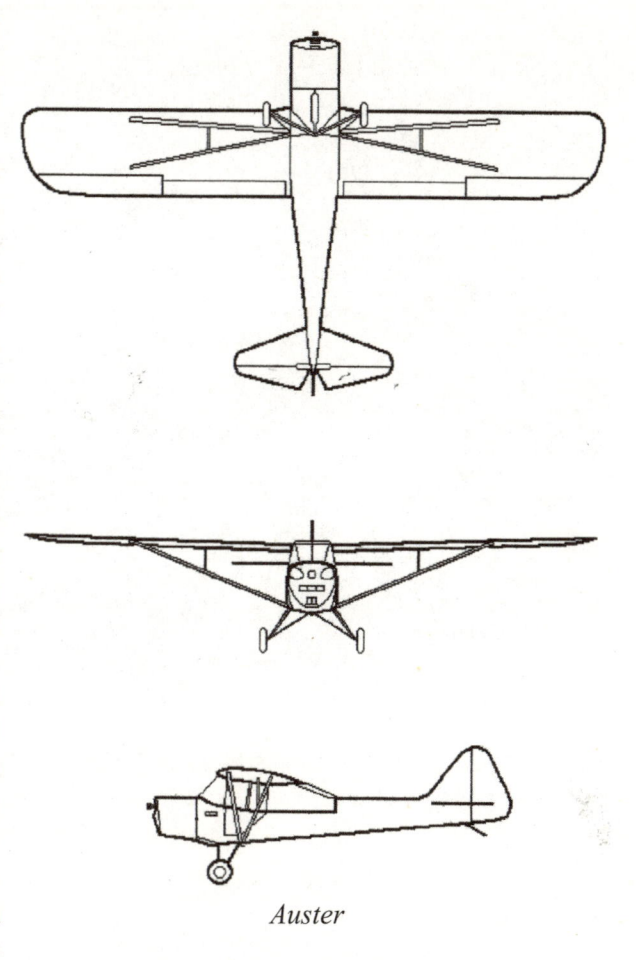

One evening I was persuaded to go out on the town by a colleague who had got to know a couple of fraüleins living on their own in a small ground-floor flat in Celle. There was a curfew in the town, and in the evenings nobody was allowed to go out on the streets, which were patrolled by the Military Police. If you went on an evening escapade of this sort you were there for the night whether you liked it or not.

We arrived at the house in the early evening and were welcomed by the two

*Auster*

*Plate 14, the daily inspection on a Spitfire XIV.*

*Plate 15, a Spitfire XIX. Note the five-bladed propeller to absorb the power of the Griffon engine on this and the Spitfire XIV opposite.*

fraüleins, but it was not long before I realized that this was just not my cup of tea: the women were blowzy, far older than myself, and might even have been prostitutes. I had no wish to stay, and curfew or no curfew I preferred to chance my luck out in the open. The trouble was that the airfield was on the opposite side of the town and some way outside it, and there was no form of transport available so late in the day. Somehow I had to avoid the patrols and yet get right round the town. Luckily it was late summer, and the night was not too dark, so I set off on foot towards the outskirts with a view to working my way round outside the built-up region.

It may sound straightforward in theory, but in practice it was incredibly difficult since it meant getting over hedges and round fields. Of course I had no map with me, and so had no idea from one moment to the next where I was or how far I had still to

*Plate 16, the author with a Spitfire XIV at Celle.*

go, or even if I was going in the right direction. I expected eventually to meet the road to the airfield, and then walk straight on from there, but the journey seemed to be never-ending. It was approaching dawn when at last I reached a distant part of the airfield without ever hitting the connecting road, and finally stumbled into my quarters just about exhausted. Ever since then I have had the greatest admiration for those prisoners of war who had escaped and made it on foot to the Swiss border or elsewhere.

A more innocent escapade was duck-shooting. Somebody managed to organize a duck shoot and invited several of us along. Where the shotguns came from I have no idea, since they are hardly the type of gun issued to the Armed Forces. Perhaps they came from the old Luftwaffe armoury, since it would not surprise me if German officers regarded wildlife shooting as a sport to which they were entitled as a form of relaxation. We went off in the back of a 15-cwt truck to some nearby marshland just as it was getting dusk, and waited for the duck to come over. My contribution to the kill was nil –

*Plate 17, a Spitfire XIV taxying out at Celle.*

I now wonder if I even had a gun – but what I mainly remember is being amazed at the masses of fireflies twinkling in the darkness on a grassy bank nearby, the only time in my life that I have ever seen them.

At that time members of the Armed Forces were given free rations of both chocolate (of terrible quality) and cigarettes. I always ate the chocolate since it was better than no chocolate at all, but since I didn't smoke I used the cigarettes for barter. The Germans were extremely short of them, so much so that cigarettes had become a form of currency, and were passed from hand to hand in exchange for goods or services, although I suppose that somebody must have smoked them eventually. Through this mode of exchange I acquired a pair of compact German military binoculars made by Hensoldt, presumably taken from a German officer, alive or dead, for which I paid 100 cigarettes. The binoculars are still in my family and although there is evidence of deterioration of the glue which holds the lenses, resolution and clarity of image are still excellent more than forty years later. I also acquired in the same way a cine camera with automatic exposure meter – unusual for that time – but I never used it and eventually sold it in England.

The RAF had a thing about sending people on courses, and after I had settled down at Celle I was sent on an Intelligence Course at an RAF centre at Highgate in London which lasted three weeks, travelling first of all as passenger in one of our own Ansons to RAF Bückeburg, and then on to Croydon in a Dakota, eventually returning the same way.

On the course we were instructed in such things as international relations, the importance of Germany as a central European country, and the dangerous political consequences of the vacuum that

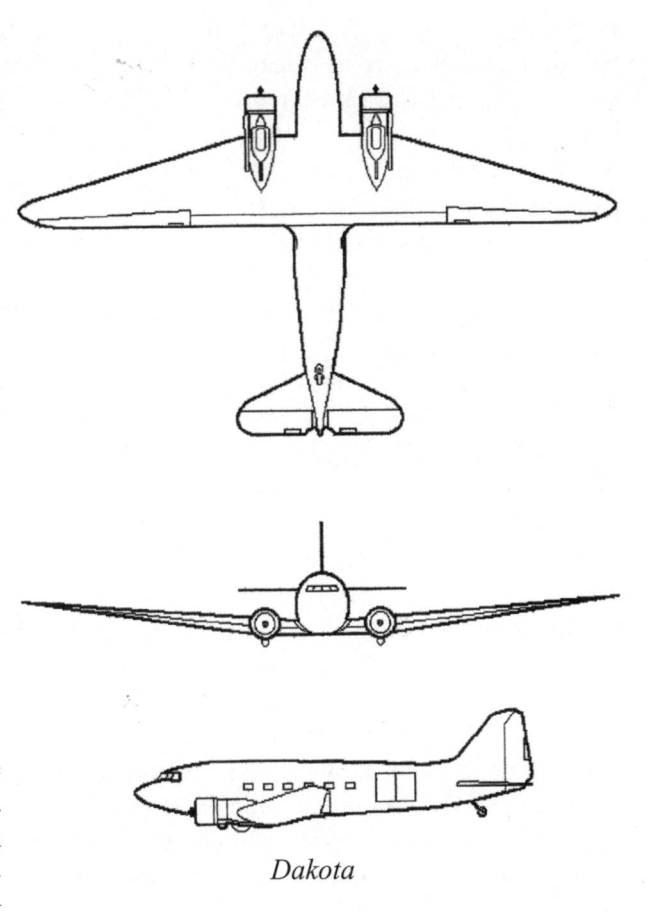

*Dakota*

would be created if Germany were not helped to stand on her own feet again; looking back over the years I now realize what remarkably good sense the lectures made. There was also more conventional instruction on intelligence matters, and I now feel that it must have been as a result of my attendance on this course that I was later made Intelligence Officer in the next Squadron to which I was posted.

While in London I bought what was then a complete innovation in the field of writing: a Biro. I give it a capital letter since that was the name of the firm which produced the first and only ballpoint pen at the time. Nowadays ballpoint pens are universal, but in 1946 they had only just been invented, and the thought of a pen which did not need refilling and wrote by means of a little metal ball in its tip intrigued me no end. It gave me quite a thrill just to see it working, silly though that may seem in these days of universal ballpoints. It cost thirty shillings, or £1.50,[1] which was a lot of money then, and the ink cartridge could not be replaced. Indeed, the plain black case had a left hand thread to discourage you from finding out how it worked. That didn't fool me, and inside I discovered a metal tube folded back on itself three times which contained the

---

1 Retail Prices Index: 1946, approximately 7; 1990, approximately 126.

ink. When it was empty I intended to keep it as an historical souvenir, but it has disappeared long since.

Another course, which was really enjoyable, was a five-day one at a gliding school at Salzgitter near the Harz Mountains. This school was one of those created in Hitler's Germany to get round the restrictions on military power imposed by the Allies after the First World War, aiming to teach potential Luftwaffe pilots the rudiments of flying.

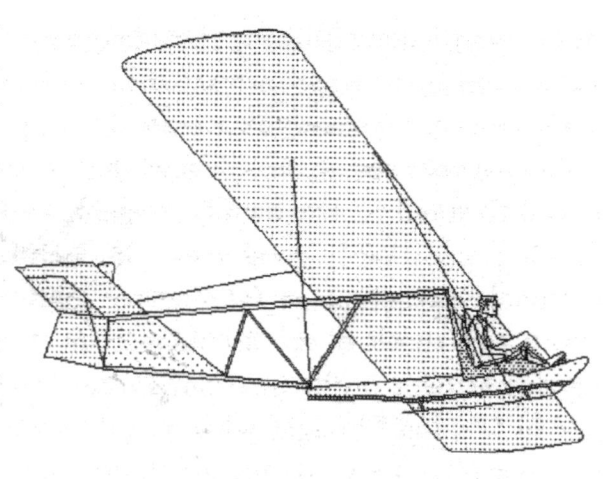

*SG 38 glider*

Several of us from Celle went there in an RAF truck, none of whom had had any gliding experience at all. Like everything else in Germany at that time this course, including accommodation, was free, while the gliders were, by the standards of the time, excellent. They were all single-seaters; gliders with dual control did not appear until considerably later. When learning to glide the pilot of powered aircraft has virtually to go back to square one, since the absence of an engine means that he has to learn a new flying technique; but he learns it quickly.

We started on a primitive glider called the SG 38,[2] similar to the British Dagling. The fuselage consisted of an open girder framework to which was attached a rectangular fabric-covered wing above and a tailplane behind. The pilot sat on a wooden seat bolted to a forward projection of the framework in front of and below the wing. He had a stick between his legs which controlled the ailerons and elevators, and his feet rested on the rudder pedals. That was all. There was no cockpit and the pilot was right out in the open, strapped to the framework, with nothing in front of him, nothing to either side, and only the seat that he was sitting on below him – rather like a Microlite, but of course with no engine. It looked a bit scary, but felt quite safe, and it gave you a real sense of what flying was all about, far more so than even the Tiger Moth.

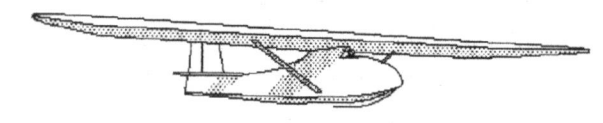

*Grunau glider*

Since there were no instruments, speed was judged by the noise of the air across the rigging and wings, and by the feel of the controls. The approach to the stall was indicated by the dying away of this noise, the stall itself being no more than a gentle dropping of the nose. As an efficient glider the SG 38 was terrible. There was no attempt at reducing drag or increasing efficiency; it was simply a workhorse for teaching

---

2 SG is short for Schulglitter, meaning literally school glider.

*Plate 18, an SG 38 glider at Salzgitter. Note that the pilot has nothing between him and the world around except the seat hs is sitting on.*

the basic elements of flying.

There were also at Salzgitter some Grunaus, German high efficiency sailplanes. By present-day standards they were not aerodynamically very efficient since they had open cockpits and a strut on each side joining wing to fuselage, both of which increase drag, but they were one of the best sailplanes of the time.

The school and the hangars were set on the brow of a hill, at the bottom of which was a flat field from which we flew. Every morning each glider was hauled out of its hangar to the top of the slope, and a cable which stretched away on both sides attached to the nose shackle. The glider was launched down the slope of the hill by several people holding on to the cable on either side at an angle of about 45 degrees to the glider's heading and running down the slope. It was landed in the field at the bottom so as to be ready for the day's gliding. Here the gliders were launched into the air by a petrol-driven winch at the windward end of the field which hauled them forward by means of a wire cable. When high enough, the pilot released the cable and went on to soar or land depending on the weather conditions.

We Spitfire pilots had to start almost at the beginning with a Low Hop in an SG 38, just rising briefly into the air to get the feel of the controls before settling down on to the ground again. Next was the High Hop where the pilot was allowed to go considerably higher, but still landing straight ahead. Finally we were allowed to make a circuit, banking round to the left after releasing the cable and then flying parallel to the edge of the field, eventually landing at the starting point. We would then switch to the Grunau and go through the same procedure. For those who had never flown before, there would be a stage before the Low Hop, when the glider would be pulled slowly along the ground without getting airborne, the pupil simply getting the feel of keeping the glider upright with the ailerons only. This was all very different from the way it is done now with dual control, when the pupil can get into the air straight away.

To see the sort of progress made by those who could already fly, I have laid out details of my own flights at Salzgitter (Table 2). I had hoped that I might manage to catch a thermal and stay up for a reasonable time, but the weather was mediocre. I obviously had beginner's luck, since the first time I went up for a circuit in the Grunau I was in the air for nearly seven minutes, which suggests that I had indeed briefly found a thermal.

| Day of the course | Glider | Type of Flight | Duration of flight |
| --- | --- | --- | --- |
| 1 | SG 38 | Low hop | – |
|   | SG 38 | High hop | – |
|   | SG 38 | 3 Circuits | c. 2 min. |
| 2 | Grunau | 2 Low hops | – |
|   | Grunau | Circuit | 6 min 47 sec |
|   | Grunau | Circuit | 2 min 50 sec |
| 3 | Grunau | Circuit | 3 min 53 sec |
| 4 | Grunau | Circuit | 2 min 5 sec |
|   | Grunau | Circuit | 1 min 30 sec |
|   | Grunau | Circuit | 1 min 30 sec |
|   | Grunau | Circuit | 2 min 18 sec |
| 5 | Grunau | Circuit | 3 min 2 sec |
|   | Grunau | Circuit | 2 min 6 sec |
|   | Grunau | Circuit | 3 min 16 sec |

*Table 2, Details of my flights on the Salzgitter Gliding Course.*

On the journey back from Salzgitter to Celle we went through Brunswick, and it was an eye-opener to see from the ground the type of devastation which I had already seen of Hanover from the air. Like Hanover the town was almost completely destroyed – ruin upon ruin, with only the shells of buildings standing. I still cannot comprehend how the Germans were able to recover so rapidly from the virtually complete ruin of their cities.

Back at Celle one not unpleasant duty that I was given one day was to act as duty officer supervising the flying at an air-to-ground firing range. This range was a large expanse of heath near Fassberg to the north of Celle (see Fig. 3, page 56). It was used by fighter squadrons to practice bombing or shooting at ground targets. I was accompanied by a few groundcrew, and spent my time on a wooden tower or platform with radio facilities which enabled me to talk to the pilots – in this case from a Belgian Squadron – over the radio, directing their flying, mostly with the purpose of avoiding collisions. I was fairly high up with a good view all round and it was a good opportunity for getting some close-up photographs of low-flying aircraft. Perhaps I took my duties

*Plate 19, the ruins of Brunswick in 1946.*

less seriously than I should have done, since I asked one of the pilots on the radio to do a 'beat-up' of the observation tower. He was more than happy, since that is the kind of mad flying that Belgian pilots liked to do, and I got what I wanted. The photograph on the next page shows a Spitfire XVI, not very far away, coming head-on for the camera. I was so intent on taking the picture that I really did not appreciate how close he came, but out of the corner of my eye I saw the groundcrew beside me duck as with a roar the Spitfire just skimmed the tower. I thought afterwards that things might after all have been getting a little too dangerous!

*Plate 20, a mad Belgian in a Spitfire XVI aiming directly for me in the observation tower at Fassberg - a bit scary!*

While I was at Celle I was sent on a week's leave to the town of Bad Harzburg, a small health spa on the edge of the rolling forested Harz Mountains. A large comfortable hotel, the Harzburger Hof, had been commandeered by the British, and was used as a relaxation and pleasure centre for commissioned officers. It really was luxurious and, like the gliding, all free.

While there I would sometimes wander into the local hills on my own with my camera. The walking was easy going and took me up to the tops of small hills where I might find a clearing with a view over the whole area or back towards the plains below. In the distance there was one hill which rose slightly higher than the rest and which had a tall cairn or monolith on top: the Brocken (3,747 feet) of Brocken Spectre fame.

On one occasion a colleague and I walked to the dividing line between the British Zone and the neighbouring Russian Zone (later East Germany). Exactly where the border was we never found out, because we decided that, the Russians being what they were and also rather trigger-happy, it was wiser to go no further than a large wooden notice which had on it in large letters BRITISCHES GEBIET indicating British territory and in Russian characters ANGLEESKAYA ZONA.

Another time I took a bus to a small village called Altenau in the depths of the Harz mountains. It was a fairytale setting. The village was set deep in a small isolated valley with meadows on the hillsides rising up towards the forest encircling it above, rather like a softer Switzerland. It was idyllic and peaceful, with half-timbered houses set

*Plate 21, a colleague at the border between the British and Russian zones of Germany (1946).*

among streets lined with beech and chestnut, and a little tinkling stream running through it all. There might never have been a war.

Eventually my pleasant time at Celle came to an end. It appeared that a couple of Spitfire pilots whom I had known at Benson had been killed while flying with a photo recce squadron in India and had to be replaced. One, Arthur Chin, had hit a concrete hut while trying to go round again after a failed landing. The other, Ali Leheta, had plunged into the ground from a great height after his oxygen system had become obstructed by frozen water vapour just as happened to Bill Strachan, mentioned briefly in the last chapter. (Oxygen is stored under pressure and should be quite dry; if there is any moisture, the water will condense and freeze as it emerges to the lower pressure outside and the ice so formed may block the narrow outlet tube.) I was to replace one of these two. I was enjoying life at Celle, and did not in the least want to go to an outlandish place like India, but in retrospect this posting turned out to be one of the great events in my life, the nine months which I subsequently spent in India being an unforgettable experience.

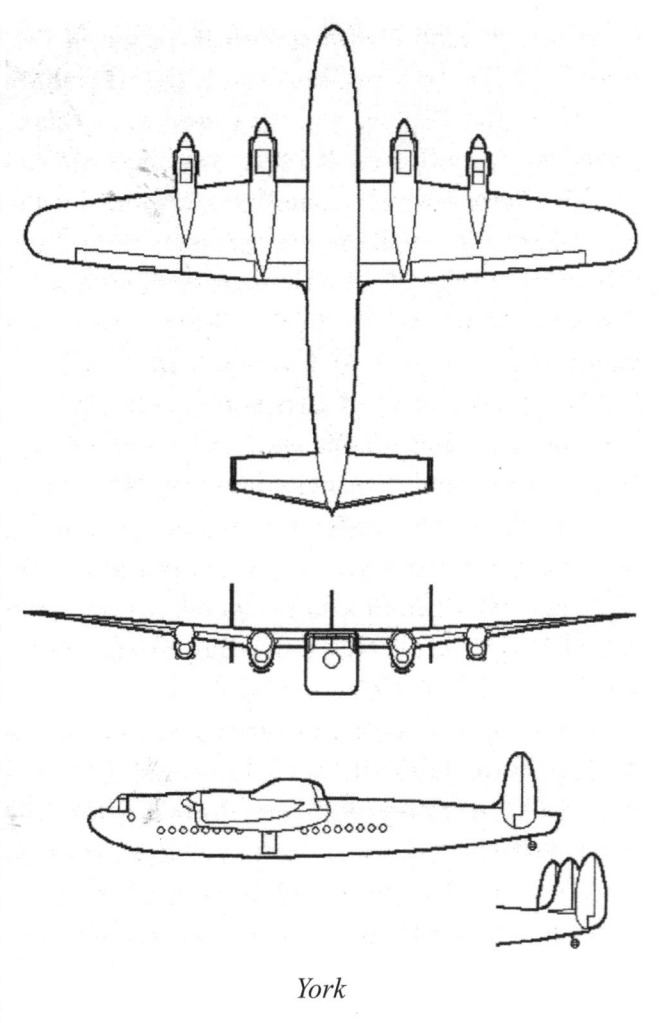

*York*

I left Celle after a stay of about four months. Like most postings it was just a matter of collecting together my few belongings and going where I was told. But I had a small problem of how to get my cigarette-bartered binoculars home. It was not a good idea to take them myself, since I did not at that time know whether I would be given time to visit home before going on to India. So I made them up into a parcel and asked a colleague who was going back to the UK on leave if he would take them for me – perhaps not declaring them at Customs – and post them when he got there, to which he agreed. They duly arrived home safe and sound, but in retrospect I am amazed, firstly at my temerity in asking somebody else effectively to smuggle something through

Customs, and secondly at his agreeing to do it for me. Was this because both of us were young and naïve?

Off I went once more to RAF Bückeburg, from where once again I travelled with several others in a Dakota back to the UK. This was one flight I did not enjoy. We sat on bench seats placed along the inside of the fuselage of the Dakota when suddenly the person next to me started being airsick, which continued on and off throughout the rest of the journey. Needless to say I started to feel a bit peculiar myself.

We flew first to RAF Membury just south of Lambourn in Wiltshire,[3] which took two and three-quarter hours, and then back to RAF Manston on the coast of Kent, another thirty minutes. From there I had to go to RAF Hornchurch in Essex from where I had originally gone out to Germany. Here I had more jabs, this time adding yellow fever to my record to prepare me for the Far East.

As it turned out I did get some leave, after which I went to RAF North Weald near Epping just north of London, another old fighter airfield which had now become a transit camp, before a final journey to RAF Lyneham in Wiltshire for the 'plane to India. Lyneham was the RAF's main centre for long-distance journeys. These journeys were mostly carried out by the four-engined York, flown either by the RAF for the Armed Forces or by BOAC (British Overseas Airways Corporation) for civilians. The York was based on the Lancaster bomber, but had three fins and rudders, and a much more spacious fuselage. It was a lovely aircraft, and I looked forward to flying in one, but it was going to be a long journey.

---

2 As far as I can make out the site of Membury airfield is now the Membury Service Station on the M4 motorway.

# 7

# India

*The flight to India was on an Avro York, a transport aircraft whose wings, tail, undercarriage and engines were derived from the famed Lancaster bomber. Typically, the York carried 21 passengers.*

The journey to India[1] took three days. Apart from the fact that the long-distance piston-engined aircraft were slower than the present-day jets, flying was only carried out during daylight hours, with overnight accommodation at the intermediate stops of RAF Luqa in Malta and RAF Habbaniya in Iraq, which was then a British Protectorate.

The pilot of the York was an RAF officer whose rank was no higher than my own. This rather surprised me, since I considered that flying a large number of people – men and women from the various Services – a quarter of the way round the world carried considerable responsibility. But then in any walk of life rank is not necessarily related to technical ability, and as long as he was a competent pilot that was good enough for me.

We left Lyneham in the middle of November 1946 and flew over France and Sardinia, landing at Luqa after a non-stop flight of seven and a half hours to find the sun shining out of a clear evening sky, a pleasant change from the chilly and overcast autumn day that we had left behind.

The next day we flew east along the Mediterranean, then over the dry landscape of Palestine with a view of the bright green thread of the valley of the river Jordan twisting its tortuous way south, and finally across the sandy brown of the deserts of Syria and Iraq to land at the isolated outpost of Habbaniya after eight and a half hours in the air.

RAF Habbaniya was an island of comfort set against the left bank of the Euphrates about 50 miles west of Baghdad. It was virtually surrounded by desert, relieved only by the local greenery bordering the river just at the edge of the airfield, and it seemed a desolate place at which to be stationed. Luckily it was not particularly hot at the time, although in the summer the region can become intolerable.

It was here that I got my first introduction, described by a fellow-traveller, to one of the hazards of India: the loose-wallah. This is a native who creeps into your bedroom in the dead of night to filch any valuables that he can lay hands on, even taking articles from under your pillow while you sleep. He enters stripped naked and with his body greased all over so that it is virtually impossible to get a grip on him if he should be caught on the job. I began to wonder what the RAF was letting let me in for!

---

1 In this and subsequent chapters I shall be using the name 'India' to refer, as it did then, to the whole of the subcontinent under the jurisdiction of the British. Other names used will also be those of that time.

The last leg of the journey took us to Karachi on the west coast of northern India, flying first of all south-east towards the Persian Gulf where we crossed the green and watery swampland stretching inland from its head, then down the Gulf itself, before finally turning eastward to land after eight hours at the RAF airfield of Mauripur just outside Karachi.

As I climbed out of the York the heat hit me like a blast furnace, an introduction to India that I have never forgotten. Yet looking back the sensation must have been more in contrast to the coolness of the York since at that time, the end of November, the temperature at Mauripur was low compared with what I would experience later on. Before me stretched the airfield beyond which was a flat sandy semi-desert landscape with a few scrubby bushes disappearing into the heat haze and the sun blazing down from a blue sky – a hot dryness typical of much of India for a large part of the year. Because India is so different from anything which the newcomer from the UK may have known, I will try and give some picture of the country where I was to live for the next nine months.

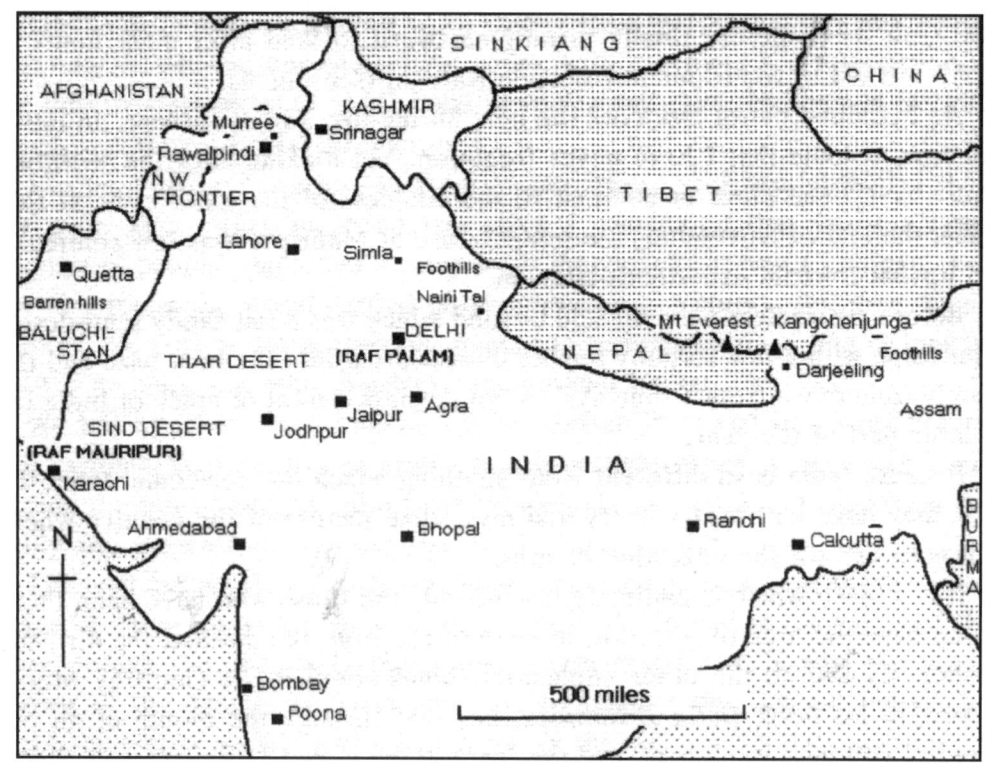

*Figure 4, Map of north India (this map is unavoidably distorted.)*

It is a place which is endlessly fascinating, and those who have been there often have the urge to revisit it, in spite of the heat, the disease, the dirt, the dishonesty and all the other unpleasant things about it. As Geoffrey Moorhouse, in his book *India Britannica*, has said through the mouth of an old hand: 'I still miss it, y'know; and the funny thing is that I miss most of all the things I didn't much care for when I was there, like the smells and the noise of all those crowds pushin' and shovin' their way through the bazaar.' This is all too true; you ignore the bad bits and get a strange yen to return. I have felt it strongly myself. What a country, that it can get such a grip on those who have lived there!

India was, and still is for much of its population, a relatively primitive society. The rich Indians have always lived well, but the standard of living has in general been extremely low compared with that in the UK, and because labour was cheap, the British were able to keep large native staffs in their homes and elsewhere. Indeed, a large staff was unavoidable, since the Indian servants had a strong sense, often related to religion, of what tasks each person could and could not do. As a result there were sub-hierarchies of servants all down the line so that each type of menial task could be done by only one type of person.

**The climate**

It is the climate which hits the visitor first, as it did me, although its effect depends on the time of year. In much of the country the winter months are pleasant and somewhat similar to a good dry English summer, but during the spring, from about March onwards, the temperature rises progressively until for a large part of the day it may be well over 100°F (37°C) – the dry or hot season – after which until late autumn the climate becomes humid but a little less hot – the wet season. Indeed, the hot season is so unpleasant that in the earlier days of the Raj the staff of the Government would move lock, stock and barrel to the cooler climate of Simla, a hill station about 7,000 feet up in the foothills of the Himalayas, to continue their governing at a more equable temperature; according to Brian Montgomery in his book *Monty's Grandfather* this continued as late as 1940. He says that round about 1850 the families of the senior administrators might move to the hills with their retinue of perhaps 40 servants who would go all the way on foot, and with all their furniture packed on to something like fourteen camels and various other pack animals, to stay there for five months, before reversing the whole process.

In the hot season the temperature rises higher in the inland parts of the country than on the coast, but this is often compensated for by a much lower humidity which increases the cooling effect of sweat. Provided that the air is moving over the body it is possible to keep reasonably comfortable, and it may be better to keep on the move than to sit still. The air inside many buildings is circulated by electric fan – with air conditioning virtually non-existent when I was there – but in the previous century the air had been wafted to and fro by a *punkah* (a word used also for the electric fan) which was a sheet of woven cloth suspended from the ceiling. This was moved by a menial called a *punkah-wallah* who pulled it, so it is said, by means of a string attached to his big toe while he lay half-asleep on the verandah outside.

My own experience of the weather where I was subsequently stationed not far from Delhi, may show some of the vagaries of the Indian climate. Delhi is in the middle of northern India and about as far from the sea as you can get. The humidity was low, and although we sweated a great deal during the day as the hot season progressed, I never had that feeling of exhaustion which in a heat wave in England is caused mainly by the high humidity. However, some places on the coast, such as Calcutta and Madras, are always humid, and I found Calcutta even in April to be intolerable; a fan going all night did not alleviate the discomfort.

During the winter months there was no problem, since the temperature in the shade was only in the seventies or eighties Fahrenheit even with the sun blazing down outside. As winter gave way to spring and then to early summer the days became progressively hotter, not always with a clear sky. I have photographs showing plenty of cloud in March during the dry season, with thunder and lightning in the evening. On many days in the early summer the temperature regularly reached 110°F in the shade, and once rose to 116°F (46°C). Under these conditions, if you just rested your arm on a desk or table it was soon sitting in a pool of sweat. If your arms were not touching anything and if there was a breeze it was not so bad, since the sweat evaporated immediately and cooled you in the process. Riding in a 15-cwt truck – our standard form of transport – was all right, if you kept your elbows off your knees, since the breeze kept you dry, but if you rested your arms for a moment there was again a puddle underneath. I soon got into the habit of keeping out of contact with anything, and of finding the place with the greatest breeze. The backs of people's shirts, particularly of the groundcrew who worked out in the open on our aircraft, often had a dark patch of sweat surrounded by a white incrustation of salt.

This kind of weather continued until the middle of June, when the monsoon arrived, bringing rain and a fall in temperature. Although only one monsoon is usually referred to, there are in fact two, a north-west one and a south-west one, related to different airstreams occurring at different times of the year.

The north-east monsoon brings dry air from the Asian land mass north of the country and is associated with the progressively rising temperatures of spring and early summer. The air is then on the whole dry so that the whole of the north-west, and much of the northern and central parts of the country are brown and dry. Except for surviving scrub there is, at least from the air, an appearance of semi-desert over the whole central area; indeed one large region, between Delhi in the middle and Karachi on the west coast, is genuine desert, comprising the Thar and Sind Deserts.

The south-west monsoon, which brings warm moist air from the Indian Ocean south of the country is the one commonly referred to as the monsoon and with it comes heavy rain. Sometimes it fails and the parched countryside is then deprived of the rain it so much needs.

**The people of India**
The people themselves provided a kaleidoscope of colour and appearance, often as a result of differences in religion, which affects dress as well as habits. The main religious groups were the Hindus, of varying sects from the high-caste Brahmins down to the Untouchables (the Outcastes or Harijans), the Moslems, the men moustached, the

*Plate 22 (RAF) a street-seller in Karachi, India.*

women veiled from top to toe in a white burqa with only a cloth grill through which to view the outside world, and the Sikhs with their dark impressive beards. There were also various minor sects, such as the Parsees – highly successful in business, but mostly limited to the region of Bombay – and holy men, some of whom have renounced the trappings of the world.

Clothes were a constant fascination; from the coverings of the head down to those of the feet the variety was endless. The commonest headgear of the men was the puggaree – a form of turban – which is a length of white cotton material wound rather untidily round the head. In the more formal atmosphere of the RAF Mess the various Indian servants wore a more colourful and neater version of turban, and I now wonder if the individual style of these might have had some relation to status.

The Hindu men often wore a loose white shirt and a *dhoti*, a length of white cotton cloth wound loosely round the body and falling almost to the feet, the end drawn up again between the legs. The Hindu women's clothing was much more attractive; it consisted mainly of a sari, a length of vari-coloured cloth wound round the body and over the shoulder, rather like a Roman toga, with a fold brought over the head. The large area of colour gave the women a brilliance seldom seen in other countries. The better-off women, as is often the case wherever you are, wore garments whose colour scheme was simpler but more subtle; the most attractive sari I saw, worn by a woman who was clearly well-off, was made of a filmy material, delicate emerald green in colour, which certainly caught the eye.

The men had one ubiquitous and unattractive habit: the chewing of the betel nut which stained their teeth red. The residue was eventually spat out, so that the pavements in the towns were covered with red blotches. *Everyman's Encyclopaedia* says that betel nuts are derived from the fruit of the betel-nut palm; they are 'boiled, sliced and sun-dried. Each piece for chewing is wrapped in a leaf of the betel pepper-vine, with some lime and often an aromatic flavouring. The betel reddens the mouth and blackens the teeth, but preserves them.' They were sold by itinerant pavement traders; the vine leaves were laid out in front of them, and in the middle of each was a reddish paste containing the nut.

The people as a whole were pleasant and quiet, but as shown by the violence which could be produced by riots, religion-inspired brutality and cruelty were not far below the surface. There have been riots of one sort or another since the early days of the British occupation of India; these were often against the British themselves, but, as Independence approached, the Moslems and Hindus turned instead against each other,

*Plate 23, (RAF) the barber's shop, a main street in Karachi, India.*

resulting sometimes in severe massacres. The worst of these occurred when these two religions attacked each other at the time of Partition in 1947, when about a quarter of a million people were killed. Some Hindu-Moslem riots occurred not far from the airfield near Delhi to which I was eventually posted, resulting in the destruction of whole villages, a particularly sad sight in view of their inherent poverty.

It might be thought that there would be considerable antagonism against the British as the dominating race in India, and this had in the past been so, but once the departure of the British was definitely on the horizon in the 1940s such antagonism became more sporadic. I was there during the nine months immediately preceding Independence, and never once did I have any sense of being threatened. I often wandered on my own through the countryside or some parts of towns, and still felt perfectly safe. That does not mean to say that there was no danger. There have always been some members of the population who might kill you for your money or even for a religious principle, but these seemed to have diminished over the years. The days when it was not safe to walk on isolated roads because of the risk of being killed by *dacoits* or *thugs* – who practised a kind of religion called *thuggee* – were long in the past.

Nevertheless the native quarter of towns, including the ancient town of Old Delhi, was mostly out of bounds to troops, probably because if there was any violence to the British, that is where it would be most likely to occur. Although most of the Indians who came into contact with the British could speak English, you did not have to go far off the beaten track to find that you were not understood. Most of us picked up a few words of Urdu, the main language of northern India, but no more than the commonest of words and phrases, such as *tik hai* for all right; we would have been useless in a wider Indian context.

**Servants and living conditions**
The British in India seemed to live, as I have implied, with a multitude of servants, as I soon discovered at Mauripur. The RAF Station was for me no more than a transit camp where I would stay for a fortnight until somebody at Air Headquarters in Delhi told me where to go. Even for this short time I was allocated a bearer, as personal servants were called. This worried me, since I did not want a personal servant; however, it was not only routine, but essential to have one. Wherever you went in India on a permanent or semi-permanent basis you had to be allocated a bearer, whom you might share with someone else. In a sense he was the equivalent of the Army batman, but he was really much more than that. He looked after your room, your kit, your laundry and all other immediate aspects of living. He guarded the contents of your room from thieves, he woke you in the morning, he brought morning tea if required, and generally acted as an intermediary between yourself and all the other essential services of the place, particularly those carried out by Untouchables, who acted as general dogsbodies, *sweepers* (cleaners), *dhobi-wallahs* (laundrymen), and so on. Without a bearer as intermediary it was impossible to get anything done.

The whole set-up of servants was one of established hierarchy and delegation. Every kind of service had to be carried out by a specialist in that service and no other type of person could or would do it. The water-tight compartments seen in British unions are nothing compared with those in India, where everything was broken down into what seemed like the smallest possible units. Without a bearer I could not have got my clothes washed, my drinking water supplied, or my room cleaned. As it was, all this was done frequently and remarkably efficiently; clothes were cleaned, laundered and starched. A complete set of clean clothes was laid out each day as routine, an apparent luxury which became a virtual necessity as the heat increased during the summer.

I was lucky when I first arrived at Mauripur in being allocated a really excellent bearer. He was a fine-looking man, in late middle age, with plenty of experience behind him. He must have had something of the Pathan (pronounced P'tarn) in him – he came from Murree up in the northern hills – since there was nothing subservient about him, and the Pathans, who come from the North West Frontier region, are a very independent people.

One sometimes hears of off-hand and degrading treatment of Indians by the British, but I only saw it once. This was a few months later when an RAF officer shouted at an Indian taxi-driver and generally treated him like dirt; it was shameful behaviour. In my experience the British were mostly courteous to the Indian servants and these were courteous back. Although most of us were only there on a relatively short-term basis and referred to Indians as *wogs* – a term which never meant anything more than any other form of Service slang – we got on well with the various Indian servants whom we came across. Those employed by the British were probably better off than many of their compatriots, but they still had low wages and poor accommodation and were usually far from homes which might be in some distant part of the country.

The various RAF Officers' Messes in India were on the whole quite good and in most cases the rooms had an electric fan in the ceiling for creating a breeze in the hot weather. We slept on the native *charpoy*, a not uncomfortable wooden bed framework with a criss-cross string weave for support. Baths did not exist, there were only showers. The toilets in the more modern concrete blocks, such as at Mauripur, were of the standard flush type, but in squadron Dispersals and in the living quarters of some RAF and Indian Air Force Stations which I visited they were a usually a variation of the thunder-box of the Army. You sat on the lavatory seat and below you was a metal tray to catch anything that fell. When you had performed, the tray was removed through a hole behind you (normally closed by a flap) in the outer wall of the building by a member of the Untouchable sect who was permanently watching and waiting and who disposed of the contents I know not where. (There was always the worry that it might be removed prematurely!) What happened when you had diarrhoea I hate to think; luckily I did not need to find out. But at least this was better than the local lack of sanitation in some villages; for example, Paul Scott, the author, staying with a leading citizen of a village in India, had to squat out in the fields like the locals (see *Paul Scott* by Hilary Spurling).

As regards luggage, the accepted practice when moving around in India, even temporarily was to take with you your bedding, including a thin mattress, the whole known as a bedroll. Only the *charpoy* was left behind. This was all made possible by the multiplicity of servants who looked after your needs. (It rather reminds me of the way in which Royalty in England used to moved around the country in mediaeval times when the whole of the king's household equipment accompanied him.) Accordingly there was little provision for supplying bedding to visitors staying at a strange place for a night or two; they were supposed to have brought their own sleeping equipment with them. In the course of flying around India I often had to stay a night at another airfield, but there was only space in the Spitfires for the bare minimum; even a holdall was a squeeze. As a result it sometimes caused considerable confusion when I turned up with no bedding whatsoever; the country was just not geared to such visits, but somehow the essentials were always produced without serious complaint.

*Plate 24 (RAF) a goat herd in a main street in Karachi. Members of the RAF personnel can be seen in the background.*

## Health

A big problem for white people in any tropical country is that of health, the main risks in India being heatstroke (so-called sunstroke), dysentery, and to some extent malaria. I will ignore yellow fever and typhus against which in any case we were immunised, since I never heard them mentioned. The appalling health problems with which Europeans used to live in the country in the nineteenth century seemed to be a thing of the past. In those days the living conditions of troops stationed in India were appalling and resulted in unnecessary loss of life simply from poor hygiene; the death rate in the British Army in India over many years was about 7 out of 100 men every year just from disease (see *Florence Nightingale* by C. Woodham-Smith). As hygiene improved and understanding of cause and effect increased, many of the diseases disappeared among the British population, and in the sheltered environment of an RAF Station I never heard of anything serious.

In its original guise, sunstroke was supposed to be caused by exposure to too much sun, and you were supposed to keep the back of the neck covered. This was a misinterpretation of what in most cases was heat stroke, caused largely by depletion of sodium from the body as a result of excessive sweating; by drinking only water when thirsty the sodium is not replaced and, if not treated, heatstroke will progress eventually to death. It can be prevented by taking salt tablets regularly; these were put out routinely at meals in the Mess, and we religiously helped ourselves to one every day. And as for the problem of the sun on the back of the neck, we used to go swimming in the heat of the day, and sunburn was the only thing we worried about.

*Plate 25, (RAF) a main street in Karachi with holy Hindu cows occupying the pavement.*

Dysentery is a disease mainly of hot countries, but I never heard of a case in the RAF, although we were certainly warned about it. The main rules which we were given were: (i) do not eat salads, and (ii) rinse any fruit in potassium permangate solution – which was supplied – before you eat it. I never suffered from any intestinal symptoms during my stay, and I attribute this mainly to the supervision of the cooking in the various Messes at which I stayed; the cooking was carried out by Indian cooks but was under the direct eye of a British catering officer.

Another disease of many tropical countries is malaria, and one great legacy which the British gave to the Indians was what seemed like progress towards its almost complete eradication. When flying to distant parts of the country I often had to stop overnight at places situated far apart and almost at the extreme limits of the subcontinent: west as far as Karachi and Baluchistan, east to Calcutta, south to Bangalore, and – on holiday – to the hills in the extreme north. The only time that I had to have a mosquito net at night was at the RAF airfield of Yelahanka outside Bangalore in the extreme south. Indeed, an Indian who was attached to our squadron near Delhi, which was a malaria-free area, had to use a mosquito net so that he, who had had malaria in the past, would not infect the local mosquitos. It is a sad sequel to this success story in public health that the Indian-run civil service which took over when the British left did not continue to keep malaria at bay and most of the country became malaria-infested again.

I ought to mention also prickly heat, from which some of us suffered, although I was thankful to be free of it. This is an irritating rash which develops mostly in the creases of the skin where sweat does not easily evaporate. It is most common in people with particularly fair skin, and there is nothing they can do about it except keep out of the sun and try to keep as cool as possible.

**More of life at RAF Mauripur**
I had arrived in India in RAF blue uniform, but I now had to get kitted out with a khaki drill uniform, consisting of khaki bush shirt and shorts, together with long woollen below-knee socks, and a bush hat of Australian style. Apart from the need for cool, light clothes it was important that they be made of material that could be washed daily in view of the great amount of sweating. When I arrived towards the end of November it was still warm enough to wear khaki drill, and although as winter progressed we would go back into blue battledress I would certainly need khaki drill the following year.

On the RAF Station there was a small shopping area which contained a shop run by an Indian tailor, so I went along to him and got measured up, expecting to have to wait several days before trying on the new uniform. To my surprise it was ready the very next day! Not only that, but it fitted perfectly. This was my introduction to one incredible aspect of Indian life – the efficiency of some of the small traders when it comes to making something to specification. Indian tailors are renowned for their ability to make anything out of anything and to do it quickly and cheaply. They are also said to be good at copying articles of clothing, even to the extent of including unwanted faults.

I also bought some comfortable Indian footwear. Standard black shoes were the official footwear with khaki drill, but it seemed sensible to have something more comfortable off duty. So I bought a pair of *chapplis* and a pair of *chappals*. *Chapplis* are sandals of a type that can be bought in the UK and which have a couple of interlinked straps crossing at the toes and going round the heel. The *chappal*, on the other hand, has no heel strap, and consists of a leather strap or cross straps across the front of the foot, attached to the sole at the nearest point. They are comfortable with bare feet, but with socks they keep sliding off.

One pleasant surprise which I had as soon as I arrived at Mauripur was to see bananas again. A peculiar thing to remember, you may say, but during the war tropical fruits were just not seen in England. There had been no oranges, no lemons, no grapefruit and no bananas since about 1939, simply because they had to be imported and the import of non-essential goods had been banned. So imagine my surprise at my first breakfast in India to find a whole basketful of bananas on the table. I had one every morning – what luxury!

I enjoyed going into Karachi, about four miles away, to look around the shops. There was a good bus service between the RAF Station and the town, although the buses themselves were ramshackle, and typical of the Indian motor trade. One wondered how they kept going although they never seemed to break down. They had no glass in the windows, but this was intentional so as to allow a cooling draught to pass through.

Karachi was my first introduction to Indian life and was endlessly fascinating. Being then a part of the unified country of India it was probably more polyglot than it would be now with the predominantly Muslim population of the subsequent Pakistan of which it became the capital. It was a strange mixture of ancient and modern, with camel-carts and the supercilious-looking camels walking sedately along a broad street through which an MG sports car might be trying to push its way between crowds of people. Occasionally a holy Hindu cow might stand motionless in the road and temporarily stop the traffic. No matter, time was unimportant.

In one part of the street in the warm of the afternoon people were lying on the pavement fast asleep, while in another there was a gathering of beggars holding up bowls for a free issue of cooked rice. Once I saw a bearded holy man, stark naked, walking along the pavement, with nobody taking any notice; it was all part of life.

Approaching the shops in Elphinstone Street, the main shopping area, I was surrounded by a crowd of *chikkos* (children) crying 'Baksheesh, sahib!' I had learned that the answer to this was '*Jallo!*' (Go away!) – or, more colloquially, '*Jow!*', but at that time it had little effect. It was said that the children who roamed the streets could tell from the colour of your knees that you were a newcomer, hence the admonition from old hands to 'Get yer knees brown!' There may be something in this, since when I visited Karachi again several months later I was troubled by children hardly at all. Or was it that my khaki drill no longer had that brand-new look about it?

The shops along Elphinstone Street were like those of any sophisticated Indian town of the time – a mixture of old and new. Some were glass-fronted and conventional in the Western sense, while others had that ramshackle appearance of anything typically Indian, with wooden shutters ready to close them off after hours. But many of the shops were no more than booths or small open unglazed compartments in the wall of a building, and some of the trade was simply carried on in the street.

*Plate 26, (RAF) a scribe on the pavement in Karachi.*

In one booth grocery provisions of various sorts were being sold, with grain and pulses of untold variety; in another, fruit and vegetables; in yet another a *mochi*, or cobbler, was carrying on his trade. There was also an itinerant grain-seller walking along the pavement with a wooden pole over his shoulder from one end of which was suspended a circular metal container divided up into compartments for different types of grain, from the other end the trader's cashbook, money and so on hung in a basket (Plate 22). In some cases the pavement itself was the shop. Sitting nearly in the gutter was a pair of barbers, the customers being shaved sitting cross-legged on the pavement in front of them (Plate 23).

In another part of the street was a *char-wallah* or tea-seller, with his canteens of hot tea, while around him, squatting in traditional Indian fashion, were his customers. Nearby, a flock of black goats was being driven gently along by a couple of boys each of whom was holding a baby goat in his arms (Plate 24), while another part of the pavement was occupied by some lethargic cows belonging, as far as I could see, to nobody in particular (Plate 25); since the cow was holy to the Hindu, they could do what they liked and nobody was going to move them on. Against the wall of an adjoining building a scribe was writing a letter for another Indian squatting in front of him (Plate 26). The whole made up a fascinating variety of people of all ages and types and occupations.

It was from a booth beside the pavement here that I bought a Parker 51 pen which I still have, although outmoded now by ballpoint pens. At the time they were all the rage, having a reputation for providing comfortable writing, and looking quite different from any pen before them. I think I paid somewhere between £2 and £3, which seems a lot now,[2] but at that time, just after the war, they were a new design and in short supply and therefore expensive, but I certainly paid less than I would have done in the UK. My main worry was that I might be swindled and the pen not work, but it turned out to be the best pen that I ever possessed.

My photography provided one amusing experience when I tried to photograph some of the interesting characters in Karachi. Before going to India I had bought a right-angled view-finder which clipped on to the top of the camera, so that when the camera was pointing towards the subject, you yourself were actually facing at right angles. The idea was that you could photograph people from close quarters without their being aware of it. My results at Karachi? Every single person that I tried to take unobtrusively in this way knew perfectly well that they were being photographed. I quickly gave up using the thing and obtained just as good photographs without it.

While at Mauripur I first discovered the delights of swimming in a tropical sea, and the thought of cooling off from the warmth of the day appealed to me. One day several of us managed to get a lift to a place a mile or two along the coast where there was a long sandy beach. The sea was beautifully warm, about 80°F, a pleasant change from the cold swimming baths or sea of England that I had experienced up to now. We plunged and splashed about to our hearts' content.

Another place which we found good for swimming were the premises of the Karachi Boat Club who allowed us to use their facilities. The club was set on an inlet called Chinna Creek on the other side of which was a mangrove swamp with the mangrove roots projecting down into the water. Where we swam was on the edge of what must be a most unhygienic city, with drains presumably going directly into the sea. The one-inch map I have of the district shows it to be hemmed in by the city on the north, a long mole with numerous railway lines on the west, and south, and otherwise surrounded by mangrove swamp and mud! I now wonder at our temerity at swimming in what must have been a most unhealthy site. Or were we, in our first days in India, just plain ignorant of the squalor of much of the place? But none of us suffered any ill-effects.

If you walked in the direction of the coast from the edge of Mauripur airfield you came to some large square reservoirs of seawater, each perhaps 50 yards across, acting as salt pans for the evaporation of sea water to obtain salt. And beyond them, nearer to the sea, was a great mass of pink which on closer inspection turned out to be a large flock of flamingoes.

One advantage that Karachi had over many other places in India was a built-in wind in the form of a permanent sea breeze. Every day this wind would get up and blow off the sea at a constant 25 mph. As a result, even when the air turned hotter you could still walk about the place and keep reasonably cool. This wind was also useful for flying; I once landed at Mauripur in a Spitfire several months later and it was a great help

---

2  Retail Prices Index: 1946, approx. 7; 1990, approx. 126.

in slowing down the aircraft.

Shortly after I arrived at Mauripur a crazy thought passed through my mind. I had read books about the climbs among the great mountains of the Himalayas, and I knew that Mt Everest was near the northern border of India. With a bit of luck, I thought, perhaps one day I might just catch a distant sight of that great peak away in the distance if I am stationed within reasonable range; but at that time just the idea of seeing it even from far away was no more than an idle dream.

Eventually after about two weeks somebody made up their mind that I still existed, and that it was time to send me somewhere so that I could be useful. I was to be posted to RAF Palam, about six miles south-west of Delhi, where I would join the only photo reconnaissance squadron in the country.

# 8

# Getting Settled In

I flew to Palam in a Dakota in December 1946, which was the best time of year for settling in. For a month or two there would be the pleasant winter temperatures while getting used to everything before the hot weather started. Palam was a busy airfield by Indian standards. It not only had the photo reconnaissance squadron which I was joining, but also a small communications squadron for liaison with the Army, and a transport squadron with a large number of Dakotas. In addition the airfield served Delhi, five miles or so away, as an airport for which it accepted civilian airlines, and there were frequent comings and goings of the four-engined Yorks of BOAC and of the two-engined Vikings of Indian National Airways. We always enjoyed watching these civilian aircraft landing, since there was a great difference in performance between the two organizations: the BOAC pilots always made beautifully smooth landings which were a joy to watch, while the Indian National Airpays people tended to bounce around a bit. But then who am I to talk – I wasn't all that hot at landings myself!

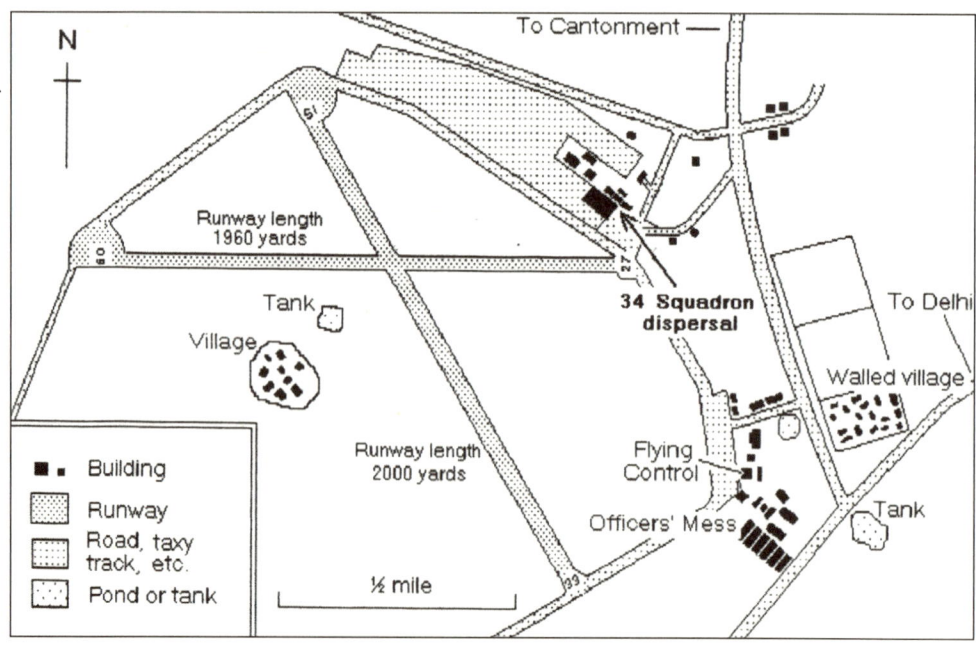

*Figure 5, Map of Palam Airfield.*

# GETTING SETTLED IN

*Plate 27, photo reconnaissance image of Palam Airfield and neighbouring cantonment, made up from a number of overlapping photographs – taken by the CO, Gerry Fray.*

Because of Palam's function in serving Delhi we were given the opportunity of watching one of the great events of Indian history: the send-off, with a multi-gun salute (my photograph, page 91, shows at least eight guns) of Field-marshal Wavell as ex-Viceroy by his successor Lord Louis Mountbatten who had arrived as the last ever Viceroy to sort out the problems of Independence and Partition. Wavell was given an RAF York to himself to take him back to the UK.

The buildings of the Officers' Mess at Palam looked much the same as those at Mauripur: both consisted of white concrete blocks with verandahs whose style of architecture gave them a definite Eastern flavour. The RAF seemed to have built their permanent accommodation in India all to much the same local style just as they did in the UK.

When I arrived I was allocated a bearer to myself, a moustached Muslim who unfortunately always smelt strongly of garlic. He was a cheerful but rather cocky person, and tried unsuccessfully to teach me Urdu. I found the odour of garlic which always accompanied him rather repugnant, and eventually managed to replace him with a bearer called George – an English nickname because of the problem of pronouncing his real name – who was already working for somebody else. He was happy to work for two of us at the same time in spite of the extra work and was quiet, efficient and good-humoured. Although his English was limited, this did not seem to matter. Indeed, there was another bearer by the name of Gwalam, who looked after somebody else a couple of rooms away, who could not speak a word of English. Yet he was highly efficient and somehow always anticipated the needs of the officer whom he looked after, putting out the appropriate clothes for different occasions without having to be told. He never seemed to put a foot wrong in spite of the language problem and I have sometimes wondered if this was an example of the reputed sixth sense of some Indians.

*Plate 28, Flying Control (left centre) and one of the residential blocks of the Officers' Mess (right). Two hot water boilers can be seen on either side of the doorway of the residential block.*

I had a ground floor room which was to be my home for the next eight months, my longest continuous stay anywhere in the RAF. The room had a door on to the verandah and contained a charpoy, or string bed, a table, a chair and a chest of drawers. In one corner was a *chatti*, a porous earthenware jar holding drinking water, which was filled every day by my bearer. The porous nature of the earthenware allowed slow evaporation of the water and so kept it cool; as with so many things in India it was simple, yet effective. The building had showers and flush toilets, although I did not immediately appreciate the latter until later on when I encountered the more primitive alternatives at other RAF Stations.

One thing about our living quarters at Palam which intrigued me was the way the water was heated. The boiler was a Heath Robinson affair which made use of discarded aircraft engine oil. It consisted of a hot water tank fixed against the outside wall at the end of each residential block – see photograph above. On either side of this tank were two reservoirs, one for oil and the other for water, each with a pipe complete with tap leading down to a metal tray directly beneath the boiler. The metal tray was initially heated in the conventional way with matches, paper and wood, and when hot enough, i.e. at a temperature above the flashpoint of oil, the taps were opened just enough to allow the water and oil to drip on to the tray in suitable proportions. The mixture of oil and water then burned and crackled with almost explosive violence, heating the boiler above, with practically no smoke, and producing piping hot water. I have never seen the like of this system anywhere else and I admire the person who devised it, since it was simple, effective, cost nothing and got rid of waste oil.

Not far away in the cantonment was an Officers Only club called the 'Chota Club' (i.e. Little Club) which had a swimming bath. We in the Officers' Mess were made honorary members and as the weather became warmer several of us would often go there in the afternoon to cool off in the water and disport ourselves (in the hot weather work finished at noon). For some twisted reason I would frequently try and swim two lengths under water – which was not too difficult since the swimming bath was small. Here I got to know quite a number of people whom I might otherwise have only encountered infrequently; some were from Flying Control and others from various administrative jobs around the station. It all helped to give the place a friendly atmosphere. When the weather got really hot the hygiene of the swimming bath was liable to get rather out of control and the water turned green with algae; the bath was then closed for protracted periods.

*Plate 29, Field-Marshal Auchinleck (left), Commander-in-Chief in India (left) and Lord Louis Mountbattern (right), the new Viceroy, at Lord Wavell's departure from Palam.*

After meals at those times of the year when the station effectively closed down at mid-day owing to the heat, the members of the Officers' Mess would gather on the lawn in front of the building to have a pint or two and a chat with colleagues that they normally didn't come across during working hours. It was all a remarkably friendly and contented place.

*Plate 30, colleagues off duty relaxing on the verandah of the residential block.*

*Plate 31, the Officers' Mess at Palam.*

## Number 34 Photographic Reconnaissance Squadron

The squadron at Palam which I was to join was 34 Photo Reconnaissance Squadron, and unlike 2 Squadron at Celle it had no fighters; its purpose was purely photographic reconnaissance. During the war in the Far East it had been stationed at Kuala Lumpur in Malaya, but afterwards was moved to Palam. The CO, Squadron Leader Gerry Fray, was a pleasant person although tending to keep himself a little apart from the rest of us. It was he who had taken from a Spitfire the famous photographs of the Moehne and Eder dams in Germany after they had been breached by the 'Dam Busters'. He also took the definitive survey photographs of Palam shown in Plate 27.

I was the most junior of the pilots, being only a Flying Officer, whereas all the others, apart from the CO, were Flight Lieutenants, one rank higher. But that didn't seem to matter, since the atmosphere was friendly and informal and we all got on well with each other. Most of them come into this story in one role or another and so I will run through their names.

There was 'Robbie' Robinson, the oldest of us, who had three gongs or medals, 'Jimmy' James, who had more gongs than Robbie, but looked much younger, Derek Turner-Ettlinger, an old hand from 2 Squadron at Celle, who was a fanatical birdwatcher and was more usually known as T.-E., Johnny Rees, a permanently cheerful soul, and, an Indian attached to us from the Indian Air Force, Johnnie Shukla, a most delightful person. When I joined the Squadron T.-E. promptly gave me the nickname Nemesis which stuck to me for the rest of my time in the RAF.

There was also the Squadron Engineering Officer, Flying Officer 'Blackie' Black, who was responsible, with the help of Warrant Officer Baldwin, for keeping the aircraft

*Plate 32, T.-E., Robbie and Johnny Rees.*

and their engines in good trim and us in the air. He was fair-skinned and fair-haired, both ingredients for prickly heat from which he suffered badly. He often had rather a despondent air about him, although in fact he was cheerful enough. To support the seven or so pilots in the squadron and keep them flying there were about 50 ground staff. A pilot attached to the squadron in a loose sort of way was Flight Lieutenant Piggott who flew Austers for the Communications Squadron and with whom I flew once or twice. He constructed a balsa wood radio-controlled glider with a wing span of about six feet which he hoped to get flying in thermals, but unfortunately his collaborator, a radio expert, was posted elsewhere before full-scale tests could be made.

There were also numerous Indians who did odd jobs around the place, not to mention the Untouchables who looked after the toilet facilities and the general cleaning. Most of these people could speak a little basic English, but they were not so good at writing, and usually got somebody else to write any formal request. This could prove quite amusing; for example, one letter which we received from an Indian asked for compassionate leave to visit his mother because 'she is quite unserviceable'!

*Plate 33, Johnnie Shukla and Blackie.*

We were also visited regularly by the char-wallah or tea-seller who brought two or three large tea-urns and a tray of sticky buns for anyone who wanted to buy refreshments; as was common with Indians he carried out the transactions in the typical squatting position. He was certainly popular with the groundcrew, who needed the liquid to replace what they had lost while working on the aircraft in the heat – the British are always thirsty, but these even more so. We always knew when the char-wallah was coming, because we could hear from afar his typically Indian high-pitched long drawn-out wailing cry of 'chaaarwallaaah'.

I must not forget the squadron dog who went by the name of Rocky, a cheerful but scruffy mongrel. I call him the squadron dog, but he was not on the official list; he happened to be around most of the time and was probably owned by one of the groundcrew and was just fun to have around. And with a name like Rocky, what more could you ask for? The trouble was that I knew somebody a few years later with the surname of Rocky and whenever I met him I always thought of the dog first.

*Plate 34, Number 34 Squadron. Only three pilots were available, and not away on sorties: from left to right (second row in peaked caps) they are T.-E., 'Jimmy' James and myself. To my left is 'Blackie', the engineer officer, and to T.-E.'s right is Warrant Officer Baldwin*

The Squadron Dispersal consisted of a hangar and a few small one-story white-washed buildings situated half-way round the periphery of the airfield (see Figure 5). The Squadron offices were in one of these buildings, with a covered verandah in front. Behind it were the ablutions and toilet, also looking smart and white, but the toilet itself was of the primitive type which I described in the previous chapter, with a metal tray under the seat. Somewhere behind the ablutions building there would be a sweeper on permanent duty waiting to remove the metal trays.

Thirty-four Squadron was a particularly happy one, and I think that this was partly because there were so few of us that we got to know each other much better than on a larger squadron, and partly because operationally we were still very active. After the end of the war most other squadrons flew only practice exercises, but we were still fully operational in the sense that we were carrying out purposeful work. For example, the Government of India had asked for a complete survey of the coast, which we never seemed to catch up with. We also took survey photographs of towns and other subjects for the military and civil authorities and in one case for an expedition surveying the Himalayan foothills. There was thus a serious purpose to the flying, and at any one time there were always several of us away on some sortie or other.

The aircraft which we used for the photography was the same as at Celle: the Spitfire XIX, of which we had six. The ones at Palam looked really lovely. Apart from having the beautiful lines of the Spitfire, the upper surface of the long nose was painted black, while the rest of the aircraft was silver. This made them look bright, sleek and full of life.

Although there were no fighter aircraft on the strength we did have one or two other machines. There was a Harvard, mainly used for familiarizing new pilots with local conditions, and for a brief time a Spitfire XI. There was also an Auster, flown mainly by Piggott, mentioned earlier, who acted as liaison officer for the Army and was sometimes asked to reconnoitre riot areas from a few hundred feet up.

*Plate 35, the squadron char-wallah. Note the padlocks on the canteen.*

I have already mentioned that the Spitfire XIX was fitted with a Griffon engine, more powerful and larger than the Merlin of the photo recce Spitfire XI which I had flown at Benson. The difference in the engines produced some anomalous effects which I noticed for the first time at Palam. The Griffon engine rotated anticlockwise whereas the Merlin rotated clockwise, and this produced a torque in opposite directions. Since the Griffon engine was particularly powerful the Spitfire XIX always tried to swing off the right-hand edge of the runway as the throttle was opened up at take-off. It was therefore essential at the beginning of any take-off to give hard left rudder, and this just about kept the aircraft straight; as speed increased the problem disappeared owing to the greater effectiveness of the rudder. In contrast, the propeller of the XI rotated to the right, and so this aircraft swung to the left on take-off, although the swing was not as strong as with the XIX. When changing from one type to the other the instinctive reaction was to use the rudder movement for the previous type, and as a result you were quite liable to overcorrect, so that the aircraft might swing from one side of the runway to the other as it started its take-off run. (Why did Rolls-Royce, the manufacturers, not make the engines rotate in the same direction, I wonder?)

The powerful torque of the Griffon engine probably contributed to the death of Arthur Chin, the member of the Squadron whom I had been sent out to replace. As I

*Plate 36, wheeling out a Spitfire XIX. Note the port for the oblique camera just in front of the roundel.*

have said, he was killed by hitting a concrete hut to one side of the runway when trying to go round again after a failed attempt at landing. I once walked across the airfield to look at the remains of his Spitfire, which had not yet been removed (Plate 39). It was a mess. The wings had been torn off, the fuselage on the underside of the engine had been ripped away, there was no sign of the propeller blades, and the propeller shaft itself was bent and ragged. The hut which he hit was still there off to the right of the runway, in the direction to which the torque would have swung him.

Another difference of the two Marks was the method of starting the engine. The Merlin was started by means of a trolly-acc, a huge accumulator battery on wheels – standard airfield equipment – which enabled the engine to be turned rather after the fashion of the self-starter in a car. The Griffon in the XIX (and also in the XIV) on the other hand, was started by means of a Koffman Cartridge. This was an explosive cartridge, rather like a much enlarged cartridge of a 12-bore shot-gun, held in a revolving barrel within the engine cowling somewhat after the fashion of a six-shooter gun. There were places for six cartridges in the holder which could be rotated from the cockpit to fire each in turn if necessary. After adjusting the throttle and mixture controls in the cockpit a cartridge was detonated by pressing a button in the cockpit. The explosion turned the engine round to the accompaniment of a loud bang and a cloud of smoke, and with luck the engine would fire. If it did not you had to repeat the whole process. The main advantage of this method was that it was independent of both trained ground-crew and trolly-acc equipment, so that the engine could be started on any strange airfield, but it was of course important to take plenty of spare cartridges when away from home.

Although I enjoyed flying both types of Spitfire, there is no doubt which I preferred: the XI. This, I think, was solely due to the difference in the engine. The Griffon of the

XIX always ran rougher than the Merlin, which was as smooth and gentle as you could ask for. It is rather like comparing a thoroughbred racehorse with the old family hack; you are never quite sure what the racehorse will do next. And, although it may sound strange, this was always the kind of feeling that I had about the Griffon. It was a superb engine and never let any of us down, yet the smoothness of the Merlin in the XI always produced a greater feeling of confidence.

*Plate 37, two Spitfire XIXs at the Dispersal, seen through the undercarriage of a Dakota. Note the fire extinguishers just visible on the ground on either side of each aircraft.*

There were no serious accidents after I arrived, just the occasional minor mishap, such as when a tyre burst while Gerry Fray, the CO, was taking off, so that he had to come in to land knowing one wheel to be defective. His skill enabled him to bring the landing off without mishap, and I took a photograph of the otherwise undamaged aircraft and of the burst tyre (Plates 40 and 41). I myself did a small piece of minor damage to a Spitfire once, owing to landing too fast. I often came in rather high for landings on the most commonly-used runway at Palam, runway 27 (see Figure 3), which unfortunately started just beside the Squadron dispersal; there was a small blockhouse some distance short of it, and I was always afraid of hitting it if I approached too low. As a result I tended to land too far up that particular runway and often had to use the brakes fairly firmly to stop before the end. One day, to avoid running over the far end I had to make a ground-loop – swinging the aircraft sharply round with hard rudder – and this put too much strain on the undercarriage leg, so that the whole thing had to be replaced. Did I have a red face!

One problem with the Spitfire in India was caused by the hot climate. The struts of the Spitfire's undercarriage were directly in front of the engine cooling radiators so that the latter were partly masked when the undercarriage was down and there was

*Plate 38, two Spitfire XIXs taking off together for some formation practice.*

then a risk that the engine would overheat. As the weather grew hotter it became ever more important to spend as little time as possible on the ground after starting up, and we had to do our routine engine checks, taxi out to the take-off point and get airborne as quickly as possible. The radiators had flaps at the rear which automatically opened to expose more radiator to the airstream if the coolant got too hot, but this was still inadequate when the undercarriage was down. Even when in the air at low altitude these radiator flaps might stay open even with the undercarriage raised; indeed, I have a photograph taken from the ground of myself a few hundred feet up which shows this, a sufficiently unusual event for me to have commented on it in my photograph album.

Our working hours in the cooler weather – December and January – were much as in the UK, with flying, if required, both morning and afternoon. But in the hot weather we had to get up in time to be on duty at 6 a.m. and then knocked off at 12 noon, since the morning was the only time when it was cool enough to be able to work. Flying was then confined to the morning hours, whether flying from Palam or from other airfields, since the whole aircraft, including engine and fuel, became much too hot sitting

*Plate 39, the remains of Arthur Chin's crash. A rare photograph of the two camera ports used for vertical photography visible in this view of the underside of the fuselage. The building which he hit can just be made out in the background.*

on the ground to be sure that it would function satisfactorily.

Most of the time during the hot season the best altitude to fly for personal comfort was about 20,000 feet; when the heat was really unpleasant on the ground, the temperature in the cockpit at that height was just right. I often remarked to myself when up there how intolerable it must be for the many people forced to stay on the ground who could never cool off in this way. In addition, at that height the air was smooth, whereas lower down the turbulence caused by the heated land made flying extremely bumpy.

*Plate 40, Gerry Fray's Spitfire after landing with a burst tyre. Note the blood waggon (ambulance) in the background ready for the worst.*

*Plate 41, the burst tyre.*

## Round and about Palam

The countryside around the airfield was dry and dusty, appearing to consist mostly of large areas of long dry grass with a scattering of trees. At first sight there appeared to be no cultivation, but this was an illusion owing to the dryness, since an aerial photograph of the region shows the countryside to be broken up into cultivated fields (see left edge of Plate 27) which would probably sprout all kinds of plants when the Monsoon came.

Palam was served by a tarmac road which ran from New Delhi, past the cantonment and airfield, and then on towards a disused airfield, Gurgaon, about three miles away. On the opposite side of the road from the airfield was a small rectangular walled village made of mud-brick houses (see Figure 5), brown and dusty like the rest of the area and looking very poor. The area enclosed by the wall was quite large, but the aerial photograph of Palam shows that only part of it was built on, the rest being cultivated. Women would walk in and out through the entrance gate in their colourful saris with water pots on their heads, sometimes one pot on top of another with no visible means of support, while the men often loitered about with apparently nothing to do. They all used the grass verge and the monsoon ditch beside the road as their toilet, and the villagers, both men and women, could often be seen squatting near the ditch, gathering their clothes around them as best they could for modesty. Not far away but next to the road was the village pond in which there were always several water buffalo keeping cool.

Whether the village was officially out of bounds to British troops I never knew, but it surely must have been. It looked so dirty and dusty that the thought of going beyond its walls never entered our heads. This all came back to me when a year later I read Hagen's book *Indian Route March* in which the author was stationed in India during the war, and with three others spent a night with Indian girls in a village just outside their camp, in spite of Hagen's own adverse comments about Indian dirt and disease. The book describes vividly what India is really like when you have left the glossy brochures behind. After reading it I inserted a written note to the effect that 'it gives my feeling on India completely, and shows it for what it really is – hot, smelly, sweaty, dusty and filthy, which one tends to forget after having been away from it for some time.'

Sometimes I would go off on my own into the local countryside, although such forays were limited to the earlier months of the year before it became too hot to do so in comfort. Once I hired a bicycle and followed the local road as far as the derelict airfield of Gurgaon. I went no further, since the countryside did not change, and it didn't seem worth the effort in the heat of the afternoon, but there was much to see on the road itself. There were the usual Indians walking from somewhere to somewhere else – even far from anywhere you always saw someone on foot. A train of camels would be carrying I knew not what from one distant place to another, while a farmer might be fast asleep on top of his cart piled high with hay or straw, the oxen pulling the cart plodding slowly along. Beside the road was a well, with its opening raised above the level of the surrounding country and a ramp leading to its rim. Pairs of oxen, urged on by the shouts of the men driving them, would take it in turns to walk down the ramp pulling up a large water container by rope and pulley-wheel, the whole supported by

*Plate 42, ruins near Palam.*

huge carved stone pillars.

Another time I walked across the open countryside to some buildings I could see on the horizon – Plate 42 above. These turned out to be the remains of architectural gems, presumably from the times of the Moguls, small buildings of various kinds made from blocks of stone, with some of their walls, arches, turrets and cupolas still intact. The site was now derelict, and was used by the local farmers to shelter their produce; surprisingly it did not look as if much stone had been taken for local building.

Walking back from these ruins I saw the nearest things to a ghost that I shall ever see. Moving through the dry brown grass beside me I heard a queer rustling sound while the grass itself moved as if something invisible were passing through it. It was in fact no more than a dustless dust-devil, a rotating region of air being carried along by the slightest of breezes.

Around Palam there was quite a lot of small-time wild life. But let me say straight away that I never saw an elephant or a tiger. Nor did I see a snake in the wild, although I was always expecting a visit from the small and lethal krait at any time. There were occasional tiny scorpions, perhaps an inch or so long, in the grounds of the Mess – so small that I felt that they could not provide much more than the equivalent of a wasp's sting. But there was one unpleasant type of beastie which we had in our living quarters: a large hairy spider, perhaps nine inches across. It looked positively evil, but I never discovered if it really was poisonous; to be on the safe side we killed them by dousing them with petrol.

Flying insects were prolific. In the hot weather they would swarm round outdoor electric lights in the dark of the evening, eventually dying in the process, so that next morning there was a pile of bodies under each light. The type of insect making up these piles varied from month to month; sometimes they would be beetles, another time there would be more ordinary flying insects, each type taking it in turn.

There was one little animal called a tree-squirrel which I found most endearing. It was less than a foot long, with stripes along its head and back, and a long fluffy tail, and was probably identical with the American chipmunk. There were several of them which played up and down and around the local trees and skittered across the ground in front of the Mess.

Two other animals which abounded were the pi-dog, or pariah dog, and the jackal. The pi-dogs were mangy-looking scrawny creatures which mostly lived around the native living quarters, scavenging among the refuse, all of them looking diseased. The jackals could be heard howling at night but I never saw any. One other animal once appeared which was never identified. A few of us were charging down one of the airfield runways in a jeep at about dusk (I wonder why – probably just for the hell of it!) when suddenly a large animal bounded out of the long grass on our right, crossed in front of us and disappeared into the long grass on our left. We decided that it might have been a wildcat, but none of us ever saw it again.

It was the birds which I found the most fascinating. They varied from the huge vultures soaring high up in the sky to the small brain-fever bird whose single note would go maddeningly up and up and up until you felt that something must snap, when suddenly it stopped. The smaller birds would keep their beaks permanently open throughout the hot weather, simply for better ventilation to keep them cool.

The vultures, of which the finest looking was the white Egyptian vulture, were past masters at soaring, and circled effortlessly, without a flap of their wings, in the many thermals which came off the hot land. But when on the ground they were just ugly bald-headed clowns. I once saw a group of these birds gathered round the carcase of a cow. The cow, being holy to the Hindu, could not be used for food and so the dead animal was left out in the open for the vultures to dispose of (how daft can a religion get in a country with so much poverty and shortage of food). The vultures were putting their heads inside the fresh carcase as they tore away at the flesh, regardless of blood and guts. They were so greedy that they just went on eating until they had gorged themselves so much that one or two of them were unable to take off because of their increased weight. I was able to get close to these without any trouble at all; the only response was an attempt to flap a bit further away. Those that had not gorged themselves quite so much did eventually manage to clamber into the air, but only after an inordinately long take-off run.

Another bird which was even greater fun to watch was the kite-hawk (or shite-hawk as we called it), more commonly known simply as the kite. These birds were a bit like the vultures in their ability to soar in thermals, but were more attractive close to, with the head of a hawk. They were great scroungers and frequented the area around our buildings, flying down and picking up any food that might be lying around. I have heard that they will even take food from your plate while you are eating outdoors if you are not careful, although ours were a bit too shy for that.

Being fellow-flyers we admired the skill with which they would pick up in their talons without interrupting their flight any food that we threw on the ground, and then feed on the wing. We would tease them by putting out a piece of food attached by a length of string to a paper glider. They would snatch up the food and away they went with the glider following along behind. We also took advantage of the fact that one bird might mob another in the air and try to steal its food. We would put two pieces of food on the ground joined by some string. When a kite-hawk picked up one of the pieces the other piece would follow dangling behind. This of course would be spotted by another bird, which would then chase the first, and the whole thing was liable to end in a flurry of wings and feathers.

*Plate 43, the Viceroy's Palace in New Delhi. Black and white photographs do not do justice to its beautiful two-tone cream and warm red sandstone.*

Occasionally one or two of us would go into New Delhi. This, quite separate from the hustle, bustle and noise of Old Delhi, is a new town designed by Lutyens and Baker in the 1920s, laid out in a hexagonal grid pattern. It is mostly residential, with the bungalows of the well-to-do set in their own gardens, the focal point being the magnificent Viceroy's Palace, of beautiful cream and red sandstone of varying shades and set on a slight rise at the end of a long broad avenue. New Delhi was built to provide a city for the seat of Government (which had been moved from Calcutta) rather similar to the building of Canberra in Australia. All the buildings are widely separated, and from the air the hexagonal pattern is most attractive. At one end was the main shopping centre, Connaught Circus (now renamed Indra Chauk), where we would sometimes go and shop. It consisted of a circle of Western-style buildings with arcaded glass-fronted shops at pavement level, the whole enclosing a large green.

To get from Palam to Delhi we took taxis, mostly battered American Dodges, but for short distances within Delhi itself the main form of transport was the horse-drawn carriage. There were two types, the *ghari* and the *tonga*. The *ghari* was a four-wheeled carriage, which might in the UK have at one time been called a landau. The *tonga* was a two-wheeled carriage, which of course cost less to hire, but did not have the panache of the *ghari*. These have since been replaced by noisy motorised vehicles. (Although the name *ghari* refers to a horse-drawn vehicle it was also used in India by the RAF as a slang name for any form of motorized transport, but particularly for the ubiquitous 15-cwt truck, that maid-of-all-work of the Armed Forces.)

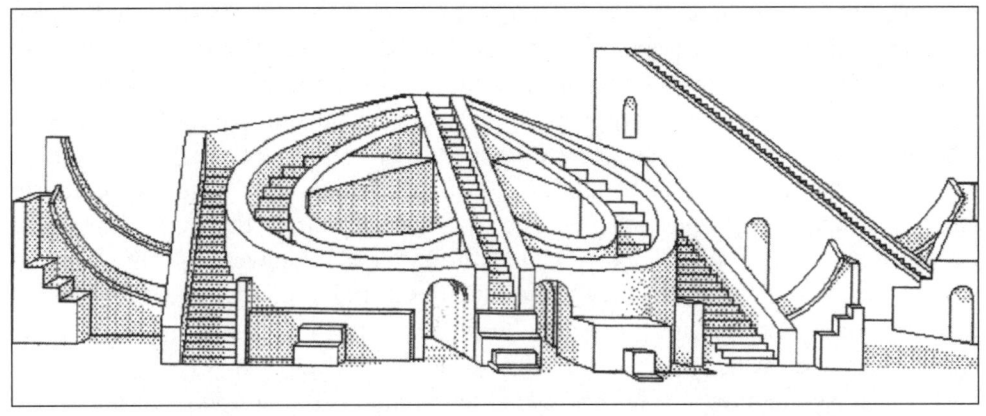

*Figure 6. Jantar Mantar, the ancient observatory in Delhi built by the Maharajah Jai Singh II.*

The main tourist attraction of the city, the Red Fort, I never visited. Instead, I went to have a look at Jantar Mantar, an ancient astronomical observatory built in about 1725 by the Maharajah Jai Singh II, of Jaipur, where he built a similar observatory. The observatory in Delhi was still in excellent condition. It consisted of surrealist-looking platforms, circles, quadrants and other peculiar shapes all built in the red sandstone of the district, and had been designed for observing the movements of the heavenly bodies in the sky. Although looking like some marvel of modern architecture, the structures were strictly functional, the tallest being a sundial 55 feet high, shown in the background of Figure 6 above.

Occasionally we would visit a Western-style cinema in Delhi, which would show not-so-old films; but the best of it was that the cinema was air-conditioned, so that we escaped from the heat outside into the chill of the interior. It was the only air-conditioned building that I ever encountered in India. We would also sometimes try an open-air cinema, mainly for the British troops, in the subsidiary shopping centre or bazaar of the cantonment near Palam. It had plain hard chairs to sit on out under the night sky, but it served its purpose, and the films shown were only a little older than those in Delhi.

The cantonment shopping area had a few other forms of entertainment. For example, one of our number had the courage to have his fortune told by one of the many Indian fortune-tellers in which the country abounds. And it was there that I saw my one and only cobra, a tame one fighting with a mongoose for the entertainment of the onlookers.

One morning before the hot season had set in three of us decided to go a bit further afield. Johnnie Shukla, Blackie and I set off on hired bicycles to the Qutb Minar,[1] a famous local monument about seven miles away by road. On the way the road passed through Mahrauli, an Indian village rather larger than the one beside Palam. This was the first time that I had actually been inside an Indian village, and what left the greatest impression on me were the flies. I have never seen so many. They were just a thick buzzing mass everywhere, the road included, and we had to cycle right through them.

Away in the distance we could now see the Qutb Minar, a huge red sandstone tower about 230 feet high rising up from ancient ruins around it. The fluted sides were carved with Muslim writings, and there were four sculptured balconies around it at various heights. By climbing a staircase inside you could get right to the top, or walk out on to the platforms at the various levels. It was a quite remarkably preserved and beautiful structure. Apparently since Independence the upper levels of the Qutb Minar have been closed to the public who can now only go as far as the lowest balcony; this was to discourage, so it was claimed, potential suicides from jumping off the top, although since the lowest balcony itself is a good forty feet above the ground this seems to be rather a feeble excuse.[2]

It was there that I met the only hornet in my life. Its nest was up in a corner of one of the walls of the surrounding ruins, and it suddenly launched itself straight for me. I stepped hurriedly back, and one leg fell into a hole in the paving, my knee hitting the edge rather hard, while the hornet went off somewhere else. As a result of this I developed water on the knee, a complaint which I had had once before in childhood, and Johnnie and Blackie had to help me back to Palam on my bicycle with a bit of pushing. The Medical Officer strapped the knee up, and much to my chagrin I was put off flying for about a week. Even if he had allowed me to fly I would not have been able to climb into the cockpit with an unbendable leg.

Another place well worth going to, although much further away, was the Taj Mahal at Agra,[3] about 100 miles to the south-east. While the weather was still cool two of us decided not to miss the opportunity of seeing this famous building. So one day we set off by train from Delhi, taking a first-class compartment which was essential if you wanted reasonable comfort and not have to experience India at its worst. This was the

---

1 A triumphal tower dating from the time of the first Mohammedan rulers who lived in Delhi. It was built by Kutb-ud-din (1206-10), Altamsh (1211-35) and Firoz Shah, who added the final upper parts in 1368. (Details from *Traveller in the Orient* by Martin Hürlimann.)
2 Mentioned by M. M. Kaye in *The Sun in the Morning*, p.262.
3 A mausoleum built by the Emperor Shah Jehan in memory of his favourite wife, Mumtaz Mahal. It is an example of Mogul architecture at its peak. It is square in plan and 'is built mainly of white marble, beautifully carved in open traceries and designs, and largely inlaid with semi-precious stones, many of which have been stolen.' It took 22 years from 1630 to 1652, to build, (from *Everyman's Encyclopaedia*, edited by E. F. Bozman).

*Plate 44, the Taj Mahal, Agra.*

only time that I ever went on an Indian railway, for which I am thankful from what I have heard of the trains.

It was a lovely day with the sun blazing down from a clear blue sky when we eventually arrived at Agra, but it was still winter and the temperature was just right. After we had paid our fee at the entrance building we stepped into the grounds of the Taj. As with many preconceived notions, the real thing did not quite come up to expectations. When you first see it the Taj should be reflected in a trough of water which leads up to it across lawns and shrubberies, but on this day there was no water and the empty trough gave the whole place a drab appearance. But the Taj is a superbly proportioned building, and its marble shines white in contrast to the reddish colour of the buildings nearby, which helps to give it an appearance of perfection.

Before being allowed inside the building we had to take off our shoes – since it is Muslim holy ground – and put on large floppy overshoes which were supplied. There was not much to see inside, simply a wall of carved stone tracery surrounding the tombs of Shah Jehan and his wife Mumtaz Mahal. We found it more worthwhile to climb one of the four minarets which are placed at the corners of the square platform on which the Taj stands. From there we could look at the Taj from above and see it in perspective. Directly behind it ran the broad and muddy Jumna – the river which higher up flows past Delhi – beyond which was the flat and empty countryside of the plains of India. The Taj Mahal is certainly a beautiful building, and as we rumbled back to Delhi in the train I thought how lucky I was to have had a chance to see what must be classed as one of the architectural wonders of the world.

# 9

# First Sortie in India

The first flight which I made in India was no more than a refresher in a trainer aircraft to get me back into flying practice again. One of the other pilots took me up in the Squadron Harvard, and let me handle the controls while he pointed out the local landmarks. I was a bit ham-fisted at first since not only had I not flown for two months but I had not touched a Harvard for a year. After six months on Spitfires it was a bit strange to return to the American cockpit layout, and I found it difficult to know what to do with all the knobs and levers. But mostly I just sat and looked at the new countryside below.

I had got my camera with some colour film in it – a rarity in those days – and I wanted to try my hand at photographing the Himalayas whose foothills were only 150 miles away, so we went up through the slight haze to have a look at them. I shall never forget my first view of the mountains. Even from that distance they were impressive. As we broke out into the blue sky above the haze I could see them pushing their snowy tops into the clear air – a great jumble of peaks stretching away to the east and north until they disappeared beyond the horizon. I just itched to get near them, and after that first sight they never failed to pull at me every time I flew above the ever-present haze.

I took several photographs of the mountains, as well as of a formation of Tempests from another airfield that passed below us, and then we went back to land at Palam. I could not wait to get the film back from being processed in Bombay to see how the pictures had come out. Alas, the last I saw of that film was when I posted it; it then just disappeared. This was typical of India, and was a rude introduction to the country's ways.

All high altitude flying in the Spitfires had been temporarily cancelled until the oxygen systems had been thoroughly checked after the death of Ali Leheta – mentioned earlier – who had been killed owing to contamination of his oxygen. He went straight into the ground from about 25,000 feet on his way to carry out a photo recce sortie. Johnny Rees had gone up the same day to check the oxygen and had felt the typical symptoms of oxygen lack at high altitude. Ali, being less experienced, might well not have noticed anything wrong before he lost consciousness. Johnny reported the symptoms as soon as he landed and was at once given a medical examination which showed that the fault did not lie in himself. So we had to wait for a new, uncontaminated supply of oxygen to arrive.

Another problem with the Spitfires which arose during my first month at Palam was a report that the engine bearings in Spitfires at another airfield had been shearing, which my own are shown in Figure 7. The actual take-off routine itself was much the same as in the UK and Germany, but in India, because of the vast distances and the need to land at strange airfields, there was now a great deal more to the whole business of departure.

Various procedures had to be gone through with the people of Flying Control – often referred to as Flying Confusion – in the Control Tower. One was to coordinate the flight with other airfields where you might be landing, either to refuel or to stay the night. At the same time you collected pamphlets giving details of those airfields. These pamphlets would have a photograph and a large-scale map showing the layout of the runways and neighbouring buildings, as well as a smaller-scale map showing the local district and particularly the altitude of any high ground or obstructions in the vicinity (for example, plates 45 and 46). Other relevant details such as servicing and radio facilities were also shown. It was also important to be briefed by the meteorologists, or *met. wallahs* as we called them in India regardless of nationality, who also had their offices in the Control Tower. It was vital not only to know the kind of weather in the part of the country where you were going to fly, but, even more important, owing to the large distances, to obtain reliable values for wind speed and direction at the altitude at which you were flying so that you could allow for these when calculating the compass course to steer. The meteorologists at Palam were English, and although they were good, the Indian ones that I met at other airfields were often better since they were more familiar with the vagaries of their own country.

When the time came to take off and you had strapped yourself into the aircraft and carried out the routine cockpit checks, you had, as is the case anywhere, to call up the Control Tower and ask permission to take off or scramble – the same applied when you wanted to land or *pancake*. Each squadron had a specific call-sign and each pilot had a number, so that there might be no confusion as to who was calling; 34 Squadron's call-sign was *Roadhog* and I was number 22 (pronounced 'two-two'). I never discovered how the name Roadhog arose – obviously somebody had had a sense of humour.

The conversation at take off would go something like this: 'Hullo Tower, this is Roadhog 22. Permission to scramble. Over', to which the Tower would reply, 'Hullo Roadhog 22. You may scramble. Runway 27. Over', and I would answer, '22. Roger. Out'. If there had been an instruction, then *Roger* was replaced by *Wilco*. (Roger meant 'Received and understood' and Wilco was short for 'Will comply'[1]). The object of all this was to ensure that we did not take off or land when other aircraft were coming in, and that we took off on the correct runway – again standard procedure at any controlled airfield.

The people in the Control Tower were a good crowd; we got to know them in the Mess and might strike up friendships with them off duty. There was never the feeling, as some might think, that such airfield rituals were a bureaucratic imposition, or that Big Brother was watching us. Their purpose was to make life as safe as possible, flying being safe only as long as it is carefully regulated; if not, it can become highly

---

1 According to R. T. Bickers in *The Battle of Britain* it seems that Roger and Wilco were (regrettably) US Air Corps terms adopted by the RAF in 1943.

dangerous. In addition, the Control Tower people provided an information service which we of 34 Squadron very much needed when flying to other airfields, particularly when we wanted to know such things as what accommodation, refuelling and other facilities were available, and how long those airfields' runways were.

I will now describe in some detail in this and the next chapter my first three photographic sorties each of which was more complex than its predecessor. In later chapters I shall only describe those which had something unusual about them. It is worthwhile reading about the first one, which gives a basic idea of the problems and techniques of flying in India, but if the reader finds it boring I suggest that the second and third are skipped.

**Sortie to Shahjahanpur, 16 January 1947** (see Figure 8, Sortie 1)
When I had seen some of the countryside from the air and had got my hand in again I was sent off on my first photo reconnaissance sortie to photograph Shahjahanpur, a town about 200 miles to the south-east of Delhi – quite a short distance for India, but far enough for me, since I made only the two flights on my own to date and was far from competent at map-reading in that country. And to use a colloquial phrase, long-distance navigation in India was a whole new ball-game.

In those days the multiplicity of navigational radio aids that we now have worldwide did not exist even in England, but England at least had a recognizable coast and plenty of landmarks. In India the land was vast and there were no long-distance radio aids so that we had to be totally dependent on ourselves for navigation over long distances. We navigated by dead reckoning checked intermittently by the identification of specific landmarks or pinpoints along the route. Being a single-seater aircraft there was of course no navigator to help out. The only radio aid was the Homer, briefly mentioned in an earlier chapter. This was an airfield radio station designed primarily as an emergency service for guiding a pilot to the Homer's airfield. The radio operator of the Homer took a bearing on the pilot's radio transmission and gave the pilot a course to steer. Its range depended on the height of the aircraft but in general was between 50 and 100 miles and so covered no more than the immediate vicinity of the few airfields that there were. We were encouraged to use the Homers at all airfields as much as possible to keep the radio operators occupied since otherwise they had nothing to do, emergencies being few and far between. Besides, the Homer simplified navigation for us in the final stage of a long flight. There did come a time later when I myself needed the one at Palam badly, and the radio operator saved me from disaster – but that tale will be told in its place.

In England I had learned to map-read from the air by using various landmarks such as railways, roads, towns and rivers, all in a fairly compact setting. In Germany map-reading involved mainly the recognition of railways, with the autobahns prominent on longer flights. In India, however, the landscape was quite different; neither roads nor railways were easily seen against the dusty brown background of the Indian countryside from the height of between 10,000 and 20,000 feet at which I usually flew, so I

# PALAM

## GENERAL INFORMATION

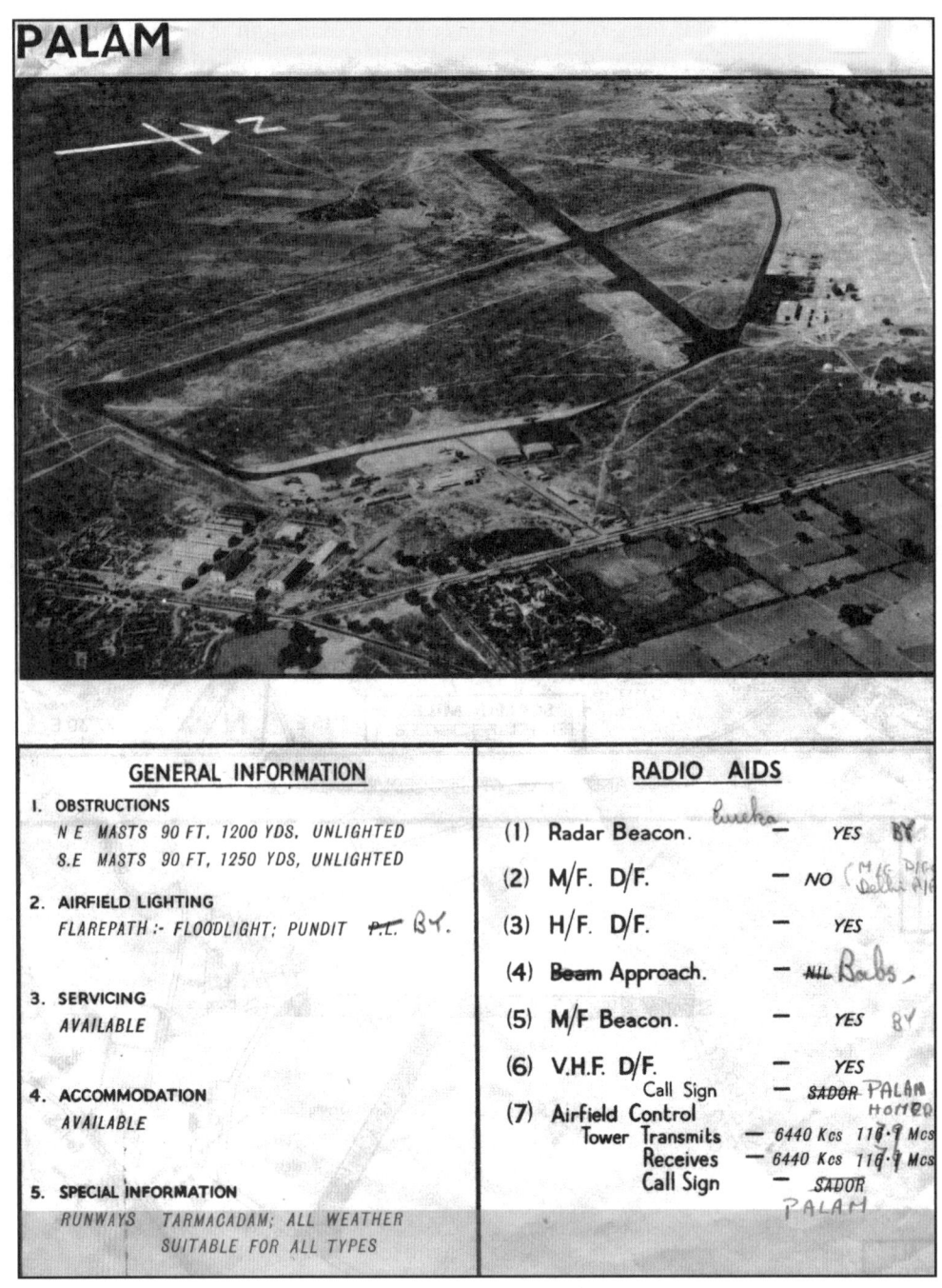

1. **OBSTRUCTIONS**
   N E MASTS 90 FT. 1200 YDS. UNLIGHTED
   S.E MASTS 90 FT. 1250 YDS. UNLIGHTED

2. **AIRFIELD LIGHTING**
   FLAREPATH :- FLOODLIGHT; PUNDIT P.L. BY.

3. **SERVICING**
   AVAILABLE

4. **ACCOMMODATION**
   AVAILABLE

5. **SPECIAL INFORMATION**
   RUNWAYS  TARMACADAM; ALL WEATHER SUITABLE FOR ALL TYPES

## RADIO AIDS

(1) Radar Beacon.  Eureka  — YES BY
(2) M/F. D/F.  — NO (M/F D/F Delhi A/F)
(3) H/F. D/F.  — YES
(4) Beam Approach.  — NIL Babs
(5) M/F Beacon.  — YES BY
(6) V.H.F. D/F.  — YES
    Call Sign  — SADOR PALAM
(7) Airfield Control  HOMER
    Tower Transmits  — 6440 Kcs 116·9 Mcs
    Receives  — 6440 Kcs 116·9 Mcs
    Call Sign  — SADOR PALAM

*Plates 45 and 46, The two sides of an information pamphlet for Palam airfield supplied by Control Towers at other airfields for the use of visiting pilots. In the photograph above, the Officers' Mess are the buildings at the lower left, with the Control Tower and neighbouring buildings above them and to the right where three aircraft can be made out on the tarmac, of which the left-hand one is a York and the middle*

# FIRST SORTIES IN INDIA

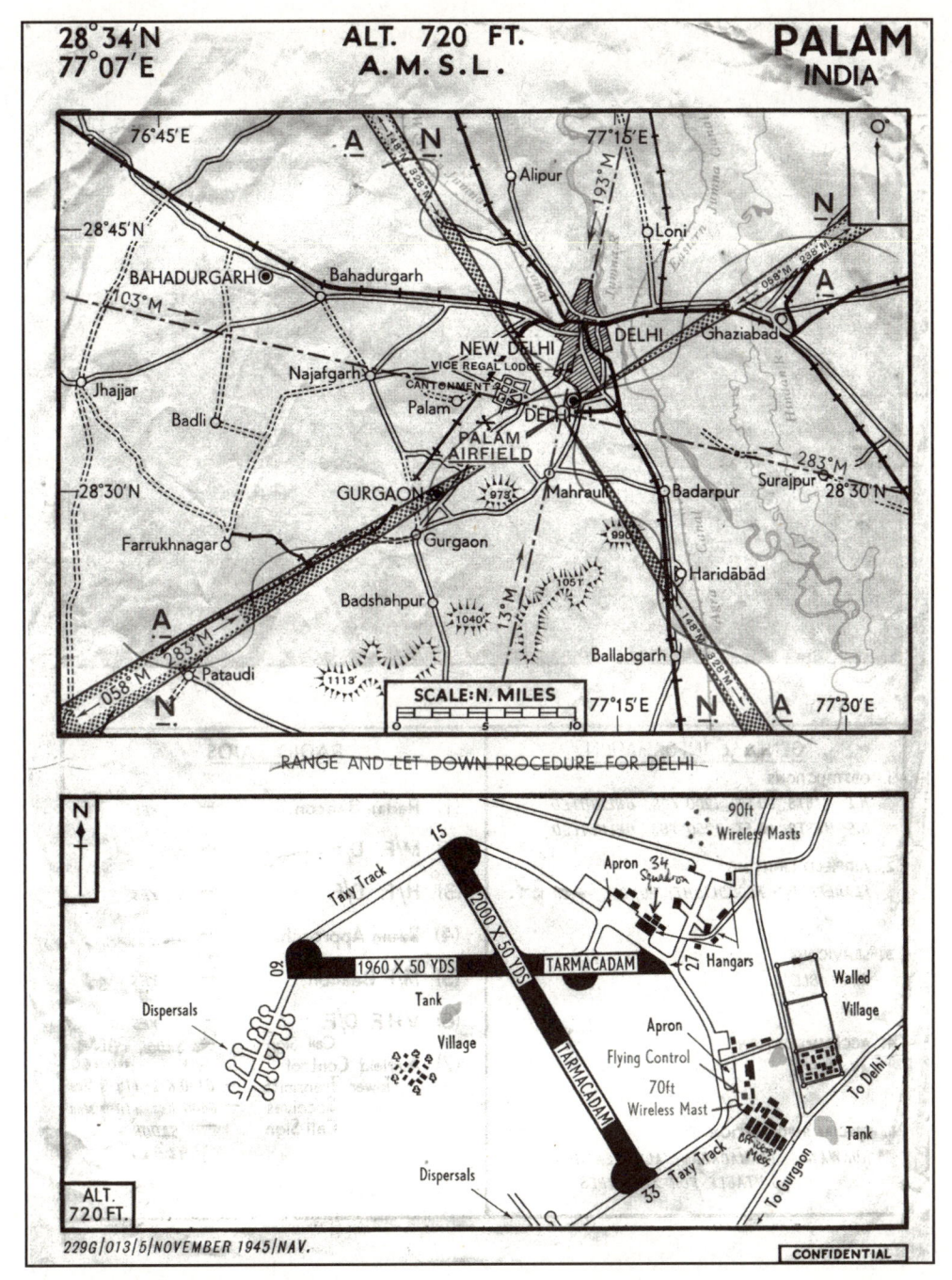

*one a Dakota. The buildings beside a dark taxy-track at the upper right are the 34 Squadron Dispersal. The local walled village with enclosed cultivation plots is at the bottom centre and lies beside the road beyond which can be seen the (dark) pool where water-buffaloes spent their time.*

never specifically looked for them on long-distance flights. In addition, even if I had managed to identify a railway, it would usually have been impossible, with no other specific landmarks in its neighbourhood, to decide exactly where I was along the length of it. Railways did sometimes come in useful for identifying towns since each town had its own characteristic pattern of lines traversing it; and occasionally railways might be useful in leading me directly to a particular town.

The main navigational landmarks were rivers. They were easily seen from the air, particularly the larger ones, and often had characteristic shapes which enabled one stretch of a river to be distinguished from another so that it was possible to pinpoint the aircraft's position along the course of the river with reasonable accuracy. Occasionally confusion was introduced when a river had changed its course and no longer matched the map.

Really long flights were sometimes broken up into legs or discrete lengths each of which led to a prominent pinpoint like a large town which would represent a turning point. How one tackled a long flight usually depended on the topography. Following a single straight line to one's destination might mean flying over a landscape with few pinpoints, but a slight deviation to one side or the other of the straight-line route could take the pilot over a series of unmistakeable pinpoints, each of which would be an identifiable turning-point, and so would make the navigation both easier and safer.

Map-reading was affected by the permanent dust haze over the country which varied with the time of year. In the early months it was fairly thin and rose up to about 8,000 feet; cloud was variable but much of the time the sky was clear. Navigation was then straightforward; you simply set a course, and there was little problem with map-reading and seeing landmarks once you got used to the type of landscape. And since the winds during the whole period of the north-east (dry) monsoon were so constant from day to day and from month to month it was often possible to anticipate the meteorologists' forecast and even suggest to them what winds might be expected on the route.

As spring and summer progressed, the heat over the dried-up countryside caused turbulence which thickened the dust haze and made flying below the top of it very bumpy; it became progressively worse as the months passed and haze and turbulence eventually extended up to 20,000 feet. At the same time the visibility became so poor that the area of ground visible from the air was reduced to a small circle immediately beneath the aircraft. Particular care was then needed in identifying landmarks to check whether you were on course. On long-distance flights, as I have said earlier, I always flew for comfort above the haze where it was cooler and the air was smooth.

Accurate navigation depended on adequate preparation with maps before leaving the ground and then using established principles when in the air, subject to the limitations imposed by India. Before the flight I would draw the flight track on one of the numerous flying maps of India with which we were supplied – 1:1,000,000 or about 16 miles to the inch – and calculate from the expected wind speed and direction the course to steer. I would then work out the Estimated Time of Arrival (ETA) at which I should expect to cross the first river; this would be my first pinpoint. Shortly before

FIRST SORTIES IN INDIA

it was due to appear I would to start to watch out for it and then note the time when I crossed it; with this established I could calculate the groundspeed – the speed over the ground – from the distance I had flown and how long it had taken to get there. At the same time I would note the exact spot at which I crossed the river to provide a check on the accuracy of my compass heading. From these two pieces of information I could calculate the time at which I might expect to cross the next river and also by how much to correct my compass course. This first pinpoint sometimes revealed errors in the

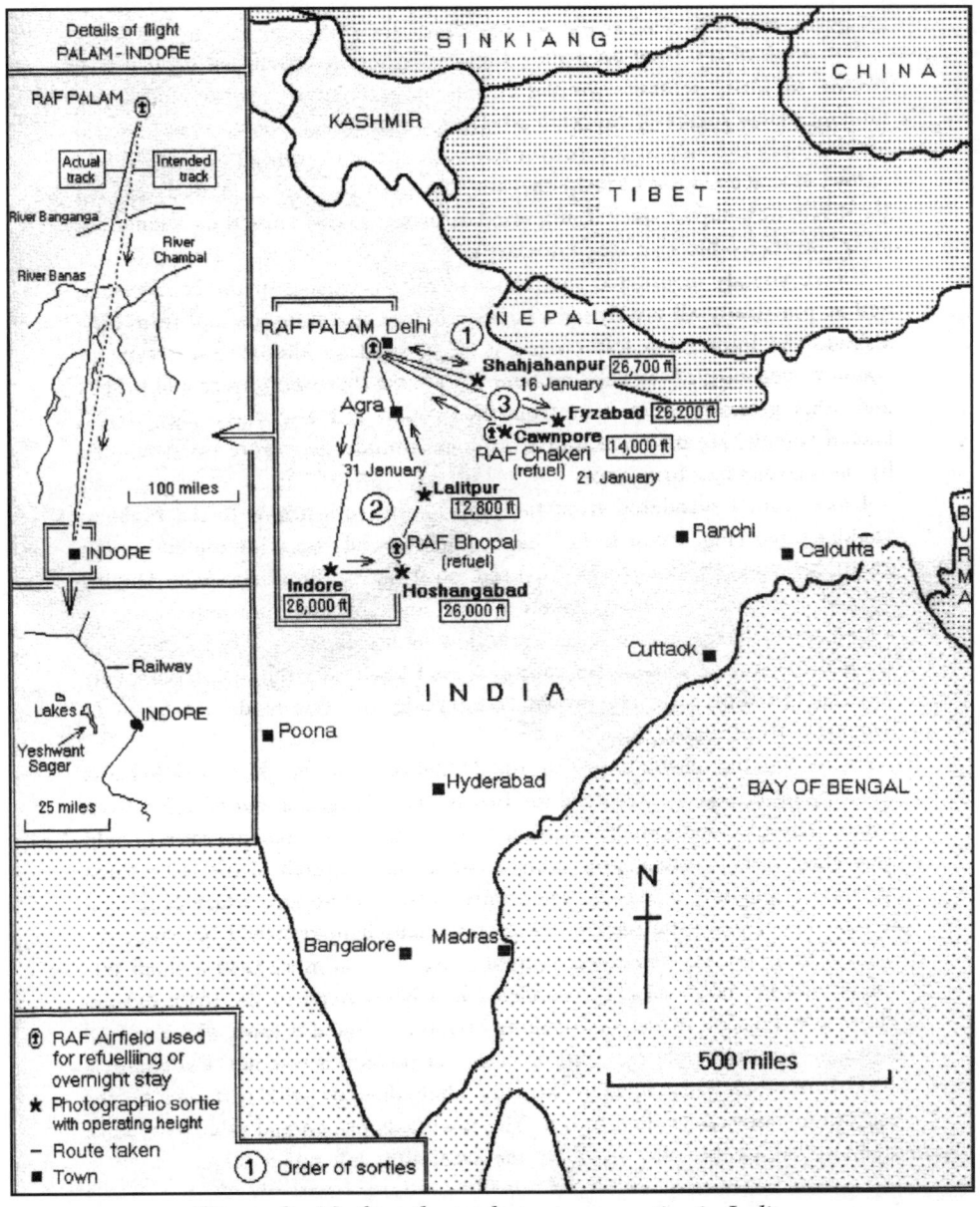

*Figure 8. My first three photo recce sorties in India.*

original calculations; with these corrections made, further errors should then be small.

To make navigation easier I later on adapted for my own use – once I had discovered by experience what was needed – an RAF Navigational Computer (Mk IIID) which was designed to be strapped to the thigh for use during flight. The computer as issued consisted of two main parts. On top was a hinged metal flap in which was incorporated a circular slide-rule for calculating speed from distance and time, and for determining true height and airspeed from indicated values; on the under surface of the flap itself was a note pad. When lifted up the flap revealed the main part of the computer which consisted of a movable grid over which was a metal ring with compass directions, the whole being designed to calculate the course to steer if you knew the wind; I never managed to learn how to use this part, so replaced it with a sheet of tough perspex over which I glued the metal compass ring. I could then slide a map under the perspex and read an accurate bearing directly off the map. I thus had a much simpler gadget: the top or slide-rule part I used for calculating the relationships between time, distance and speed, the bottom part for measuring compass directions on the map. Strapped on to my thigh it was always ready for use.

For most of the time on a long flight it was a matter of sitting back for twenty or thirty minutes waiting for the next river to appear, and doing nothing except regularly checking airspeed, altitude and gyro compass, or just looking over the side at the brown featureless countryside thousands of feet below. It was essential to keep checking the gyro compass frequently against the magnetic compass since it

*Plate 47 (and opposite). The RAF Navigational Navigational Computer Mk III, as adapted by myelf for use with maps. The compass ring mounted on perspex for taking bearings directly from a map.*

precessed or progressively altered its orientation at an unpredictable rate (see Glossary).

I have already mentioned something of the brownness of the countryside, and as practically all my flying was done before the monsoon and from high altitude the impression left on me is of a dried-up almost desert type of country over most of the subcontinent. Of course there were trees and bushes and other greenery when seen from the ground as I discovered each time I landed somewhere different, but from high altitude they were overwhelmed by the surrounding brownness.

I have rather wandered from the point, so to return now to the flight to Shahjahanpur (Figure 8, Sortie 1). This task had already been attempted but the town had not been completely covered, so it had to be done again. Having only flown locally around Palam, I had not yet had any experience in long-distance navigation in India, so, following my experience in England and Germany, I started looking for railways. As I have said, they were not easily seen against the uniformly brown countryside and this made me begin to wonder if I was getting lost.

I was climbing all the time towards 27,000 feet, the height at which I was to take photos, and soon crossed the broad river Ganges, about 80 miles from Palam. This gave me a rough position, but because of my inexperience I could only place myself somewhere along a twenty mile stretch of the river. Soon afterwards I managed to make out a railway but had no idea which of several it was. I also had little idea of what size Shahjahanpur would be, since the sixteen miles to the inch flying map showed it as no more than a small rectangle and the large-scale map which I had been given of

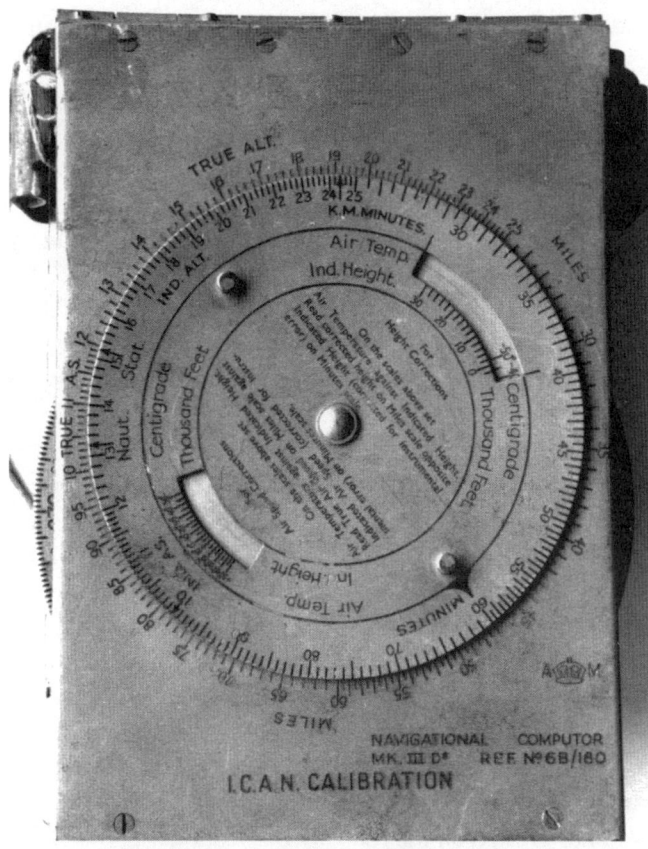

*Plate 47a. The circular slide rule ('Navigational computor'). Three of its uses were (i) the conversion of indicated airspeed (IAS) to true airspeed (TAS), (ii) the calculation of groundspeed, and (iii) the calculation of estimated time of arrival.*

the town did not show it in relation to the surrounding country. I found a town which at first I thought was the right one, but on closer inspection it was not. Eventually a little further on I managed to identify Shahjahanpur with certainty by the pattern of railways leading into it. The town was brown and otherwise much like any one of the other towns in the area, although rather larger.

I wrote the original account of this flight only a few months afterwards, and now, many years later, looking at the actual map which I used at the time, and which I still have, I am surprised that I could have had any difficulty at all in the navigation, since the various railways and the positions of the different towns are quite distinctive – but being in the air over a new and unfamiliar type of landscape is all too different from looking at a map in the comfort of your home.

I now looked at the photographic runs which I had earlier marked on the large-scale map of the town; there were three to do, all steering 360°, or due north, so without doing a dummy run – as I ought to have done, and always did subsequently – I started with the easternmost, or right-hand, run, switching on the cameras just before reaching the area to be photographed.

About half-way along the run I looked over the port side of the cockpit, and I could see the southern edge of the town appearing behind the trailing edge of the port wing. This was not right at all – it should have been directly beneath me, not over to one side. It was clear that I was drifting rapidly eastward, to my right, as the result of a strong unexpected westerly wind (see Figure 1, middle, page 42), so I immediately switched off the cameras.

I swung the aircraft around and came in again for what I ought to have done first – a dummy run with the cameras switched off. This time, to correct the drift I steered 350°, or 10° to the left of my original heading. When I had completed the run I found that I had still drifted to the right, so I came round for a third run across the town, this time steering 345°, or 15° off my first heading. This did the trick, and I now ended the run in line with where I had started. I now repeated the run but with the cameras switched on, and this time finished it and the remainder of the runs without further trouble. Since I felt that there might have been a slight gap between two of them, I did a fourth run to make sure.

While over Shahjahanpur I tried to contact the Palam Homer out of curiosity at that distance, but even at 27,000 feet I was too far away at 200 miles and heard nothing. So on the return flight I climbed another 2,000 feet to improve the range, but it wasn't until I was 150 miles away that I began to hear them clearly. After that I continued to ask for courses to steer and these brought me straight back to Palam without any further risk of navigational errors; I finally landed 2 hours 55 minutes after take-off.

When the photographs were later plotted on the map at Air Headquarters in Delhi it turned out that I had covered the required area successfully, but with the expected 15 degrees of drift so that all the photographs were angled to the left. A calculation showed that the wind at altitude had been blowing at 90 mph; no wonder I had had trouble in keeping over the target.

# 10

# Further Afield

**Sortie to Indore, Hoshangabad and Lalitpur,** 21 January 1947 (see Figure 8, page 115, Sortie 2)

My second photo reconnaissance flight was less than a week after the Shahjahanpur sortie. It was the first of many in India where the combination of great distances and the time required for the actual photography commonly made it necessary to land at other airfields for refuelling or to stay the night. The various airfields which I visited in this way are shown in Figure 9.

There were three targets on this trip, and I would have to refuel at the RAF airfield at Bhopal in central India. First of all I had to take photos of the town of Indore, about 400 miles to the south of Palam, then go 120 miles to the east and photograph the town of Hoshangabad, after which I would fly 50 miles north-west to land at Bhopal for fuel and to get a bite to eat. I would then have to take off again and photograph Lalitpur, 120 miles to the north-east before returning to Palam, 200 miles away to the north. Quite a day's work!

After my difficulty in finding my way to Shahjahanpur I was feeling a bit apprehensive. It was only my fourth Spitfire flight in India, and this time I would be completely out of touch with Palam. Still, there was nothing I could do about it, so after being briefed by Johnny Rees who was looking after the details of what photographs were required I climbed into the cockpit and set off.

It was 9.30 in the morning when I took off, and I climbed straight up to 26,000 feet, the height at which I would be photographing the first target, Indore. (Navigational details of this part of the trip are shown, inset, in Figure 8, page 115). The weather was predicted as cloudless, and there would be nothing much to do until I crossed the River Banganga, the first pinpoint, about 130 miles south of Palam. The sun shone down out of a cloudless sky, which was fairly typical of much of India at that time of year; there was a slight haze, but visibility on the whole was good.

After about 20 minutes I started to go into cloud and this I was certainly not expecting, so I started to descend through it; I didn't want to miss that vital first pinpoint, the Banganga. But there was more cloud below, and it looked as if I might not see the river at all – and there is nothing worse in a country with few identifiable landmarks than being uncertain of where you are. There was still no sign of the ground by the time I was due to cross it, so the Banganga came and went without my even catching a glimpse of it.

Luckily, 90 miles further on there was another large river, the Chambal, which would come in from port and could easily be identified by its several tributaries. This would now have to replace the Banganga as my first pinpoint.

After a little while the cloud started to break up, for which I was thankful, so I climbed back to 26,000 feet, and soon saw the Chambal down to my left. It was further away than it should have been, but in crossing a tributary, the Banas, I obtained a good idea of my position and altered course a few degrees to port. At the same time I was able to calculate my groundspeed accurately by noting the time at which I crossed the Banas. Another of the Chambal's tributaries now ran with me on my port side for part of the way to Indore and this gave me a running check for a while. I also checked my position when I passed any other recognizable landmarks and was able to calculate accurately when the town should appear. So a few minutes before the estimated time of arrival I looked ahead and to starboard, expecting to see a couple of small lakes about 10 and 20 miles respectively to the west of Indore, one of which had been given the strange name of Yeshwant Sagar (see Figure 8, lower inset). Yes, there they were, and Indore should be just to the left of them; yes, there it was as well. Just check that it was Indore and not somewhere else: one railway coming in from the north-west, another twisty one from the south-west, and the two lakes to the west – yes, that was Indore all right.

It was now time to start the photography; after the fiasco at Shahjahanpur I made sure of doing a dummy run first and this seemed to go all right. Before leaving Palam I had marked the runs on my large-scale map of the town to go from west to east, and I now started the photography on the southernmost run, beginning it over a pond next to a road. When I had levelled up and was heading due east on the gyro compass I switched on the cameras.

On reaching the end of the run, I switched the cameras off, and quickly swung round to port, banking steeply so as to be able to see where the run had ended. I found that I had drifted a bit to starboard in spite of the preliminary dummy run – this indicated that there must be a wind from the north. Still, if I followed the same heading, the rest of the runs would be parallel to the first and would still cover the required area. It would mean an extra run to cover all of it, but there would have had to be an extra one anyway if I started again from scratch.

So back again to the starting point, this time turning on to the next run a little further north than the first one, starting over what looked like military buildings (marked on the map as artillery lines). On with the cameras, hold her steady, then off with the cameras, swing round again in a steep bank to have a look at the ground directly below. Yes, that run was just about parallel with the first. Two more runs to go, making four in all... better do a fifth as well, I thought, just to make sure – that fourth run had probably missed the north-east corner of the area.

When that was finished I set course eastward for Hoshangabad, a small town on the river Narbada. It was easy to find; as I flew towards it, the river itself, the only large one for miles around, came in towards me from starboard and led me straight to the town. It was such a small place that only one run would be needed to cover it, so I thought I would fly past it to the south, come straight in from the opposite side, and do the single run heading west.

So I watched Hoshangabad pass under the trailing edge of my port wing, waited until I had got beyond it, and then swung sharply round to port to head west over the town for the photographic run. But I had delayed my turn too long and found that I was further from the town than I should have been. It was too late to do anything about

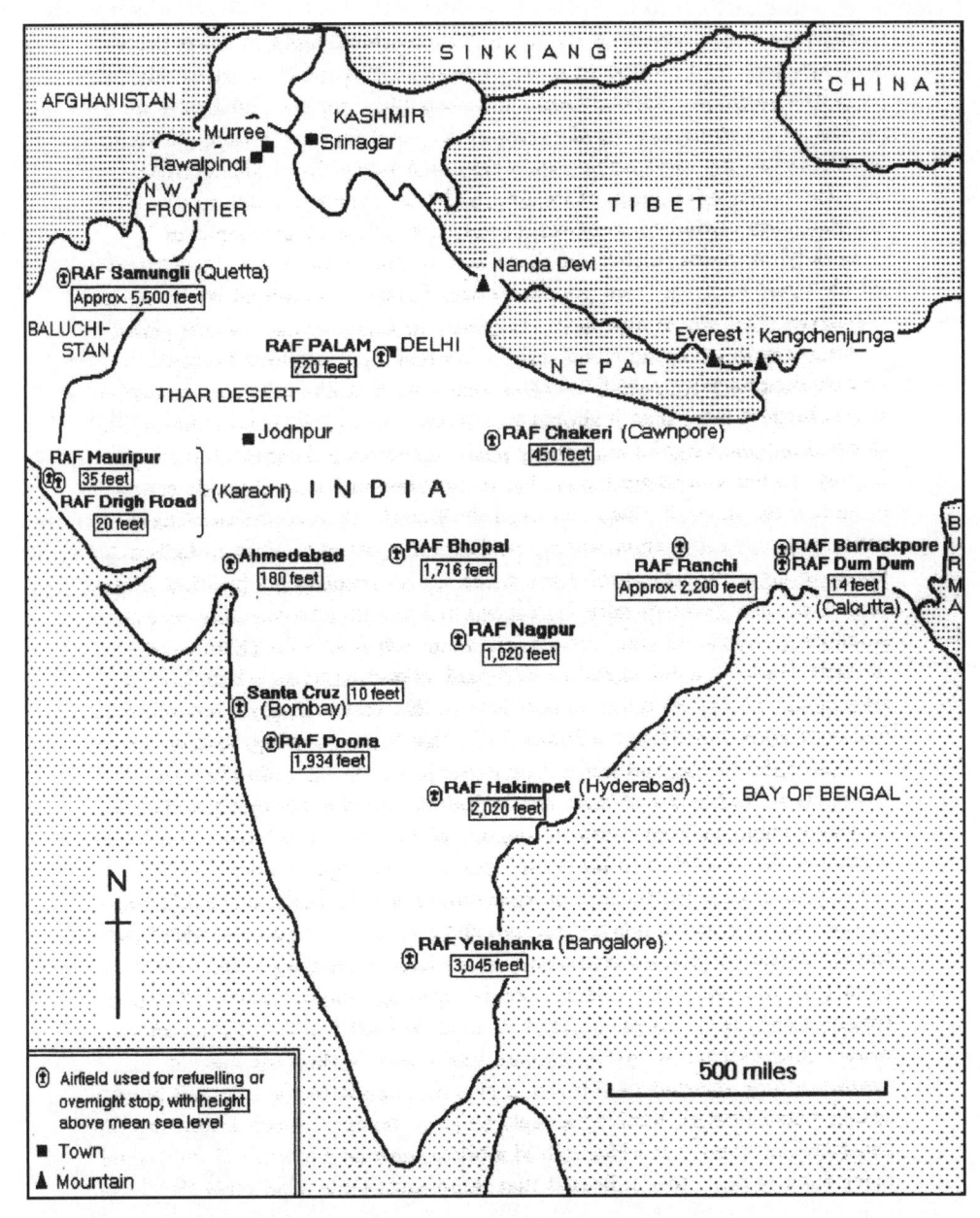

*Figure 9. Airfields in India which I visited for accommodation or refuelling.*

it, so I paused for a bit (by guesswork) before switching on the cameras. After what I thought was about the right time I dipped a wing quickly between exposures to see how far I had got – the taking of each picture was indicated on the control box and there was enough time for this – but found that I had still not reached the town, so I carried on for a little longer.

Eventually I finished the run, and, turning steeply to see exactly what I was over, found that I was badly off to the left, i.e. to the south. This was clearly the northerly wind I had encountered over Indore affecting me again. I ought to have allowed for it, but for some reason did not. Since I was getting short of fuel I continued the turn and went straight into another run heading east, in the opposite direction from the first, instead of starting all over again. That seemed to cover it, although I was a little doubtful. However, in view of the fuel problem I decided that it was time to head for RAF Bhopal, an Indian-run airfield. It was only 50 miles away and I found it without difficulty, landing after a flight of 2 hours 40 minutes.

The obvious solution to the problem of the northerly wind, looking back now, would have been to make a run due north, directly into the wind, so that there would be no drift sideways. But in this case the area to be photographed had an east-west rectangular shape so that runs in a north-south direction were really not feasible. The refuelling was soon completed, after which I went and had a chat with the Flying Control people, who were British, before making my way to the Mess about a mile away to have something to eat.

After lunch I said goodbye to Flying Control and got airborne. This time I was heading north-east for the town of Lalitpur (see Figure 8, page 115), aiming for 13,000 feet. It was easy enough to find, since about halfway to it a sizeable river, the Betwa, came in from near Bhopal and led almost straight to the town through what looked like rather swampy ground, in a countryside which otherwise appeared jungle-covered.

The target was officially just the town, but by common consent on the part of 34 Squadron it was decided that I should kill two birds with one stone, and photograph the airstrip just outside the town as well. This had not been asked for by Air Headquarters, but as it was the sort of thing that we knew by experience they would ask for at some time in the future and then send somebody all that way again especially to take it we decided to forestall them. Unfortunately they didn't quite see the joke when presented with it out of the blue. I should have been able to cover Lalitpur in two runs, but the actual runs which I did seemed to be rather too close together so I did a third to make quite sure.

I now set course north for the 200 miles back to Palam, not bothering very much about getting accurate positions, since there were no obvious pinpoints, and I could always follow the broad River Jumna which would later on come in from the east and lead me straight to Delhi. The ground directly below was at first rather swampy with rivers and small lakes, the sort of country which is anyway difficult to sort out on the map. I expected to pass over a seaplane base at a place called Gwalior near the town of Lashkar, about as far from the sea as you can get. Although I did see a lake and tried to make it fit with Gwalior on the map, I didn't manage to convince myself that that was really it; there were certainly no seaplanes visible.

As I came once again over the river Chambal which I had crossed further upstream on the outward journey I saw about 40 miles away to the north-east the whitish city of Agra, and having visited the Taj Mahal on the ground I thought it would be interesting to see it from the air. I had plenty of fuel so diverting from my original course I put the nose down and headed directly for the city, passing through a layer of wispy cloud on the way, and levelling out at 1,000 feet. As I got nearer, the Taj itself appeared, four square and glistening white. Although from the ground it tended to appear rectangular owing to foreshortening, from the air it was perfectly symmetrical, surrounded by the four minarets at the corners of a square pedestal, and looking like a child's toy.

I had a brief look at the RAF airfield at Agra, where I knew there was a fighter squadron of Tempests, and then flew on to Palam, following the River Jumna most of the way before finally, when near Delhi, veering off to port towards Palam, landing 2 hours 50 minutes after leaving Bhopal.

And what about the photos and the doubtful coverage of Hoshangabad? Luckily all three targets were covered, so there was no need, thank goodness, to have to repeat any of them. But the plotted mosaics did look something of a mess. I was clearly still very ham-fisted.

**Sorties to Fyzabad and Cawnpore**, 31 January 1947 (see Figure 8, page 115, Sortie 3) My next task was to take photos of a couple of targets some distance east of Palam. The first was the town of Fyzabad about 350 miles away, and the second the town of Cawnpore, a little nearer to Palam, and well known for the fearful massacres during the Mutiny in 1857. Fyzabad was a fairly simply task, but on a previous photo recce sortie a gap had been left between a couple of runs, so it had to done again. But I would have to land for refuelling, this time at RAF Chakeri, just outside Cawnpore (see Figure 8, page 115, Sortie 3).

So, ten days after the previous sortie, I took off and headed east-south-east for Fyzabad, climbing through the slight haze to well above it at about 26,000 feet. This was an easy route for navigation, since for about 100 miles in the earlier part of the flight the River Ganges, too big to mistake, was below the starboard wing. It then swung away from me into the distance and I almost immediately crossed one of its large tributaries, the Ramganga, at an easily identifiable spot. After that there was a maze of rivers, canals and railways.

There was no need to do much for the next half-hour, since my position over the Ganges and Ramganga had fixed my track accurately; I just let my eyes roam over the haze and pick out the villages scattered about below. And in the distance 200 miles away to my left I saw once again the Himalaya rising up in an impenetrable snowy wall stretching away into the distance; a wonderful sight.

As the end of the half-hour approached, another large river, the Gogra which drained some of the mountains in Nepal, came in from the left. Since Fyzabad lay on its south bank the river would lead me directly to the town. But I still had to keep my wits about me, since I could so easily have overshot the town, and then it would have been difficult to find out exactly how far I had gone along the river.

I had only about 60 more miles to go, and would be over the target in less than a quarter of an hour. So I watched the river weaving sluggishly about below me with huge dry sandbanks scattered along it. Yes, there was Fyzabad at last, with the two horns of land marked on my large scale map projecting into the river on the north side, and its airfield to the south.

So without much delay I started on my runs, doing them from east to west, and starting on the southernmost one. Everything went well until the last run, and then for some reason I drifted off to the south and seemed to miss the top left-hand corner of the area to be covered. So round I went again and repeated it, but that seemed to be almost the same, so I decided that I was not seeing straight, and that enough was enough. When the photos were printed later, I found that I had just covered the area, but no more. I would indeed have looked a fool if the town had not been covered the second time round.

The Himalaya was looking most enticing, and I did so want a photograph of the mountains, so although the cameras in the aircraft were designed for vertical photography I decided to have an attempt at using them in an unorthodox way. Flying above Fyzabad parallel to the mountain range I put the aircraft into a steep bank so that the cameras, looking out through the bottom of the fuselage, would now be pointing horizontally towards the Himalaya, pressed the button, and then went back to normal level flight. Then back again the other way into another vertical bank for a second photo. When I took those photos I was sure that I had done a 90° bank, so that when I had a print from each camera and fitted them together I would have a nice two-picture panorama with the mountains slap in the middle. But when I saw the subsequent prints I was incredulous. The Himalaya were nowhere to be seen, not even the foothills! There was simply a nice picture of Fyzabad below, with the countryside stretching away into the haze, and that was all. What I had thought was a 90° bank was more likely only 60°. So much for my flying skill!

I now set course west-south-west for Cawnpore to get some fuel at RAF Chakeri which was about four miles outside the city. It was about 120 miles away, but since there were no definite landmarks except railways I just steered in the right direction on the compass. I could not overshoot the area, since I would have to cross the huge River Ganges; the only problem would be to decide where along the line of the river I was. A homing would be the simplest answer, so as I flew on I got one from the Chakeri Homer, and this solved the problem of navigation as I slowly descended towards the altitude of 1,000 feet required for joining the airfield circuit. After a quarter of an hour the Ganges appeared, then I was over it, and there ahead was Chakeri, with its two white runways. After a preliminary circuit I came in and landed, finally taxying back to the Control Tower to park the aircraft.

The groundcrew got the petrol bowser out and set to work to fill her up with 100 octane petrol, and also decided to have a look at the oil level. They did not know whether the oil filler cap to be removed was the one on the top of the engine cowling or the one at the side, and I didn't either, which made me feel a complete fool! Both seemed to lead to the same place, so the groundcrew took the cap off the top one and shoved some oil in. It turned out afterwards that it should have been the one at the side, so they must have overfilled it. Luckily no harm was done, but when I got back to Palam I got 'Don't we keep the engines oiled well enough for you, Nemesis?!' from Blackie, the engineering officer.

With refuelling finished, I taxied out again and got airborne, immediately climbing to 14,000 feet, the height for photographing Cawnpore. This was a difficult task, the area to be covered being unusually large, seven miles by ten miles, which included the RAF airfield. The photographic runs were therefore particularly long, but they seemed to go all right, although I had to repeat one of them, since I thought that I had gone off slightly to one side. Then it was straight back to Palam in time for lunch. The whole trip had been completed in the one morning, the two parts taking respectively 2 hours 15 minutes and 2 hours 45 minutes.

When the photos of Cawnpore were plotted later I was dismayed to find that I had left a small gap between two of the runs over the middle of the town in spite of repeating a doubtful one. That meant that the whole lot would have to be repeated; it was not possible just to fill the missing gap, since everything had to match in the finished product, and slight differences in height, due perhaps to variations in barometric pressure on different days, would have prevented this. Although I had sorted out an earlier failure at Fyzabad, I had now given somebody Cawnpore to do again instead!

**To the south of India**, 4-6 February 1947 (see Figure 10 and Table 3)
So far I had always returned to Palam the same day, but on the next trip I would not only be landing at several strange airfields but would also be staying away for two nights, with an overall journey that would take me to the extreme south of India.

It differed from the previous trips only in the complexity of the overall route, and so I shall describe it mainly as a skeleton of times and distances to show the scale of such journeys. The whole thing covered three days, with two overnight stops, six landings at airfields other than Palam, and five photographic targets, and it is shown here in the form of a map (Figure 10) and Table 3. The whole trip was not as formidable as it might at first appear since I was now getting the hang of both the navigation and the photography.

After leaving Palam in the morning I had to refuel at the already familiar airfield of Bhopal before flying further south to Hakimpet, the RAF airfield just outside Hyderabad, where I stayed the night. The next day I photographed the three targets of Nellore, Vellore and the Kolar Gold Fields even further south, before landing at Yelahanka, the RAF airfield outside Bangalore, the main inland city of south India. Then on the same day I flew even further south to photograph Maddukarai, a site ten miles south of the well-known hill station of Ootacamunde, before returning to Yelahanka for the night. (I now have no idea what Madukkarai was; the name is not even marked on my 16 miles to the inch flying map.)

At Yelahanka I had to sleep under a mosquito net – the only place where I came across one in the whole of India. The countryside outside the airfield was much the same as many other places in the middle of the dry season: brown, rather rolling country with a few huge boulders scattered about. The next day I flew north-west to Poona to refuel before starting off on the last leg back to Palam, photographing the town of Dhulia on the way and landing at Bhopal again for fuel.

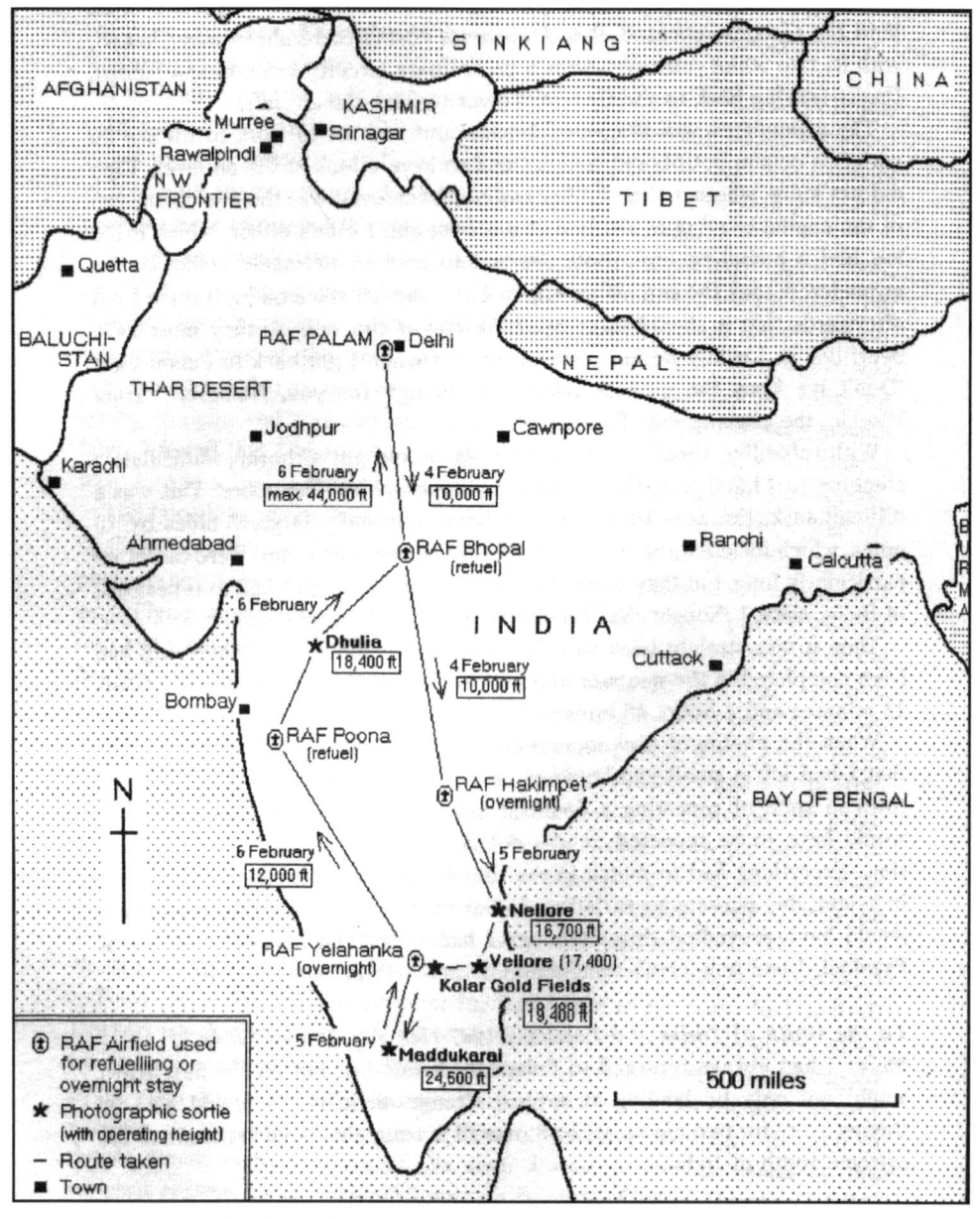

*Figure 10. The long-distance sortie to Yelahanka and the south of India.*

| Date | RAF Airfield | Photographic target | Course | Height | Distance | Flight time |
|---|---|---|---|---|---|---|
| 4.2.47 | PALAM \| BHOPAL (mid-India) | | South | 10,000 ft | 365 miles | 1 hr 20 min |
| | Land and refuel | | | | | |
| | BHOPAL \| HAKIMPET | | South | 10,000 ft | 410 miles | 1 hr 30 min |
| | Land and stay the night | | | | | |
| 5.2.47 | HAKIMPET — NELLORE — VELLORE — KOLAR GOLD FIELDS — YELAHANKA (S. India) | | SSE / SSW / West / NW | 16,700 ft / 17,400 ft / 19,400 ft | 240 miles / 120 miles / 60 miles / 50 miles | 2 hr 35 min |
| | Land and refuel | | | | | |
| | YELAHANKA — MADUKKARAI (S-W India) — YELAHANKA | | SSW / NNE | 24,500 ft | 160 miles / 160 miles | 1 hr 35 min |
| | Land and stay the night (mosquito net required) | | | | | |
| 6.2.47 | YELAHANKA \| POONA | | NW | 12,000 ft | 450 miles | 1 hr 40 min |
| | Land and refuel | | | | | |
| | POONA — DHULIA — BHOPAL | | NNE / NE | 18,400 ft | 170 miles / 230 miles | 1 hr 40 min |
| | Land and refuel | | | | | |
| | BHOPAL \| PALAM | | North | height climb 44,000 ft | 365 miles | 1 hr 30 min |

*Table 3. The journey to Yelahanka and back.*

There was one memorable event on that flight: I did another of my height climbs on the final leg. After taking off from Bhopal I pulled the stick back and just let the Spitfire climb at her own rate. Eventually the altimeter got to 40,000 feet and I was still climbing. The controls were getting sloppy at that altitude owing to the thinness of the air and it was becoming difficult to keep her steady. The rate of climb was getting less and less, and eventually when the altimeter read 45,000 feet I decided that it was about as high as the 'plane would go and settled down for the slow descent back to Palam.

When I got back I worked out what altitude I had actually reached. An altimeter only measures pressure, and the altitude shown on its dial is based on certain assumptions of air temperature and local sea level pressure so that the value needs to be corrected. Using the circular slide-rule of the Navigational Computer mentioned earlier, I converted the indicated altitude to true altitude. The indicated altitude was off the scale, but by extrapolation I worked out that I had reached a true height of about 44,000 feet.

I have heard it said that the sky at that sort of height is getting on for indigo, and that you can see the curvature of the earth. Both these statements are untrue. The sky was indeed a darker colour than when seen at sea level, but it was still a fairly straightforward blue. And as for the curvature of the earth, all I could see was the circular horizon all around, fairly sharply defined at the top of the haze about 30,000 feet below me, but otherwise similar to a horizon seen from lower altitudes. I do not remember having any problem with the oxygen, although at that height the total pressure is so low that I must have had some oxygen deficiency however well-fitting my mask might have been.

**Other sorties** (see Figure 7, page 109)
There were two more sorties in February. The weather was still reasonably cool, the dust haze had not yet thickened as it would later, and navigation was straightforward.

The first sortie was to the south, spending a night at Bhopal and then taking some vertical photos of Nimach to its west before returning to Palam. This trip was memorable for an episode in the middle of the night. I shared a hut at Bhopal with one or two of the few British officers at that Indian-run airfield, sleeping as usual on a charpoy, and covered by no more than a sheet for warmth. In the middle of the night I was suddenly woken by the feeling that something was moving over me. It was pitch dark, and my first reaction was 'It's a cobra!'; I just lay there paralysed with fear. If I moved I might frighten whatever it was, and a frightened snake bites first and asks question afterwards. So I just lay without moving a muscle. I did not know whether the thing which had woken me was still on the bed or not.

After a while I decided to move just a little, and then when nothing happened, I moved just a little more. Eventually I decided that there was no longer anything there, so I got up and turned on the light, which of course woke the others. When I told them what had happened I got a sour 'Oh, it was probably only a rat, go back to bed'. So I did. In the discussion we had about it next morning the general opinion was that it had almost certainly only been one of the rats which frequented the area, and not a snake. Was I relieved!

The second sortie that February was to the east, and took three days, landing for the night firstly at RAF Ranchi, about 600 miles to the south-east of Palam and then about 200 miles further on at RAF Dum Dum, the airfield of Calcutta which had a single really long runway of 2,500 yards (for comparison, Palam's two runways were 2,000 and 1,960 yards). One set of photographs which I had to take was of the town of Cuttack in the south of the region, and the other was of Sylhet right over to the east near the border of Assam. Unfortunately I photographed Sylhet rather late in the day when the light was poor, and the resulting pictures, although covering the target, lacked detail. With my photographic knowledge I ought to have known and waited until the next morning, but the light probably looked good enough to the eye which can easily be misled when it comes to photography.

From Dum Dum I made a fifteen minute hop to RAF Barrackpore, almost next door (see Figure 9 on page 121), and landed there before continuing on my journey. Why such a silly little flight? I have no idea. Was I delivering something, or perhaps Dum Dum lacked facilities for servicing which might be necessary on an extended trip of this sort? What is memorable is that I lost a rather nice propelling pencil in the cockpit while at Barrackpore. I was entering up some notes on the flight while sitting in the cockpit and the pencil slipped out of my hand and dropped out of sight. Unfortunately the bottom of a Spitfire cockpit had no floor to it; it was effectively part of a metal cylinder with various tubes and cables going from one end of the 'plane to the other. I upended myself in the cockpit, with my head down and with my feet sticking out of the top, but there was no sign of the pencil, and even if I had seen it I could probably not have reached it. Perhaps it is still there lying in some Indian aircraft junkyard.

## 11

## Low-Level Sortie and the Bombay Bibbies[1]

An unusual task which I was given at the beginning of March was to take oblique photos of a region of the coast for the Army, to be used by an attacking naval force in a Combined Operations Exercise. Since this Exercise was to be held in a fortnight's time the pictures were wanted fairly urgently and there was no time for mistakes.

Urgent or unrepeatable sorties were commonly given to somebody on the squadron who had had experience of something similar, and since I happened to be the only member of the Squadron who was not away on a sortie or otherwise occupied and who had taken obliques before, I got the job. The target was the south-eastern and western coasts of a peninsula nine miles long called North Salsette, fifteen miles north of Bombay, on the west coast of India. Vertical photographs of the area had been taken earlier by T.-E. as part of the Coastal Survey which the Squadron was carrying out, and prints of these had already been provided for the Exercise.

To get to the Bombay area I would have to fly first of all south-west to Ahmedabad, an Indian-run civilian airfield roughly halfway between Karachi and Bombay (see Figure 7, page 109) where I would land for fuel. (Normally we avoided landing at civilian airfields since they usually had no servicing facilities but in this case there was no RAF alternative. There had originally been an RAF airfield at the ancient city of Baroda about 50 miles away from Ahmedabad, but that had been closed down.) From Ahmedabad I would then fly south to Santa Cruz, another civilian airfield just outside Bombay.

After being briefed at Flying Control I taxied out to the end of the runway at about 8 o'clock but when I got there and made the routine take-off check of the magnetos I found that there was a slight magneto drop: the engine faltered and then picked up again when I switched off one of the two magneto switches. 'Still, it's not too bad,' I thought. 'Perhaps she'll clear herself when I get airborne'.

So I opened up the throttle, took off, and headed south-west for Ahmedabad. After climbing to my cruising altitude I checked the switches again – she had taken off all right and was running nicely – but that magneto drop was still there, so I increased the revs and boost once or twice to try to clear it, but it was no go, it just would not disappear. Unlike some civilian airfields Ahmedabad did not have an RAF Detachment, so if the aircraft broke down there I would really be stuck. There was nothing for it but to turn round and go back to Palam. Twenty minutes after take-off I was back on the ground.

---

1 *Bibby* was a slang word used by British troops for an Indian woman.

*Plate 48, the author relaxing with photo reconnaissance friend. Photograph believed to date from 1946, RAF Wunstorf, Germany.*

As I taxied into dispersal Blackie came up to me and asked 'What's wrong, Nemesis?' 'Magneto drop, Blackie, must be the plugs – I don't know whether I shall get off again today.' 'I doubt it,' answered Blackie, looking a bit despondent as usual. 'The engine'll be too hot to touch at the moment, and we've got no other kites serviceable except D [the large identification letter painted on the side of the aircraft], but that's got to have an air test first.' So that was that. After the rush and bustle of getting off on a trip, here I was back again for the night at Palam. Later that morning, when the engine had cooled down sufficiently to work on it, they took the cowling off and found that there was indeed a faulty plug.

Next morning I took off again, and climbed away towards the south-west, the engine this time giving no trouble. I settled down at 6,000 feet, the height for which I had worked out my flight plan, but found that at that height the air was much too bumpy for comfort on a long trip like this, so I climbed to 8,000 feet. The bumps disappeared, so I stayed at that height for the rest of the journey to Ahmedabad.

After crossing the nearly dry course of the Sabi River, followed by a few hills, I saw the town of Jaipur about eight miles off on my port side, looking very dry in the surrounding desert-like country (see Figure 7, page 109). I now got my last pinpoint for some little while: two railways coming out west from Jaipur, with ahead nothing but the dry dusty light-brown earth. This pinpoint had to be accurate since it was a long haul of fifty minutes to the next really good one, the town of Udaipur 200 miles further on.

The fifty minutes passed slowly, but eventually straight ahead and rising up from the dry plain, appeared a ragged wall of hills, broken by a small gap. As I crossed the gap there ahead and to starboard was Udaipur itself, white among the brown hills, its two lakes gleaming in the sun. I learned later that it is a famous and beautiful city, with a white palace set in the middle of one of the lakes, but at the time I knew nothing of that; even if I had I would have seen little of its beauty from the altitude at which I was flying. What I particularly noticed was the whiteness of the buildings in contrast to the brown of other towns which I had seen from the air.

The important thing for the moment was that I was just about on track. I had a look at the landing ground at Udaipur as I went over to check how suitable it might be for a forced landing; we always did this automatically as an important policy of always being prepared for the worst. The landing ground might have been fine for light aircraft, for which it had obviously been designed, but I decided that it was far too small for a Spitfire XIX to land on, unless with the wheels up!

The countryside continued to be broken up by hills for a further ten minutes, but eventually these dropped away to give place once again to the familiar flat brown plain. Then away to the right I could see coming in towards me the River Sabarmati, which would lead me directly to Ahmedabad, so I turned slightly towards it. I should then be able to see the airfield ahead off my port wing as it came up. Yes, there it was, with its two runways, a shorter one of 1,600 yards and a longer one of 2,000 yards, roughly similar to those at Palam. The position of the 'T' symbol on the ground in front of

Flying Control showed me that the shorter runway was the one to land on.

I had been warned before I left Palam that Ahmedabad had no radio telephony on any of our wavelengths. Just to check I called them up on the Universal Airfield Control frequency, but there was no reply. So I had to land entirely by visual contact, which meant watching out for other aircraft and also watching Flying Control for a red or green Very Light. There were no other aircraft around, no green Very Light giving me permission to land and no red one telling me not to. So I came in to land, choosing the shorter runway as directed by the T in the signals area – reminiscent of Perth and the Tiger Moth days. I did not at first notice that a wind from the left was giving me a drift to starboard, and as a result touched down with the port wheel on the runway and the starboard wheel off it. Just careless flying. So I opened the throttle smartly and went round again. This time I took a bit more care, and concentrating everything on the landing I touched down slap in the centre of the runway with just a slight bounce before rolling to a stop. Then I turned around and taxied back down the runway to Flying Control, where I was marshalled to the front of the building for parking.

An Indian Burmah-Shell bowser came out, and after checking that they were not going to put petrol into the oil I went up to Flying Control to have a chat and find out what was what. I was greeted, not with the expected facetious comment on my trouble in landing that I might have had at an RAF airfield, but with 'Didn't you see the Red we gave you?' That was news to me, and I told the Indian control officer so. Apparently they had given me a red Very Light after my first attempt, since the wind had changed direction from that indicated by the T which they hadn't bothered to change and they were then going to land me on the longer runway. But after the first bad attempt I was concentrating so much on the landing that I presumably missed the Very Light, although since the Control Tower was off to one side the chances are that I would not have seen it anyway while on the approach. (Usually Very Lights for aircraft on the landing approach were sent up by an Airfield Controller near the end of the runway, but Ahmedabad didn't have one.)

When my 'plane had been refuelled and I had signed the acceptance forms, I climbed aboard once more, taxied out and got airborne, this time heading almost due south for Santa Cruz airfield (see Figure 9, page 121). On this leg of the journey the air turbulence did not reach so high, probably because of the cooling effect of the sea, and since flying was now smooth at the 6,000 feet of my original flight plan I decided to keep to that. It was always better to fly at the height decided on back at base, since that is the one for which corrections for wind and airspeed would have been worked out.

It was an easy and uneventful flight. There was a little haze, but not enough to matter, since a line on the map from Ahmedabad to Santa Cruz goes straight down the wandering coastline. Flying down such a coast can sometimes be a little erratic since you tend to follow the coastline itself rather than the compass, and find yourself going in all sorts of directions. Still, all the pinpoints came up as expected.

About 100 miles north of Bombay there was a bit of Portuguese territory, Daman, similar to the better-known one of Goa much further south. It was in two parts, one on the coast, and one slightly inland, and I had to deviate slightly from my set course to avoid crossing these territories. It was not difficult to judge where to go, since there was a railway line shown on the map running between them, so I followed that. It is interesting to note my attitude at the time, taken from some notes written shortly afterwards: 'When I got to the piece of Portuguese territory which occupied a chunk of that coastline I found that I was heading into it, so, feeling rather virtuous, I flew round the border. Quite nuts, of course, because who would worry about an aeroplane flying over a measly little bit of territory like that at 6,000 feet?'

As I neared Santa Cruz airfield and started to lose height, I looked out to my right for North Salsette to see what it looked like, and found that it was quite clear-cut and easy to recognize. The airfield was ten miles further on; it had three runways, which was unusual for India, where two runways were usually sufficient considering the uniformity of the wind directions. I had never landed on an airfield with more than two runways and found it rather confusing having to decide which was the correct one out of six possible directions. I got it right, but only after doing two circuits first! The trip to Ahmedabad had taken 1 hour 55 minutes, but this second leg of the journey only took 1 hour 5 minutes, making a total of exactly three hours in the air from Palam.

On instructions from Flying Control I taxied back down the runway, and after a lot of zigzagging finally ended up safely at the local RAF Detachment with whom I left the aircraft for its daily inspection since the air temperature would become too hot for any more flying that day. This Detachment was no more than a Servicing Wing for looking after aircraft staying a night or two; it was later disbanded, and from then on anybody carrying out photographic sorties in that region of India had to use RAF Poona, 80 miles to the south-east. The ground crew came out and took over my Spitfire while I wandered over to Flying Control to tell them what I would be doing and how long I would be at Santa Cruz.

When I got back to the RAF Detachment I rang through, as I had been briefed to do before I left Palam, to a local Wing Commander who knew something about the task I was doing. He told me that what was wanted were not photos of the south-eastern coastline of the peninsula – which I had been told to take – but bigger and better photos of the western coastline, which looked on to the Arabian Sea. He also wanted single shots of certain pinpoints for which he gave me map references so that I could find them on the one-inch map which I had been given.

The next thing was to sort out food and accommodation. At RAF airfields there was never any difficulty in doing this, but since this was a civilian one it was rather out of the ordinary. Before leaving Palam I had had some advice from T.-E. who had already been here and had found that he could stay at the Mess of the local Detachment. So I rang them up, but they were not interested, and eventually I was informed that the best thing to do was to go to the RAF Transit Mess at the Adelphi Hotel five miles away in Bombay itself.

Luckily there was some RAF transport available, and off we went through the wilds of Bombay's outskirts. At the hotel I was told that normally they did not put people up without notice, but that by chance there was a room to spare and would I please inform the rest of my friends that they would in future like at least two days' notice. Yes, I replied, I would be glad to, making a mental note that I would have word or two to say to T.-E. about all this.

I was shown up to a superb room, with electric *punkah*, a nice soft bed – a real one, not a *charpoy* – and a BATH – the only one I saw all the time I was in India – all to myself. I have put BATH in capital letters, since it was such a rarity and such a luxurious change from the shower or tub usually provided in India that I could hardly believe it. I had one immediately. It was particularly welcome since the heat of Bombay at that time of year, March, was beginning to get sticky and it felt hotter than Palam.

At the evening meal I got talking to a medical officer, a Flying Officer Bird from the RAF Hospital at Karachi. He claimed to be a ciné enthusiast, but I decided that he had more enthusiasm than sense, since he wanted to go into the dark alleys of Bombay in the evening and get some pictures of the sordid life there. 'The lighting won't be good enough,' I said. 'The best part of the day is over and you'll find the pictures will be hopelessly underexposed, even in the brighter parts of the town.' But he was determined, so off we went together in a taxi, starting with the brightly-lit centre of Bombay, where he took some shots of the local populace outside a cinema.

Then he wanted to go to Number 5 Grant Road. This was a house of ill repute, famous throughout the length and breadth of India as the leading brothel in the country for Europeans. They were said to charge Rs 30 (£2/5s/0d)[2] just to get in, but we intended to see inside the place without paying anything. The taxi-driver did not like the idea at all, saying that it was forbidden and so on, but in the end we managed to persuade him to take us there.

Round by back alleys we drove, and down a side street which curved back almost underneath the main thoroughfare, until eventually we came to a high wall in which a gap gave on to a drive leading up to the front door of Number 5. It was surprising to find, among all the dirty and sordid-looking houses around, this detached, expensive-looking mansion, set back from the street, with trees in the garden and a circular drive up to the front door. We drove in, told the driver to wait, and went up the steps. After knocking, a pretty Eurasian let us in, and we saw the Madame of the place in the hall. Beyond her we could see dancing, and the strains of music wafted out to us. Bird asked if he could take some ciné shots of the dancing, but the answer was a firm 'No'. (He had originally suggested that he would say that he had come to carry out a medical inspection but somehow didn't quite get around to it!) He tried to argue the point, but it was no good, he just wasn't allowed to take any pictures. So out we went again, but at least we could now both shoot a line about having actually been inside the infamous Number 5.

There was no doubt about where my friend wanted to go next – the 'cages', or native brothel area. It was out of bounds to British troops, but after again persuading the

---

2 Retail Prices Index: 1947, approx. 7; 1990, approx 126.

taxi driver that it was all right we pushed on into the meanest part of the city. We found that the 'cages' consisted of brightly lit small rooms open to the street, some with curtains across, which contained Indian prostitutes on show waiting for men. Some had shutters up which consisted of vertical steel bars, hence the name 'cages'. Occasionally my companion would get out his camera expecting, as he put it, a knife in the back. He had little success, however, since the women immediately covered their faces whenever he pointed the camera at them, while the men slouching around gave us menacing looks. It was far too dark for photography and I doubt whether anything that Bird took came out. Eventually we left, both of us agreeing that we were glad to be out of it without having had our throats cut.

That escapade reminds me of a rhyming Urdu jingle about Bombay which was current at Palam: *Taura cheeni, taura char, Bombay bibby bhot ach-cha*. I have forgotten what *cheeni* means, but otherwise it may be translated as: '…some tea, Bombay girl very good'. I doubt whether it was genuine Urdu, more likely a concoction of pidgin Urdu, since another jingle going the rounds was obviously of British origin: *Pani pani subchees pani, kutch nai hai peenika pani*, which is a loose Urdu translation of 'Water water everywhere, but not a drop to drink'.

Next morning after a fairly early breakfast I paid my bill, caught the transport and returned to the airfield. My 'plane was all ready, so after ringing up Flying Control I strapped myself in, taxied out to the end of the runway and got airborne. Almost before I realised it I was over North Salsette. It took no more than two and a half minutes to get there; I had not quite appreciated how near it was. After looking it over briefly I did a dummy run to prepare for photographing the coast from the west, over the sea, but found that the sun at that early hour was shining almost directly into the camera lens. 'This isn't much good,' I thought, 'I'd better get back to Santa Cruz and wait for an hour or two for the sun to get a bit higher.' So back I went, landing again only 20 minutes after take-off.

There was nothing to do before having another try, so I killed time by wandering over to Flying Control, looking at some of the civilian airline buildings, and generally mooching around the airfield. I always found something of interest at such places, and this time I found two familiar types of aircraft, a Harvard and another Spitfire, sitting on the tarmac, as well as a Tempest.

Eventually the sun had risen high enough for eastward-facing photography, so I went back to my Spitfire, got things organized as before, and once again arrived over North Salsette. This time the angle of the lighting was much better, so I set to work and did a run down the coast at an altitude of 1,000 feet, followed by another one at 500 feet. Since the coast was irregular, it meant having to do quite a number of separate short runs, tackling each of the promontories of the peninsula separately. Below me I could see preparations for the coming Exercise already taking place. Men were being landed on the beach from a landing craft and being lined up ready for marching away. They looked up at me as I did a rather bad run and shot low over their heads.

Then it was time to concentrate on the Wing Commander's pinpoints. I had been told at Palam not to fly below 400 feet but he had countermanded that with: 'I want some photos from 100 feet if possible.' A bit much, I thought! Most of the pinpoints meant flying in from over the sea, and as it is difficult to judge your height over calm water I decided to do the best I could by altimeter (how do seaplane pilots manage to land, I wondered?). Being effectively an aneroid barometer, this meant setting the altimeter's reading at some known height – in this case the height of Santa Cruz airfield, officially ten feet above sea level – which I had done as one of the routine flight checks before take-off. However, an aneroid barometer is too crude an instrument for accurate low flying so I decided to go down to no more than 200 feet by its reading. At this indicated height I flew past a rocky promontory with a flag on top which I had been told to photograph, making several runs, and taking single shots from all sides. Another target was some kind of scaffolding in the surf; it looked like a beach defence and was the only one of its kind.

After that, my last targets were some bare hill-tops, with large white numbers in Roman figures marked on them. I have no idea what they were for, but they were big enough to be seen quite clearly from the air. Perhaps they were targets of some kind for the aerial side of the Exercise. Giving a last look round before returning to Santa Cruz, I noticed in a sort of creek to the south of North Salsette a collection of small warships congregated around an apparently permanent naval station, nicely hidden from the sea and obviously another facet of the Exercise. The whole flight took 1 hour 50 minutes, quite a long time considering the few minutes it took to fly between the target and Santa Cruz, but I had at least used up the whole film of 100 exposures which would please Blackie – he was always grumbling about the waste of unused film left in the cameras.

When my Spitfire had been refuelled and I had been briefed on the weather at Flying Control, I took off from Santa Cruz for the last time. I had decided to fly direct to Palam instead of going by way of Ahmedabad, thus shortening the journey. There had also been a headwind on the outward journey which would become a tailwind on the return journey, increasing my groundspeed and making it possible to return to Palam in one hop. Not only would I get back more quickly, but I would also avoid the risk of the aircraft breaking down when on the ground at Ahmedabad with no servicing available there. However, it was about 700 miles and I would be running it rather fine in terms of fuel.

So before I left I carefully marked on my map 50-mile distances so as to be able to work out my fuel consumption and ground speed accurately as I went along. I then drew in a couple of lines joining Agra airfield – 100 miles nearer than Palam – with two easily identifiable pinpoints on the later part of my track, and marked on these lines the distances and courses to Agra. The object of this was that if I found towards the end of the journey that my fuel consumption was higher than I had expected I could at the last moment divert to Agra, which, although about 100 miles to the east of the direct route to Palam (see Figure 7, page 109), was a fully equipped RAF airfield where I could obtain fuel and, if necessary, servicing.

As soon as I had taken off I set course and started to climb. At 25,000 feet I levelled out, and adjusted the pitch and boost so as to fly at about 200 mph Indicated Air Speed, which worked out at about 300 mph True Air Speed (see Table 18 in the Appendix for relationships between Indicated and True Airspeed). I chose this height because it gave a better range, an important consideration in long-distance flying. It had not mattered on the way to Santa Cruz, since I was refuelling at Ahmedabad, but on the one-hop journey back it was essential to economize on fuel.

Over the dry hills of the Western Ghats I flew, with the sea gradually disappearing in the distance away to the left. About 200 miles from Santa Cruz I had my first really good pinpoint, the Tapti, a large river with an unmistakeable shape. It showed me that I was a little to starboard of my intended track, so I altered course slightly to port. There was little of interest to see from 25,000 feet, just the same dry brown countryside, maybe a slightly different shade of brown here and there, but on the whole fairly uniform. Occasionally a glistening river would break the monotony with its tentacle-like branches pushing their way through the hillier parts.

My next pinpoint, a section of the upper reaches of the Chambal River – the same river that I had encountered on my earlier flight to Indore – was another hundred miles on, but in the meantime it was impossible to tell whether I was still on track or not. There were so many small rivers wandering all over the place none of which was definitely identifiable, and numerous inaccuracies on the flying map did not help. But eventually the Chambal came in from starboard, and twisted along beside me for another 50 miles. Then it gave one tortuous wrench before breaking away to starboard. That wrench was the pinpoint I had been looking for – there was no mistaking it. It showed that I was as near to my track as could be expected.

I was now getting near where I would have to divert to Agra if I was going to, so I started to work out how long it would take to get to Palam. I knew my fuel consumption, which I had calculated at each pinpoint, and when I put the time to Palam and the consumption rate together at another first-class pinpoint – where the River Banas crossed my track at right angles – I found that I could just get there comfortably. But I must not relax. I must still keep checking my distances and consumptions or a gremlin (see Glossary) would get at me and drain the fuel from my tanks.

From now on there were several rivers at right angles to my course, excellent for measuring accurate distances provided that I could identify them, but the route was now beginning to be familiar, since it was gradually converging on that of my earlier flight to Indore. Eventually I came within radio telephony range of Palam, so I called the Homer and started to descend. Soon I was in the circuit, then safely down and climbing out of my 'plane. I felt that I had been away for a week, but it had only been a couple of days. The flying time for the return trip in one hop proved to be 2 hours 20 minutes compared with the 3 hours total for the outward journey.

The photos turned out well on the whole, but there were some disappointments. One or two were slightly off-target, and the low-level ones were unfortunately blurred because of a combination of the speed of the aircraft and the closeness of the target.

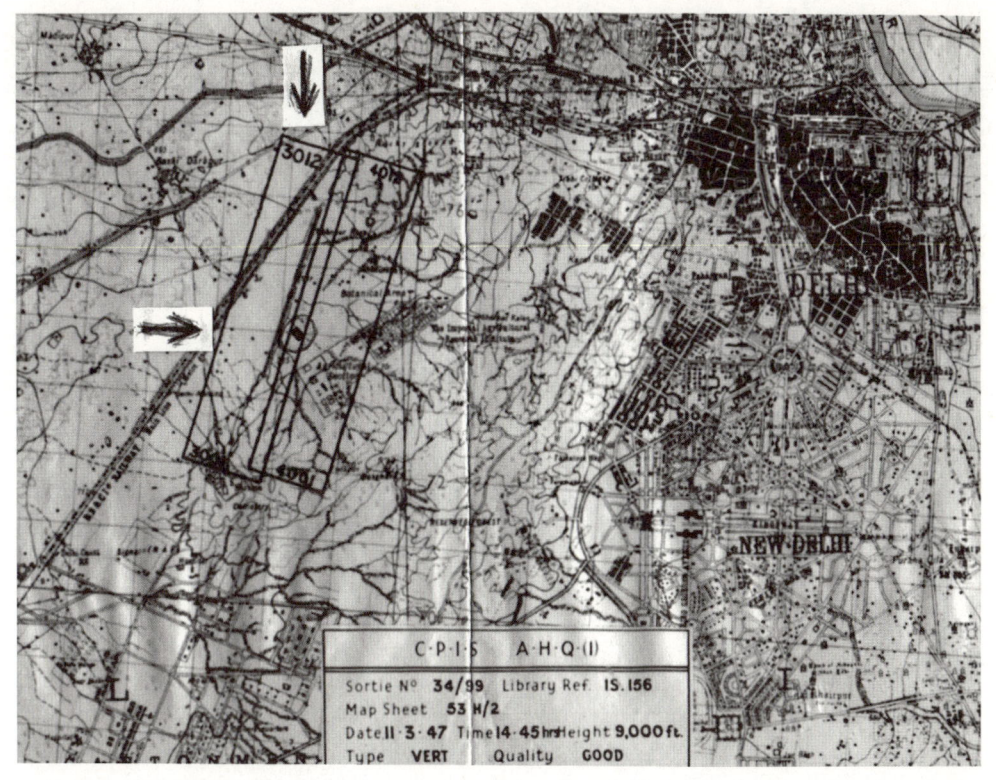

*Plate 49, The plot of the reconnaissance photograph of the Agricultural Institute just outside Delhi (see text). This should be viewed from the edge of the page, so that Delhi is on the right and the plot of the Agricultural Institute is on the left.*

## The smallest of sorties

I add here what must be the tiniest sortie ever. The object was to take, from the unusually low height of 9,000 feet, vertical photographs of the Agricultural Institute which lay about half-way between Delhi and Palam. Only one photographic run was needed. It used practically no film, and I managed to take it to perfection – a rare occasion. A copy of the plot of the run prepared by Air Headquarters in Delhi is the only one of any of my sorties that has survived the intervening years and is shown as Plate 49 above.

It shows the single run as two overlapping rectangles to the left of centre running roughly south to north, labelled 3001-3012 and 4001-4012 (the number 3001 is almost completely obscured in the photocopy), superimposed on a large-scale map of the area. The series of numbers represent the individual frames of the left- and right-hand vertical cameras respectively – twelve photographs taken with each camera. The Agricultural Institute is the small black rectangle within the overlap of the two sets of photographs, its position being indicated by the two large arrows drawn in to the left of and above the run.

Delhi is the large built-up area to the right – Old Delhi being the black area above and New Delhi the widely-spaced regular road pattern below (the small circle of roads at the top of New Delhi is the shopping centre, Connaught Circus, mentioned earlier).

The illustration is also an example of how the prints of all our photographic sorties were plotted. After the film had been developed and printed at Air Headquarters in Delhi the prints were passed to plotters who marked, as shown here, the location of the strips of photographs on a large-scale map. Usually, as shown in Figure 1 on page 42, there were several parallel runs from which several plots like this were drawn side by side and overlapping.

## 12

## Lost!

Now comes an episode which I would be happier to have forgotten, since it gave me the fright of my life, and still makes me go cold when I think of it. It happened like this. The Air Headquarters Communications Squadron at Palam had a Spitfire XI in their possession, but for some strange reason it had been laid up at another airfield. Then one day in March it was flown to Palam and was given a thorough inspection by our groundcrew. We all wanted to fly it, since we all thought it a marvellous aircraft; it was really gentle, and the lovely Merlin engine was so smooth compared with the more powerful but rougher-engined Griffon engine of the Spitfire XIX.

Gerry Fray, the Commanding Officer, went up first, and then – what luck! – I was told that I could have a flight in it. So they filled the 'plane up with fuel and I got somebody to give me a quick run-over of the cockpit instruments and controls; there were a few differences here and there from the XIX.

I climbed happily into the cockpit, strapped myself in, and got down to the routine cockpit check. It was strange starting the engine of the XI again after getting used to the XIX. In the XIX you had to press one button and this was followed by the loud bark of the Koffman cartridge as it detonated and turned over the engine. But with the XI the groundcrew had to attach the trolly-acc to provide electrical power, and then you pressed two buttons at once. This was followed by a creaking humming noise, the engine at first turning over sluggishly before finally firing.

The Merlin engine started with no trouble, and I checked over the cockpit instruments, noting particulary the fuel gauge which showed only 85 gallons. She could have held considerably more, but the wing tanks had not been filled, since I was supposed to be making only a short local flight.

I had my own camera with me, and decided that this was a great opportunity to go and take a close look at the nearest of the Himalayan mountains 200 miles away, which so far I had seen only from a distance. Since I had no oxygen I could not get really close, but it would be better than nothing. Nanda Devi was the nearest of the great peaks, and I very much wanted to see inside the Nanda Devi Sanctuary, a region enclosed by high mountains, but that was out of the question since it would have required oxygen.

I taxied out and took off at about 10 o'clock before the heat of the day developed. I had a little trouble with the take-off owing to the unfamiliar torque. (I have already mentioned that the engines and hence the propellers in the Spitfire XI and XIX rotated in opposite directions, resulting in swings on take-off in opposite directions.) I remembered to trim the rudder the opposite way from that required in the XIX, but when it came to accelerating down the runway my automatic reactions kept battling with my knowledge of what was required, and the take-off run turned out to be rather erratic.

Flying Control assumed that I was doing local flying, for which I was authorized. I did not of course want to disillusion them, so I simply cleared myself with them and climbed away steadily north-eastward. As soon as I had got above the haze at about 9,000 feet I could see the blue-white mountains away in the distance ahead. I had made no flight plan before leaving the ground to give me a course to steer; instead, I simply headed straight towards the peaks, using my map occasionally to check ground speed and position.

After 20 minutes I crossed the river Ganges (see Figure 11), not particularly wide here, and then the River Khoh, a tributary of the Ramganga which I could see winding away to my right. Then I was over the foothills, which shoot up from 1,000 feet to 6,000 feet within about ten miles. I was now at 10,000 feet and climbing slowly. The rugged foothills below were rather indistinct, just dark ridges with the silver gleams of rivers.

There were still 50 or 60 miles to go before I was as near the high peaks as I could get without oxygen. Directly ahead was the Nanda Devi group towering white and gleaming above the dark foothills, while over to the left were the twin flat-topped Gari and Hathi Parbat[1] with Kamet hidden just beyond them.

I finally reached 14,000 feet and was beginning to feel slightly muzzy-headed, a symptom of lack of oxygen. A rather low height, I felt, to start feeling such an effect, although in theory one is supposed to start being affected at 10,000 feet. So I descended to 13,000 feet where I felt better. The ridges of the foothills had now reached about 10,000 feet, only 3,000 feet below me; I could see them in considerable detail with their steep sides covered with sparse scrubby trees, quite different from the jungle that I had expected in this region.

Beyond the pass to the left of the Nanda Devi group were more white peaks rising up jagged against the blue sky – the snow-covered peaks of Tibet. I just itched to fly on and have a look at that very different country, but it was again out of the question without oxygen.

I had reached about as far as I could. Only two thousand feet separated me from the foothill peaks beneath which were getting ever higher and higher. I had been taking a few photographs of the range through the perspex of the hood as I approached, but I now began to get the camera properly to work and eventually used up the best part of a reel of film. I took several of the high peaks over to my left, including the Parbats (Plate 50) before swinging left and flying parallel to the range, getting more photos of the Nanda Devi group now on my right (Plate 51). Then it was time to go home or I would not have enough fuel left. So I swung around to port and set a rough course back to Palam.

---

1 Not to be confused with Nanga Parbat in the Hundu Kush range further north.

# LOST!

*Plate 50, The flat-topped Gari Parbat (21,747 ft) and Hathi Parbat (22,070 ft) just left of centre.*

It was now that I made two big mistakes which nearly cost the country an aircraft and me my life. The first was that I did not set myself an accurate compass course because I knew that when I hit the River Jumna I would not be far from Delhi and Palam. The second was that I did not note the time. I should have made a note of the time at which I set course for Palam and again of when I crossed the edge of the foothills, and from the difference between them worked out a groundspeed. Instead, I just set course roughly, and relied over-confidently on my map-reading alone – a foolish thing to do, particularly in India. This carelessness was without doubt due to lack of oxygen, flying as I was at too great a height. I should have remembered the coloured poster in the crew room so long ago at Cranwell which stated that 'Apathy and unconcern are symptoms of lack of oxygen'. I thought I was clever enough to tell when I was suffering from lack of oxygen, but in fact a mild deficiency is not necessarily obvious.

As I crossed the edge of the foothills I saw a river below me and assumed that it was the River Khoh which I had crossed on the way out. Soon afterwards I saw another one which I assumed to be the Ganges. So I said to myself 'Fair enough, the next river will be the Jumna [on which Delhi lies] and when I see that I'll turn south and then after a little while I'll see Delhi'. So at the next river I turned south and followed it along.

Later, back at Palam, I came to the conclusion that the first river must have been just a tributary, while the second was not the Ganges but the Khoh, so that I was now following the wrong river: the Ganges instead of the Jumna. Without a flight plan this was an easy mistake to make since the two run parallel in that region and from the air looked much the same.

I had about 27 gallons of fuel left out of the 85 with which I had started, enough for only about 40 minutes' more flying, so there was not much time to spare. Even so, I still did not check the time when I came to the river. If I had, I could have worked out how soon I might expect to see Delhi.

I continued to follow the river southwards but there was no sign of the city. Visibility was not too good owing to the dust haze, perhaps ten or twenty miles, but I knew that I should be able to see Delhi easily when it appeared, since it was large and right beside the Jumna. I was now starting to get worried, since it was becoming obvious even without timing anything that Delhi was overdue. So I called the Palam Homer to try and obtain a bearing back to Palam, but there was no reply other than a slight noise in my earphones which might have been them.

I saw a bridge down below over the river I was following, and found one on the Jumna, so although the positions did not exactly correspond I assumed this to be due to the inaccuracy of the map; these were known to be unreliable, but in this case it was just wishful thinking.

Delhi of course ought to have appeared fairly soon after reaching the river, but I blindly ignored this fact, and now started to feel a bit panicky. I could definitely hear the Homer when I called them, but they were still too faint for me to understand what they were saying. I could have heard them better if I had been able to climb to a higher altitude, but that was out of the question. So I decided that since I could now hear them I was probably after all getting nearer, and so said to myself 'If I press on a bit further I should be able to hear them better'. So on I pressed.

I continued to call the Homer, but still no joy. Fuel was now down to 20 gallons, or about 30 minutes' flying time, which is precious little when you have no idea where you are. Then at last I thought 'I have been following this river for too long; I wonder if it really is the right river? If it is, the Homer should be getting louder but they aren't. If it's not, then it must be the Ganges, and I might be anywhere along it, so if I turn to starboard I should go roughly in the right direction; but if it really is the Jumna I shall be heading straight into the Thar Desert.'

Looking over the side all I could see was the unfriendly brown earth that looked smooth enough where it was not broken up by villages and trees, but which I knew was probably covered with broken boulders and rocks, where an aircraft which force-landed would stand little chance. I began to imagine the Spitfire with me in it smashing itself to bits as I tried to bring it down with the wheels up (with wheels down I would have turned over on the rough ground). I was beginning to sweat by now and kept looking at the fuel gauge. Down to 18 gallons: 27 minutes left. Still no sign of Delhi.

The difficulty in a situation like this is to think rationally. I had built up a picture of myself flying down the Jumna towards Delhi, and since it consisted of a process of apparently logical sequences it was difficult to believe that after all I really might not be over the Jumna.

I would now certainly not get back to the airfield without the Homer's help, since I was well and truly lost. So I made the decision and swung the aircraft round until it faced west, once more looking over the side at the brown dry countryside. I had that awful feeling that a prang was now inevitable – a feeling of predestination – a feeling of 'this is it, you can't do anything now – you've had it'. A numbing fatalistic feeling. I started praying aloud, 'Oh, God, please God, let me get back, I've got to get back, I can't prang now.'

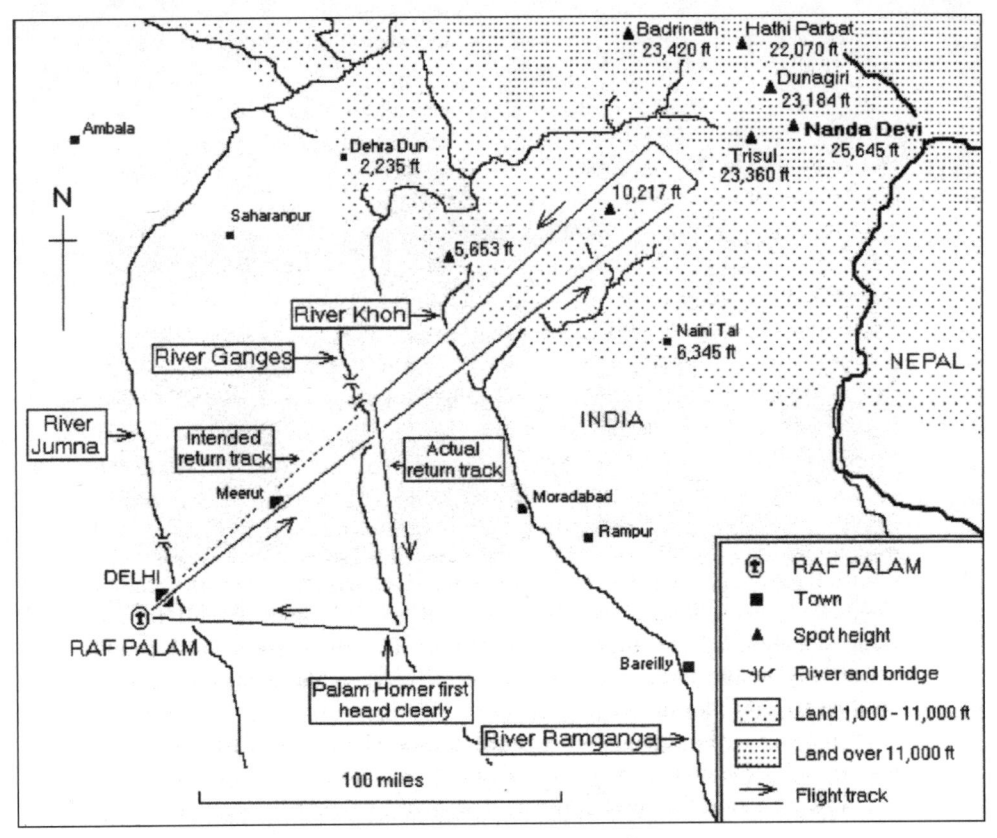

*Figure 11, The flight in Spitfire XI.*

Curiously enough, the thought that was uppermost in my mind was not my own safety – I somehow didn't feel that I would get hurt in a forced landing – but what the commanding officer would say if I crashed the precious Spitfire. If I did run out of fuel, I decided that I would not bale out, but would force-land to try and save the aircraft. I somehow felt quite confident that I could do it without hurting myself in spite of all those rocks and boulders.

But suddenly relief flooded over me. I had called up the Homer again and this time I could hear them! They immediately gave me a course to steer for Palam. Oh, the relief! Dear Homer, I thought – I could have hugged them. The only worry now was whether I did actually have enough fuel to get there; but there was nothing I could do if I hadn't. The fuel gauge said 15 gallons – about 22 minutes of flying time – and there were 70 miles to go. That ought to leave me with just a slight margin which would be useful in case I had to go round again when trying to land.

*Plate 51, The Nanda Devi group. Nanda Devi (25,545 ft) lies in what has been called 'The Sanctuary', and is here largely hidden by lesser peaks in front of it.*

The Homer gave me an accurate bearing – not in fact far off my heading after turning starboard – which took me straight back to Palam. With relief I reached the airfield and joined the circuit, landing without trouble. I taxied in, and just before switching off the engine looked at the fuel gauge: five gallons left, equivalent to about seven and a half minutes' flying time. Much too small a margin for my liking! Indeed, if I had turned towards Palam five minutes later I would not have reached the airfield.

After landing I went over to the Homer hut to thank them, but the radio operator who had brought me in had just gone off duty, so I could not thank him personally; I hope that the gratitude which I expressed to his replacement was passed on.

The whole trip had lasted 1 hour 50 minutes, but nobody noticed except Blackie who, ever watchful of his charges, realized that I had been away rather a long time for the quantity of petrol that had been put in. 'Hullo, Nemesis,' he greeted me with. 'You've stretched the fuel a bit – did you get lost?' Little did he know how right he was!

The photos which I took were disappointing. The film became jammed in the camera – another of the hazards of the bottom-loading of the Leica (see page 35) and I had difficulty in getting it out under the bedclothes on my *charpoy* which I had to use as a darkroom. Half of it was stuck in the camera, and half of it was out of it, all curled around in the darkness. I had stripped naked in view of the heat, but even so was dripping with sweat; I could feel it running down my nose to form blobs which dropped on the film. I did get one or two printable negatives from the film, but even they have marks on them. Plates 50 and 51 are the best of a bad bunch.

As for the Spitfire XI, somebody flew it next day, but sadly that was the last time for anybody. It was not needed and was overdue for inspection, so it was decided to scrap it. Ironically, I nearly did it for them.

Even now, when writing this in 2005, this episode still gives me the heeby-jeebies! If I had not made it back to Palam, I would have been alive/dead, court-martialled, and everything that followed this trip would not have happened. I would not have been able to go to medical school, and my present family would not have been. That I got back can be put down to the competence of an unknown airman operating the Palam Homer.

# 13

## Kangchenjunga and Everest

A flight which in retrospect stands out above the others, mainly because of the later publicity, was a flight to Mt Everest. At the time, it was little more than a diversion from a routine sortie, and certainly did not stand out in my mind as being particularly different from any of the other flights, except for satisfying a whim to fly close to a remarkable mountain. Indeed, a flight which I have still to describe, a low altitude air-land rescue exercise, was much more exciting.

On 25 March 1947 Air Headquarters in Delhi requested us to take some photographs of the southern slopes of the Himalaya in the neighbourhood of Darjeeling, about 300 miles north of Calcutta; these were wanted by Dr J. E. Church, an American, who was leading an expedition into that area to obtain information on snow catchment for new irrigation plans. He wanted vertical photographs of two areas, each 50 miles by 50 miles, one to the north of Darjeeling in the province of Sikkim, the other to the north-west in Nepal, and he wanted them by 1st April.

Heights in the region vary from about 7,000 feet in the foothills right up to the 28,168 feet[1] of Kangchenjunga itself, and since we could take photographs from up to 30,000 feet it was theoretically possible.

When we worked it out, however, we found that vertical photographs were just not practicable. With an average altitude of the ground to be photographed of about 15,000 feet, we would be only 15,000 feet higher if we flew at 30,000 feet, and so the coverage with each frame would only be half what it would be if we were photographing a sea level target. We also found that the large area required would be impossible with the facilities and time available. It would need 100 exposures per run, and with 500 frames in the vertical cameras a single flight would only be able to do five runs, each of which would only span about eight miles; that was assuming that we could make accurate runs, which would have been doubtful in a region with few identifiable landmarks. We would then have to return 300 miles to the local base, RAF Dum Dum just outside Calcutta, to refuel and put new magazines into the cameras. To cover the whole area would require twelve trips, each trip taking four hours. In the end it worked out at about 48 flying hours, which was about twice the flying that one pilot was allowed per month! (A survey of this kind was eventually carried out in 1984, but from 39,000 feet; see Chapter 14.)

The whole thing as it stood was therefore impossible, particularly with various other

---

1 I have used the heights marked on the maps of that time.

photographic sorties waiting to be done. It was therefore decided instead to take oblique photographs of the Sikkim region only, which mostly comprised the south-eastern slopes of the Kangchenjunga massif, and omit the Nepal region. It could then be done in one flight.

Since Dr Church wanted the photos in Calcutta within a week, there was not much time, particularly as the film would first have to be processed in Delhi and the prints then sent back to Calcutta. Because of the urgency, a quick decision had to be made in the squadron as to who was to do the trip. The requirements were the same as for the sortie to North Salsette: firstly, the person going should have taken oblique photos before, and, secondly, he should not be otherwise engaged on ground duties or photo recce work elsewhere. There were two or three of us not otherwise engaged, but of these I was once again the only pilot who had had experience of oblique photography. So it was me again. I was delighted; here was the chance to see at close quarters the giant mountain Kangchenjunga, and perhaps to get a distant glimpse of Mt Everest.

So I got my things together for an overnight stay at Dum Dum, not forgetting my camera, and climbed into one of the Spitfires. I had been given a 90-gallon drop tank in view of the extra distances involved: 300 miles from Dum Dum to the foothills and 300 miles back, as well as the time spent photographing. The extra 90 gallons would add about 400 miles to the range of the aircraft and would also allow me to make the 900 miles from Palam to Dum Dum in one hop instead of having to refuel on the way.

The drop tank was a bulky thing, attached to the belly of the aircraft between the wheels and reaching halfway down to the ground. The weight of an extra 90 gallons of petrol made take-off rather hazardous, since it increased the length of the take-off run quite considerably, and the aircraft felt as if it was barely off the ground before reaching the end of the runway.

I left Palam on the morning of 26 March and flew at 10,000 feet which, according to the meteorological people, was the best height for the strongest tail wind, reducing the time taken to reach Calcutta. They could give me no idea of what the weather would be like over the Himalaya; that would have to wait until I could talk to the local people at Dum Dum. After three hours' flying, navigating by way of Cawnpore, Allahabad and Gaya which I used as intermediate pinpoints (see Figure 12, lower part), I eventually landed on Dum Dum's single, north-south, runway.

I turned the aircraft over to the RAF groundcrew for servicing and then, putting my watch forward an hour for the new time zone, went off to sort out a meal and a bed for the night at the Officers' Mess. The next thing was to have a chat with the local meteorological wallahs about the weather over the mountains next day; here at Dum Dum they were Indians, of which I was glad, since they would know more about Indian weather than the British.

'I've got to take some photographs north of Darjeeling tomorrow. What will the weather be like then?' I asked.

'Not too good,' they replied. 'At the moment there is stratocumulus covering the foothills. The best time for no cloud is first thing in the morning, but cumulus will start building up as the day gets warmer. There's a depression over to the west which is moving eastwards. At the moment it's somewhere near the central Himalaya and it shouldn't hit Darjeeling for a few days yet. But each day there will probably be a bit more cloud over Darjeeling than the day before.'

I thanked them and went out. A depression in a day or two didn't worry me unduly, since by the time it reached Darjeeling I should be back at Palam. The cloud build-up during the day was disconcerting; to avoid it I ought to get there really early, but the light would then not be good enough for taking photographs. So it would have to be a compromise: set off as early as possible next day, yet late enough for there to be sufficient light when I got there.

I went along to the Mess to relax for the rest of the day. I had stayed a night at Dum Dum in February on an earlier sortie, and it had then been rather humid, but now, no later than the end of March, the humidity was really high and it was pretty horrible – sticky, sweaty and hot. Even a table fan blowing on me at night could not keep me cool.

I made the acquaintance for the first time of a praying mantis, an insect which was fascinating to watch with its fully-articulated neck enabling it to turn its head in various directions in quite a human sort of way. Another new experience was the noise that the crickets and bullfrogs kept up through the evening, which was quite something. I supposed that if you lived in that region for any length of time you might get used to it, although it seemed doubtful. That night it took me a long time to drop off.

Next morning I got up fairly early, but with a minimum temperature of, I suppose, 75° or 80°F and a high humidity my clothes were damp when I put them on. After breakfast I paid a visit to the meteorological wallahs.

'Yes,' they said. 'It's the same story as yesterday, and there's no guarantee how fast that cloud will build up. With luck you ought to be all right up to about 10.30.'

Off I went to my Spitfire, which I had asked should be ready early, and made sure that everything was all right. I climbed in with my parachute, checked everything in the cockpit, started the engine, turned on the oxygen and taxied out to the runway.

After a further routine cockpit check I opened the throttle and was off; the time was ten minutes past eight. With the extra 90 gallons of petrol the take-off was sluggish and the machine lumbered down the runway, eventually getting airborne and climbing slowly away. I was grateful for the length of the runway at Dum Dum – 2,500 yards – but it was just as well that it never entered my head at the time what a mess there would be if my engine cut just after I had taken off and I had to do a belly landing with a drop tank full of petrol underneath!

Kangchenjunga was about 360 miles away, and I expected to be there in about an hour and a quarter. I climbed slowly to 20,000 feet, the aircraft being held back by the weight of the extra petrol and the drag of the drop tank. There was nothing to do except watch the compass and airspeed indicator and keep the climb steady. Occasionally I looked over the side to try and do a bit of map-reading, but there was only the thick dust-haze typical of that time of year and I could see little down below. Above me it gradually thinned as I climbed until at 12,000 feet I slowly emerged into a clear blue sky.

There was not a cloud to be seen except for some cirrus high up and far away. The top of the haze slowly dropped away, looking like a great grey-brown woolly rug, with no sign of the earth except directly beneath if I dipped a wing. I peered ahead, for I knew that there lay the Himalaya. And then I saw it – a single white peak directly in front: Kangchenjunga. From that distance it looked small, just rising above the horizon of the haze with the blue of the sky as backcloth. As I climbed still higher I began to see more and more of it, so that the mountain appeared to ride on a great buttress of

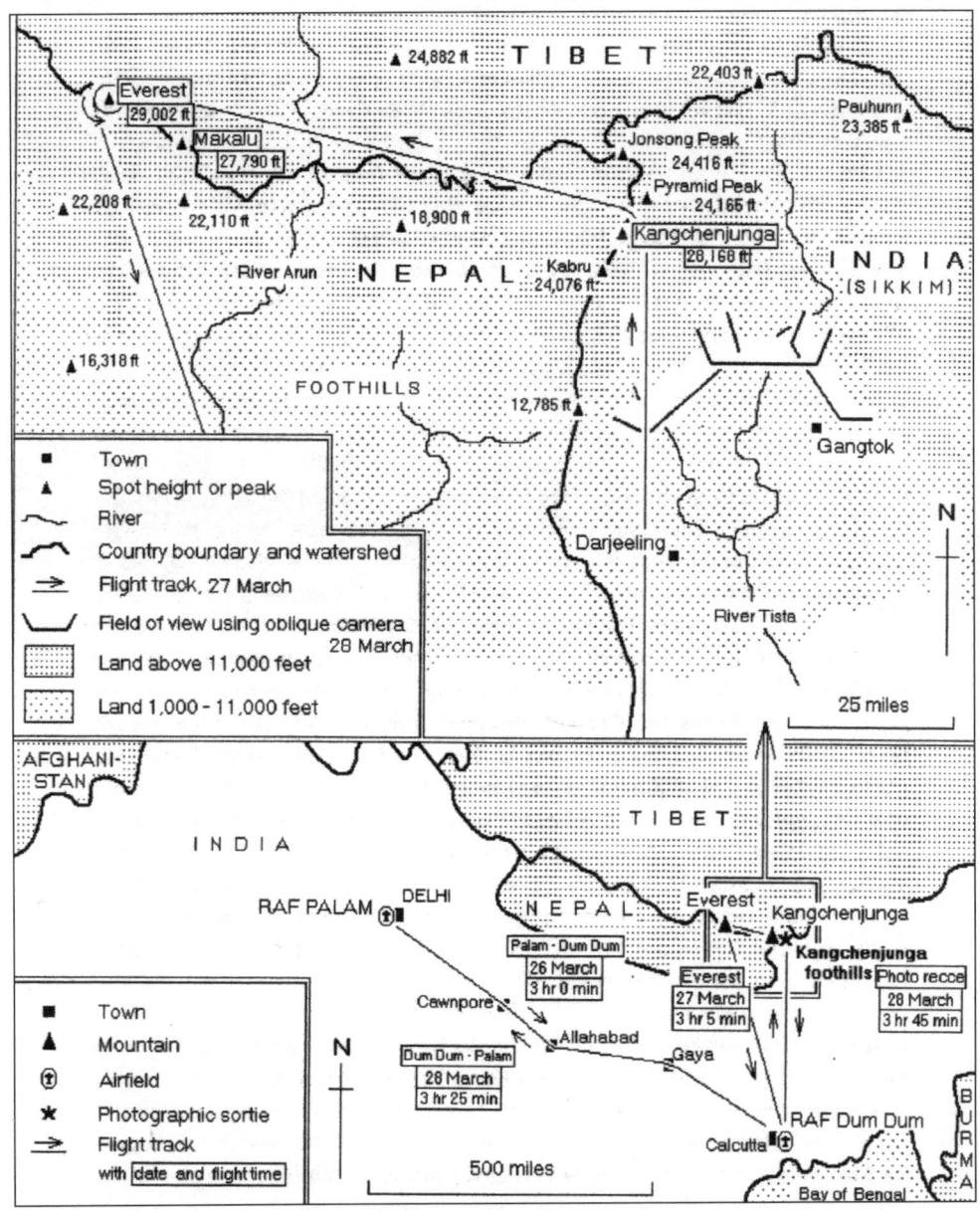

*Figure 12, the flights to Kangchenjunga and Everest.*

snow, with lesser peaks supporting it on either side. Then still more until there was a great broad base spreading out to left and right – a mixture of whites and blues, culminating in the summit of the huge peak itself.

Suddenly, before I had really got used to the great mass of Kangchenjunga ahead I saw, far away to the left and much further off, a group of three small peaks clustered together, standing up above the main range. They looked insignificant compared with the much nearer Kangchenjunga, but I knew from the way they rose above everything else, that one of them must be Everest; perhaps one of them did seem to be slightly taller than the other two.

*Plate 52, view eastward during the approach to Kangchenjunga. The prominent peak to the right of centre is Chomolhari (23,977 ft), and just visible to its right on the horizon is Kula Kangri (24,780 ft), 150 miles away.*

I now gazed along the huge range of the Himalaya – a continuous jumble of peaks stretching from one horizon to the other. Only one other peak really stood out: Chomolhari, over to my right. I had now reached 20,000 feet, the height at which I was to take the photographs for Dr Church, so I levelled out. I was still only half way, with about 180 miles still to go, but there was now no further need of compass and map; I could fly with the nose of the aircraft pointing at Kangchenjunga and just gaze at the snowy range ahead.

Before I go further I had better explain exactly what was required by Dr Church who, according to India's *Sunday Statesman*, was President of the International Snow Survey Commission. In the modified form of the sortie, as decided back at the squadron, I was to fly above the foothills and take photographs of the various parts of the mountains so as to show all the snow from the snow line to the topmost peaks, getting as much as possible on the 100 frames which the camera held. The snow line was important, since Dr Church wanted to know the lowest extent of the snow for the time of year.

*Plate 53, looking north over Tibet from near Kangchenjunga. The range of peaks in the middle distance include Sentinel Peak (21,700 ft), second from left. Beyond is the Tibetan plateau with an altitude varying between 14,000 and 17,000 feet.*

At Palam I had worked out the runs methodically, determining where to take the photos from and the best height at which to fly – 20,000 feet. When I got to the target area I realized that at that height the nearer peaks would hide some of those further away and that it would be necessary to take the photographs instead from 25,000 feet. All my careful calculations had to be thrown out of the window, and I came to the conclusion that it would be much easier and better in practice to judge it all by eye.

But to return to the flight. So far there had been no sign of cloud below, just the all-enveloping haze, but as I got nearer to the foothills, which stretched for about 60 miles south from the mountains, I could begin to see ahead, level with the top of the haze, patches of stratocumulus which became denser until the cloud stretched from the edge of the foothills to just above the snow line, with puffs rising to about 13,000 feet. Since Dr Church had specifically wanted the snow line on the photos, there seemed little point in taking any pictures that day. 'Well,' I decided, 'that's that – have to leave it till tomorrow and hope it's better then.'

With that decision made, what should I do next? The correct thing would have been to go straight back to Dum Dum. But with Everest only 100 miles away, plenty of petrol and my own camera, could I go back? The thought didn't even enter my head. Up to now I had wanted no more than just to see the mountain but this was the chance to get close.

So I pushed the throttle forward and climbed still higher so as to be well clear of the highest mountains, this time aiming at 30,000 feet as my new cruising altitude. I got out my own camera, along with the separate exposure meter of the time, and started taking pictures to right and left. There was a new 36-exposure film in it camera, so there was no need to economise.

One problem was how best to take photographs. In a Spitfire XIX it was essential at all times to have one hand on the stick, since the uneven balance of fuel in the wing tanks did not allow you to fly hands off, so I only had one hand available to hold the camera. It was also impossible to take photographs with the hood open; not only was there the risk of frostbite, but more important from the point of view of photography the buffeting from the slipstream would have shaken the camera. Yet the perspex hood was scratched and was by no means as clear as glass. All in all, there was only one way in which I could take pictures, and that was by holding the stick with my left hand and the camera with my right, putting it as close as possible to the clearest part of the perspex, and hoping that any scratches would be so out of focus as not to appear in the final pictures.

My map was the standard sixteen miles to the inch aeronautical one, and so I could not have identified any of the lesser peaks even if I had wanted to. Kangchenjunga and Everest were the only names which I knew at the time, and since they stood up clearly from the rest of the range I could use them as reference points. I decided to pass round the far side of Kangchenjunga and then point the nose at the Everest group.

As I approached Kangchenjunga I continued to take photographs, some of general views (Plate 53) and some of any nearer peaks which looked interesting. How far could I see as I climbed towards 30,000 feet? It is difficult to say. Theoretically the furthest distance visible from that height is 212 miles if the horizon is at sea level, or 150 miles if it is at 14,000 feet, the height of the Tibetan plateau. Thus Lhasa, 200 miles away in Tibet, would have been over the horizon. But the snow peaks of the Himalaya rise to twice that height and so could be seen from further away even though their base may be below the horizon. From my photographs I have identified one peak, Kula Kangri (24,780 feet), 170 miles to the east near the Bhutan-Tibetan border (Plate 52), but the eye can make out more than standard photographs show, and on the flight from Dum Dum Kangchenjunga was clearly visible from 180 miles. Perhaps I might have seen peaks as far as 250 miles, but identification would have been impossible.

Below me now, rearing up out of the cloud, were the supporting peaks of the Kangchenjunga massif, and the huge Zemu Glacier with its sandy-coloured moraine stretching away from the east face, while everything else was a mass of white snow and jagged peaks. Occasionally I thought about what would happen if the engine cut, but the snow looked so deceptively soft and flat in a lot of places that I did not particularly worry. I had visions of working my way down snow slopes and trekking along glaciers, but since my engine seemed all right such thoughts did not really trouble me, although I was certainly more aware than usual of how the engine was behaving.

To the north, ahead, was the great rolling plain of Tibet, looking reddish brown and horribly dry, like some burned up land from another planet. And yet I realized that people lived down there in that desolation, and that expeditions had crossed it from India; even that some people thought it a pleasant place. But from where I was sitting in my cockpit, detached from the world, it looked like some desert hell where nothing was ever meant to live.

*Plate 54, the Kangchenjunga massif, looking west, with the Zemu glacier running towards the camera. The peak of Kangchenjunga (28,144 ft) is in in the top right-hand corner. (Taken with the RAF oblique camera as part of the snow survey.)*

After getting a close-up photograph of Kangchenjunga as I swung round it (Plate 55) I aimed for Everest 80 miles away to the west (Figure 12, upper part). I was still climbing, but with an indicated airspeed of 180 knots the aircraft did not seem to want to climb at more than a couple of hundred feet a minute, held back as it was by the extra drag of the drop tank. Below me was a vast area of jagged white peaks stretching to the foothill clouds on the left and the brown dryness of Tibet on the right.

The original group of three peaks away to the west now resolved itself into one peak nearer and slightly to the left (which I later identified as Makalu, 27,790 feet) and a separate closely-knit pair, of which one was Everest, straight ahead. Everest is roughly 29,000 feet high and I had reached 31,000 feet but still it seemed to be above me. When I got to 32,000 feet I decided that I was now just above it, and that the sea level pressure must have changed a bit since leaving Dum Dum, so that the altimeter reading was wrong.

I now began to feel a little dizzy and my eyes would not register properly. 'Curse it,' I thought, 'oxygen lack.' So, after checking from the supply indicator that the oxygen flow was all right, I realized that my mask was not fitting tightly enough and that some of the oxygen was escaping. I held the mask tightly over my face while I went down to about 31,000 feet, at which height I knew that I had been all right, and took my hand away. Yes, that was better.

As I drew nearer, the illusion that Everest was above me disappeared; it was now definitely below. 'Good show,' I thought, 'the altimeter's OK after all.' So I dropped still lower to about 30,000 feet and carried on with my photographs.

*Plate 55, looking down on Kangchenjunga from the north. Its peak is in the bottom right-hand corner. In the background is the cloud over the foothills.*

But I now became confused by the two peaks still ahead. They were close together, almost a double peak, and appeared to be of identical height although there is actually a difference of about a thousand feet between them. One was Everest, but which one? All the photographs of the mountain which I had seen – from the north, that is, from the Tibetan side from which previous expeditions had approached – showed one peak standing up alone at the head of the Rongbuk valley in Tibet. So why were there now two? The trouble lay in my sense of direction. From Kangchenjunga to Everest is roughly west, and there is a large glacier, the Kangshung Glacier, flowing due east from Everest – towards me. This I mistakenly – and now, looking back, idiotically – took to be the Rongbuk Glacier, which was the only Everest glacier that I knew about and which actually flows due north.

Although I did not know it at the time, the second peak was Lhotse (27,890 feet), Everest's twin to the south, separated from it by the now famous South Col and about a thousand feet lower. It is completely hidden by Everest in photographs taken from the Tibetan side, which explains my discomfiture. I had brainwashed myself into

*Plate 56, Mt Everest from the west. In the foreground is the peak of Everest (29,002 ft), with Tibet on the left and Nepal and the South Col on the right. Beyond and to the right is Makalu (27,790 ft).*

thinking of Everest as a single mountain with a single glacier, the Rongbuk. Since I was now confusing the Kangshung Glacier with the Rongbuk it was natural that I should wonder why there were two peaks. If I had looked at my compass or even noticed the direction of flow in relation to Tibet I should have realized my mistake immediately.

The confusion between the two directions ninety degrees apart, particularly when I had both a compass and the orientation of the line of the Himalaya to guide me, I attribute mainly to oxygen lack, which had got me into trouble once before (see Chapter 12; also see oxygen lack in the Glossary). The fact that I felt all right in myself does not, as is well known, mean that I was not suffering from it. The problem of the two peaks was only solved much later when I had printed the photographs and compared them with maps and photographs taken from the ground.

Since I had no idea which was Everest I thought that the best thing would be to take photographs of both; luckily Everest was the one of which I took the most pictures.

As I came over the north-east ridge of Everest the aircraft received a terrific kick. This was clearly a violent updraught and cured me of any desire actually to fly directly over either of the peaks. Because of the oxygen problem I did not want to go any higher and what was the point of flying directly over the top, anyway? Also at that height the thinness of the air combined with the effects of the drop tank (which reduced the stability of the aircraft) made the controls rather sloppy, so it was better to keep a safe distance away, and concentrate on taking photographs.

What surprised me most was the colour of the mountain. I had always imagined from black and white photographs that it would be grey, but it was not; it was sandy in colour, with the various strata appearing in darker and lighter shades. Its glaciers, too, except where the cold white ice was exposed near the mountain flanks, were covered with moraine of the same sandy-brown colour. Even colour photographs do not do justice to the lovely blends of colour of the rock which are better seen in T. H. Somervell's paintings, one of which appears in E. F. Norton's *The Fight for Everest: 1924*.

That day the famous plume of driven powder-snow was absent so that there were clear views of both peaks from all angles; there was just a tiny puff of vapour about a mile away on the leeward side of Everest.

I flew round the two peaks a couple of times, taking photographs all the while, still, of course, having to hold the camera close to the perspex with one hand. I had intended to take close-up pictures of the north face – the only climbing face of the time – but since I had no idea which mountain was which this had to be shelved. As it happened I did get several good shots of the north and west faces, as well as one which was almost a duplicate of a photograph taken by the Westland-Houston Flight[2] in 1933 (Plate 56); also, which was more important for the future, albeit unwittingly, one of the South Col and the south face (opposite).

It was now time to start back on the 380 miles to Dum Dum, so I set the compass, put the aircraft on the right course and settled down for the return journey, finishing up the film by taking photographs of the lesser peaks to left and right as I headed south. Although I had a fair amount of petrol left I was not going to waste time playing around the peaks any longer, particularly with the poor visibility over India. The return flight would take less time than the outward one since I would be descending instead of climbing, but I was not going to take any chances.

I crossed the foothills of Nepal at about 10 a.m. and saw that, just as I had been warned, the stratocumulus cloud was now beginning to give place to cumulus. The rest of the flight was uneventful, with a gradual descent into the obscuring haze as I approached Dum Dum, making full use of their Homer in the final stretch to guide me. I landed at about 11 o'clock, 3 hours 5 minutes after take-off, and with about 50 gallons of petrol – a good margin – still in the tanks.

After handing the aircraft over to the groundcrew I went along to the meteorological wallahs to tell them what sort of weather I had found and to ask them what I could expect next day. 'There might be a little less cloud over Darjeeling tomorrow,' they said, 'otherwise it will all be much the same. Don't forget there's that depression to the west still moving along. It'll hit Darjeeling in a few days and the whole region will then be shut in by cloud.'

There was no point in having another try that day, since the cumulus that I saw

---

2 See illustration opposite page 154 in *The Pilots' Book of Everest* by the Marquess of Douglas and Clydesdale and D. F. McIntyre (full details in the Bibliography).

*Plate 57, Mt Everest from the south. The large white patch at the bottom of the near slope is the South Col. Tibet is in the background.*

would have continued to build up strongly and would eventually hide most of the lower peaks. It would have to be tomorrow whatever the weather.

I then went along to the Flight Office of the RAF groundcrew for a chat with the sergeant about the 90 gallon drop tank, which had developed a leak – apparently a common thing. He told me that it would be all right if they filled it up last thing before I set off again next morning.

He also reported another mishap: the glass window in front of the oblique camera had got broken by somebody's carelessness. Luckily the windows for the vertical cameras, which were not being used on this trip, were the same size as for the oblique, so they switched one of them. They also found that the oblique camera itself was loose, and that the window would not shut, so got me to deal with that and reset it. I had no idea what to do, but sorted it out as best I could; the result was that the photographs taken with that camera all had a very slight tilt.

That afternoon it was too hot and sticky to do much. I would have liked to go and see Calcutta, but decided that the heat would make such a trip really unpleasant; instead, I just did nothing. A pity; I now regret not having seen that famous city, particularly after reading Geoffrey Moorhouse's book *Calcutta*.

I decided that I would get off earlier on the morrow in the hope that the foothills might be clearer of cloud. After another hot and sticky night in spite of the fan in my room going at full revs I had breakfast and went to see the meteorological people again. They confirmed what they had told me the previous day and implied that I had better get moving!

I took off this time at twenty minutes past seven, 50 minutes earlier than the day before, but when I reached the foothills I found that the cloud over them was already much the same as then: stratocumulus with tops at about 13,000 feet covering the snow line, but with no cloud above that height. Away to the west Everest still looked exactly the same, with no sign of the famous plume.

I now got to work with the RAF oblique camera at 25,000 feet, using the standard technique: start a run, turn on the camera control knob in the cockpit, hold the heading, and then turn it off again at the end of the run. Each run had to be straight, so I made several runs in different directions resulting in an overall arc covering firstly the mountains to the north-west of Darjeeling, then those to the north, and finally those to the north-east (see bracketing frames in Figure 12, upper, above and to the right of Darjeeling).

When I had finished I found that I still had some film left in the aircraft's camera which I might as well use up. So I headed up towards the snow mountains and Tibet, and took some pictures of Kangchenjunga looking up the huge Zemu Glacier (Plate 54), then some of the extreme northern passes of the area, and finally back to the southern foothills of the mountain, photographing a little further to the westward of where I had started.

As I started back towards Dum Dum I noticed that the cloud was again behaving as it had done the day before, with the stratocumulus slowly being replaced by cumulus, perhaps today a little more so.

I landed after a flight of 3 hours 45 minutes, 40 minutes longer than the previous day, the difference being accounted for by the time needed for the photography in spite of my not having gone out of my way this time. This shows that the official photography itself took something like an hour. There were 40 gallons of petrol left in the tanks, ten less than the day before, but still a safe margin.

I handed the aircraft over to the faithful groundcrew for refuelling ready for the return journey to Palam that afternoon and then went and had a last chat with the meteorological wallahs to tell them what kind of weather I had found over the foothills; finally I made my way to the Mess to wait for lunch time.

After a meal I got back into the cockpit and took off again, following the same route back to Palam as on the outward journey (Figure 12, lower), taking 3 hours 25 minutes – rather longer this time owing to a headwind. I landed at Palam safely, set my watch back an hour, and climbed out to be greeted by T-E: 'How did it go, Nemesis?'

'Oh, fine, but I delayed a day because of cloud over the foothills. It was still the same today when I got around to taking the pictures, so I doubt whether they will show all that's wanted.'

Next morning the film was rushed to Air Headquarters for developing and printing, but when it was developed it was found that the film had become jammed in the camera, and that only 60 out of the 100 exposures had come out. Luckily the successful ones were good. There had been some doubt about whether the exposure would be correct. Warrant Officer Baldwin, who was in charge of photography, had never had any experience of photographing snow scenes with the aircraft's cameras, and had set the aperture by guesswork; to his credit it had turned out to be just right. The pictures were of course far better than the ones I took with my own camera, and so they should have been with a much larger size of film and camera. The background of Tibet was clear in every detail, whereas on mine it was dark and murky. It may have been helped by the use of a more suitable filter: the RAF camera had a yellow filter for haze penetration, while I had used a green one.

The prints were rushed to Calcutta, and we heard no more until four months later when I read an account of the Snow Survey expedition in the Indian *Sunday Statesman* of 1st August, telling of Dr Church's objectives, and what he had done. Included was a short statement about the flight: 'A Spitfire plane sent up by the RAF on April 1 [it was actually March 28], revealed a vast panorama of dazzling white peaks above clouds that veiled their base to 13,000 feet, and the Everest and Kangchenjunga that towered at the heads of the two valleys still looked "like marble sentinels from our trails along the Nepal-Sikkim boundary",' none of which came from me.

And what did everybody on the squadron say about my illicit flight and the photographs taken with my own camera? Nothing, because I told nobody. If I had, I could well have been court-martialled for flying unauthorized over a foreign country, Tibet. (Flying over Nepal might have been excused since part of the original task had been to photograph the part of the eastern end of that country.) I kept quiet until I was out of the RAF and interest was again being shown in climbing Everest, when my photographs and an account of the flight came out into the open (see next chapter). As one of the press reports of the time stated: 'Boy on National Service just dare not tell!'

# 14

## Everest – the Aftermath

*Wing Commander E. Bentley Beauman (1891-1989) was an experienced mountaineer and skier (he became a member of the Alpine Club in 1920). He had been considered for the 1933 Everest expetion, but was judged too old. He was a keen supporter of the formation of the RAF mountaineering club in 1947 so, in all, he had more than a passing interest in Everest.*

What happened to the photographs which I took of Mt Everest with my own camera? Even though the flight at the time was little different from routine, the photographs were, I felt, good enough not to let them just rot away in a drawer. After I had left the Air Force and was safe from court martial (I hoped!) it seemed a pity not to be able to do something with them.

So in 1948, two months after I had left the RAF, I took them to the Air Ministry to find out the position. There I saw a Wing Commander Beauman, who, although officially retired, was still working for the Air Ministry. He was particularly interested in the pictures, since he himself had climbed in the Himalayas, and in the 1930s had taken part in an expedition to Kamet, a mountain to the west of Nanda Devi. He wrote to me a week later to say that permission to publish the photos had been refused:

> Referring to your visit here last week I have now taken up the question of the Everest photographs, and under the circumstances Air Ministry permission for their publication cannot be given…

This did not surprise me, since Beauman had pointed out that publication might have prejudiced the outlook for yet another expedition to Everest by way of Tibet which was being mooted at the time. (In the end the proposed expedition was refused entry through Tibet for political reasons.)

Everything then lay dormant until 1951, when Eric Shipton led a reconnaissance expedition which approached Everest from a new direction: the south. For the first time Nepal was allowing an expedition through her territory. In August of that year Beauman, who had now left the Air Ministry, wrote to me:

> You may remember coming to see me at the Air Ministry a few years ago with some photos you took of Everest from a Spitfire. You will probably have read of the new attempts on Everest from the Nepal side, which is taking place shortly.
>
> We thought that some of your photos might be useful for this, and I was wondering whether you could kindly lend me the films for the Himalayan Committee. It also might be desired to publish some of them at a later date if you had no objection – you would of course get paid for any publication.

# EVEREST - THE AFTERMATH

*Plate 58, the two photographs from my Everest flight combined by 'The Times' and published on the back page of the issue of 8 September 1951.*

*Plate 59, the title page of an account of my flight published in 'Lilliput'.*

A little later Beauman acted as negotiator between me and *The Times* newspaper, which resulted in the publication on 8 September 1951 of three of the photographs; these took up the whole of the main picture space on the back page of the paper. Two of them were cleverly combined to create a broad panorama. At the time, I insisted that I remain anonymous, since I still felt that there could be repercussions, although, looking back, I was probably overcautious.

Various newspapers and magazines then asked to publish the photographs and accounts of the flight, and eventually anonymity became pointless. Details of the various publications in which these appeared are shown in Table 4. below.

Interest in the photographs continued until 1953, when the mountain was finally climbed by Hillary and Tensing of the British Expedition, led by (later Sir) John Hunt.

| Date | Publication | Author's title | Material published | Fee |
|---|---|---|---|---|
| 8 Sep 1951 | The Times | Anonymous | Three photographs | £52 10s 0d |
| 1951 | The Times Reconnaissance Supplmt | Anonymous | One photograph | £5 5s 0d |
| 22 Sep 1951 | Illustrated London News | Anonymous | Four photographs | - ? - |
| Oct 1951 | Geographical Magazine | Anonymous | One photograph | £2 12s 4d |
| 30 Aug 1952 | The Field | Anonymous | One photograph | £2 2s 0d |
| 1952 | The Mount Everest Reconnaissance Expedition (E. Shipton) | Anonymous | Three photographs | £8 8s 0d |
| 12 Jun 1952 | BBC Television (+ attendance of my wife Marion and myself at the studio) | Anonymous | One photograph | £3 13s 6d |
| 29 Jul 1952 | Daily Express* | Kenneth Neame | Article + one photograph | £17 17s 0d |
| Jul/Aug 1952 | St Mary's Hospital Gazette** | 'Nemesis' | Account of flight + four photographs | Nil |
| 30 Aug 1952 | The Field | Anonymous | One photograph | £2 0s 0d |
| Oct/Nov 1952 | Lilliput*** | Kenneth Neame | Account of flight | £35 14s 0d |
| Feb 1953 | Lilliput Spanish edition | Kenneth Neame | Account of flight | £2 2s 0d |
| 3 Feb 1953 | The Times | Anonymous | One photograph | £5 5s 0d |
| Mar 1953 | The Times | Anonymous | One photograph | £4 0s 6d |
| Mar 1953 | St Mary's Hospital Gazette | 'Nemesis' | Article on Everest + one photograph | Nil |
| 17 Apr 1953 | BBC Radio Newsreel**** | K. D. Neame | Talk by me: 3 min 40 sec | £2 15s 2d |
| 18 Apr 1953 | The Sphere | Anonymous | One photograph | £4 4s 0d |
| 7 May 1953 | Le Monde | K. D. Name [sic] | Two photographs | £6 6s 0d |
| 11 Jun 1953 | Point de Vue | L'Anglais Name [sic] | One large, four small photographs | £8 8s 0d |
| Jul 1953 | Camping Plein Air | Anonymous | One photograph | £5 5s 0d |
| 12 Jul 1953 | American Weekly | Kenneth Neame | Account of flight + one photograph | £33 8s 0d |
| 23 Oct 1953 | Panorama (Dutch) | Kenneth Neame ('de Engelse Oorlogspiloot') | Account of flight + one photograph | £3 0s 0d |
| 8 Jan 1954 | Journal of the Royal Society of Arts | K. B. Neame [sic] | One photograph | £2 2s 0d |
| 1955 | The Mountain World 1955 (M. Barnes, ed.); also Italian edition, Montagne del Monde 1955 | Kenneth Neame | Chapter 'Alone over Everest'; pp. 133-144 (no photographs) | £13 18s 0d |
| 1955 | Du Mont Blanc à l'Himalaya (G. Rébuffat) | K. D. Neame | One photograph | £4 12s 0d |

*Table 4. Publication details of text and photographs of my Everest flight.*

**Notes to Table 4**
For comparison of payments with later values, the Retail Prices Index for various years are:

        1951    9.7
        1953   10.3        1990   126.7
        1955   11.0

**Marked entries:**

\* The headline above the article in the *Daily Express*, in large capitals, read: 'Lone Pilot keeps Secret Five Years', followed by 'Boy on National Service just dare not tell'. The article starts in good journalese: 'A secret flight over Mount Everest in a Spitfire was made by an RAF pilot on National Service in India. He wanted some photographs for his album. The pilot, Mr Kenneth Neame, kept his secret for five years because he made the flight without permission...' True enough!

\*\* The Editorial of the *St Mary's Hospital Gazette* (I was now a medical student at St Mary's Hospital Medical School, London), written by a fellow student, Kenneth Mole, makes amusing reading:

> On the 7th of September last year, one Friday afternoon, Nemesis [my pen name for the occasion], who contributes the article appearing on page 130 of this issue, fiddled a little bashfully with his stethoscope, and said, 'Look in tomorrow's *Times*; there'll be some interesting photographs of Everest on the back page.' We looked, and sure enough there they were, among them a magnificent view of the south face, hitherto unphotographed. The caption beneath said simply that the photographs were taken on an unrecorded flight, nothing more.
>
> How had Nemesis known one day what *The Times* would do the next? It took until Monday before the penny dropped. We said to Nemesis, 'Did you take those photographs?' and Nemesis, changing from diaphragm to bell [stethoscope switches] said, 'Yes, I did'.
>
> It is always other people who go to the North Pole, or who win the men's singles at Wimbledon, not someone whose turn it is to fetch the coffees. Even now it seems a little improbable that Nemesis, whose practical physics notebook we have borrowed, with whom we have sweated over *Johnsons's Synopsis*, had really been high up in the sky over Everest on that unrecorded flight.
>
> A few of his photographs are reproduced here. They were eagerly examined by Eric Shipton before he made his trip to Everest last winter, for they showed for the first time the south side of the mountain block, the region now hitting the headlines as containing the most likely route to the summit. All sorts of journals, British and foreign, have published these photographs before us, and they have been shown on television, but in the *Gazette* for the first time is the story of the flight itself. It is not often that the editors of the *St Mary's Hospital Gazette* get the chance of publishing a world scoop, but this is it – exclusive.

\*\*\* I hate to admit it, but the account in Lilliput was ghost-written by a journalist of the magazine. But it does read rather better than my own writings of the time; see also Plate 59.

\*\*\*\* The BBC Radio Newsreel talk was read by myself; the script was in rather journalese style:

I saw two peaks. Not one. Now, when you're flying at thirty thousand feet and you haven't checked over your oxygen mask and are suffering from the effects of rarefied air you begin to wonder of indeed you are seeing double. But there were two mountains. One was Mount Lhotse; the other Everest. All the pictures I had seen of Everest were taken from the north side, and Lhotse, the smaller of the two mountains, was hidden behind it.

Another thing, I had expected Everest to be grey, perhaps because all the photographs show it as grey and white. But it wasn't grey. It was a sandy brown colour, in light and dark layers, with a paler band, the famous yellow band at about twenty-seven thousand feet or two thousand feet from the summit.

It was the same with the glaciers; they weren't as I had expected them to be. They encompassed Everest and her neighbours, pressed upon their bases and poured down their flanks, rivers of contorted ice which must in places have been thousands of feet thick and they certainly cover thousands of square miles. I had imagined they would be white. But they were white only around the base of the mountains, and for the rest they were mainly of a sandy colour because of the rock debris with which they were strewn.

I approached Everest from the east and could clearly see the snow-covered South Col – that's the shoulder between Everest and Lhotse where the present British expedition plans to pitch one of its camps. I could also see part of the Western Cwm up which it will, all being well, make its laborious way.

As for the east face itself, I'd say this was utterly unclimbable. It's pretty well sheer; a white precipice eleven thousand feet high.

The north side was broken by ridges and gulleys. It looked pretty fearsome, and thinking back, I'm not surprised that the Everest expeditions of the old days failed to reach the summit because they tackled it from this side. The south side was the steepest of them all. Practically clear of snow, it dropped almost sheer to the western valley seven thousand feet below and it was broken by great buttresses of rock.

But there's a ridge between the south and east faces of Everest which isn't so steep, and it's towards this ridge that the present Everest expedition will make its way. From the air it appeared as a not too badly broken slope that stretched to within five hundred feet or so of the steep rock pinnacle that is the summit – a summit that to me seemed almost to overhang the immense east face of the mountain.

At one time I was a bit muzzy in the head because of lack of oxygen and I was, well, just a little put out once or twice by the air currents – they're pretty violent in the neighbourhood of Everest. But then everything in this part of the Himalayas seemed to be extreme. Looking down upon it as I did I saw nothing but thousands of square miles of rock and ice and snow contorted quite beyond description.

## Mount Everest: Other Flights

Other flights to Mt Everest, apart from my own, of which I am aware, were the highly organized Westland-Houston Expedition of 1933, an unauthorized flight by a Mosquito in 1945, an authorized flight by the Indian Air Force to take photographs of the mountain shortly after it was climbed in 1953, and an authorized photographic survey in 1984.

## The Westland-Houston Expedition, 1933

Mt Everest was flown over for the first time in 1933 by two single-engined Westland biplanes each with two open cockpits. It was a great feat in its time, and required massive organization. Numerous photographs were taken by the observer in each aircraft using a large and heavy camera in the rear cockpit under formidable conditions. Not only was there the cold and buffeting of the open cockpits, but the use of oxygen at high altitude was still in its infancy. I need say no more about this flight, since it is well documented,[1] except to remark that over the next ten years high altitude flying made such progress that by the time of the Second World War it had become little more than routine to be able to make high altitude flights over long distances.

## Mosquito Flight, 1945 [2]

This was a flight of which there are few details and no official record. It was made on 11 June 1945, apparently by a Mosquito XVI of 684 Squadron stationed at Alipore on the southern outskirts of Calcutta.[3] Some photographs were taken, and of these only six survive. From the data on these it seems that they were taken with an RAF F.14 oblique camera and were processed by the RAF in the usual way. The photographs have sometimes, wrongly, been referred to as the '1945 Spitfire photography'. It has been suggested that this flight may have been made as a joyride to celebrate the end of the European war the previous month. According to Unsworth in his book *Everest* the crew were C. G. Andrews, a New Zealander, and C. Fenwick, who was British.[3]

---

1 *First Over Everest – The Houston-Mount Everest Expedition 1933* by P. F. M. Fellowes, L. V. S. Blacker, P. T. Etherton, The Marquess of Douglas and Clydesdale and *The Pilots' Book of Everest* by the Marquess of Douglas and Clydesdale and D. F. McIntyre.

2 I am indebted to Mr. P. K. Clark, MA, Keeper at the Royal Geographic Society, London, for information on this flight.

3 The pilot and photographer was British RAF Flt. Lt. Peter Racey who was a member of the Photographic Reconnaissance Unit from 1944 and took the photographs of Everest when Squadron 684 flew over the Himalaya in 1945. This was confirmed by Dr. Michael Ward, Medical Officer of the successful 1953 Everest expedition, who originally discovered the images at the Royal Geographical Society. It was also confirmed by Dr. Michael Ward's widow in 2013, by his sister Meg Arnold, who had copies of the photographs and her brother's letters from the time, and by his son Nigel, from family papers and discussions. The flight was not a joyride but was unrecorded because it was a spying mission related to concerns about Russia's intentions after the end of the Second World War in Europe on 8 May 1945.

## Indian Air Force Flight, 1953

I have no details of this flight, except for a copy which I possess of one superb photograph taken from several miles away over Nepal.

## Photographic Survey, 1984[4]

A photographic survey of Mt Everest was made on 20 December 1984 from 39,000 feet by Bradford Washburn and a team of map-makers after four years of planning. They took off from Katmandu in Nepal in a Learjet fitted with a survey camera and made seven runs, each overlapping the next by 30 per cent, while the photographs in each run overlapped by 80 per cent. They positioned their runs accurately by the use of pinpoints based on satellite photographs.

## Flights Directly over the Summit of Mt. Everest

The Westland-Houston Expedition of 1933 flew directly over the summit of Everest, but I have no evidence that anybody else has done so, except possibly the 1984 Survey Flight as part of the survey. I did not.

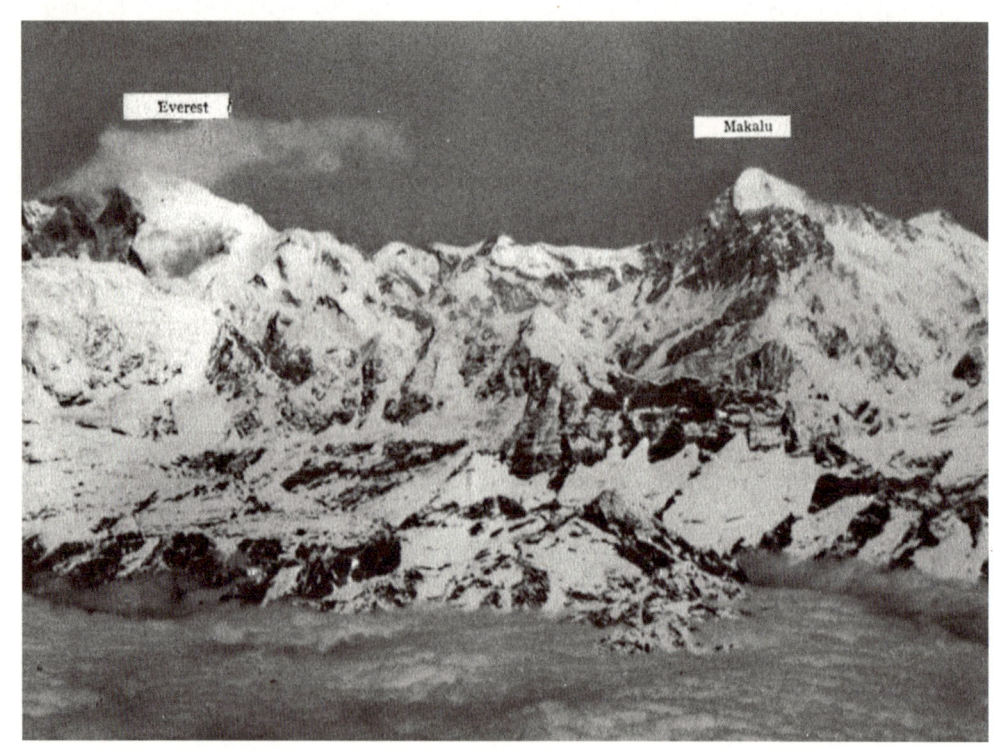

*Plate 60, photograph from 'First over Everest' showing, far left, Chamlang with Everest behind it (labelled in the original) and Makalu (also labelled) on the right. It was taken on the return flight from Everest.*

---

4 *Measuring the Roof of the World,* transcript of a *Horizon* programme of the British Broadcasting Corporation transmitted on 25 March 1991.

# 15

# Wild Hill Country

*Baluchistan is now Balochistan, Pakistan.*

About a month after the flights to Kangchenjunga and Everest, that is, towards the end of April, I had to do a trip which was much more challenging owing to the unusual terrain over which I had to fly.

Among our photo reconnaissance tasks was one which had been on the waiting list ever since I had arrived at Palam: a survey of several areas in the hill country of Baluchistan, a province close to the border of Afghanistan and immediately south-west of the better-known North West Frontier Province. This whole area of India was tribal hill country, renowned in its northern regions for the almost continuous running battles between the Indian Army and the tribesmen of the district, mostly Pathans, a ruthless and wild people in their native territory.

Baluchistan itself is a wild and arid region of mountains and valleys with little rainfall, so that not much more than scrub grows over most of it and from the air the whole countryside looks brown and desolate. Much of it lies at not less than 5,000 feet, and the whole region is geologically unstable and subject at times to severe earthquakes; its capital, Quetta, the site of the Army Staff College, was devastated by one such earthquake in 1935 with great loss of life.[1]

The proposed photographic survey consisted of several different tasks using the vertical cameras, and since the area was hazardous to fly over it was decided to do them all in one go. Navigation was particularly difficult owing to the lack of landmarks in the desolate mountains of the region. The result of engine failure hardly bore thinking about in such inhospitable country. In most places it would have been impossible to force land, and the only alternative – baling out – was not much better, since distances were large and the population negligible, while the tribes which lived there might just as well have cut your throat as look at you, although in Baluchistan they were more peaceable than in the North West Frontier Province further north.

T.-E. had already attempted the tasks but something had gone wrong with his cameras and he had had to come back before he had barely started. Since he had experience of the terrain he would have been the obvious person for the job, but at the moment he was not available, so the Commanding Officer decided that I should be the one to go.

My base in Baluchistan would be RAF Samungli, an airfield not far from Quetta and right in the middle of mountains bordering Afghanistan. To get there I would have

---

1 As recounted in *Thirty Seconds at Quetta* by R. Jackson.

to fly 425 miles across the Thar Desert west of Delhi, then 130 miles across some barren mountains rising up to over 5,000 feet, and finally follow the line of a difficult and twisting gorge north-west for another 85 miles before reaching Quetta and Samungli (see Figures 13 and 14).

Why did I not set course direct for Samungli, or even aim for it after crossing the Indus? Because once across the Indus and over the barren and desolate hills of Baluchistan there would have been no landmarks for checking my position and I might all too easily have missed Samungli and become lost.

The 300-mile crossing of the Thar Desert would be straightforward, with the junction of the Indus and Panjnad rivers on the far side providing a good pinpoint, although over the desert itself there would no means of checking my position. Beyond the rivers navigation would again be difficult once I started flying over the rugged hills.

After reaching the Indus I would aim for Sibi, a disused airfield near the entrance to the gorge leading to Quetta which provided about the only good landmark after crossing the rivers. I would then bradshaw (see Glossary) by following the railway and road running along the floor of the gorge. It was essential over the last part of the journey to navigate in this normally scorned way, since if I set course directly for Quetta and missed it, I would almost certainly get lost. One valley looked much like another, and it was no good relying on a homing from Samungli airfield since the surrounding high mountains would mask the radio signals.

After getting my things together for a couple of nights away I took off from Palam and climbed to 12,500 feet before levelling out. I was below the top of the dust haze, but I could not fly higher since that would have meant using some of the oxygen needed for the sorties ahead. Above me I could see a patch of blue sky, but practically nothing below except for the thick sandy brown haze stretching right down to the deck, so it was pointless to try and think of getting intermediate pinpoints for navigation. Even if there had been no haze there was nothing but empty desert: just miles and miles of dry sand, one or two railways crossing it and virtually no habitation, in spite of the scattered villages marked on the map. I could do no more than check the gyro compass frequently against the magnetic compass, hold a course of 273° and resign myself to waiting for about an hour and a quarter until the Indus appeared below.

I have been asked whether I wasn't bored on long flights such as this when there was nothing to see through the haze. The answer is definitely 'No'. Apart from just enjoying being in the air there was always a certain amount to check in the cockpit; there was no autopilot to do it for me. The whole time it was necessary to adjust the aircraft's lateral trim by keeping an eye on the amount of fuel in each wing tank, to watch the reading of the gyro compass so as to maintain an accurate heading, to check the gyro compass against the magnetic compass (there was always precession of the gyro compass to be corrected for), to keep a constant watch on airspeed and altitude, to check the time so as to be ready for the next pinpoint, and to keep an eye on the instruments generally.

At long last signs of cultivation showed that I was approaching the rivers. It was a strange experience. First of all the dust haze gradually thinned out so that I could begin

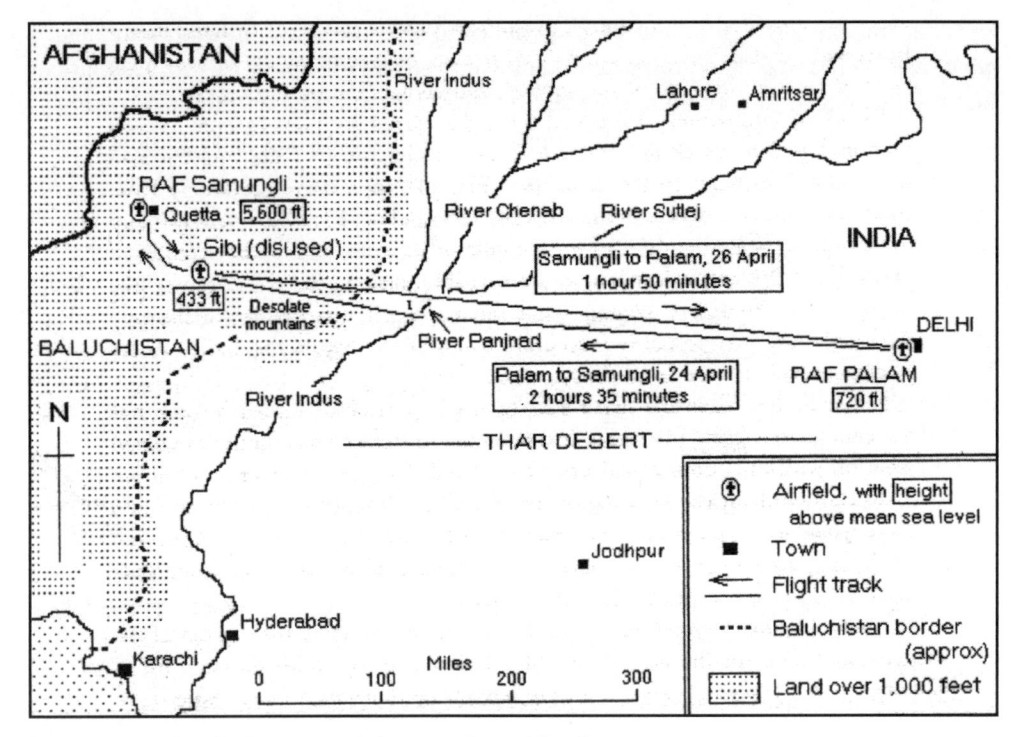

*Figure 13, The flights to RAF Samungli and back.*

to see details of the desert, still brown, uninviting, monotonous. A railway appeared, running northeast-southwest along the edge of the desert, and then quite suddenly beyond this there were signs of habitation – fields and canals. They, too, were dusty brown, but the demarcation was quite clear: desert on one side of the railway and civilization on the other.

I held my course until I reached the Indus about 30 miles further on, and then managed to check my position from the junction of Indus and Panjnad rivers about ten miles to the south; then more accurately from some characteristic curves in the rivers directly below. Even so, it was difficult to be precise, since both rivers were a mile or so wide, and neither contained much water. Numerous sandbanks were visible, making the rivers rather like the rest of the landscape around, while the map itself, apart from not showing the sandbanks, was probably inaccurate owing to the liability of Indian rivers to change their course from time to time.

I came to the conclusion that I was slightly to port of my intended track, but not enough to suggest that there had been any serious change in the predicted wind on which my course had been calculated. I made a correction of about 3° to starboard for the next leg of the journey, 150 miles to Sibi. Once again there would be no pinpoints to look out for – the intervening country appeared on the map as a large area of barren mountains. But the haze was behind me and I could now see the landscape around.

About 30 miles beyond the rivers the mountains suddenly rose up out of the plain, and then for the next 25 minutes I flew over the most desolate bit of country that I have ever seen. I may have forgotten much since those days, but I can still remember that region clearly. Where numerous small rivers were marked on the map there was nothing except a few dried-up water-courses. The whole area was just a jumble of barren rocks – cliffs and precipices in colours ranging from reddish-brown to sandy yellow. And it looked so hot that I felt that anyone entering that area would soon be shrivelled up. If I had had to bale out I would not have lasted more than 24 hours. It reminded me of artists' impressions that I had once seen of the surface of the planet Mercury, sun-scorched and oven-hot. Was I relieved when the far side of the range appeared! With only one engine to keep me in the air I had one ear permanently cocked for any change in its note while crossing those mountains.

T.-E had told me before I left Palam that I could not miss the airfield of Sibi, and that the mountains I was now crossing would suddenly stop and give place to a stretch of flat desert beyond which would be more mountains. Sibi would be in that bit of desert.

Just as he had said, the mountains ended as suddenly as they had begun, and I immediately began to look for the airfield. At first I couldn't see it although down below to the left were the unmistakeable road and railway which ran together for 130 miles from Shikarpur away to the south near the Indus until they separated somewhere beneath me not far from Sibi. Below me I could see where the road crossed the railway which, according to the map, should be eight miles south-west of the airfield. Ah, yes, down there to starboard I could now see Sibi itself, the same sandy colour as the country around and not immediately obvious, while just to the west of it was Ibis, its twin airfield, also deserted, with the railway running near it (see Figure 14, bottom right hand corner). A rare collection of pinpoints in this barren region.

Changing course for the last leg of the journey I now steered approximately north-west and once again entered a region of mountains, ready to follow closely the course of the railway line which entered the gorge to Quetta and was the only means of identifying the correct valley (the road went initially by a different route, joining the railway higher up).

Because of the narrowness of the valley it turned out to be more difficult to follow the railway than I had expected. If I flew over the middle of the valley I could not see the railway because it was then directly beneath the aircraft. And I could not very well go off to one side, since I was now flying at 11,000 feet and the mountains went up to over 8,000 feet on one side of the gorge and on the other to over 10,000 feet, leaving too little margin for safety. On the other hand if I had flown much higher so as to be able to get to one side and obtain a better angle of view it would have been difficult to distinguish the railway from the sandy ground on either side; but that was out of the question since it would have meant using the precious oxygen which I had to keep for later.

At one point I did follow a wrong valley, but luckily soon realized my mistake. Even then it was not easy to find my way back, since all the valleys looked alike and

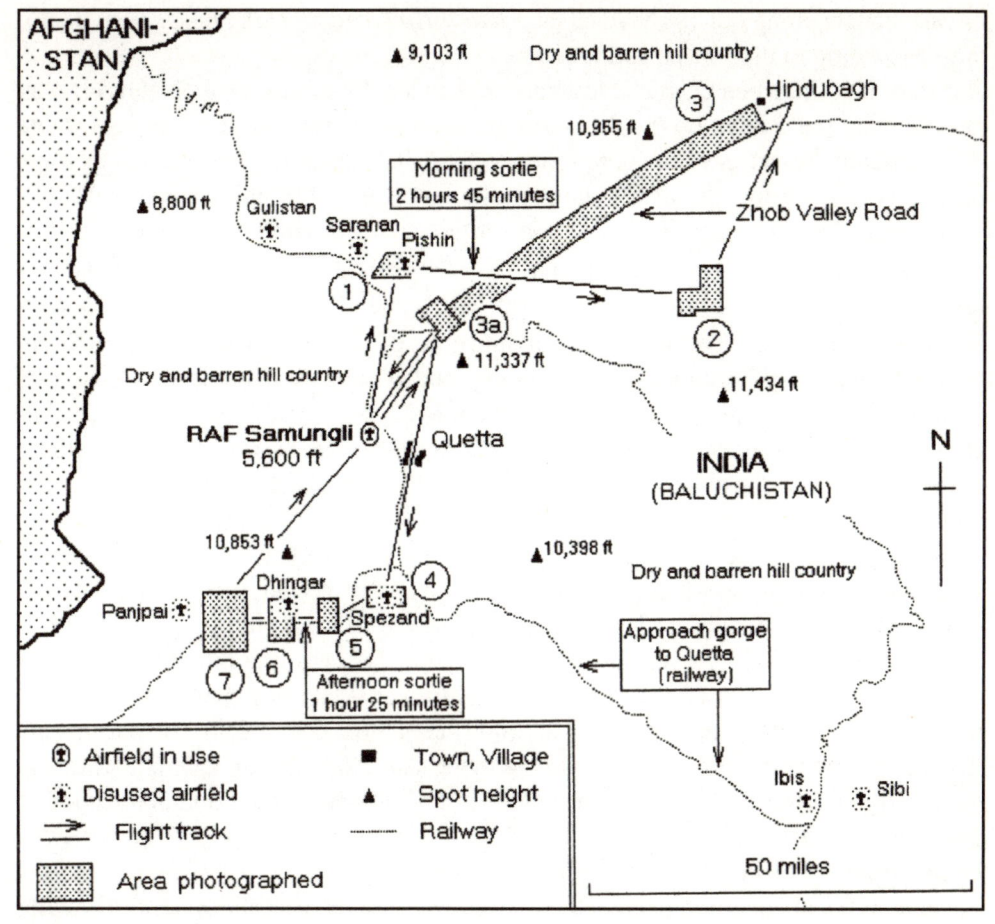

*Figure 14, The areas photographed with RAF Samungli as base. The circled numbers, referred to in the text, indicate the order in which I photographed the targets.*

ran higgledy-piggledy all over the place. After a short panic I eventually found the railway again, and from then on concentrated even harder on not losing it. I could certainly not afford to get lost in that sort of country.

From the height at which I was flying the valley from Sibi to Quetta, although narrow, did not look like a gorge, but from the ground it is dramatic and forbidding, as Evelyn Hart portrays it in her novel *Spring Imperial*. The railway line slowly climbed, she writes, 'turning and twisting up the graded incline of the 67-mile Bolan Pass… a marvel of engineering', while on either side the view was 'blocked by barren rocky contours of heights and ravines from which the line had been blasted. The cliffs excluded any breeze.' At Mach the train stopped to take on water, and 'started up again towards Spezand at the zenith. The only vegetation… was an occasional straggly sage bush: no trees, no shade, no shelter from the blistering sun. The arid land of red-gold soil was broken occasionally by the appearance of black goats from over a hill…' At the Spezand stop the train started up again 'and gathered speed into a barren wilderness of vast plain opening out… The level land was surrounded by rocky bastions of mountains ascending to the sun-pulsating sky.'

I was thankful when Quetta at last appeared ahead; I had a quick look at its civilian airfield and then carried on the five more miles to Samungli, the RAF airfield (Plate 61). Samungli Tower gave me permission to land, but asked me to be careful of some people working at the end of the runway, although it was not quite clear what I was supposed to do about it. Just over 2½ hours after leaving Palam I touched down, without running anybody over, on to my highest-ever airfield, 5,600 feet above mean sea level, just another of the hazards of this trip. The higher the airfield the trickier a landing will be, since the air is thinner and landing and take-off speeds are correspondingly greater than at lower altitudes. I consequently landed rather fast, but luckily there was quite a head-wind to slow me down. I taxied in to Flying Control and handed the machine over to the groundcrew (Plate 62); I felt that at least it was giving them something to do, since there was no sign of any other aircraft there, and the whole place looked quite deserted.

Samungli was the kind of airfield that gave you the shivers from the flying point of view, apart from the problem of the high altitude and of getting there. It was set in a broad shallow valley surrounded by mountains rising in the distance up to 6,000 feet above the valley floor – a serious hazard to flying. To the north and only about five miles away was a line of hills rising up to 3,000 feet (Plate 61), and immediately to the south more hills rising gradually to 2,000 feet above the airfield. Beyond Quetta to the east were still more mountains rising to the same sort of height. Only to the west were there no mountains nearby, the sandy valley floor widening out and becoming quite flat, eventually curving away behind the hills to north and south, although away in the distance were yet more hills, dry and brown.

Samungli had one saving grace: the runway was laid out east and west, and the prevailing wind came from the flatter region to the west, so that for most days of the year the take-off was in that safer direction.

As I looked around and took all this in, the wind was blowing steadily from the west at about 25 mph. Indeed, it continued to blow like that all the time I was there – a built-in wind like the one at Karachi – which helped to reduce the otherwise fast landings at this high altitude. It came, dry and warm, from the plains of Persia (as it was then called) and raised dust devils all over the valley. At any one time it was possible to see at least four of these. They might be small, just wisps of sand whirling round, or huge things going up to 2,000 feet or so. Once when I was in the circuit at 1,000 feet preparing to land I saw a dust devil nearby which stretched out of sight well above me.

The Mess at Samungli was a cheerful little place – there were not more than about half a dozen people there, consisting of the Commanding Officer, a Flying Officer, a visiting padre, a warrant officer and some sergeants. The station was so small that the Sergeants' and Officers' Messes were combined – a freak which I never came across anywhere else, but which seemed to work well. However, I did not envy them living there. It was a desolate spot, and to travel between Samungli and any civilized place other than Quetta meant going down the long, hot, dry, dusty gorge which I had followed so rapidly on my way up. In fact, one of the sergeants was going to take a couple of trucks the 500 or so miles to Karachi in two or three days, with probably bad roads all the way; I was thankful that I was not going with him.

The climate of Samungli in April was a pleasant change from the heat at Palam at that time of year; owing to its altitude it was much cooler. For the first time for two months I had a sheet over me at night, and even blankets on top.

The next day I was up at about 8 o'clock, and after breakfast got a lift in a truck down to my aircraft. It had been serviced and was all ready, so, after telling Flying Control that I would be away for about three hours, I strapped myself in and set off.

The first of the several tasks was to photograph Pishin, a deserted airfield about 20 miles north of Samungli in an extension of the valley in which Samungli itself lay (see 1 in Figure 13). T.-E.'s cameras had worked for this particular job, but he had failed to cover it, not through any fault of his own, but because the demand map that he had received from Air Headquarters had been marked wrongly! Pishin looked as desolate as anywhere else in the region, with a couple of runways and some deserted buildings. I sometimes wonder how anyone managed to get runways built in such a place so far away from the normal facilities of civilization. After checking the layout I did four runs over it from a height of 17,500 feet – or 12,000 feet above Pishin – and then climbed up to 30,000 feet for the next job.

*Plate 61, the desolation that was Samungli. Looking north over the airfield towards the neighbouring hills. The airfield buildings can be seen in the centre of the picture, with the airfield itself just beyond. The whole region was brown semi-desert scrub country.*

This was to photograph a rather obscure area slap in the middle of the mountains, and which consisted of a kind of pass between two parallel roads about ten miles apart (see 2 in Figure 14); it was not easy to identify but somehow I found it. I started by doing a dummy run from south to north, but found that there was a strong wind from the west which blew me off course. The resulting drift made things rather difficult, particularly since most runs here had to be south to north. The area to be photographed was in the shape of a reversed L, so I had to do some east-west runs as well and it all became rather complicated. I was glad when I had completed it, since there were no landmarks to help me locate the start of each run, the region just consisting of a muddle of valleys. The third task was to take photographs of something which had been hanging over our heads at Palam for a long time: the Zhob Valley Road (see 3 in Figure 14). We were required to photograph a 55 mile stretch of the road joining Quetta with Fort Sandeman nearly 200 miles away to the north-east. The part to be photographed bent gently in a continuous curve throughout the whole of its length. Its width was narrow enough to fit within the field of view of the two vertical cameras, and so in theory it could have been covered in one run, but this was not feasible because of both the curve of the road and its length.

The start of the run was to the north-east of where I now was, so I steered in that direction until I came to the Zhob Valley. It was important to have a landmark to identify where to start the photography, and it was fortunate that just at the right place the map showed a village by the name of Hindubagh. But when I came to look for it there was no village to be seen; knowing the unreliability of our maps this didn't surprise me. Nor was the road itself easy to see since the valley was shallow and the road was the same sandy colour as its surroundings. At first all I could see were dried-up watercourses running into the valley, but eventually I managed to make out the road. There was still no sign of Hindubagh, but I saw a characteristic bend in the road itself which looked like the right place.

So around I went and after the usual dummy run began the first photographic run, steering just south of west. I knew that it would be impossible to follow the curve of the road, so I gave myself a set time during which I would fly a straight course covering a limited stretch of it. Then I switched off the cameras, a quick whip round and a steep bank to see whether I was still over the road – yes, I was, so at least that run was all right. But there now below me was Hindubagh itself without any doubt – brighter yellow than the rest of the valley, and consisting of a motley collection of small buildings with some larger ones among them. The map was right and I was wrong; I had simply started photographing about ten miles too early!

With Hindubagh located and with a bit more confidence I started a second run of about 22 miles, trying to introduce a slight curve in my flying. This was more difficult than it sounds. I could not just slew the aircraft round as I went along; everything had to be done with the knowledge of what lay below. The time interval between individual exposures, which I had set on the control box in the cockpit, was seven seconds, and this gave me just time to dip a wing right down, see where I was in relation to the road below, note where it was going next, and then get straight and level again before the next exposure was taken. Each 'take' was indicated by a light on the control box enabling me to coordinate my 'dips' between exposures. When necessary during an interval I could turn the aircraft the necessary number of degrees by gyro compass, and then bring it back straight and level on the new course. I do not know how this might have affected the quality of the photographs themselves since I never saw them; it's possible that some could have been blurred. All I did see later was the plot, which showed that I had managed to cover the whole road satisfactorily.

After photographing most of the road I found that my fuel was getting a bit low,

*Plate 62, my Spitfire being refuelled at Samungli. Note the concrete block holding the wing down – a precaution against violent winds in the harsh climate of the place. The neighbouring hills can be seen beyond.*

which meant that I would have to return to Samungli and come back to finish it off later. The airfield was only about 20 miles away, but I had to descend from 30,000 feet, and this took a little time. I was glad at last to get down, after 2 hours 45 minutes in the air, since for some reason I had been feeling slightly sick while at high altitude. There was no reason for it, since I had not had any alcohol the evening before, and the breakfast had been all right. It disappeared once I was on the ground and stayed away for the rest of the trip, which was just as well, since there was no provision in a Spitfire for being sick.

I went along to the Mess to have some lunch while my aircraft was being refuelled, and then set off again in the afternoon to finish the Zhob Valley Road (see 3a in Figure 14). It was soon done, and I set course for the rest of the targets, using the railway line once again to guide me. These targets were a group close together about 20 miles to the south of Samungli and had to be photographed from the same height as Pishin, that is, 17,500 feet. The first was another disused airfield called Spezand, named after the settlement where the train halts on its way from Sibi to Quetta; it was easy to find since it was just to one side of the railway (see 4 in Figure 14). It had one runway about 2,000 yards long and another of 1,000 yards and looked just as desolate and deserted as Sibi, Ibis and Pishin. It was set in what looked like a great area of sand, about ten miles across and most of it as flat as a pancake with nothing discernible except for a few vague dried-up water-courses and the railway just to the east; but to the west, only three miles away, were mountains rising 2,500 feet above the airfield – yet another flying hazard for the pilots who had once used the airfield.

Once again I had great difficulty in finding a pinpoint on which to start my runs, and eventually used a large silted-up delta from the dried-up mountain streams. I was not the only one who realized how featureless the area was, because when the photographs of Spezand had been printed and plotted on a map back at Air Headquarters in

Delhi a comment had been written at the bottom of the plot: 'Owing to lack of topographical detail no accuracy can be guaranteed [in plotting the photos]'!

The final task consisted of three areas to the west of Spezand (see 5, 6 and 7 in Figure 14). One of them included another airfield called Dhingar, but I don't think that it was specifically for the airfield itself, since the three areas, although of different sizes, were rather similar to each other, and seemed to consist of almost featureless countryside. I have no idea at all why photographs of these apparently featureless areas were required.

The westernmost of the three areas took me to within fifteen miles of the Afghan border and when I had completed it I thought of flying just over the border and adding to my record of countries flown over, but it was so easy to get lost in that mountainous country that I decided against it.

I often wonder what the numerous airfields in this area had been used for. In the general area the map shows eight first class airfields with runways, of which only one, Samungli, was still in use, and even Samungli was due to be closed down shortly. (I do not count Quetta airfield, which was a civilian airfield and probably third-rate, since it was marked on the map as no more than 'landing ground'.) These airfields were all in the most desolate of places, with clearly a problem of water supply and general communications. Perhaps they had once been staging posts for aircraft going to the war in the Far East. One particularly strange thing about them was that they were a group on their own; the map shows no other airfields within hundreds of miles. It also shows more railways in the region than would normally be expected in such a desolate area, one even going as far as the border with Afghanistan (see Figure 14).

I landed back at Samungli about an hour and a half after take-off, and left the aircraft with the groundcrew for the routine daily inspection. One more night at Samungli and then the following morning I set off on the journey back to Palam. I decided to do a rapid climb after taking off just to show those down below what the Spit XIX could do. (A week before, some Tempests from Peshawar had dropped in at Samungli, and I could not compete with them for beat-ups, but the Spitfire XIX had a good rate of climb in compensation.) So I took off, pulled back the stick, and shot upwards, banking round over the Mess, and finally heading back for Sibi.

Since I had adequate oxygen left, I thought that I might as well fly at 20,000 feet, my favourite cool height in the hot season. I also thought that in view of the mountains it would be interesting to check on the range of the Homer at Samungli, so as I climbed on my way to Sibi I kept calling them up. I lost contact when about half-way to Sibi, which gives the Homer a range of only 40 miles, about half that over flat country; clearly it would not have paid to get lost even fairly near the airfield.

From Sibi I set course direct for Palam, with everything the reverse of the journey out (see Figure 13), except that the desolate mountains didn't look quite so formidable from my new height. I met the familiar dust-haze shortly after crossing the Indus, although now I was well above it – its top was at 15,000 feet – but that of course was no help in seeing the ground. When I was within radio range of Palam, I called the Homer for a course to steer and started to descend. I was a bit ahead of my estimated time of arrival and off track to port, but that no longer mattered with the Homer to guide me. I landed only 1 hour 50 minutes after leaving Samungli, as compared with 2 hours 35 minutes for the outward journey; the groundspeed on the return journey worked out at 340 mph as compared with 240 mph. This difference was the result of a combination of wind direction and altitude: I had a head wind on going which became a tail wind coming back, and which would be stronger at the higher altitude.

When I had landed and the groundcrew had taken the film out, Blackie, in charge of unloading the cameras, wandered up to me with 'Well, Nemesis, it's a nice change to find somebody using up just about all the film that we put in.' This was a bone of contention on his part, since we always asked for more film than we actually needed so as to allow for errors, and almost invariably came back with some unused. As a result there were always surplus lengths of film too short to do anything useful with, and this offended Blackie's dignity. At last he had something to be cheerful about!

# 16
# Holiday in Kashmir

'Time for you to have four weeks' leave in the hills, Nemesis,' the Commanding Officer, Gerry Fray, said to me one day towards the end of May. 'The place we go to is Lower Topa, up in the north, and there's usually a Dakota laid on to take people most of the way.' I was glad to hear this, since it would provide a break from the continuous heat of the plains.

I have mentioned earlier the Government's summer move to the hill town of Simla, but there were several other hill stations to which the British and the more well-to-do Indians usually went: Darjeeling, Naini Tal and Mussoorie in the foothills of the Himalayas, for example, and, in the far south of India, Ootacamunde in the Nilgiri hills.

I would be going further north than any of these, to the foothills of the Hindu Kush, where there was another group of hill stations based on the small hill town of Murree, 30 miles north of Rawalpindi – or 'Pindi as it was colloquially known (Figure 15, lower). I still have a three inches to the mile map of the Murree area which shows that the whole district was based on the military. Within an area of about ten square miles it shows seven settlements, with, in addition to Murree and Topa, names like Gharial, Kuldanna, Barian, Khatra Gali and Changla Gali, all of which have military designations of one sort or another attached to them, such as Cantonment, British Military Hospital, Officers' Mess, Sergeants' Mess, Regimental Bazaar and Sandes Soldiers' Home, while one of the minor settlements goes by the name of Sunny Bank, and there is even a Military Dairy Farm.

Lower Topa – officially known as No 1 Hill Depot, RAF Lower Topa – was a collection of buildings about four miles beyond Murree with its own Officers' Mess. When I heard the name Murree I remembered that this was the home town of my bearer back at Mauripur when I had first arrived in India. At that time I had never heard of the place, and in my ignorance thought that it was his peculiar way of pronouncing Meerut.

A Dakota was to take several of us from Palam to the RAF airfield of Chaklala, just outside Rawalpindi, a town lying in the plain below the foothills. Thank goodness for the RAF, I thought; the alternative form of transport would have been the railway, which most ground-based people, such as the Army, had to use. The thought of being cooped up in an Indian train in the hot season to travel the 350 miles to Rawalpindi appalled me, and it would probably have taken more than a day to get there.

When George, my bearer, heard where I was going he asked if I could find him a place on the 'plane, since his home town was Murree – do all bearers come from Murree? I wondered – and he had not seen it for some time. So I went to the person in charge of the flight and a place was found for him; clearly this was one of the perks of

## HOLIDAY IN KASHMIR

being attached to the RAF.

We set out from Palam on 27 May, at the height of the hot season. Although we left fairly early in the morning the sun had risen sufficiently to make things uncomfortable, and the inside of the all-metal Dakota was already like an oven. There was a slight delay, and by the time we eventually trundled down the runway the heat was becoming

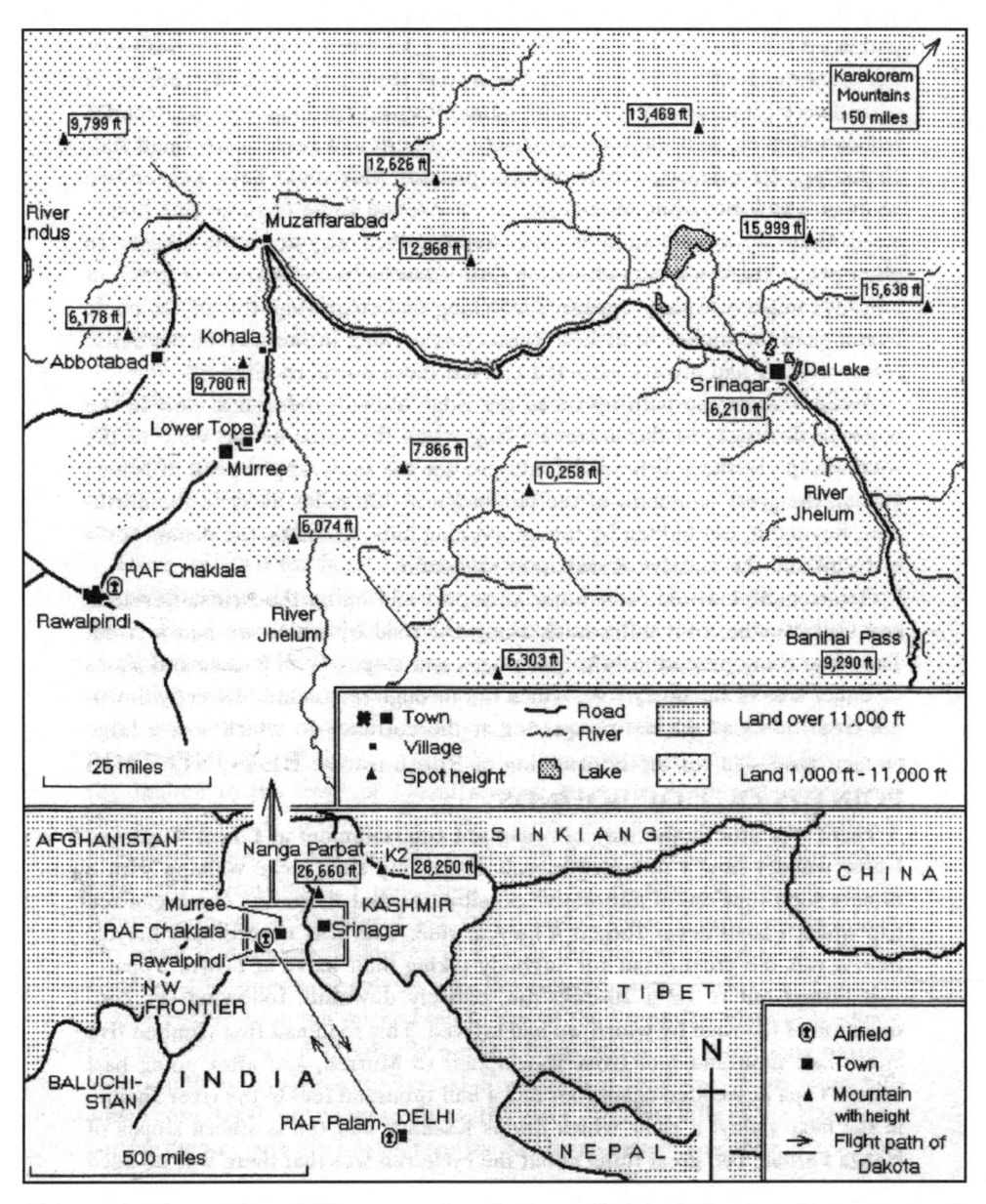

*Figure 15, The northern hill country; in relation to Palam (below) and in more detail, showing the route to Srinagar (above.)*

unbearable; we were glad when we had climbed to a cooler altitude.

On landing at Rawalpindi we found that somebody had laid on a *ghari* in the form of a 15-cwt truck to take us into the hills, so after a mid-day meal all those who were going to Lower Topa piled in.

Before we left I was regaled by some of the local RAF people with fearsome stories of the goings-on in towns such as Peshawar (pronounced P'shaar) situated right at the bottom of the Khyber Pass in the North-West Frontier Province. The tales might have come out of Kipling, except that they were worse; they told of decapitated bodies lying on charpoys with their heads placed on top of them, and of what the tribal women did to any captured British that they got their hands on, such as sewing their testicles into their mouths and throwing their bodies, sometimes still alive, back over the wall of the local fort! It always seemed to be the women who thought up and carried out the more gruesome practices. As with many so-called romantic places such as the Khyber Pass, the real-life version could be horrific.

It was hot in the truck, but its movement soon created a breeze and it was not long before we left the plains and started climbing into the coolness of the hills, up and up, twisting and turning, until after about 30 miles we reached Murree, 7,000 feet up on the side of one of the hills. We drove through it and then along a shallow ridge to arrive at Lower Topa, 500 feet lower, also set on a hillside and surrounded by numerous steep hills and valleys. At that height the temperature was just right, similar to an English summer.

The settlement faced south with a view down the steep valleys which ended in the plains of India hidden by the distant heat haze. It was said that arriving suddenly at that altitude you got short of breath easily, although I never experienced this; but then I was never one to take much violent exercise.

I spent much of my time wandering around the district with my camera. It was all very pleasant and quiet, with numerous paths through the open conifer woods which clothed the hillsides. Scattered here and there were small flat-roofed primitive houses where lived a peasant who might have one or two goats or a cow browsing among the trees. Around some of these tiny homesteads there were cultivation terraces stepping their way down the hillside. In other places there was no cultivation, just scattered trees in which a group of monkeys might suddenly appear, screeching and chattering, too shy to come nearer than the higher branches. There was nothing in the way of the dense forest which I had always assumed clothed these northern hills.

A climb along the path up on to the ridge above produced a view in the opposite direction, to the north, looking much the same as the view to the south. In the furthest distance I could just see the snowcapped peak of Nanga Parbat, the great mountain of the Hindu Kush, 100 miles away to the north-east. Beyond it, but hidden by the intervening hills, would be the distant town of Gilgit and the massive Karakoram mountains.

Occasionally I would catch some transport laid on by the British Services, and visit Murree, four miles back along the road by which we had arrived. The town clung precariously to the ridges and slopes, with houses and shops on either side of the dusty road which ran through the middle. Directly downhill from this was the native quarter at the entrance to which was a large circular road sign for the information of British troops: BEYOND THIS POINT IS OUT OF BOUNDS.

There was little in the way of organised entertainment at Lower Topa and I now wonder how I occupied myself during my stay, since walking with a camera soon runs out of alternative possibilities. But there was one organized trip which I shall never forget: a bicycle ride. This was no ordinary bicycle ride; it was the great event for anybody taking their leave at Lower Topa.

It turned out to be a 20-mile run, entirely downhill, following the continuation of the road by which we had arrived. This road had first climbed five and a half thousand feet from Rawalpindi to Murree, and after going past Lower Topa descended again four and a half thousand feet to the River Jhelum in the next valley, a river which drains Kashmir and the southern slopes of Nanga Parbat. The great thing about the cycle run was that there was no need to pedal once, the road descending continuously as it twisted and turned around and across the hillsides, until at the bottom it reached the tiny village of Kohala where it crossed the Jhelum before continuing on its journey north and then east to Kashmir.

We free-wheeled the whole way, which was just as well, since the air got warmer as we descended – the lapse is about 3°F for every thousand feet – and pedalling might have become rather hot. When we arrived we ate packed sandwiches which had been provided, and then were taken back up the hill, riders, bicycles and all, in a ramshackle Indian lorry which had been laid on. Where else could one cycle 20 miles without moving a muscle!

While at Lower Topa I discovered that it would be possible to spend part of my leave in Kashmir, a country which I had heard was of great beauty. Not wishing to miss a chance when so close to it I decided to go there for the third week of my leave.

Kashmir is to the east of Lower Topa, and lies directly against the foothills of the western Himalayas; it is a kind of Shangri La,[1] topographically isolated from the rest of India. It is the site of an old lake bed, now a flat plain set at about 6,000 feet and ringed entirely by mountains or high hills rising thousands of feet higher.

There are two roads into Kashmir. One is a direct route from the south which climbs to about 9,000 feet over the Banihai Pass; the other – the one I took – is a rather convoluted route approaching from the south-west by way of Abbotabad or Murree (see Figure 15, upper). The Murree road was the one by which we had come and down which we had cycled to Kohala.

So one morning I set off in a weekly transport laid on by the British Services which followed the road to Kohala, then continued along the far side of the Jhelum to the town of Muzaffarabad. Here the river and road turned sharply south-east to follow the river's gorge which cut through a barrier of hills rising up to 12,000 feet, the road itself

---

1 This name comes from James Hilton's book *Lost Horizons*.

liable at times to be blocked by rock falls. Surprisingly, I remember no details of that journey, nor of the return journey a week later. I say 'surprisingly', since from what I have read the route is dramatic, following as it does the narrow gorge of the Jhelum river for 130 miles as it cuts its way through the mountains.

Eventually the gorge opened out to reveal the broad flat plain of Kashmir, covered with rows of Lombardy poplars lining roads and tracks and presumably acting as windbreaks. Beyond it, distant in the haze, were more hills which rose 9,000 feet or more above the plain – the last hills of the Himalayas barring the way between Kashmir and the Karakoram mountains 150 miles beyond.

The road wound across the plain to arrive at Srinagar (pronounced 'Sirrinnugga'), the capital of Kashmir. I do not know if any hotels existed in Srinagar, but I had been booked into a houseboat, the standard type of accommodation for visitors. Anyone from outside the country who wanted to go and live there, either for pleasure or to set up in the hotel business, was not allowed to buy property, but instead had to make do with one of the numerous houseboats scattered among the many waterways of the district. Anyone who wished to rent accommodation with or without full board automatically stayed in a houseboat.

The houseboat in which I was staying was tied up to the bank of the River Jhelum on the edge of the town. It was looked after – probably owned – by an Indian, Juma Paktoon, and his teenage son, who lived in an adjacent houseboat, and they provided me with full board. They were a pleasant pair, and did all they could to make my stay enjoyable.

Srinagar is a little like Venice in being surrounded by water; the River Jhelum borders it on two sides, while around the rest of it there is a mixture of cultivated marshland and lakes. On the lakes there were what were called floating gardens; these were freely floating masses of matted vegetation on which a certain amount of cultivation was carried out, with the lotus plant seeming to be predominant. Everything on these floating gardens was made use of in one way or another, since I frequently saw flat wooden boats being paddled around, piled high either with lotus plants which had been collected up, or with a mass of other vegetation. Some of the boats were rather like elongated punts, on which it seemed that nothing more than waterweed was being collected. Reeds of course might be used for thatching, but I believe that the waterweed itself was largely used as fertilizer. It would certainly not have been wasted.

All the waterways must have been shallow, since the main method of propulsion, even across the lakes, was by punt-poles which often appeared to be no more than the branches of trees.

The first thing I did when I arrived was to explore the immediate surroundings, including the local hill which stood just outside Srinagar, and provided a superb view of the whole of the Vale of Kashmir. Apart from this one hill and the circle of mountains hemming it in, the whole plain, 80 miles by 20 miles, was quite flat.

Immediately below the hill was Srinagar itself, a ramshackle collection of buildings typical of any Indian town, but with the glint of water all around. Spreading out beyond was the flat floor of the Vale, green and fertile in contrast to the brown dryness of so much of the rest of India, and with water predominating. The hills and mountains on the far side were hidden in haze, but immediately behind me the grass-covered hills of the Himalayas rose high above.

As I stood there and looked around I felt that as a place of great beauty Kashmir was disappointing. Compared with the dry, dusty and sweltering plains of India its greenness and its waterways were most attractive and to anybody who had never seen anything else there was no doubt that it would seem to be a paradise, tucked in among towering hills. But in my mind I was comparing it, not with the Indian plains, but with England, and realized that it lacked the variety and beauty of the English countryside, where every turn in the road shows something different and where there are trees, woods and fields of all sizes and descriptions.

Shortly after settling in I was visited by an old school colleague who by some strange bush telegraph had learned that I was there in spite of our never having had any contact with each other since leaving school. He was in the Army, and was also taking a holiday on a houseboat. We had known each other quite well, although we had not been close friends, and it was pleasant to meet somebody English to talk to. I forget his name, so I shall simply call him Harry.

We both felt that it would be a good idea to see the sights together, and on one occasion we visited a silk factory – an industry for which the district was famous – with, in its grounds, the mulberry trees on which the silkworm grows and upon which the trade depends. But much of the time we seemed to spend on the water. We found out that on one of the lakes beside Srinagar, called the Nagin Bagh (Plate 63), sailing dinghies could be hired, so we decided that we ought to have a go, although neither of

*Plate 63, the Nagin Bagh in Kashmir. Houseboats can be seen againt the far shore.*

us had ever sailed in our lives and knew not the first thing about it. But we were game to try. To get to the Nagin Bagh we had to hire a water taxi, many of which plied for hire in the various waterways of the district. Some of the more expensive ones were quite luxurious, with canopies overhead, but those that we hired were little more than the standard punt-like flat-bottomed boats (Plate 64).

When we got to the lake we found it simple enough to hire a sailing dinghy, with no questions asked about previous experience. Obviously as far as the Kashmiri proprietor was concerned, the money in his pocket was what mattered.

We set off into the middle of the lake with a gentle breeze behind us, and at first managed the boat quite well, even if a bit ham-fistedly. Inevitably pride comes before a fall, and a sudden need to change direction forced us to gybe rather violently. Round we went, across swung the boom, and over went the boat. We could both swim, so after disentangling ourselves from the various lengths of rope that were curling around us, we hung on and waited for help. We were eventually hauled from the water and the boat was righted, but the proprietor was not pleased, and quite rightly wanted extra baksheesh for the trouble of sending out the help. After some haggling, we agreed on a price, and everyone was happy, while Harry and I had learned a lesson the hard way. We made quite sure that it didn't happen again.

Kashmir is renowned for its wood-carving and back at Palam I had been intrigued by hand-carved wooden boxes sold by a peripatetic native of Kashmir, and had bought a couple. They had been made in Srinagar, then only a name to me, but now that I was there I realized that I had the chance to see where they actually came from. I asked Juma Paktoon about this and he arranged for the peripatetic traveller, who happened to be in Srinagar, to show me round, which he was quite willing to do, hoping, of course, for a sale.

He took me off with my camera to the native part of Srinagar where the workshops were. Although they were called 'factories', that title is far too grandiose for what was nothing more than a small room or two where the carving was done. To get there we had to go through the back-streets of the town, and just walking through the native quarter was an education in the life of such a town, with the women all wearing their heavy white burqas. The workshops were fascinating, too, with men and boys of all ages squatting Indian-fashion on the floor as they chipped away at blocks of wood to make anything from the simplest designs to the most complicated. My camera worked overtime.

Finally, of course, we ended up at the display shop which had the grand title of Kashmir Art Chamber, and I had no hesitation in buying several wooden articles, such as a box with carved dragon designs and a lamp carved like a lotus, and also some Kashmiri embroidery, most of these articles costing in the region of £1. Since it all turned out to be quite bulky they said that it would be quite easy to post everything direct to the United Kingdom, so I paid for it then and there and left them to it; I did, however, take with me the embroidered articles since they were easy to carry. This of course sounds too trusting of me. Did I expect the goods to arrive? Having got to

*Plate 64, on the way to the Nagin Bagh in Kashmir.*

know India and its ways, I knew that there was a chance that they might never leave Srinagar, but it was a gamble that I was prepared to take since it would have been impossible to carry them. I ought to have seen the articles packed up, and posted them myself, but this was right at the end of my stay, and there was not enough time. Instead, I asked Harry, who was staying on a bit longer, if he would check up for me that everything was posted, to which he agreed.

I never saw any of those purchases again. I met Harry a couple of years later and asked him if the parcel had been posted, but he remembered nothing about it, so that was that. My immediate reaction is to blame the dealer himself as a thieving Kashmiri, but that may be maligning him. It could just as easily have been stolen in the mail, as had happened earlier to the colour film which I had sent to Bombay for processing.

The week in Kashmir passed all too quickly, and soon I was off back to Lower Topa for the remaining week's leave, before returning down the road to Rawalpindi and getting a flight back to Palam. There the heat hit me with a vengeance. Life was back to normal.

# 17

# The Search

Thirty-Four Squadron was much the same as usual when I got back from Lower Topa, although, as the departure of the British from India approached, photo recce flights became fewer. I now sometimes flew with Flight Lieutenant Piggott of the Communications Squadron in carrying out riot recces for the civil authorities – low level reconnaissance to investigate the results of local riots which had been occurring. These were no longer against the British, as they had once been, but were now between Moslem and Hindu. With Independence and the division of the subcontinent into Hindu India and Moslem Pakistan not far off, Hindus and Moslems were being incited to attack each other, resulting in bloodshed and destruction. Piggott had been told to investigate from the air how much damage the local villages had suffered.

With him as pilot flying the Auster or me as pilot flying the Harvard we flew over quite a number of villages at 500 feet or less (see Plates 65 and 66) and for the first time I saw the countryside at really close quarters instead of from high altitude. I was surprised how poor the villages looked. Most consisted of flat-roofed rectangular dwellings, but some were of small thatched huts and occasionally round African-style

*Plate 65, an Indian village photographed from the Auster.*

*Plate 66, a country railway station photographed from the Auster. In the foreground are numerous people, a few bullock carts and fourteen camels.*

ones. We found a few riot-stricken villages, sad and deserted, the buildings mere shells.

At the end of one such flight, Piggot decided to show off the ability of the Auster to land in a small space. The runway on which he should have landed that day was on the far side of the airfield, so instead of wasting time having to taxy a long way back, he decided to land on the very end of the runway which ended just next to our Dispersal, even if it was the wrong one. As the wind was blowing at right angles to this runway it meant that he would have to land across it, the thought of which intrigued me. He brought the Auster in across the grass bordering the runway, touched down gently on the concrete and pulled up well before the far side; and there was still plenty of room to spare!

**Air-Land Rescue Exercise**

A flight which was simply good fun was an exercise in searching for a crashed aircraft. Unlike other trips, where we were always on our own, on this occasions several people were involved, which made a stimulating change. On our air base there was what was called an Air/Land Rescue Service, a name which conjures up visions of a vast organization like the Air/Sea Rescue Service of Britain. But at Palam it was nothing of the sort, just a single room in the Control Tower containing some air/land rescue equipment: emergency rations, flares, and so forth. There was officially somebody in charge of it, but it is doubtful whether he would have known what to do should anyone actually force-land out in the *bundu*.[1] At the moment the person in charge was a Flight

---

1 Indian countryside.

Lieutenant who went by the nickname of Bender owing to his proclivity for alcohol. If anyone did force-land it was he who was supposed to do something about it. Since he was said to be on the booze nine times out of ten, that would have been virtually impossible, and, since no exercises had ever been held, nobody else would have known what to do.

One day the Station Commander suddenly decided that there ought to be an exercise based on the Air/Land Rescue Service, and he decided that it would be held on 16 July which was just about at the height of the hot season. Thirty-four Squadron – that was us – was to carry out the exercise in conjunction with Flying Control and a member of the Communications Squadron. After a delay in organizing things – as always in such cases – it was decided that T.-E. (who wanted a chance to get in some wildlife shooting) and Flight Lieutenant Haynes of the Communications Squadron together with a couple of the groundcrew, would go off into the wild in a *ghari* – in this case a signals waggon – to represent a crashed aircraft. They could go where they liked. Another pilot from 34 Squadron would search for them in a Spitfire.

Before they left, T.-E. would work out a flight plan for the imaginary aircraft and a time for its crash, put the details into a sealed envelope and hand this over to Flying Control. (In real life Flying Control would have obtained the necessary details from the pilot's flight plan, routinely given to them before he took off.) T.-E. and his crew would then leave Palam and eventually park their *ghari* somewhere near where, according to the flight plan, the 'aircraft' should have crashed. To add realism this could be some distance from the predicted spot.

At a predetermined time after T.-E. had left, Bender, in Flying Control, would open the envelope and after working out the general position of the 'crash', would set off with a colleague in a jeep in its general direction. They would have a radio with which to keep in contact with Flying Control and attached to the jeep would be a trailer containing emergency equipment. At the same time the contents of the envelope would be telephoned through to 34 Squadron, and the pilot doing the air search would work out more accurately the expected site and take off in a Spitfire. When he had found the *ghari* he would radio the position to Flying Control. They in turn would relay the pilot's message on to the jeep, which would then go to that position and 'rescue the crew'.

The big problem here was that three radios, that of the pilot, that of the jeep and that of Flying Control, would all have to be in working order at the same time. Owing to some peculiarity of technical administration the radios of jeep and aircraft used different wavelengths and so they would not be able to communicate with each other directly. And in the days before transistors there was no guarantee that all three radios would work at the same time.

It turned out that I was to be the one to do the flying since I was the only pilot available. The commanding officer and Jimmy James, for example, were both on holiday in Kashmir. So on 16 July T.-E. and Haynes set off at about 6 o'clock in the morning, taking with them my camera to see if they could get some shots of me from the ground.

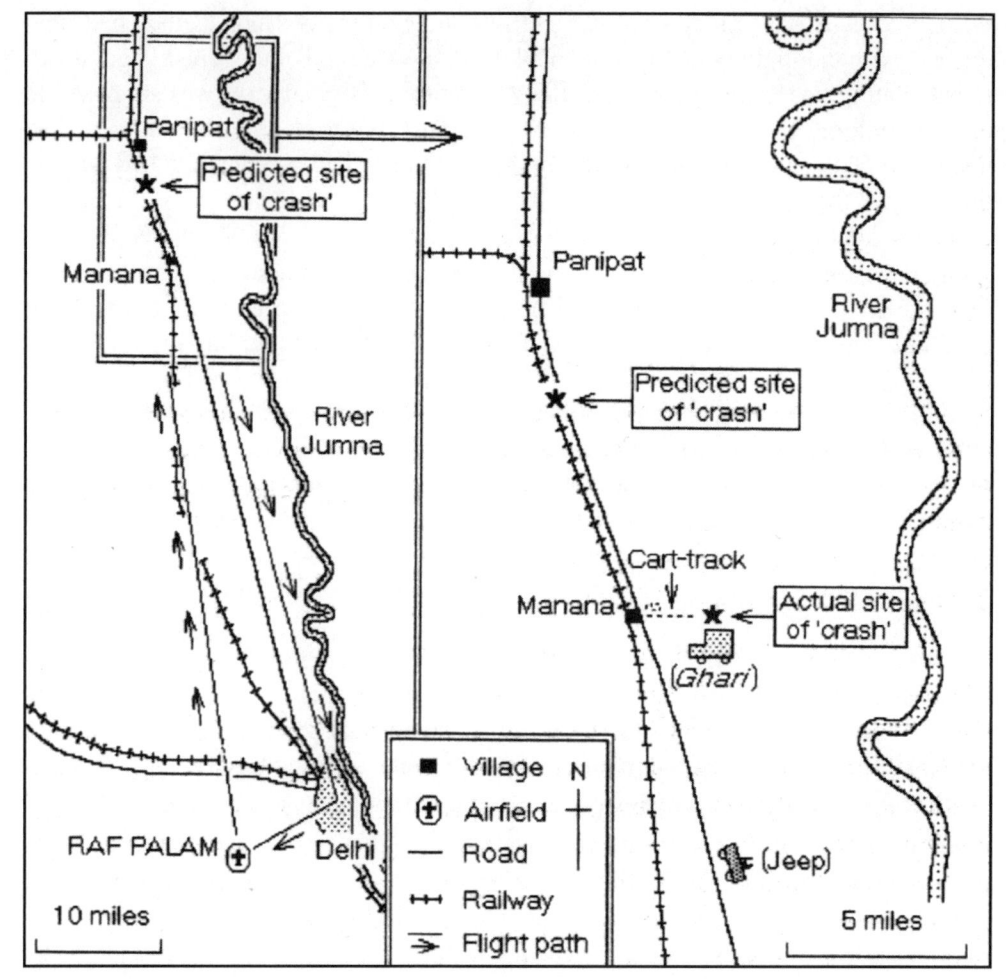

*Figure 16, the search area; general location (left) and in detail (right).*

Even at that time of day it was getting warm, and as the morning progressed it would become really unpleasant for them; still, it was all expected to be over by midday before the real heat got going.

My Spitfire had been made ready, but there had been some delay in finding something suitable for dropping messages. (Dropping anything out of an aircraft was against regulations, but nobody was taking any notice of that when 'lives' were at stake). In the end I managed to scrounge from the Communications Squadron some oiled bags of the type used for being airsick into; these would be ideal for holding messages, so I took several and put in each a piece of paper ready for writing a note on. At the same time a member of the ground staff managed to obtain some lengths of red cloth normally used as indicators for locked controls on aircraft; these I could tie on to the bags before throwing them overboard so that they would be easily visible. I stuffed everything into a clip in the cockpit and got my maps, parachute and flying clothing ready, so that I could be off at a moment's notice.

At 8.30 T.-E.'s envelope was opened in Flying Control. As soon as they had rung through with the flight plan, the time of take-off and the time of the 'crash' I got down to calculating where the prang[2] might have occurred. The 'aircraft' was supposed to have been doing a training flight to Ambala, about 125 miles north of Palam, and had just had time to call up on the R/T to say that the engine had cut, but they had not had time to give their position.

I calculated the site to be just south of the small town of Panipat, about 50 miles north of Palam (Figure 16). As I have said, T.-E. would have assumed an uncertainty of the exact position of the 'crash' when parking his *ghari*, so I could not expect to find him exactly at the calculated spot; he might be anywhere within a radius of ten miles.

After I had checked my calculations a couple of times, off came my shirt and trousers to avoid getting too hot and on went my flying suit. I was going to fly at 400 feet, which somebody had said was the best altitude for carrying out a search; at that height it was still going to be too hot in just flying suit and pants (keep in mind that I normally flew at 20,000 feet at that time of year for a comfortable temperature), but we were forbidden to fly in just pants alone owing to the need for protection in case of fire.

The next thing was to ring up Flying Control and tell them that I was just off. Bender had already shot past in his jeep about a quarter of an hour before for his ground-based search, since all he needed to know was which road to take in the general direction of the 'crash'; he would then follow my instructions relayed to him by Flying Control.

I climbed into the kite with my parachute on – strapped myself in – tied the log pad round my knee – made the routine cockpit check – signed to the groundcrew on 'contact' – pressed the tit for the Koffman starter, and she started on the first cartridge. No need to get the engine warmed up – she would do that easily enough while taxying out in this heat, even with the radiator flaps open. Just check the radio – yes, that's O.K. Now I'm at end of the runway – brakes on – check the magnetos – yes, they're O.K. – set the gyro compass. Green Aldis lamp from the airfield controller at the end of the runway – one last check on temperatures and pressures – out on to the runway – straighten up – throttle slowly open – hold her straight with left rudder – tail up – steady – we're off – feels safely airborne – undercart up – pitch back – then up to 1,000 feet. Check with the radio for airfield clearance. Steer 338° by gyro, check with the magnetic compass. Then just wait till I see the road and railway to Panipat, which come in from starboard (see Figure 16, left).

I didn't close the hood because at 1,000 feet it was too hot even first thing in the morning. I already felt pretty warm even with it open, although not uncomfortable, since there was plenty of draught to dry the sweat, and everything was flapping in the breeze. I had become airborne at about 9 o'clock and now flew towards Panipat at 270 mph. When I got to where the road and rail ran close together I closed the throttle

---

2 Crash.

a bit, dropped down to 400 feet and flew from then on at about 200 mph, since I was almost at the place where I had worked out that the 'crash' should have occurred.

I now flew up between the road and railway towards Panipat, weaving slightly and looking on both sides. It is amazing how comparatively useless the Spitfire, or for that matter any low-winged fighter, was for searching for something on the ground when compared with a high-winged aircraft like the Auster. The view ahead was completely blocked by the nose to about 20 degrees on either side, and the wings blocked the view further back from about 70 degrees to 110 degrees. At the same time to look behind the trailing edge of the wing involved such prolonged neck-bending that it was almost impossible to do anything but give a casual glance in that direction.

The snag was that most people on the ground, although possibly not experienced pilots, would send up a signal rocket or Very Light when the aircraft was abreast of them, which would of course have been the worst possible moment. I hoped that T.-E. would have more sense than to do that.

I now realized that it would be quite impossible to find a vehicle simply by looking for it in so large an area; I just wouldn't see it. So I looked instead for white smoke from a flare or Very cartridge, which is fairly easy to detect. I was at first misled by smoke from numerous bonfires dotted around the countryside, but I soon recognized them for what they were.

I reached Panipat, had a brief scout round to the north of it, and seeing nothing, came back and started in earnest, thinking that the best plan would be to do a square search, that is, methodically searching along the edge of imaginary squares of ever-increasing size. So I flew down southward just along the east side of the road, looking hard on both sides, and then, coming to where the road and railway diverged, banked round to starboard through 180° and went up northwards just to the west of the railway. Nothing there, so once again down the east side of the road, this time a little further out.

When half way down that leg I suddenly noticed just ahead of the port wing what looked like a thin trail of smoke. Another look and – yes, it was the *ghari*! So I whipped over and did a steep dive towards it, then climbed round in a circle so that I could recognize landmarks again and pinpoint them on the map.

The *ghari* was about two miles or so east of the main road at the end of a kind of cart track which joined the road at what was presumably a small village – there were some houses on one side of the junction but not on the other (see Figure 16, right). Having found an immediate landmark the next thing was to find a more obvious one. That was easy; between the road and railway was a large-sized village, named on the map as Manana, and easily recognisable.

To digress for a moment. When I discussed it all with T.-E. afterwards he told me that he had originally intended to park near the River Jumna, just about on the edge of the ten-mile radius, but luckily for me the ground was too difficult for his *ghari*. If he had done that I might never have found him.

To show how difficult it is to locate people on the ground there are two points which

I discovered after the exercise when I talked to T.-E. The first concerns the smoke which I saw from the flare which they fired. This apparently was not the first; they had originally fired one when I passed by going north, and I had missed it in spite of keeping my eyes skinned (perhaps T.-E. had fired it when I was abreast of him!) The second point is that they had laid on the ground some white strips, a standard part of the survival kit of the time designed to attract attention; they were installed rolled up in all our Spitfires for just such an emergency. But on all the flights that I made over T.-E. and his fellow 'survivors' then and subsequently, I never recognized them for what they were; they were too small and I realized after the exercise was over that I had mistaken them for a picnic cloth.

Now back to the exercise– the next thing was to notify Flying Control so that they could transmit to the jeep the position of the *ghari*. I climbed up to 3,000 feet for better reception, closed the hood and called them up over the R/T. They were receiving me all right, so I gave them the message, describing the position as best I could from a quarter inch map which I had with me. Although it may sound quite a simple thing to do, it actually took quite a time, several words needing to be repeated and then the whole message having to be read back.

While I was doing this I saw a huge wall of blackness approaching from the north – a wall of cloud stretching from some distance above me right down to about 800 feet, clearly an approaching storm. Below the cloud was a wall of dust kicked up by the turbulence of the air. I did not quite appreciate its significance at the time, and it simply seemed to me to be just a storm working its way southward. It was in fact the prelude to the monsoon!

As soon as I had given my message I wrote a short message to T.-E. to tell him that I had contacted Flying Control: 'Have informed RAF Palam of your position'. I put it into one of the bags, wrapped it up and tied a red streamer round it. It was a bit tricky doing all this one-handed, since with the other hand I had to keep the aircraft on a more or less even keel. Then I opened the hood again – I had had to keep it closed for all this, otherwise the slipstream would have blown everything over the side or into the irretrievable bottom of the cockpit – and dived down to the main road, turned right at the buildings on the corner, then along the farm track, and there was the *ghari* again.

After manoeuvring the kite round I got down to about 100 feet – I could not go much lower as there were too many trees around – reduced my speed to about 160 mph, and lowered the flaps to help keep the speed down and also improve flying stability at the lower speed. Then I headed for the *ghari* and, just before reaching it, hung the message over the side and let go. A slight turn to port, open with the throttle, and a quick look down behind me. I saw somebody run across the ploughed field to get the message – about 200 yards away from the *ghari*. It had fallen short of them because I had allowed for forward momentum as if it were a bomb, forgetting that something light simply flutters straight down.

The next thing was to go and find the jeep which should still be moving along the main road from the direction of Delhi. So after climbing to a safe height I whipped up

# THE SEARCH

the flaps, did a mild beat-up of the *ghari* and went back to the main road again.

Steering south I kept the main road on my port side and flew at about 400 feet, positioning myself so that I could look out for it about 45° to port. I kept the speed down to about 180 mph so as to have plenty of time to look for them, but not so slow that the controls started getting sloppy. Quite a few vehicles of various sorts were moving along the tree-lined road, including now and again a bullock cart. Then after several minutes' flying I saw the jeep. It was an unmistakeable bright yellow and batting along at a pretty good speed; for the first time I realized what a good colour yellow is for showing up against the landscape.

I immediately whipped round to show them that I had seen them, while at the same time they shot up a Very Light to attract my attention. I thought I would drop them a message – although it was not necessary in view of their radio contact with Flying Control – just to give them the information first-hand, so after seeing them pull in at the side of the road I climbed for height, closed the hood and set about getting something down on paper. I drew a rough map of the road, the village, the houses and the cart track, and marked the position of T.-E.'s *ghari*. It was just as well that I did all this, since when we all got back to Palam we found that Flying Control had been unable to contact the jeep – apparently the jeep's radio had failed. So if I had not dropped the message poor old Bender in the jeep would have had no idea of where T.-E. was. Indeed, I might have gone straight back to Palam after sending my message to Flying Control without even looking for the jeep, but for the fun of it I wanted to see the thing through and keep in direct contact with those on the ground. To add further confusion – although I was not aware of it at the time – my own R/T had packed up after I had transmitted my message, so Flying Control could not have told me that they were unable to contact the jeep; indeed, nobody could have told anybody anything!

After I had written out the message I opened the hood again and went down to look for the jeep. But could I find it? Not a sign of it. I went up and down that road three or four times before I eventually saw it tucked away at the side. I had hoped that they would let off another Very Light, but they thought that I was only manoeuvring for position. Anyway, once I had seen them I got the airspeed down to 160 mph, put the flaps down, descended to 100 feet, and headed for them, dropping the message this time about 70 yards away from the target. I had the satisfaction of seeing somebody run for it, and after raising the flaps and doing a brief beat-up I pushed off back to T.-E. to tell him that I had contacted the jeep.

The approaching storm was now between the *ghari* and myself and to reach it I had to plough through it. As soon as I hit the storm everything became dark, and whirling sand appeared to surround me; turbulence caused the aircraft to bump around, and then it was pouring with rain. In a moment I was through the murk and under a heavy overcast. Then a turn to starboard down the cart track and there I was back at the *ghari*. A climb to gain height, and another message: 'Have contacted jeep, they are not very far now'. There was not a sign of anybody out in the open, although I did see somebody run out to get the message. I discovered afterwards that they were a bit mad at me for coming in the middle of a storm; they were all sheltering from the downpour.

A couple of beat-ups and back to the road again to look for the jeep. I found it easily this time, beat it up, and then returned to T.-E. My idea was to indicate to each group how far away they were from each other by the amount of time I took to go away and come back. So back to T.-E. for another beat-up and then back to the road again.

Like a fool I had not timed myself along the road to see how long it took to reach the jeep, and this time I missed it and flew on for several minutes before realizing that I must have shot past it. They would have seen me go by anyway, so I turned round, and there they were waiting at the junction of the cart track with the main road. Good, they had understood my rough map, and were waiting for me to come and check their position. So waggling my wings I banked round in order to get into position in line with the cart track. I flew out towards the west first, then headed straight back across the railway, across the big village, down to 100 feet, and along the cart track, zooming up when I got to the *ghari* to show the jeep where it was.

I circled round and repeated the manoeuvre but the jeep had disappeared, so after two more runs with still no sign of them on the cart-track or the main road I thought I would go and look for them. I flew up and down the main road a few times looking into the country on either side, but still no sign. They had to be somewhere around, so I continued zooming down on the *ghari* followed by a steep climb, which should continue to give the jeep some indication of its whereabouts. A few more runs along the cart track, and then I decided to circle the *ghari* in case I had been too low on each run-in for them to see me. So I climbed to 1,000 feet and started circling, but then found that the circles were really too large to be useful, and also I hardly ever seemed to get the *ghari* in the middle of the circle.

While I was doing the runs and beat-ups I had visions of T.-E. taking photo after photo of me with my camera, but I discovered afterwards that he had only taken three pictures at the beginning when I was only doing mild beat-ups at about 300 feet, and had then gone off into the *bundu* with his gun, leaving the camera in the hands of Haynes. I will admit that a Leica in the hands of someone who has never handled one before is rather a fearsome object, especially with the long-focus 10.5 cm lens which I had put on it for the occasion, and T.-E. found that really he was unable to cope. He did point the camera in the right direction when I started coming in low, and the resulting few photos, although a bit lop-sided, were not at all bad. But then he got muddled in winding on the film; he tried to turn the wrong knob – the rewind knob – which of course would not turn. So, afraid that he might break something he wisely left it alone. I do at least have four photos of that trip: three rather small ones of me, and one of the locals who had gathered round the *ghari*.

But to continue with my tale. After a bit of circling I decided to go and look for the jeep again. So I flew off in the rough direction of the main road and after bit of searching eventually found it. They were some way off to the north, coming over what looked like the roughest country imaginable; from the air it appeared as a series of thickets, ploughed fields and ditches. What had apparently happened was that they had tried the cart track, but not far along it they found that owing to the downpour it now ran through what had suddenly become the village pond, which I hadn't noticed, so they had had to turn back.

The only reason why I found the jeep again was because they fired a Very Light. I was searching around and then saw what appeared to be a smoke trail, so I took a second look, and there was the jeep at the bottom of it. I discovered afterwards that the Very Light had not been intended for me, but was to attract T.-E. so that he would fire one in exchange and give them a line to steer on. From then on it was easy – I just did straight runs between jeep and *ghari* to give the direction. At last the jeep reached the *ghari*, and there must have been much rejoicing and celebrating with the hooch that Bender had brought.

I wrote my last message: 'Well done – cheerio – Ken', went down as low as I dared with all the trees around, and dropped the message, as I learned afterwards, slap in the middle of them. I had at last learned – a bit late – not to allow for the momentum of the aircraft.

By this time there was a large crowd of locals all round the *ghari*, and as I came in on my last run I saw what looked like a yellow flag waving around on the end of a very long bamboo pole. In fact it was the kite aerial for the dinghy radio that the crew had brought with them, bouncing around in the wind, which shows how difficult it may be to identify some things from the air.

Climbing away gently, I raised the flaps, did one last beat-up and then set course for Palam. I thought that I would go by way of Delhi to make the navigation a bit simpler, which, as it transpired, was just as well. When eventually I reached it I steered direct for Palam, expecting to encounter the cantonment on the way. But could I see it? I thought that I was going in the right direction, but there was no sign of it; all I could see was a rather swampy area which I didn't recognize. Then suddenly it dawned on me; the cantonment was virtually under water – all the roads looked like rivers, and all the gardens like paddy-fields. Once I had realized that, I found Palam quite easily. I had not seen the airfield from a greater distance because of poor visibility but the airfield too now looked something like a swamp, with great pools of water on the runways, and the monsoon ditches on either side filled to overflowing, glistening in the rather murky light. It had apparently only just stopped raining, and the clouds all around still looked ominous.

I was unable to contact Flying Control because, as I have said, my R/T was now useless, so I followed a Harvard which happened to be in the circuit, and then, getting no 'red' – a Very Light warning not to land – came in to do one of my best landings ever, which was lucky, since the runway was slippery and I doubt whether I could have pulled up in time on the brakes if I had been going too fast.

I landed at 12.30, taxied along to Dispersal, stopped the engine and climbed out. I had been 3 hours 35 minutes in the air and could have flown for another half hour if necessary – and that was without a drop tank. This very low fuel consumption was due to the height at which I had been flying and the low speed: the range would have been poor, but the endurance was good.

I went along to Flying Control, and the Flying Control Officer's comment was: 'We were just going to send off a search aircraft, as we hadn't had any word from you, and everyone was starting to panic, especially with the monsoon turning up like this. Incidentally, if you had turned up a little earlier or the rain had been a little later we would have had to divert you to Agra or somewhere. We certainly couldn't have taken you here'. Not that they would have been able to tell me that without a functioning radio, although they would have tried their best with a red Very Light. And if the rain had been a little later I would not have had enough fuel to reach Agra, so I do not know what would have happened. Such is the luck of flying. To think that all the dust and rain and bumps that I had been flying through unconcernedly had been the monsoon, that horror of fliers. Perhaps if I had know it I would have gone straight back to Palam without more ado!

As a sidelight on flying in India, this was the only time that I came across an airfield being closed because of the weather, and then it was only for a brief time. This is in marked contrast to Great Britain, where the weather frequently prevented flying by clamping down with rain, fog or low cloud.

The rescuers and rescued arrived back safely that evening, and we had a good post-mortem about it before going to bed. The conclusions were rather depressing. To find anything on the ground without something to attract attention appeared to be virtually impossible because of the small scale when seen from the air and the uncertainty of where exactly to look. The only satisfactory answer seemed to be to create lots of smoke; from the air this could be seen for miles. The white strips for laying on the ground were just a waste of time. And, as I have said, a low-winged monoplane would be a poor choice for making a search; a high-winged aircraft like the Auster would be best. But to use an Auster for anyone who had disappeared on a long-distance flight in a Spitfire in India would have been impossible owing to the Auster's short range.

In fact, looking back on it now after all these years, I doubt whether we would ever have been found if any of us had force-landed or baled out over such country as the Thar Desert or Baluchistan. Most of the rest of India would probably have been all right, since it was fairly well populated. But it is frightening just to think what might have happened if any of us had come down in the Thar. The distance across it was 300 or so miles. Since we were out of radio contact with any airfield after the first 100 miles nobody would have known at what time we came down – we might have been anywhere along the next 200 miles. And the further we were from base the greater the error on either side of the track. Probably on a flight over the Thar Desert or Baluchistan the chances of being found would have been just about nil. It was lucky that the Spitfires kept going!

# 18

## Farewell to a Spitfire – and to India

*While many Spitfires were handed over to the Indian Air Force after independence, the photo reconnaisance Mk XIXs from Palam were scrapped.*

The last flight I made in India was the saddest: ferrying a Spitfire to another airfield for disposal. Independence Day, 15 August 1947, was approaching, when the British would officially leave the country. Squadrons would be disbanded, and airfields and aircraft handed over to the new Government.

What would happen to our beloved Spitfires which had served us so well? Nobody seemed to know, but there were three possibilities: they would be handed over to the Indian Air Force, they would go to the RAF Maintenance Unit at Drigh Road airfield just east of Karachi away to the south-west (see Figure 9) to be stored for an indefinite period with an unknown future, or they would be broken up at our own airfield, Palam.

After delays and uncertainties it was eventually decided that they would be ferried to Drigh Road[1] and that on 22nd July T.-E., Jimmy James and I would take the first three aircraft that were serviceable. So on that day we each climbed into a Spitfire. Jimmy was unable to get his started, so T.-E. and I took off without him, leaving him to follow when he could.

We aimed to fly at 6,000 feet in open formation with T.-E. leading. After take-off I positioned myself a little way off on his starboard side, and we set course along the southern edge of the Thar Desert for Jodhpur, which was the standard intermediate pinpoint on the way to Karachi (see Fig. 7). Unfortunately soon after take-off my radio packed up, so that I couldn't talk to T.-E.; from then on I had to be especially careful to keep one eye on his aircraft and the other on the map. We had also known beforehand that his gyro-compass was precessing badly so it was important to keep our wits about us. After about 25 minutes I saw T.-E. signalling to me, so I closed up on him. He was making strange signals with his hands and was patting his ears, so I concluded that his own radio was not working either. I therefore nodded and patted my ears, to show that I was in the same position (although of course he could have interpreted this as showing that there was nothing wrong with my radio). Then he started to make circling movements with his hand and pointing at me and I realized that he wanted me lead him back to Palam.

Round I went and set course for the return journey while he formated on my starboard side. I knew roughly where we were, and since we had been flying for less than

---

1 Pronounced Drigg Road.

25 minutes it should be straightforward to get back to Palam on my compass, although with my radio out of action I couldn't get a homing signal. Eventually, more by good luck than anything else, we came slap over Palam and I veered sharply to port to show T.-E. that we had arrived.

At that time I had a bad cold, and my sinuses were rather congested. As a result the rapid reduction in height from 6,000 feet to 1,000 feet, the height of the airfield circuit, gave me a bit of trouble. I had never before had any problem of this sort, except of course the normal clearing of ears with change in altitude, but this time as I descended I got a severe jab of pain in the top of my nose, although luckily it soon disappeared.

After a mild beat-up of Flying Control and rocking my wings to show that I had no radio I came in and landed. I stopped about two-thirds down the runway, but then I did a really silly thing. Usually, with Flying Control supervising us on the radio, we would taxy back along the runway and turn off at the intersection with the second runway to shorten the route back to Dispersal (see Figure 5). But now, without any radio and with T.-E. in the circuit I should have kept rolling to the end of the runway. Instead, without thinking, I turned round in the middle as usual, expecting T.-E. to do another circuit before landing. As soon as I had turned I saw T.-E. on the approach coming in to land, so I quickly got to the edge of the runway ready to whip off it with a burst of throttle if he didn't see me. The Airfield Controller in his hut near the end of the runway should have given him a red Very Light, but he had probably not noticed what I was doing – he would have had his attention on T.-E.

Luckily T.-E. saw me and went round again, while I taxied on to the other runway feeling very sheepish and wondering what he would say when he got down. When he did eventually arrive back at Dispersal there was quite a torrent of language: 'You bloody fool, what the hell did you think you were you doing – trying to kill us both?!' And then no more was said about it.

Jimmy was still on the ground; he had not managed to get his aircraft started at all, and had given up for the day. The groundcrew confirmed that T.-E.'s radio had indeed packed up, so we would not have got far with his faulty gyro-compass if we had got lost, particularly with my thinking that his radio was all right. Accurate navigation was vital at that time of year, since it was still the season of thick dust hazes and extremely poor visibility, so we had to be particularly careful.

Next day we tried again with the radios put right. With Jimmy now joining us we taxied out again. Jimmy jibbed at the end of the runway and turned back. We discovered afterwards that this time it was his radio that had gone out of service, but we all privately thought that it was really that he didn't want to be away from his girl friend Madeleine. He seemed to be very much in love with her and on the slightest excuse would stay at Palam. None of us blamed him, and we passed it off as a great joke; he was later vindicated by marrying her.

Once airborne T.-E. and I set course for Jodhpur, with T.-E. again leading. This time he had decided to fly at 20,000 feet because we had been told that there would be a great deal of patchy cloud below that height. I did not like the idea after my sinus trouble of the day before, but we pressed on. I really ought to have stayed on the ground because of it, but only once in the RAF did I ever do so when an aircraft was available, and that was elsewhere after a colossal hangover. I was not going to let a sinus stop me from getting into the air. I had tried to persuade T.-E. to go at deck level, but he would not hear of it; he was adamant about going above the cloud, and since he was leading the formation it was he who had the last say.

At about 20,000 feet, after 20 minutes of climbing through patchy cloud, we were surprised to find ourselves now going into thick cloud; according to the meteorological people there shouldn't have been any at that height but we were still climbing and it stretched above us. I lost sight of T.-E. in the cloud, and it seemed to me that we might not get above it until about 30,000 feet. My sinus was bubbling away as we climbed and it was a bit worrying not knowing how high we might have to go and how quickly I could descend without severe pain. I didn't like it at all, and felt that I ought to take the opportunity of descending slowly while I still had plenty of time in which to do it.

So I turned back and started to descend. At about 15,000 feet the red-hot pains in my nose started to appear again, so I climbed a little until they had disappeared. From then on I descended more gradually without much pain until at 10,000 feet I found myself just below the cloud and could see the desert below. I decided to carry on towards Jodhpur at that height; I calculated that I still had enough fuel to get to Drigh Road.

I knew only vaguely where I was, so spent a little time checking the ground below me. Eventually I found a railway running across the desert, but not knowing which one it was I followed it south for a little while until I could fit its curves to a railway marked on the map. This showed that I was considerably to starboard, or north, of my intended track, so I followed it a little further southwards until I was quite sure of its identity, and then broke away south-westward to hit the Jaipur-Jodhpur railway. Soon after that I came to Merta Road, a very obvious junction of four railways (see Figure 7).

All this time I was slowly descending because of the cloud, and eventually came over Jodhpur at about 4,000 feet. I called up Jodhpur Tower on all channels, and it was only after considerable perseverance that I got an answer. I had passed that way once before and had found similar difficulty; indeed, we all agreed that Jodhpur did not have the best set of operators. They had once caused an Anson to crash through lack of fuel by giving it a reciprocal bearing on a homing so that the pilot flew away from Jodhpur airfield instead of towards it. Anyway, we had been warned before we left Palam that their homer was unreliable. It was a pity, because it would have been comforting when crossing the Thar Desert, on whose edge Jodhpur lies, to know that if anything did go wrong there was somebody down there who knew that you had passed overhead. But since this was an Indian service, and therefore rather lackadaisical at that time, the chances were that (i) no records would have been kept and (ii) nobody would have been able later on to find the operator who took the message.

After Jodhpur I started checking my fuel more carefully. I worked out that I could just get to Drigh Road if I didn't get lost; so I now repeatedly checked the amount of remaining fuel, the rate of consumption and the groundspeed. I worked out that I should have 35 gallons left when I arrived at Drigh Road, just enough for a spare half-hour's flying at 200 mph indicated airspeed (the best speed for economy; see Table 17 in the Appendix). Anyway, I decided to recheck again carefully just before the half-way mark, so that I could turn round and go back to Jodhpur if absolutely necessary.

Stratocumulus cloud with a base of about 3,000 feet had now appeared, so I descended further and flew on just below it. My next pinpoint, a large lake in the middle of the desert, was 140 miles from Jodhpur, and at the navigational briefing for my earlier trip on that route I had been told to look out for it as a prominent landmark. It turned up just slightly north of me, so my heading was not too bad, and I held my course; it was not worth trying to make a correction of what would have been no more than one degree.

The desert beneath – the Sind Desert which merges with the Thar – looked pretty horrible. Just miles and miles of uneven sand, with occasional evidence of past cultivation in the form of old field outlines; it looked just like the Thar further north that I had flown across on my trip to Baluchistan.

Soon the Jodhpur-Hyderabad railway, which would now wander to and fro across my track, came in from the left. This gave my position to be about halfway between Jodhpur and Drigh Road, so I checked my fuel and decided that I could make it, once again provided that I didn't start getting lost. After a little while the desert suddenly gave way to cultivation and I could check my position. Yes, I was still a little way off my intended track, but decided not to alter course until I reached the River Indus 80 miles ahead where I could get an accurate pinpoint.

I flew on across canals and brown fields for what felt like hours. The river seemed long overdue, and I was getting worried in case I had suddenly gone too far south for some reason, and would not hit it until it was too late. But I really had no reason to be concerned since I had proved by the earlier landmarks that the course I was steering was satisfactory, and if I kept to my compass course I must inevitably reach somewhere near the next pinpoint. But when you have got nothing but mile after mile of empty countryside below you that sort of logic does not always bring peace of mind. I now wonder why I did not bradshaw by following the Hyderabad railway which would eventually cross the Indus near my track, and although somewhat meandering would not have involved much extra fuel. The railway was easily visible from this low altitude, but perhaps I trusted my compass more than the vagaries of the railway or the possible inaccuracies of the map. Before leaving Palam I had marked on my map my intended track between major pinpoints, but had not prepared a proper flight plan since I was expecting to be following T.-E.; still, I felt more comfort in aiming to following a prepared straight line on the map than branching out into the unknown.

Suddenly out of the haze appeared Hyderabad, white and squashed together, the houses appearing all jumbled up in disorder. And there was the Indus just beyond (see Figure 7), with easily recognizable road and railway bridges across it; ten miles beyond was its tributary the Baran River with its own distinctive bridge. These all showed me that I was several miles north of where I should have been, so I changed course a few degrees to port, and then immediately I was once again over desert with no more pinpoints for 60 miles. The cloud was now down to 2,000 feet and getting lower. Ahead I could see some hills, all the same sandy colour as the desert, which the map said were 1,000 feet high; I would clear them easily.

Twenty miles from Drigh Road the River Malir appeared below, not very large, but recognizable, and about five minutes later Karachi Airport, the city's civilian airport with a single runway, three miles short of Drigh Road. The cloud base had descended still further and was now down to 1,000 feet, so I descended to 900 feet and turned slightly starboard to conform with the circuit around Karachi Airport. Drigh Road, easily identifiable by its three runways, soon came into view, and was I glad to see it!

In the airfield circuit I could see a Tempest and another Spitfire – surely that was T.-E.? Then over the radio transmission on universal frequency I heard: 'Hullo Drigh Road Tower, this is Roadhog 21. Permission to join circuit and pancake. Over.' And from Drigh Road Tower: 'Hullo Roadhog 21. You may pancake. Runway 26. QFE 1005.[2] Over.' '21. Roger. Out.' Yes, that was T.-E.; 'Roadhog' was our Squadron call-sign, and T.-E.'s number was 21. What a coincidence that we had both arrived at exactly the same time after going by quite different routes and altitudes.

I watched T.-E. land, and then came the Tempest's turn. Meanwhile I joined the circuit at 900 feet, occasionally disappearing into wisps of cloud, until at last my turn came. 'Hullo, Drigh Road Tower, this is Roadhog 22 [my own call-sign]. May I join circuit and pancake? Over.' 'Roadhog 22, join circuit and pancake. Runway 26. QFE 1005. Over.' 'Roadhog 22. Roger. Out.' Then once round the airfield in the circuit and a further call to the Tower: 'Roadhog 22. Downwind. Over.' 'Roger, Roadhog 22. Call Finals. Over.' '22. Wilco.' And then on the final approach: 'Roadhog 22. Finals.' Then close the throttle, ease slowly back on the stick, check with the stick… check… check… and bump, I was down. On the radio again from Drigh Road Tower: 'Hullo, Roadhog 22. Turn starboard at intersection of runway, and taxi down to Dispersal until you see the other Spitfire.' '22. Wilco.'

When I had parked my Spitfire level with T.-E.'s I switched off and climbed out. 'Hullo, Nemesis, fancy meeting you here,' exclaimed T.-E. 'Where did you get to?' 'Oh, I came down to 3,000 feet because my sinus wasn't feeling too good,' I replied. 'I kept below the cloud all the way. What happened to you – did you get a homing or something?' 'Well, it's a long story,' said T.-E. 'after you disappeared I pressed on up and levelled out at 26,000 feet. I came out of the cloud after a little while – it was just a dirty great wall of it – and pressed on. My gyro was precessing badly, so I kept checking it frequently. I couldn't see the ground, so I turned at my Jodhpur estimated time of arrival and just before Drigh Road estimated time of arrival I called Mauripur (the main RAF Karachi Airfield) on the homer. I don't think Drigh Road have got one. Anyway, as I descended they gave me a good homing. I had ended up a little way out

---

2 Barometric pressure at ground level, measured in millibars.

to sea, and they pulled me back to land. As I broke cloud there was Mauripur below, so then I pressed on here, and you know the rest.' 'That's not a bad bit of dead reckoning for a type like you,' I commented. 'Damn good in fact, all that way for three hours and a quarter (which was the time that it had taken both of us to get to Drigh Road from Palam) on a precessing gyro! By the way, what fuel have you got left?' 'Forty gallons – and you?' 'Thirty gallons,' I replied. 'Which goes to show the difference between 26,000 feet and 3,000 feet at similar speeds. Mind you, you covered more distance, what with going out to sea and everything.'

Although I didn't realize it at the time that was my last flight in India. I now wonder how T.-E. would have fared if his radio had packed up again without a second aircraft to back him up. He couldn't have got a homing and he would have been descending through cloud with no knowledge of its base which was in fact only 1,000 feet. And not more than 30 miles away were hills with peaks of over 1,000 feet. Ugh, it doesn't bear thinking about!

We had some char and obtained receipts for the aircraft. Then T.-E. suddenly got into a panic, because he realized that the Viceroy's Dakota was leaving Mauripur for Palam empty and he wanted to get on it. He had no wish to stay the night at Mauripur – the only place with suitable accommodation – and the Dakota was leaving in about half an hour. Somehow he quickly organized some transport – a 15-cwt truck – to take us both to Mauripur, and after saying goodbye to the test pilots at Drigh Road, who check the serviceability of aircraft dumped there, we scrambled aboard with our overnight kit, humping our bulky parachutes over our shoulders.

After passing through Karachi we eventually arrived at the familiar airfield of Mauripur, and found that the Dakota was not only still there, but would not be leaving for another hour, so we made ourselves comfortable in the Mess along with several others who were also going to Palam. While I was waiting I saw several people with whom I had done my flying training, so I wandered over to have a chat with them and hear their news. They were members of Number 5 Squadron and had been stationed at RAF Risalpur, 25 miles from Peshawar near the foot of the Khyber Pass, flying Tempest fighters. They were now to be disbanded and had been moved to Mauripur before leaving India. It might have been one of their Tempests which I had seen in the circuit at Drigh Road.

That was one of the pleasures of Service life; as you got moved around from place to place you kept meeting people whom you knew from earlier days. Eventually we set off in the Dakota, climbing to 7,000 feet. As we went up I could feel my sinus bubbling, but as we reduced height for landing at Palam I was grateful for the first time in my life for the slow rate at which the transport people descend. Thanks to them the journey remained comfortable, and we were soon back on the ground at Palam.

And what happened to our trusty Spitfires, which had carried us to all the corners of India? It was sad to see such old friends go; I had become fond of them, and it seemed wrong simply to send them away to an unknown future. I discovered later that they were eventually broken up – a terrible fate for such lovely aircraft.

## What of the future?

The time was coming, in about a year, when I would be demobbed and I had been wondering what to do when I returned to civilian life, since I had now definitely decided that I did not want to stay on in the RAF, with the prospect of less flying and more administration and bullshit – a problem which I have already discussed in Chapter 2.

I discovered later that it was just as well that I did not stay in the RAF, since as the years passed into the 1960s less and less money was available for the Services. I read in the Press that so-called permanent RAF officers were being thrown out of the Service to fend for themselves as civilians while still only in their forties. And of the members of the Squadron who were supposed to be in the Service permanently, T.-E. was out within ten years, and Johnnie Shukla, who continued in the Indian Air Force for many more years, eventually ended up in civilian life before he was fifty.

Meanwhile the Indian Air Force had asked whether any of us in 34 Squadron would like to transfer to them and fly Dakotas. We all turned it down flat. So what was I to do when I got out? I had become intrigued in a rather limited way by the medical aspects of flying, particularly the effects of high altitude and low atmospheric oxygen, as well as the bends. I say 'in a rather limited way' since I had no more insight into the subject than that provided by direct experience. But I had a cousin who had become a medical student, and the idea of following him into the world of medicine slowly took root.

At this time the RAF was providing education and vocational training assessments for those who were to be demobbed and who wanted guidance on what to do in 'civvy street'. These assessments were based on what are more commonly known as intelligence tests, similar to those I had encountered three years earlier at Aircraft Receiving Centre, and were accompanied by an interview. I thought that it would be a change from routine to have a go and see what they might reveal.

I was surprised to find that the officer running the tests was another person, like Harry in Kashmir, that I had known quite well at school and had not heard of again until now. He sat me down with pen and paper and I got on with the written tests; then he gave me the interview in which we discussed various possibilities. Finally he wrote the following report:

> Flying Officer Neame approached the Vocational Advice Service and took the psychometric tests. The results showed him to possess an exceptional intelligence and correspondingly high mechanical and mathematical aptitude; they also indicated a pronounced bias in favour of non-routine work with opportunity for the exercise of initiative and responsibility. He appears to have a good critical faculty and a methodical mind.
>
> With altruistic inclinations, he appears, as far as the tests can show, to be well-suited to the medical profession. He is advised to apply without delay for admission to a university as a medical student in October '48. The Further Education and Training Scheme was outlined to him.

On qualifying there was a chance of his employing his pilot's experience in Flying Doctor work in one of the Dominions. Alternatively the Colonial Medical Service might appeal to him.

Photography [as a career] was also discussed. For reasons given at the interview, it was felt that he should be more suited to the medical profession.

I have often wondered how the so-called intelligence tests are supposed to be able to show suitability for a life's career such as the medical profession; all that they can really do is to pick out one or two limited abilities, such as recognizing patterns, or knowing the meanings of words. In spite of their title they surely do not assess 'intelligence', whatever that may be. Most of the conclusions in the above assessment were more on the results of the interview.

This was in June 1947, so if I was to do anything constructive towards becoming a medical student at the end of the following year I would have to get things moving. But it would have to wait until I got nearer to the UK and was available for interviews at medical schools.

**Farewell, India!**
Life in India meanwhile had to continue, if only for a short time with Independence Day not far off. Thirty-four Squadron was to be disbanded and its members dispersed. I had earlier been appointed as Intelligence Officer in the Squadron and so I was responsible for its records, a copy of which had to be sent to the Air Ministry in London every so often. The copies held by the Squadron itself now had to be burned, which provided us with an excuse for a huge bonfire. I kept all my flying maps of India, which now provide a sixteen miles to the inch memento of just about the whole of the subcontinent. A portion with Palam airfield and Delhi and marked with parts of the tracks of my various flights is shown in Plate 67, opposite.

Shortly before leaving Palam somebody introduced me to the RAF Stores, which appeared to have all kinds of goodies. One thing that particularly took my fancy was a *kukri*, the short, heavy, but beautifully curved slashing knife of the Ghurkas, although why such equipment should be in the RAF Stores I never discovered. I had seen a lovely one owned by somebody in the Mess: it was of polished steel and so hard that it would easily chop through a large nail. So if there were *kukris* going begging, I wouldn't mind having one. The one which I acquired – and I presume that it was standard issue quality – was by no means as hard as the one I originally saw, and a nail would dent the *kukri* rather than the other way round. But I had no complaints; it was just a pleasure to look at.

Two days after the flight to Drigh Road I was suddenly posted to join Number 5 Squadron at RAF Mauripur, some of whose members I had recently met there. I could now add another squadron to those I had belonged to, even if, as it turned out, it would only be for a couple of weeks. It was good to see Mauripur and Karachi again, and to have some time to wander around the town now that I knew India rather better than when I had first arrived nine months before. Having 'got my knees brown' I was hardly pestered at all by the street children for *baksheesh*.

At the end of a fortnight those temporarily at Mauripur were flown down to Santa Cruz, the airfield just outside Bombay from which I had flown the sortie to take low-level photographs of North Salsette. From there we were whisked off to the local transit camp, RAF Worli, in Bombay, which provided temporary accommodation for those going to and from the UK by sea.

Here we were put through our final medical examination, which consisted mainly of lining us up in a row with our khaki shorts around our ankles to check whether any of us showed evidence of VD. I do not believe that anybody did. I still have my medical record card which has on it a bright red circular stamp RAF WORLI, FFI standing for 'Free From Infection', the infection in this context always referring to VD.

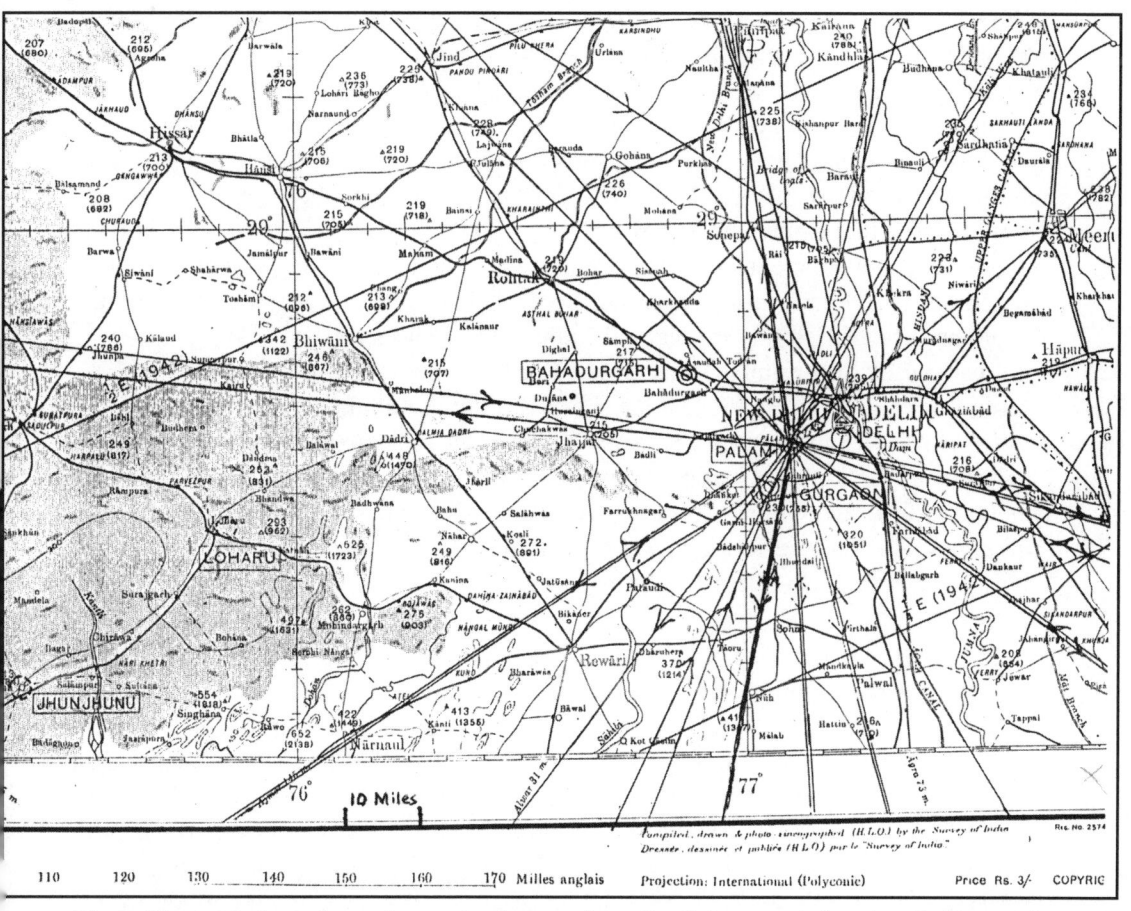

*Plate 67, A portion of my sixteen inches to the mile flying map showing Palam and Delhi. The straight arrowed lines are the local portions of the tracks which I drew for the flights to various parts of India. The line going horizontally to the left is that for the flight to Baluchistan and the next one downwards is for a sortie to Karachi and for the final flight to Drigh Road. The shaded area on the left is the Thar desert.*

I had with me a green tin trunk, an old ammunition box scrounged from somewhere, which was full of the various things accumulated since I had first arrived in India. It weighed about a hundredweight and I have never forgotten seeing it hefted up by a skinny, wiry Indian coolie and lifted on to his head apparently as easily as I would have lifted a full kitbag. I have always wondered how such a thin, weedy-looking individual, whose diet cannot have been all that good, managed it, but then one thing about India is that it is always full of surprises.

While I was at Worli, I anticipated my future feelings about India, and said to myself 'You will look back with nostalgia to your stay in India, but however strong the nostalgia may be, remember that it's a bloody awful place.' And how right I was. I have often since then been pulled by India, have wanted to go back and see it all again, although I have never returned. There is something about this kaleidoscope of a country which gets into you – I have seen it in other people who have been there. You forget the bad bits – the intolerable heat, dishonesty and inefficiency – and remember mainly the fascination, the variety, the seething life of the place.

I now wondered what it was specifically that made me make that statement to myself. After all, we in the RAF were to some extent isolated from much of the country and its ways. I think that much of it was the heat. You can make allowances for and avoid most of the unpleasant side of a region when living on an RAF Station, but one thing you cannot escape from is the heat; it is with you night and day, sometimes more, sometimes less. I arrived in the cool season and left in the hot season; I wonder if I would have felt differently if I had left India in the cool season.

I had parted from some good friends, as always when moving in the RAF – T.-E., Robbie, Johnny Rees, Jimmy James, Blackie, Johnnie Shukla. The first five would also shortly be leaving for the UK, while Johnnie Shukla, one of the best, would return to the Indian Air Force. It was only now, as always too late, that I realized that I really knew very little about him, except that he was married and had opted for the Christian religion – was it this, effectively a partial Anglicization, which put him on much the same wavelength as the British members of the Squadron and made him fit in with us so well?

Eventually along with a great mass of troops of all kinds we boarded the ex-cruise liner on which we were to return to the UK, the MV *Georgic*, launched in 1931 and This was a large troopship shuttling between India and the UK, now being used to carry back a large number of the British vacating the country. The date was 16 August 1947, two days after the Declaration of Independence at midnight on 14 August. Strangely, I recollect nothing of the celebrations that must have been going on in Bombay. Perhaps the four days that I was at Worli were so full of administrative processes such as the medical examination that there was no time to get outside the camp and see the sights.

It was exciting going on board this vast ship, since I had never been on anything larger than the ferries which crossed the North Sea, and it had then always been overnight. I was to be on board this liner for nearly three weeks. But, the Georgic was

*Plate 68, The stern deck of the MV Georgic.*

about as far in comfort from a cruise liner as you could get. Our sleeping quarters consisted of a large unpanelled metal-sided room with a low ceiling – it was too vast to be called a cabin, and might well originally have been part of the hold. We slept in hammocks slung two deep one above the other between vertical pillars, and although there was a moderate amount of space between the hammocks, there was nothing to sit on; there was insufficient space for such a luxury.

As usual in the Services, commissioned officers were accommodated separately from the rest and in more comfort. We were also on higher decks than they, and there was no mixing whatever. Towards the rear end of the upper deck we overlooked the Other Ranks on their deck at the stern where they were extremely crowded. With 6,000 troops on board it is not surprising if space was a bit limited; this was four times the number of passengers a cruise ship of that size would normally carry (she was built for 1,400 passengers). The photograph above which I have of the stern deck shows the overcrowding; but two people can be seen sitting in metal-framed deck chairs which they must have brought aboard – somebody obviously had initiative and foresight.

There was nothing for us to do on deck other than lounge around, leaning on the rail, or sitting on hatch coamings, talking or playing cards. Nevertheless, somehow we seemed to be content with the life. We travelled by way of the Red Sea, the Suez Canal, and the Mediterranean, and finally berthed at Liverpool.

The Red Sea was the hottest part of the journey, with the sun blazing down from a cloudless sky, although the slight breeze made by the motion of the ship did give some relief. There was no air conditioning, and the Red Sea would have been intolerable if we had had a following wind. We all started to get sunburnt, out on deck all day stripped to the waist. To some extent we had become inured to the sun in India, so it was not as bad it might have been, although in India we did tend to keep covered up.

The Suez Canal was fascinating. It has no locks, and so ships can go straight from the Red Sea to the Mediterranean without fuss. However, they do have to go in convoys, since the canal is not wide enough for two ships to pass in opposite directions and there is only a limited number of passing places. The Canal appeared as a straight line of water disappearing into the haze ahead and into the haze astern. On either side was desert as far as the eye could see. The cloudless blue sky provided a contrast to the yellow sand which bordered the canal. A railway ran along beside much of the length of it, punctuated occasionally by halts and small villages. Once we saw a lonely tent perched on the sand, and at one place there was a group of Egyptians who watched us from the path alongside; one of them lifted up his *jellaba*[3] and exposed himself with a roar of laughter, much to our amusement. 'Big buck!' we shouted at him.

At the northern end of the Canal we stopped at Port Said, but were not allowed ashore. Instead, the ship was surrounded by bumboatmen. These floating barrow-boys kept in their small boats all kinds of goods which they hoped to sell to passengers on any ship that stopped at Port Said. They would come up against the hull of the ship, and throw ropes up to the various decks. Then, with much shouting on both sides, bargaining would start. Somebody at the rail would ask to see something, perhaps a bit of Egyptian pottery, or simply some notepaper or a pen, and this would be sent up on one of the ropes to which a basket had been attached. The recipient would examine it and then haggle with the bumboatman below. If he wanted to keep it he would send down the money in the basket; if he did not the article would be sent back the same way by which it came. On both sides there was an unwritten law of honesty and mutual trust.

After leaving Port Said the weather grew cooler as we moved west through the Mediterranean. The few times that I have seen this sea it has always looked black when far from land – perhaps this is what was meant by Homer when he wrote of the 'wine-dark' sea. It was certainly looking black now, and the weather became quite stormy. The waves on either side seemed huge, and at one time I put them at about thirty feet from crest to trough. Eventually it calmed down again, and we passed through the Straits of Gibraltar without stopping. I was amazed at the formidable appearance of the Rock, with its massive cliffs and the great concrete slabs covering the eastern face to collect rainwater.

Shortly after this my faithful Leica gave trouble for the first time. The shutter jammed, probably as the end-result of excessive exposure to the heat of India; how lucky I was that it had not happened earlier. When I got to London, I took it to the UK

---

3 Ankle-length robe.

*Plate 69, going through the Suez Canal.*

branch of Leitz and asked them to mend it, which they did, giving it a further long lease of life. I have it still, battered but working after 40 years of use by various members of my family.

We sailed on through the Bay of Biscay, calm in spite of its bad reputation, and up through the Irish Sea to Liverpool. This was my first visit to that city and it was raining at the time, which, with the general drabness of the quay, did not exactly make me enthuse about the place. What did boost my morale was the sight of a real British policeman on the dockside, complete with traditional helmet. There had been police in India, but there was always the feeling that they were corrupt and inefficient, and did little to maintain the peace. So it was with delight that I gazed on this British one, to me a symbol of law and order; I felt that I was now back in a basically honest country.

I was a bit concerned about going through the customs, since I had bought two Weston Master II exposure meters remarkably cheaply in Karachi and assumed that, if declared, I would be charged duty on them, which would have cancelled their cheapness. They were fitted with long cords, so I slung these round my neck and let them dangle uncomfortably inside my clothes. I felt remarkably guilty as I said that I had nothing to declare, but my luggage was passed and I walked out of the customs shed a free man.

From Liverpool I was sent to RAF Burton Wood, a transit camp between Liverpool and Warrington for those returning from overseas. From there I went home for a welcome seven weeks' leave.

# 19

# Germany Again

*Between V-E day and the end of 1947, over four million service personnel (over 10% of the working age population) were returned to civilian life.*

When my leave came to an end I was sent back to Number 2 Squadron in Germany, which still had its Spitfire XIVs and XIXs. In my absence it had moved from Celle to Wunstorf, 50 miles to the south-west.

Looking up the details of the journey in my log book it now amazes me what a circuitous route I had to take before eventually arriving at Wunstorf, although wanderings of this sort were quite normal. From my home in Kent I went back to Burtonwood near Liverpool, and then on the same day all the way down to RAF St John's Wood in London where I spent the night. Next day I boarded the overnight ferry, m.v. *Parkeston*, at Harwich which took me to the Hook of Holland from where I went by train to Air Headquarters at Bückeburg in Germany. I stayed there for two days and then went to 84 Group Headquarters at Celle for another overnight stay, after which I eventually travelled to Wunstorf. Six days to get there, by way of four different RAF Stations and four changes of accommodation!

The RAF Station at Wunstorf was a pleasant place, rather similar to Celle; it was another permanent ex-Luftwaffe airfield but unlike Celle it had a concrete runway.[1] In addition to 2 Squadron and its Spitfires there was a squadron of Tempests. I never ceased to enjoy watching these aircraft coming in to land, simply because they looked too heavy to stay in the air.

Many of the original members of the Squadron were still there and shortly after I arrived I was glad to welcome my old friend T.-E. back from India. But sadly one or two colleagues from my earlier days had 'gone for a Burton' – been killed – during my absence (see Table 20 in the Appendix).

It seemed that the Squadron was no longer carrying out photo recce. At least, according to my log book I did nothing at all in that line over the three months that I was to remain in the Squadron before going back to civvy street. This was one of the developing faces of the peacetime Air Force. Flying now consisted solely of routine exercises of one sort or another: cross-country flights (Figure 17), height climbs (reaching 36,000 feet this time), and quite a lot of formation flying – all very tame after the long-distance sorties in India, but still enjoyable.

There were various duties on the ground at Wunstorf which we had to perform in addition to the flying. One of these was to act as Flying Control Officer, which I had

---

[1] It was here that large numbers of Dakota were based a year or two later for the celebrated Berlin Airlift, during which No 2 Squadron was dispersed to other airfields in Germany.

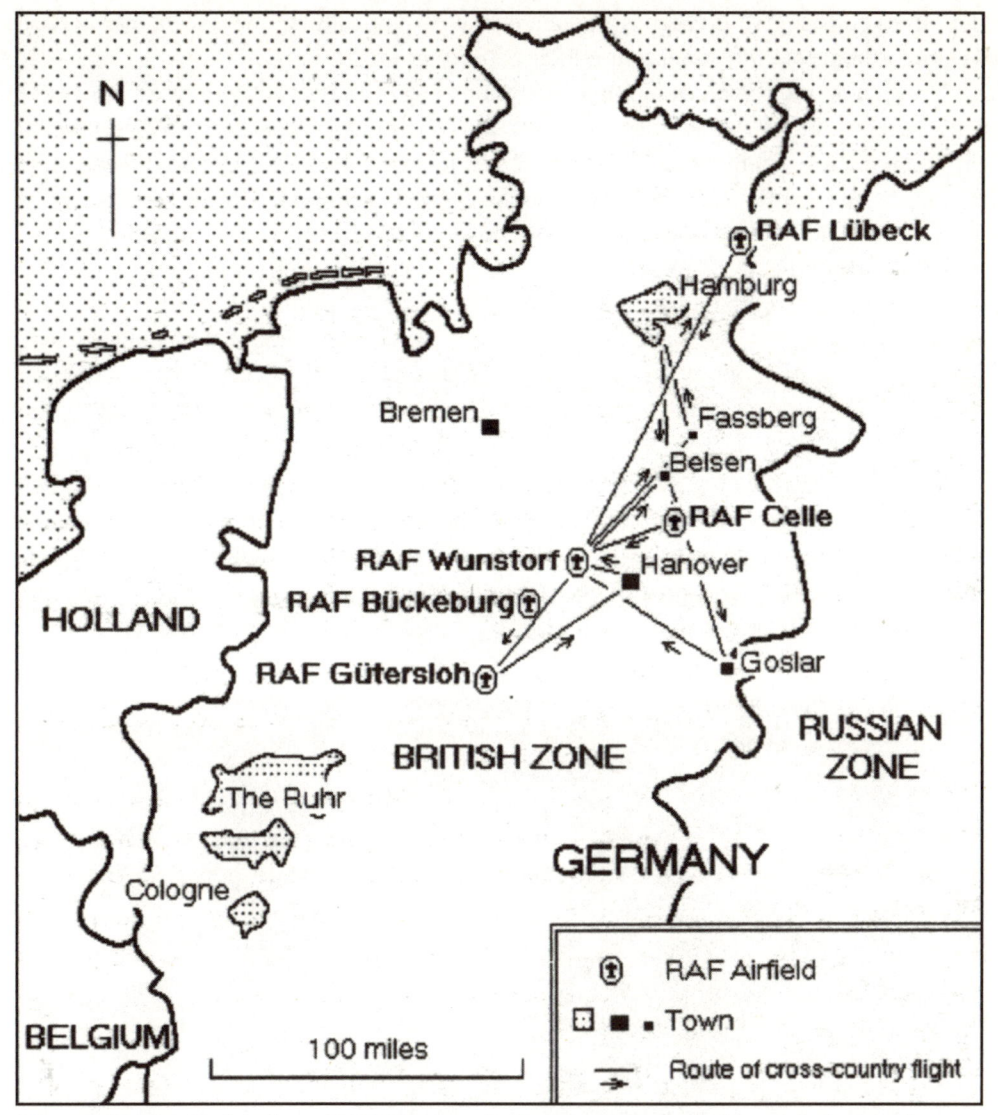

*Figure 17, the flights from RAF Wunstorf. Compare these flights with those of a year before, shown in Figure 3.*

never done before. It consisted of sitting, much of the time alone, in the upper floor of the Control Tower at weekends in case any aircraft decided to drop in (see Plate 70). None would be taking off from the Squadrons based at Wunstorf, since the place closed down on Saturday and Sunday, but somebody had to be around to keep a watch on the airfield.

The room in the Control Tower was rather barren, its walls mostly windows looking on to the airfield. It contained not much more than a communications radio, a microphone looking like a pre-war pillar telephone with the earpiece on a hook, and a loudspeaker for receiving messages from aircraft either in the circuit or on the ground. The duty itself consisted of giving visiting aircraft, what few of them there were, permission to land or take off, and supervising their activity in the circuit.

Nowadays one thinks of Control Towers as buzzing with activity, with a mass of radar screens, but there was none of this, just a radio and a few pieces of equipment for emergencies. There were so few aircraft in the air in those first years of peacetime that there were no flight corridors across the country, and control of the movement of aircraft, now that the war was over, was a purely local affair for each airfield.

With no flying at weekends, a corner of the airfield was often turned over to gliding. An official gliding club had been formed at Wunstorf by the time I arrived; it possessed two German gliders of the same types as those at the Gliding School at Salzgitter where I had learned gliding on my previous stay in Germany, an SG 38 and a Grunau. Gliding was something which I really enjoyed; it was so peaceful, and depended entirely on individual skill.

The gliding club was well-organized, and the turn-round of gliders was rapid. It had to be, since there were only two. The method of launching was the standard one of the time, with somebody operating a winch on the far side of the field to pull the gliders into the air by cable. As soon as a glider landed it was hauled into the take-off position again, somebody else got in, the cable was retrieved and off the glider went again.

*Plate 70. A weekend stint in the Control Tower at Wunstorf. Note the antiquated type of telephone for transmitting messages. A couple of aircraft (Tempests) can be seen parked on the tarmac.*

It is interesting to compare this with the inefficiency of British civilian gliding clubs which I have noticed since then, where most of the time the gliders commonly seem to sit around near the take-off point with nobody appearing to be interested in getting into the air. As a result, a member of a gliding club might get no more than one flight at a weekend. This has been confirmed by members of gliding clubs with whom I have discussed it. After leaving the RAF I had thought of joining a civilian gliding club, but after seeing one or two in action it just did not seem worth it. To show what can be achieved by good organization, I have laid out in the table below my own gliding flights at Salzgitter and at Wunstorf.

| Day | Number of flights | |
|---|---|---|
| | Salzgitter Gliding School | Wunstorf Gliding Club |
| 1 | 1 | 2 |
| 2 | 4 | 1 |
| 3 | 4 | 4 |
| 4 | 1 | 3 |
| 5 | 4 | 2 |
| 6 | 3 | 6 |
| 7 | - | 2 |

*Table 5, number of my glider flights on each flying day. The Wunstorf Club had only two gliders, an SG 38 and a Grunau.*

I never managed to stay in the air for long, which I like to I think was more due to lack of thermals than to incompetence. This was perhaps just as well at Wunstorf in view of the limited supply of gliders: my maximum at Salzgitter was just under seven minutes, while that at Wunstorf was just under five minutes, not a very prepossessing record.

I still loved flying Spitfires as much as ever, but towards the end of my time at Wunstorf I developed a peculiar apprehension before each Spitfire flight which I had never had before. This took the form of discomfort in the pit of my stomach together with diarrhoea. It was clearly a form of fear, but as soon as I was out on the tarmac and sitting in the cockpit it disappeared. In the past I had been apprehensive before such events as the first flight in a Spitfire, but that had never been more than a form of excitement, and had never taken this extreme form. The symptoms were nothing to do with flying as such, since after leaving the RAF I flew Austers with pleasure and without apprehension.

A possible though unlikely contribution to these peculiar symptoms may have been the sight of a couple of crash-landings at Wunstorf, although nobody was hurt, and I was never conscious that they had any effect on me. One of these was when a pilot in a Tempest from one of the other Squadrons who was unable to get one wheel down. After flying around for a while to use up surplus fuel he eventually came in as slowly as possible with the one effective wheel lowered, holding the wheel-less wing higher than the other. As he touched down and his speed dropped that wing gradually fell until it touched the ground, when there was a terrific noise of grinding metal as the wing-tip ground its way along the runway, the whole machine eventually slewing round. We had all been watching apprehensively from Dispersal and were glad to see none of the signs of disaster such as the aircraft pitching forward on to its nose or fire breaking out. The blood-waggon, or ambulance, rushed out together with various other vehicles, but it was not needed.

The other case was one of our own Spitfires in which the pilot could not get his undercarriage down at all. He was instructed by the commanding officer, who had by now gone to the tower to speak to him on the radio, to use up as much fuel as possible, and then to do a wheels-up landing on the grass beside the runway. Again we all stood outside, watching as he brought her in gently, getting as close to the grass as possible before closing the throttle and switching off the ignition to reduce the risk of fire. Beautifully judged, the Spitfire touched the ground with turf flying from the whirling propeller blade, and then drew rapidly to a halt, pitching slightly forward and bending the five propeller blades almost out of recognition before finally coming to rest at about 30° to the horizontal. A small but important point that I have never forgotten was that although the pilot would have tightened his straps as much as possible, his body still pitched forward violently, although he was unhurt.

Watching these crash-landings gave me direct experience of the violent forces brought into play under such circumstances. Had I seen them much earlier in my flying career they would have enabled to me to decide what to do in the event of engine failure in a Spitfire. The choices would be to land with the wheels up, to land with the wheels down or to bale out. Once I would have said that, given suitable terrain, it would be best to land with the wheels up (with wheels down and the ground at all rough the aircraft would most likely tip over on its back or the undercarriage would buckle, with disastrous results). Perhaps baling out might always have been the better bet.

It was at Wunstorf that the only occasion arose during my time in the RAF when I positively did not want to fly. One evening I found myself drinking rather an excess of rum, so much so that the next morning I felt terrible, with a severe headache and feeling thoroughly sick. I had to go to the Squadron Dispersal as routine, but when I got there I just went into the locker room where we kept our parachutes, climbed up on top of the lockers and lay down out of everybody's way. For the rest of the morning I neither knew nor cared what was happening around me. Luckily the morale and rapport within the squadron were so good that this was just accepted; nobody suggested that I fly and nobody hauled me over the coals for putting myself out of action. If it had been wartime things might have been different; I might have been up on a charge for getting myself into such a condition as to be unfit for duty. But at least it cured me of drinking rum for the next twenty years; during that time I couldn't stand the smell or taste of it!

*Plate 71. An evening on the bottle. I am the middle one.*

In off-duty hours I did not, as often at Celle, go into the local town; in fact all the time I was there I do not think that I ever once went to Wunstorf. Perhaps the habits of my colleagues had changed in the intervening months, since I have no memory of their going there either. Instead, I would occasionally go off for a walk on my own into the country which surrounded the airfield: a flat, monotonous moorland. Since it was not at all attractive, I wonder now why I did so. Probably because I always liked to get some idea of what the surroundings were like wherever I might be stationed.

It was now time to try and organise my future civilian life. As I have said, I decided in India that I wanted to do medicine, and the time had come to try and get a place in a medical school, aiming to start in the academic year beginning in late 1948. I had arrived at Wunstorf at the end of October 1947 and was due to be demobbed in February 1948, so there was not much time.

Those who had originally entered the Forces from school were at an advantage by generally being given a preference in further education over those now coming into it straight from school. My first choice, Cambridge University (chosen simply because my medical student cousin John had gone there) were just not interested, and I had to look elsewhere. My next choice was St Mary's Hospital Medical School, Paddington, in London, and here things looked better. I was asked to go for an interview, so back I went to London by train and boat early in December 1947.

I had an interview with the Dean, Dr Denis Brinton, and then joined several other candidates to write an essay on some aspect of current affairs, probably to see whether we could write English. And that was that; then back to Wunstorf to carry on with Squadron life. About two weeks later I received a letter from the Dr Brinton to say that I had been accepted as a student for the beginning of the 1st MB BS Course (commonly known as 1st MB) in October 1948. My immediate future was now settled.

Eventually it was time for me to be demobbed. I see from my log book that on the very day before I left the Squadron I flew twice on formation practice. This must have been a sympathetic Flight Commander allowing me a last fling before leaving squadron life for ever. That was on 10 February 1948. I left Wunstorf the next day, travelling by train to the Hook of Holland, by ferry to Harwich, and then by train to the demob centre at Burtonwood near Liverpool. I was demobbed on the 12 February – remarkably quick by Service standards. At Burtonwood I was offered a rather limited choice of (free) civilian clothes and chose a grey-blue pinstripe. The material was the same rather coarse material as standard battledress: mutton dressed up as lamb. But I was now a civilian again after nearly three and a half years in the Air Force.

I was sad to leave the Squadron, a cheerful and friendly collection of people, sad to leave the flying that I loved, and sad to leave the Spitfires. Even now, after all these years, when I see that rare sight, a reconditioned Spitfire either in the air or on the ground, a sense of yearning comes over me, and in my imagination I am once again in the cockpit, with my right hand on the stick, my left on the throttle lever, my feet on the rudder pedals and the instrument panel in front of me.

I took with me some of my flying equipment: a pair of wool-lined flying boots, a pair of dark glasses and my flying goggles, but not, surprisingly, my flying helmet. These had all originally been signed for in orthodox Service fashion, and now had to be returned or else paid for. I also kept my much-valued modified RAF Computer with compass bearing ring. And of course I kept my flying log book which, although officially the property of the Air Ministry, we were all allowed to keep without charge. The flying boots turned out to be useless in civilian life, but all the rest I still have, along with my Indian flying maps: a few precious mementos of an unusual period in my life.

Looking back on it all I was extremely lucky. I had not only learned to fly, but had flown much of the time in that paragon of aircraft, the Spitfire. I had seen Germany, and had spent several months in India doing something which was really worthwhile as well as enjoyable, and at the same time experiencing life in a remarkable country. And it was all mostly after the war had ended, so that there was no risk of getting killed by the enemy. Flying is a dangerous business, and I could easily have followed in the steps of some of my colleagues who had suffered from 'finger trouble' (see Glossary) and killed themselves (see Table 20 in the Appendix), since I was by no means immune from this fault myself, as the reader will by now be aware.

We never thought of flying as something which might kill us, although we were always taking precautions, such as being on the lookout in India for secondary landing strips in case of engine failure. It was probably the same dictum which says that it always happens to the other person, and that if you're careful you'll be all right. But according to Max Hastings in his book *Bomber Command* the losses in the war during flying training alone were appalling: '5,327 officers and men were killed and a further 3,113 injured in RAF training accidents 1939-45'. I suspect that this was mostly in training on multi-engined aircraft with a crew of several persons aboard, which would multiply the deaths in a single accident. In contrast, there were no serious accidents to any of my colleagues during our training days; it was only when they got on to fighters that anybody was killed.

Part of this belief in survival probably resulted from the enjoyment of flying. I do not think that I met anybody who flew who didn't enjoy it. There is something about just being in the air which gets into your blood.

It may be of interest to anyone who flies aeroplanes to see my flying record of those days (Tables 9-11 in the Appendix). It is analyzed in several ways: in terms of aircraft, in terms of flights per week or day, and in terms of flying hours, so that comparisons can be made from any aspect. There are also in the Appendix details of performance, etc., of certain of the Spitfires I flew (Tables 13-19) for comparison with present-day aircraft.

After all that, did I continue to fly when I had got into civvy street? Yes, for a brief while. Even before I left the RAF I had obtained a civilian pilot's flying licence or 'Certificate of competency and Licence to fly Private Flying Machines', as it is officially called, since I intended to keep on flying, expensive thought it might be. To obtain and keep a licence you had to pass a yearly medical examination and to have flown solo for at least three hours each year, which was just about the limit that I felt I could afford. My licence was first dated 5 February 1948 (a few days before I was demobbed) and this qualified me to fly 'All types of landplanes'. I didn't need a flying test, simply a medical check.

To qualify for my second year's licence I only needed to do about one hour's flying since between the original date of the licence and leaving Wunstorf I had already flown 2½ hours of the three required. I flew that hour from Lympne in Kent in an Auster, taking my brother Roger as passenger.

By the time that the licence again needed renewing for a third year I had decided that, as a penurious married medical student (which I had now become) I really couldn't afford it. In that second year I made only a single one-hour flight, this time from Rochester airfield, taking Marion, my fiancée as she was at the time, as passenger. That was the last time I flew as a pilot, and my licence lapsed. But flying is an addiction, and like all addictions it took some time to get it out of my system – in my case about two years.

It was at about this time that I received a breath of fresh air in the form of a letter from one of the friends I had known at Wunstorf. It gives a flavour of the RAF of that time and so I end this tale with it as a fitting finale to my years in the RAF (see next page). The Jerry Fray mentioned was the ex-Commanding Officer of 34 Squadron in India.

Letter from Wunstorf:

Saturday 18th [September 1948] Gütersloh

Hi there Major,

Well, well, Doc, how's this very cheery world treating you?

I really must apologise for the delay in answering your very excellent note (plus photos). Twas indeed good to hear from you.

I distributed your snaps, and amidst many cries of thanks one low groan was heard: That of Woodhouse – who said 'B... [sic] awful' – needless to say we all said it was very lifelike.

Thinking along, I reckon the odd spot of abbreviated news would be the best for you:

So – The Sqdn has suffered many moves indeed since this jolly 'Airlift' [the Berlin Airlift] commenced. We went to Wahn, then Uterson, and now Gütersloh. Half the Sqdn has been posted to Berlin for Air Traffic Duties (for as long as the Air Lift continues) and T. E. [Derek Turner-Ettlinger] has been posted to Central Flying School for an Instructors' Course – We don't know whether he was keen or not – but we think the influence of a certain female in Hanover has taken some of the keenness.

We still have the odd session in our rooms, and follow with a shooting match down the corridor – Alas – I'm sure someone is going to get clobbered someday.

Your course starts in October, eh? Mm! Bags of work now.

We have heard that Ian McCrae is really getting married – Heaven help the poor wench!

Needless to say the subject of the Sqdn's talk hasn't altered and grog and women are right up there.

I have enclosed a couple of gash photographs. They may help your stock of the 'boys'.

Needless to say I was slightly 'under the weather' when I took the one of Deryk. One small excuse – the train was moving at a fairish lick.

Well, Ken, I must away – the characters send their regards and if there is a sess [drinking session] organised in town we shall definitely get in touch with you.

We are all pressing out to Bad Salzuflen tonight. – Women beware! The '2nd' Pursuit is on the sess-path.

Cheers Ken.

Alka Selzter.

Joskin.

P.S. Allen-Rowlandson's today a proud father, and Jerry Fray too!

# Postscript

Kenneth Neame finished medical school during which he married Marion and had a son, Peter. He and his family moved to Sheffield where he earned a PhD, working on transport of amino acids (the building blocks of proteins) into various tissues and had two further children, Jillian and Julia.

The family then moved to New Zealand, largely paid for as part of a recruitment package and recapitulating, in reverse, part of his trip back from India. This time, however, it was not a troop ship but First Class accommodation on the SS *Orsova*. He continued his research in New Zealand (Dunedin) and then, after two and a half years, moved back to the UK and a post at the University of Liverpool. The attention to detail and analytical thinking which kept him alive in India served him well in research. His research resulted in many publications, a book on membrane transport in cells and a book on the techniques for measuring radioactivity (scinitillation counting) in biological experiments.

In his later research career, he looked at changes in the behaviour of blood cells that have been infected by malaria and also sought explanations for why some drugs work differently in different variants of malaria. He retired in 1981.

# Appendices

## Dates of Major Postings

| Location | Dates |
|---|---|
| **As a civilian** | |
| *Pre-flying* <br> Durham University Air Squadron | April - September 1944 |
| **As an Aircraftman Second Class/Cadet** | |
| 7 ACRC, Torquay | October - December 1944 |
| ACOS, Hereford | January - March 1945 |
| *Flying training* <br> 11 EFTS, Perth | March - June 1945 |
| *Official end of the war in Europe, 8th May 1945* | |
| 19 FTS, Cranwell | June - December 1945 |
| *Official end of the war in the Far East, 12th September 1945* | |
| **As a Commissioned Officer** | |
| 8 OTU (16 SPR), Benson | March - May 1946 |
| *Squadrons* <br> 2 Squadron, Celle, Germany <br> 34 Squadron, Palam, India <br> 2 Squadron, Wunstorf, Germany | June - October 1946 <br> December 1946 - July 1947 <br> October 1947 - February 1948 |

*Table 6. My major postings.*

## My medical records

| Medical categories | 1943 | A1B (N.V.O.), A8B (Turret N.V.O.), A8B (Vision) (1943) |
|---|---|---|
|  | 1946 | Fit OS |
| Night visual capacity | 1944 | 25 |
| Blood group | 1944 | 40 |
| Immunizations:<br>    Vaccination (smallpox)<br>    TABC (typhoid)<br>    ATT (tetanus)<br>    Typhus<br>    Yellow fever |  | 1944, 1946, 1947<br>1944 x 2, 1946, 1947<br>1944 x 3, 1946, 1947<br>1946 x 2<br>1946 |

Table 7. *My medical records; taken from the results of the initial Medical Board (Form 58) and from my Paybook (Form 64). Across the entries page in the Paybook is a large red circular stamp with the legend RAF WORLI FFI (see page 207). There is also an interesting statement in the Paybook about an allowance for treatment by a Civilian Medical Practitioner when on leave; the allowance for a visit to the Surgery was 3s.0d., or 4s.6d. if more than two miles away, equivalent to 15p and 22½p respectively.*

## Sizes of units to which I was attached

| Location | Number of personnel | |
|---|---|---|
| | Cadets/pilots | Supporting staff/groundcrew |
| Durham University Air Squadron | 60 | 1 Wing Commander<br>4 Flight Lieutenants<br>4 Warrant Officers<br>1 Sergeant<br>2 Corporals |
| 7 ACRC, Torquay | 42 (Squadron)<br>8 (Flight) | 1 Wing Commander<br>1 Flying Officer<br>1 Corporal |
| ACOS, Hereford | 45 | No information |
| 11 EFTS, Perth | No information | No information |
| 19 FTS, Cranwell | 42[1] | No information |
| 8 OTU (16 SPR), Benson | 3 | No information |
| 2 Squadron, Celle and Wunstorf | No information | No information |
| 34 Squadron, Palam | 7[2] | 1 Engineer Officer<br>1 Warrant Officer<br>1 Flight Sergeant<br>5 Sergeants<br>2 Corporals<br>46 AC2s |

*Table 8. Details of personnel of various groups.*

---

1 Numbers of Cadets who obtained their Wings and were commissioned. No information available on number who started the course.
2 Variable from time to time.

**My flying record (extracted from my Pilot's Flying Log Book)**
**Analysis of flights during training**

| Aircraft | Solo | | Dual | |
|---|---|---|---|---|
| | Flying time hr.min | Number of flights | Flying time hr.min | Number of flights |
| *Elementary Flying Training School, RAF Perth* | | | | |
| Tiger Moth | 32.00 | 45 | 40.05 | 61 |
| *Advanced Flying Training School, RAF Cranwell* | | | | |
| Harvard II | 54.05 | 57 | 76.55 | 76 |
| Tiger Moth | - | - | 0.50 | 1 |
| Subtotal | 86.05 | 106 | 117.50 | 137 |
| *Operational Training Unit, RAF Benson* | | | | |
| Master II | - | - | 2.40 | 4 |
| Spitfire VII | 4.45 | 4 | - | - |
| Spitfire IX | 1.00 | 2 | - | - |
| Spitfire XI | 23.50 | 10 | - | - |
| Grand total | 115.40 | 122 | 120.30 | 141 |

*Table 9. Flying time and number of flights in various aircraft during training. Time to first solo: Tiger Moth, 9 hours 5 minutes; Harvard, 9 hours.*

## Flying record in terms of flights

| Location | Number of flights ||||| Duration of flights ||
|---|---|---|---|---|---|---|---|
| | Total | Average per week | Maximum in one week | Average per flying day | Maximum in one day | Average hr.min | Maximum hr.min |
| 11 EFTS, Perth | 106 | 8.5 | 15 | 2.3 | 5 | 0.40 | 1.40 |
| 19 FTS, Cranwell | 133 | 6.0 | 10 | 1.7 | 4 | 1.00 | 2.00 |
| 8 OTU, Benson | 20 | 1.8 | 5 | 1.2 | 2 | 1.37 | 3.30 |
| 2 Sqdn, Celle | 35 | 2.4 | 7 | 1.4 | 3 | 1.33 | 3.00 |
| 34 Sqdn, Palam | 68 | 2.5 | 7 | 1.3 | 3 | 1.56 | 3.50 |
| 2 Sqdn, Wunstorf | 17 | 1.1 | 3 | 1.1 | 2 | 1.07 | 2.00 |

*Table 10. Frequency and duration of flights. Actual time on duty was used for the calculations. The term 'flying day' refers to days when flying was 'on', and omits days when the weather, particularly in the UK, was unsuitable for flying. Flights as passenger are omitted.*

## Flying record in terms of aircraft

| Aircraft | Solo[1] | | Dual[2] | | Passenger | |
|---|---|---|---|---|---|---|
| | Flying time, hours | Number of flights | Flying time, hours | Number of flights | Flying time, hours | Number of flights |
| **Training aircraft** | | | | | | |
| Tiger Moth | 32 | 45 | 41 | 61 | - | - |
| Harvard II | 58 | 59 | 78 | 77 | - | - |
| Master II | - | - | 3 | 4 | - | - |
| **Operational aircraft** [3] | | | | | | |
| Spitfire VII | 5 | 4 | - | - | - | - |
| Spitfire IX | 2 | 2 | - | - | - | - |
| Spitfire XI | 27 | 12 | - | - | - | - |
| Spitfire XIV | 24 | 18 | - | - | - | - |
| Spitfire XIX | 177 | 94 | - | - | - | - |
| **Gliders** | | | | | | |
| SG 38 | <1 | - | - | - | - | - |
| Grunau | 1 | - | - | - | - | - |
| **Communications aircraft** | | | | | | |
| Auster | 2 | 3 | - | - | 7 | 7 |
| Anson | - | - | - | - | 4 | 4 |
| Dakota | - | - | - | - | 17 | 6 |
| York | - | - | - | - | 24 | 4 |

Table 11. *The number of flights and the total flying time in various aircraft. Times have been rounded to the nearest hour. First solo in Tiger Moth was after 9 hours 5 minutes, and in Harvard was after 9 minutes; the dual flying in a Master before being let loose in a Spitfire was 1 hour 40 minutes.*

---

1 Includes piloting of aircraft with passenger.
2 Under instruction in aircraft wiht dual control.
2 Spitfires VII, IX and XIV were fighter versions, XI and XIX photo reconnaissance versions.

## General details of aircraft in which I flew

| Aircraft (in order of wing-span) | Maker | Engine | Wing-span feet inches | | Length feet inches | |
|---|---|---|---|---|---|---|
| York | Avro | Merlin | 102 | 0 | 78 | 6 |
| Dakota | Douglas | Wasp | 95 | 0 | 64 | 5 |
| Anson | Avro | Wasp | 56 | 6 | 42 | 3 |
| Oxford | Airspeed | Cheetah | 53 | 4 | 34 | 6 |
| Hotspur (glider) | General Aircraft | - | 45 | 11 | 39 | 9 |
| Grunau (glider) | (German) | - | 44 | 6[1] | - | |
| Harvard II | North American | Wasp | 42 | 0 | 28 | 0 |
| Spitfire VII | Supermarine | Merlin | 40 | 2 | - | |
| Spitfire IX | Supermarine | Merlin | 36 | 10 | 31 | 6 |
| Spitfire XI | Supermarine | Merlin | 36 | 10 | - | |
| Spitfire XIX | Supermarine | Griffon | 36 | 10 | - | |
| Auster IV | Taylorcraft | Lycoming | 36 | 0 | - | |
| Master II | Miles | Mercury | 35 | 8 | 30 | 2 |
| Spitfire XIV (clipped wing) | Supermarine | Griffon | 32 | 7 | - | |
| Tiger Moth | De Havilland | Gipsy Major | 29 | 4 | - | |
| SG 38 (glider) | - | - | - | | - | |

*Table 12. Technical details of aircraft mentioned in the text. From 'The Aircraft Recognition Manual' by C. H. Gibbs-Smith, and from 'Origin of Species - I' in 'The Aeroplane' by J. Smith.*

---

1 Dimensions uncertain.

## Technical data of Spitfires

From *Pilot's Notes for Spitfire XIV and XIX*, from *Spitfire* by J. Quill, and, where stated, from my own records.

*Pilot's Notes* states, 'The Spitfire PR Mk XIX is basically an F. Mk XIV aircraft [with standard wings] and differs from it only in the fuel system. Later aircraft are fitted with a pressure cabin [which was no longer effective by the time I was flying them]'.

### Normal maximum weight
For take-off, landing and all forms of flying: 8,600 pounds

### Engine

| Mark | Engine | Horse-power | Propeller blades |
|------|--------|-------------|------------------|
| VII  | Merlin 64 | 1710 | 4 |
| IX   | Merlin 70 | 1475 | 4 |
| XI   | Merlin 61 | 1565 | 4 |
| XIV  | Griffon 65 or 66 | 2035 | 5 |
| XIX  | Griffon 65 or 66 | 2035 | 5 |

*Table 13. The engines of the various Spitfires which I flew. The two types of engine rotated in opposite directions, producing a marked difference in torque on take-off. The power of the Griffon engine is illustrated by a remark in 'Pilot's Notes for Spitfire XIV and XIX': 'Whenever possible open the throttle slowly up to +7 lb./sq. in. boost only. This is important as there is a strong tendency to swing to the right and to crab in the initial stages of the take-off run. If much power is used tyre wear is severe.'*

## Fuel capacity (100 octane petrol)

| Tank | Gallons | |
|---|---|---|
| | Spitfire XIV | Spitfire XIX |
| Main tanks | | |
| Upper | 36 | 36 |
| Lower | 49 | 49 |
| Wing tanks | | |
| Port | 13 | 66 |
| Starboard | 13 | 66 |
| Total | 111 | 217 |
| Drop tanks (options) | 30 | |
| | 45 | |
| | 50 | |
| | 90 | |

*Table 14. Fuel capacities of Spitfires XIV and XIX. A discardable drop tank could be attached beneath the fuselage; it reduced longitudinal and directional stability.*

## Rate of fuel consumption

| Operating conditions | Approximate gallons per hour |
|---|---|
| At 5,000 feet: | |
| Weak mixture, low gear | 60 |
| Rich mixture, low gear | 130 |
| At 20,000 feet: | |
| Weak mixture, high gear | 70 |

*Table 15. Fuel consumption of Spitfires XIV and XIX. Gear refers to the setting of the two-speed two-stage supercharger.*

## Range

| Operating conditions | Air miles | |
|---|---|---|
| | Without drop tank | With 90-gallon drop tank |
| Climb, say 23 gallons fuel | 30 | 30 |
| Subsequent cruise | 890 | 1,350 |
| Total disance, say | 920 | 1,380 |

*Table 16. Estimate of range of unpressurized Spitfire XIX, allowing for a reserve of 20 gallons fuel. Calculated for 20,000 feet, 2,000 rpm, at 200 mph. Indicated Airspeed; this would give a petrol consumption of 5.1 miles per gallon in level flight.*

## Flying speeds

The Airspeed Indicator of the Spitfires XIV and XIX was calibrated in mph.

| Flying trim | Indicated airspeed | |
|---|---|---|
| | m.p.h. | knots |
| Climbing | 180 | 155 |
| Cruising, for maximum range | 200-210 | 175-185 |
| Maximum permitted speed<br>  Diving<br>  Undercarriage/flaps down | <br>470<br>160 | <br>410<br>140 |
| Approach speed for landing, flaps down<br>  Engine-assisted<br>  Glide | <br>100<br>110 | <br>87<br>96 |
| Stalling speed, with engine off<br>  Flaps up<br>  Flaps down | <br>85<br>75 | <br>74<br>65 |

*Table 17. Flying speeds of Spitfires XIV and XIX. The conversion between knots and miles are approximate. See table 18 for some relationships between Indicated and True Airspeed.*

## Flying speeds (continued)

| Altitude, feet | Indicated airspeed | | True airspeed | |
|---|---|---|---|---|
| | m.p.h. | knots | m.p.h. | knots |
| 1,000 | 200 | 175 | 205 | 180 |
| 10,000 | 200 | 175 | 240 | 210 |
| 20,000 | 200 | 175 | 280 | 240 |
| 30,000 | 200 | 175 | 340 | 295 |

*Table 18. Relationships between Indicated Airspeed and True Airspeed. Conversions have been made by means of the RAF Navigational Computer Mark IIID, assuming a temperature at 1,000 feet of 70°F and a lapse rate of 1°F for every 300 feet. Other speeds at these altitudes would be in the same proportions.*

## Spitfire XIX - data for some single flights from my own records

| | Range of values | Average value |
|---|---|---|
| Flight times | 1 hr 20 min - 3 hr 45 min | 2 hr 11 min |
| Flight distances | 360 - 800 miles | 560 miles |
| Groundspeed | 210 - 340 mph/180 - 295 knots | 260 mph/225 knots |

*Table 19. Data from my own flights. Values are derived from flight times recorded in my Flying Log Book for seventeen long-distance non-stop flights in India at various altitudes. Flight times and groundspeed are from take-off to landing; variations in groundspeed partly reflect differences in wind velocity. Airspeed was usually that which gave maximum range.*

## Fatal flying accidents

This Table lists fatal accidents of colleagues; all occurred after the end of the war some time between 1946 and 1948. I witnessed none of them; the only major accidents which I saw were two controlled crash landings at Wunstorf in which nobody was hurt (see page 215). It is interesting that out of the ten deaths, seven were caused by what we would have called 'finger trouble' (see Glossary), but now called 'pilot error'.

| Aircraft | Location | Accident |
|---|---|---|
| *Technical fault* | | |
| Spitfire XI | UK | Oxygen iced up at high altitude |
| Spitfire XIX | Palam, India | Oxygen iced up at high altitude |
| Tempest II | Berlin, Germany | Oil cut; pilot killed on forced landing |
| *'Finger trouble'* | | |
| Spitfire XIV | Celle, Germany | Mid-air collision doing 'turnabout' manoeuvre in formation |
| Spitfire XIX | Celle, Germany | Mid-air collision doing 'turnabout' manoeuvre in formation |
| Spitfire XVI | UK | Spun in on landing |
| Spitfire XIX | Palam, India | Hit building after abandoning landing |
| Tempest II | Agra, India | Dived into ground when flying at night |
| Tempest V | Lübeck, Germany | Dived into sea during air-ground firing practice |
| Mosquito | UK | Stalled in cloud (crew of two) |

*Table 20. Fatal flying accidents of colleagues whom I knew during my time in the RAF.*

# Glossary

For general RAF slang, see *A Dictionary of RAF Slang* by Eric Partridge

## Air Force and General Vocabulary

| | |
|---|---|
| AC1, AC2 | Aircraftman First Class, Aircraftman Second Class, the lowest ranks in the RAF. |
| ACOS | Aircrew Officers' School at RAF Credenhill just outside Hereford. The School provided courses for bringing some discipline and efficiency back into the lives of aircrew. |
| ACRC | Aircrew Receiving Centre; the starting point for aircrew, where candidates were tested for flying aptitude and their prospects as aircrew assessed. |
| AFC | Airfield controller (*q.v.*) |
| Airfield controller | A person attached to Flying Control who occupied a hut at the end of the runway. He was the final arbiter for permission to land or take off and gave his instructions in the form of a red or green Aldis Lamp or Very Light. |
| Airman | A rather loose term, usually referring to AC1 and AC2 (see above). It did not usually relate to flying personnel, who were referred to more specifically as aircrew, etc. |
| Airspeed | Speed in relation to the air mass through which an aircraft is moving. See also Indicated airspeed and True airspeed. |
| Air Training Corps | A youth corps aiming to give young people the fundamentals of flying and of Service discipline. |
| Aldis lamp | A bright lamp by which a green (= OK) or a red (= not OK) light was flashed to an aircraft in the air or on the ground. It was also, particularly in the Navy, used for sending Morse Code. |
| ATC | Air Training Corps (*q.v.*) |
| Auster | The Taylorcraft Auster was a small communications aircraft for low-level reconnaissance or for ferrying one or two passengers. It handled rather less well than the Tiger Moth. It had a single high wing and an enclosed cockpit where pilot and passenger sat side by side, but did not have dual control. |
| **B**AFO | British Air Force of Occupation (*q.v.*) |
| BAOR | British Army on the Rhine (*q.v.*) |
| Bevin Boys | One out of ten National Service conscripts during the later part of the Second World War were drafted to the coal mines. These conscripts were referred to as Bevin Boys and were named after Ernest Bevin, the politician who originated the scheme (see *The People's War* by A. Calder). |

| | |
|---|---|
| Blister hangar | A simple form of hangar consisting of little more than a curved roof reaching to the ground on either side. |
| Blood waggon | Ambulance. |
| BOAC | British Overseas Airways Corporation. |
| Bowser | See 'Petrol bowser'. |
| Bradshaw | A slang word derived from the railway timetable book of that name. It was used disparagingly of pilots who navigated by following the course of linear landmarks such as roads and railways instead of flying in a straight line. In the case of the flight to RAF Samungli (Chapter 15) bradshawing was accepted as the only sure way of getting to the airfield on the final leg of the flight in view of the absence of other identifiable landmarks. |
| British Air Force of Occupation | The RAF contribution to BAOR (British Army on the Rhine), the British Army of Occupation in Germany after the end of the Second World War. |
| British Army on the Rhine | The British Army of Occupation in Germany after the end of the Second World War. |
| Bull | Short for bullshit (*q.v.*) |
| Bullshit | Excessive spit and polish, attention to detail, or formality; commonly shortened to bull or bulsh. |
| Burton | See *Gone for a Burton*. |
| Camera | The photographic reconnaissance cameras in a PR Spitfire were either two cameras for vertical photographs containing enough film for 500 exposures or one camera for oblique photographs containing film for 100 exposures (see Chapter 5 for more details). See also *Oblique camera* and *Vertical Camera*. |
| Circuit | The anticlockwise route arounbd an airfield at an altitude of 1,000 feet above it, taken by aircraft preparing to land. |
| Circuits and bumps | Practice repetitions of taking off, joining the airfield circuit, and landing. |
| Civvies | Civilian clothes. |
| Clamp, clamped down | Clamp meant weather that was so bad or unsuitable for flying, particularly rain, low cloud or mist. Clamped down meant that the weather had deteriorated to this condition. |
| Clot | Idiot, fool; a term of disparagement |
| Clottishness | The property of being a clot |
| CO | Commanding Officer |
| Compass | See *gyro compass* and *magnetic compass* |
| Course | The direction taken in the air, usually as a compass bearing (c.f. *track*). Also a scheme of instruction. |
| Crate | See *kite*. |
| Cwt | The standard abbreviation for hundred weight (*q.v.*) |

## GLOSSARY

| | |
|---|---|
| **D**aily inspection | A minor inspection of aircraft carried out as a daily routine; more usually referred to by the initals DI. |
| Dakota | The Douglas Dakota was an American medium-sized twin-engine transport aircraft widely used by various Air Forces and was a reliable workhorse. The civil version was the DC3. |
| Dead reckoning | The theoretical calculation of the position of an aircraft deduced from the course followed by compass after allowance has been made for the expected speed and direction of the wind and of the speed of the aircraft through the air. |
| Deck | Ground; flying on the deck = flying very low. 'Deck level' could also mean a thousand feet or more when the general context is in tens of thousands of feet. |
| Deviation | See *magnetic deviation*. |
| DI | Daily Inspection (*q.v.*) |
| Dispersal | The region on the airfield where aircraft were finally made ready for the pilots. |
| Dope | A varnish used for tautening and making airtight the wings and tailplane of fabric-covered aeroplanes and the envelopes of airships. It has an aromatic smell rather like that of nail varnish, and was the predominant smell in hangars which housed fabric-covered aircraft like the Tiger Moth. |
| DR | Dead reckoning (*q.v.*) |
| Drop tank | An extra fuel tank fitted below the fuselage which could be jettisoned in flight, hence the name. Those for Spitfires could be of 30, 45, 50 or 90 gallon capacity. |
| **E**FTS | Elementary Flying Training School (*q.v.*) |
| Elementary Flying Training School | The school at which the first stage in flying was taught, using (in those days) the Tiger Moth as trainer. It was more usually known by its initials *EFTS*. |
| Estimated Time of Arrival | The expected time of arrival at one's destination as calculated from various navigational data. |
| ETA | Estimated Time of Arrival (*q.v.*) |
| **F**FI | Free from infection; this abbreviation always referred to veneral disease. |
| Finger trouble | Carelessness, inefficiency, pilot error; also associated with the phrase 'Get your finger out!', meaning 'Snap to it!', 'Wake up!' etc. (see *The Life and Times of Pilot Officer Prune* by T. Hamilton). |
| Flight | A small unit of aircraft (say, three or more) or of personnel (say, half a dozen or so persons). |
| Flight path | See *track*. |
| Flying Training School | As the abbreviation *FTS*, this name referred to the school in which the second stage of flying training was taught, in which the Miles Master (a British aircraft) or the North American Harvard were used as training aircraft. Thosw who graduated at this level were presented with their Wings. |

| | |
|---|---|
| Foot, feet | 1 foot = 0.3048 metre. |
| Formate | Get into formation. *Formate on*: position oneself behind and/or to one side of a leading aircraft. |
| FTS | (Advanced) Flying Training School (*q.v.*) |
| G | The technical abbreviation for the force of gravity on the body. A person standing on the ground experiences 1 *g*. A pilot pulling out of a dive is pressed towards the floor of the cockpit and experiences more than 1 *g*; if he were doing the same manoeuvre upside down then *g* would be negative. If sitting upright he may black out if *g* increases to more than, say, 5 or 6. |
| Gone for a Burton | A euphemism for being killed; literally 'gone for a glass of beer, or Burton' thus accounting for a person's absence. |
| Gong | A medal. Even I eventually had one gong to my name, pointless thought it was: the 1939-45 Star which was given automatically to anyone with 28 days full-time service in the Second World War. I later mislaid it. |
| Gremlin | A mischievous sprite, held by the RAF to be responsible for all mishaps. |
| Griffon | The name of the Rolls Royce engine fitted to most of the higher marks of Spitfire. There were numerous versions, those fitted to the Spitfire XIX being of 2035 horse power. The torque was opposite to that of the Merlin engine. |
| Groundcrew | The personnel involved with servicing aircraft. |
| Groundspeed | Speed in relation of the ground, c.f. *Airspeed*. |
| Grunau | A German high-performance sailplane of the pre-war and wartime years. |
| Gyro compass | A compass which was essentially a gyroscope, maintaining a constant orientation in space regardless of the position of the aircraft. It had no directional property of its own and no connection of any kind with the magnetic compass, but had to be set manually from the reading of the latter. It appeared in the instrument panel as a broad slit through which numbered vertical lines, representing the heading, were visible. Unlike the magnetic compass the gyro compass did not oscillate and its response to change in direction was immediate; it was the compass used routinely for holding a steady heading. However, it suffered from precession, or progressive error, caused partly by the friciton in its pivots and partly by the rotation of the earth; this error appeared as a slow and increasing inaccuracy in its reading and the rate varied from instrument to instrument. It therefore had to be checked frequently against the magnetic compass. In some cases the precession was intolerably fast and the gyro compass then had to be replaced. |
| **H**arvard | The North American Harvard was one of the main single-engined advanced trainers in the Second World War. It was all-metal, had an enclosed cockpit, intercom and retractable undercarriage. Instructor and pupil sat one behind the other. |
| Heading | Compass direction towards which an aircraft is pointed. |

## GLOSSARY

| | |
|---|---|
| High hop | One of the stages in learning to fly a glider without dual control. The glider was pulled by a winch sufficiently fast for the pilot to rise quite high into the air; after releasing the towing cable, he glided to a landing straight ahead. |
| Homer | The Homer was a ground-based direction-finding radio station usually somewhere on an airfield. It was designed to lead pilots directly to the airfield from up to 100 miles away. It was particularly useful in bad weather or in emergencies, as I had good reason to be thankful for. There was a risk of an aircraft's being given a reciprocal course to steer by mistake, which meant that the aircraft would then fly directly away from the airfield for which it was aiming instead of towards it. This was unlikely with experienced radio operators, but it was always a possibility that had to be kept in mind. |
| Hotspur | The General Aircraft Hotspur was a training glider for army glider pilots who would later fly troop-carrying gliders. |
| Hundredweight | 112 lbs or 50.8 kg. The usual abbreviation is *cwt*. |
| IAS | Indicated airspeed (*q.v.*) |
| Inch | 25.4 mm |
| Indicated airspeed | This was the reading of the airspeed indicator and did not necessarily correspond to the true airspeed, particularly at different heights (see Table 18, page 233). |
| Instrument flying | Flying entirely on instruments, when the pilot had no other indication of an aircraft's altitude and progress. Instrument flying was unavoidable when the ground or horizon could not be seen, such as when flying in cloud or at night. It was practised either i) in the air, when the cockpit occupied by a pupil pilot in an aircraft with dual control such as the Tiger Moth or Harvard was completely covered by a hood so that the pupil was unable to see outside, or ii) on the ground in a Link Trainer (*q.v.*) (More recently, with side-by-side seating, the pupil's vision of the outside world may be masked by the use of suitably tinted goggles). |
| Intercom | Electrical intercommunication system within an aircraft. |
| Jabs | Preventative inoculations or immunizations against certain diseases; the routine ones were against smallpox, typhoid and tetanus. |
| Kite | An aeroplane. This word was used almost universally in conversation as a substitute for *aircraft* or *aeroplane,* but it is now outdated, and I have only left the word in the text here and there to give flavour. Sometimes the word *crate* was subsituted. |
| Knot | One nautical mile per hour; see *nautical mile*. |
| Lapse rate | The decrease of any quantity, usually temperature, with height. For temperature it is about 1°F in 300 feet, or 0.6°C in 100 metres (see *Meteorology for Aviators* by R. C. Sutcliffe). |

| | |
|---|---|
| Line-shoot | A slang phrase for a tall story or piece of bragging. See also *shoot a line*. |
| Link trainer | An artificial ground-based cockpit, with controls and instuments, set in a crude aeroplane body, designed to provide practice in instrument flying without having to go into the air. The cockpit was covered by a hood and the body could be tilted in various directions to give the impression of pitch and bank. It was cheaper to use, had none of the risks of practice in the air, and provided a simple form of training. It was the forerunner of the present-day flight simulator. |
| Low hop | One of the stages in learning to fly a glider without dual control. The glider rose off the ground just sufficiently for the novice to get the feel of the controls in the air. |
| **M**ag drop | Magneto drop; the fall in the engine revolution rate sometimes seen when switching off one of the two magneto switches – a standard check before taking off. It always indicated a fault in the engine, usually a faulty sparking plug or dirt in the magneto; in the latter case, a few seconds of running the engine at high revs might clear it. |
| Magnetic compass | The compass in the aircraft which pointed to magnetic north. This compass was not usually used for sterring the aircraft, since there was always a lag in the movement of the needle when changing the aircraft's heading, and althought the compass was damped it also oscillated slightly. The magnetic compass was used mainly as a reference for setting the gyro compass. It was about six inches in diameter and placed horizontally below the instrument panel (see Plate 8 on page 49). |
| Magnetic deviation | The compass error due to the effect of metal in an aircraft. It is measured in degrees and is peculiar to each heading and to each aircraft. A card with corrected readings was provided in the cockpit; this had to be updated at regular intervals. |
| Magnetic variation | The compass error due to the difference in angle from the observer between the magnetic pole and the geographical pole. It is measured in degrees and may be shown on maps as a line joining places with equal variation. It changes very slowly with time. |
| Master | The Miles Master was one of the two main advanced single-engined trainers of the Second World War. It was British and had an enclosed cockpit, electrical intercom and retractable undercarriage. Instructor and pupil sat one behind the other. |
| Merlin | The name of the Rolls Royce engine fitted to the earlier marks of Spitfire (it was also fitted to many other aircraft). There were numerous versions, those in the Spitfire XI, for example, varying from 1475 to 1710 horse power. The torque was opposite to that of the Griffon engine. |
| Met. | Meteorological; an abbreviation usually used in conjunction with a noun, as in met. office, met. officer and met. *wallah*. |
| Mile | Miles are quoted in English miles. 1 English mile = 1.6093 kilometres or 0.868 nautical miles. |

# GLOSSARY

| | |
|---|---|
| MO | Medical Office |
| MPH | Miles per hour, see *mile*. |
| MT | Motor transport, usually referring to the section of the RAF which supplied four-wheeled vehicles. |
| NAAFI | The Navy, Army and Air Force Institute, a club for Other Ranks where they could eat or otherwise relax in company. A NAAFI could be found at most RAF stations, but they were rather dull places. |
| Nautical mile | 1.1515 (or 76/66) English miles. |
| NCO | A non-commissioned officer. The term comprises the ranks of Warrant Officer, Flight Sergeant, Sergeant and Corporal. |
| Oblique camera | A camera, referred to as the F.14, which, in the Spitfire, was fixed in the fuselage behind the pilot; it pointed out to port and also downwards at an angle or about five or ten degrees. It was used for low-level oblique photography, see also *Camera*. |
| Operational Training Unit | Where the third stage of flying training took place. Here pilots who had already gained their Wings learned to fly operational aircraft and to train for operational flying in the RAF. It was more usually known by its initial OTU. |
| Other Ranks | Those who were neither Commissioned nor Non-commissioned Officers. |
| OTU | See *Operational Training Unit*. |
| Oxford | The Airspeed Oxford was a small British twin-engined transport aircraft which also served a trainer for pilots going on to muli-engined aircraft. |
| Oxygen | Oxygen had to be used from 10,000 feet upwards. On any flight to higher altitudes it was switched on before leaving the ground. A well-fitting oxygen mask was important. Above about 35,000 feet an atmosphere of 100% oxygen with even a well-fitting mask is inadequate owing to the low total atmospheric pressure. The Spitfire XIX was originally built with a pressure cabin to ensure adequate oxygen partial pressure at high altitude, but by the time I was flying it the cabin seals had deteriorated and the pressurisation no longer worked (see *Oxygen lack*). |
| Oxygen lack | If the partial pressure of oxygen in the lungs becomes too low, caused either by interference in the supply, by an ill-fitting oxygen mask, or by excessively high altitudes even with an oxygen supply, symptoms of oxygen lack appear. These are dizziness, confusion and apathy; in extreme deficiency unconsciousness and death result. What is particularly dangerous is mild oxygen lack: the pilot may notice nothing, but is liable unwittingly to make mistakes as I twice discovered (see chapters 11 and 13). |
| Pancake | In the civilian world this means *crash,* but in contemporary squadron language it was synonymous with *landing,* and in conversations with the Control Tower it would be used as part of the ritual jargon used when requesting permission to land. |

| | |
|---|---|
| Petrol bowser | Vehicle supplying petrol to an aircraft. |
| Photo recce | Photographic reconnaissance (*q.v.*) |
| Photographic reconnaissance | The photography of ground sites from the air using either vertical or oblique cameras. In the early years of the Second World War it was carried out by various twin-engine aircraft, but later on was carried out mostly by Spitfires until the Mosquito came into service and took over a fair proportion of the oblique photography. |
| Pinpoint | An arbitrary but unambiguous landmark identifiable from the air and used as an aid to an aircraft's location. |
| Pitch | See *variable pitch*. |
| Port | This was originally a naval term for *left*, but was adopted by the RAF and was used in all aspects of aviation; *left* was never used to indicate direction. *Port* and *starboard* are unambiguous in interpretation, whereas *left* and *right* seem at the time of writing to be used in civil aviation and the ambiguity may have contributed to at least one major crash. |
| PR | Photographic reconnaissance (*q.v.*) |
| Prang | This term was used in place of *crash* (noun or verb), usually of aircraft, but it was also used for damage to almost anything. |
| Precession | Progressive increase in error of the indicated heading of a gyro compass (see *gyro compass*). |
| Prop | Propeller. |
| Prune, Pilot Officer | A fictional character immortalized in the aircrew magazine *Tee Emm*, who, with his dog Binder, did foolish things when flying; his escapades were intended to be salutary lessons to aircrew. |
| PSP | Perforated Steel Plating, or, according to P. Congdon in *Per Aruda ad Astra,* Pierced Steel Planking. It consisted of interlinked perforated strips of heavy metal laid out to form a temporary runway. |
| PT | Physical training. |
| **RAFVR** | Royal Air Force Volunteer Reserve, comprising, between the two world wars, those who limited their participation in the RAF to evenings and weekends. Most of the aircrew who entered the RAF during the Second World War were classified as RAFVR. (Not to be confused with the Royal Auxiliary Air Force which, although also on a part-time basis, was more highly organized and had its own squadrons). |
| Range | The distance an aircraft can fly for a given amount of fuel. A maximum range, such as that in Table 16, must be arbitrary since it has to allow for take-off, climbing, descending, landing and a reserve of fuel. In *Pilot's Notes for Spitfire XIV and XIX* range is therefore given not as an absolute distance but as air miles per gallon under various combinations of Indicated Airspeed, engine rpm and height. |
| Recce | Reconnaissance. |

# GLOSSARY

| | |
|---|---|
| Revs | Revolutions (per minute). The abbreviation usually referred to engine rotation, but might be applied colloquially to other rotating equipment. |
| RIAF | Royal Indian Air Force. |
| Roger | Code word in radio communication for 'Received and understood.' |
| Rpm | Engine revolutions per minute. |
| R/T | Ratio Telephony, or radio using speech (in contrast to W/T or Wireless Telegraphy which was limited to morse code). There was a small radio in the cockpit with press buttons for changing frequency. It had two main frequencies, the local one for use at the home airfield and between squadron aircraft, and a universal one for using at other airfields. The maximum range between an aircraft at 20,000 feet and a ground station was about 100 miles. In India the sets seemed to be reliable when we were away on sortie, but mainly seemed to go wrong when at or near our own airfield. They were of course valve sets, notorious for unreliability when subjected to disturbance or when being frequently switched on and off. |
| Run | In photographic reconnaissance, a continuous series of photographs between switching on and switching off the cameras. |
| **SBA** | Standard Beam Approach (*q.v.*) |
| Scramble | Take off. |
| SG38 | A German low-performance training glider with no pretence at aerodynamic efficiency. It consisted mainly of a seat for the pilot, an open girder fuselage, and fabric-covered wings and tailplane. There were no instruments. |
| Shoot a line | Boast or exaggerate, often with tongue in cheek; see also *line-shoot*. |
| Sortie | In photographic reconnaissance, a flight in which photographs are to be taken. |
| Spitfire | The Supermarine Spitfire is too well known to need a description. The marks ranged from Mark 1 to Mark 24. Although there were exceptions, the Rolls Royce Merlin engine was in general fitted to Spitfires up to Mark XI and the more powerful Griffon engine to the higher marks. The commonest of the photo reconnaissance Spitfires were Marks XI and XIX. |
| SPR | Spitfire photographic reconnassance. |
| Squadron | A unit comprising several Flights (*q.v.*) |
| Standard Beam Approach | A method of directing an aircraft to an airfield by menas of a radio beam. |
| Starboard | This was originally a naval term for *right,* but was adopted by the RAF and used in all aspects of aviation; *right* was never used. For more details see *Port*. |
| Stick | The control column in an aircraft which operated ailerons and elevators. |
| Swing | In the present context swinging refers to the manual rotation of the propeller to start an aircraft's engine or to an inadvertent turning of an aircraft on the ground. |

| | |
|---|---|
| T | The *T* was a group of white boards placed in the signals area of an airfield (an area on the ground used for indicating the airfield status) and laid out in the shape of a *T* to show the direction of landing. It did not always correspond to the direction of the wind as shown by the wind sock, either because the wind was erratic or because the Control Tower personnel had not updated it. |
| Target | In photographic reconnaissance, the area to be photographed. |
| TAS | True airspeed (*q.v.*) |
| Taxy, taxi | This is a verb (or adjective, as in *taxy track*) used to refer to the movement of an aircraft on the ground from one place to another under its own power. |
| Tiger Moth | The De Havilland Tiger Moth, or DH 82A, was the primary trainer for the RAF throughout the Second World War. It was a British biplane with two open cockpits one behind the other, no electrical intercom, and when on the ground the engine could only be started by swinging the propeller by hand. |
| Tit | Any finger-pressed button. With the Spitfires XIV and XIX it usually referred to the button which operated the Koffman starter cartridge, but in operational fighter aircraft it also referred to the button on the control column which operated the guns. |
| Toc H | A club for Other Ranks which provided good food. It was a Christian organisation whose name was derived from the old army signallers' designation for the initials T.H., standing for *Talbot House*. It was first opened in Flanders in 1915 as a club for soldiers. |
| Track | The path over the ground actually followed by an aircraft, in contrast to *course* (*q.v.*). It will not usually be the same as the course owing to the effect of wind. It is synonymous with *flight path*, a term not then in use in the RAF. |
| Trailing edge | The rear edge of a wing or other aerofoil. |
| Trolley-acc | A large accumulator battery on wheels used for starting some aircraft engines. |
| True airspeed | The actual rate of motion of the aircraft through the air (c.f. *indicated airspeed*). |
| Type | Officially this word referred to a *type* of aircraft, but in colloquial language it meant *person*. |
| Undercarriage | The wheels of an aircraft and their supporting structure; colloquially called *undercart*. |
| Undercart | See *undercarriage*. |
| U/S | Unserviceable, unfit or unsafe to be used. *Put u/s:* classed as unserviceable. |

# GLOSSARY

| | |
|---|---|
| **V**ariable pitch | On a simple aircraft like the Tiger Moth the propeller blades are fixed to the drive shaft. On more sophisticated aircraft they can be swivelled about their axes by means of a pitch control lever in the cockpit. The pitch is the angle at which the blade is presented to the airflow; with *fine* pitch the angle is large and with *coarse* pitch the angle it is smaller. Fine pitch is used in taking off and landing while coarse pitch is used for cruising, in much the same way as low and high gears are used in a car. |
| Variation | See *magnetic variation*. |
| V-E Day | The day on which the European part of the Second World War officially ended: 8th May 1945. |
| Vertical camera | A camera, always one of a diverging pair, and referred to as the F.24, which, in the Spitfire, was fixed in the fuselage behind the pilot and pointed vertically downwards. Photographs were taken with it from high altitude and were used for map-type surveys. See also *camera*. |
| Very Light | A green or red flare shot from a specially designed large pistol usually as a message to a pilot in the vicinity of an airfield or on the ground, the green flare giving the go ahead, the red flare the opposite. Named after E. W. Very, a US naval officer (1852-1910). |
| V-J Day | The day on which the Far Eastern part of the Second World War officially ended: 12th September 1945. |
| **W**AAF | Women's Auxiliary Air Force. It was a full-time service acting as a counterpart of the RAF and coordinated with it. |
| Wilco | Code word in radio communications for 'will comply'. |
| Wing | A unit comprising several Squadrons (*q.v.*) |
| Wings | The symbol of the qualified RAF pilot, represented by the embroidered RAF Wings worn on the left breast. |
| **Y**ard | 0.9144 metre |
| York | The Avro York was a large British passenger-carrying four-engined aircraft modelled on the Lancaster bomber, and was used by RAF and BOAC on long-distance overseas routes. |

## Indian Vocabulary

The words shown here are either Urdu, or Urdu modified by British troops, or English words peculiar to Indian and comparable countries.

| | |
|---|---|
| *Baksheesh* | A gratuity or tip. |
| Bearer | Personal Indian servant; the word may also apply to a servant who looks after a group of people. |
| Bibby | Native woman. A slang word used by British troops and derived from *bibi,* meaning 'high class woman'. |
| Bed-roll | Complete bedding rolled up for portability. In India personal bedding normally accompanied personnel from place to place. |

| | |
|---|---|
| *Bundu* | Indian countryside |
| *Burqa* | A one-piece white garment covering the entire body, with an eye-level cloth grill. Worn in public primarily by most Moslem and some high-caste Hindu women. Also spelled *bourka* and *burka*. |
| **C**antonment | The local military residential area. |
| *Chappal* | Sandal without a heel-strap. |
| *Chappli* | Sandal with heel-strap |
| *Char* | Tea |
| *Char-wallah* | Man selling cups of tea. |
| *Charpoy* | The standard Indian form of bed, consisting of a wooden framework supporting a cross-weave of string or webbing. |
| *Chatti* | Water-pot made of earthenware; being porous it allowed evaporation which kept the water cool. |
| *Chikko* | Child |
| *Chota* | Small |
| **D**acoit | Robber, may be one of an organised gang. |
| *Dhobi* | The clothes wash. |
| *Dhobi-wallah* | Washerman |
| *Dhoti* | Loose loincloth worn by Hindus. |
| **G**hari | A four-wheeled horse-drawn passenger vehicle in India. The term was also used as slang when referring to service motorised transport. Also spelled *gharry, gharri*. |
| **H**arijan | See *outcaste*. |
| **INA** | Indian National Airways. |
| India | The name used in these memoirs for the whole of the Indian subcontinent, the single country then under the jurisdiction of the British, and bordered by Persia, Afghanistan, Sinkiang, Tibet, Nepal, China and Burma. |
| *Jallo!* | 'Go away!' |
| *Jellaba* | Ankle-length robe worn in North Africa. |
| Jumna | The river on which lies Delhi; now Indianized to Yamuna. |
| **KD** | Khaki drill, the standard cotton khaki uniform of the tropics; it consisted in India of an open-necked shirt, shorts and thick woollen socks, together with an Australian-type bush hat. |
| **M**et. *wallah* | Meteorologist; the phrase refered to both British and Indian personnel. |
| *Mochi* | Cobbler. |

# GLOSSARY

| | |
|---|---|
| **O**utcaste | The lowest of the Hindu castes, given the lowest of jobs. Also called *Harijan* and *Untouchable*. |
| **P**athan | A member of one of the many tribes in the region of the North-west Frontier; pronounced P'tarn. |
| Pi-dog | Pariah-dog, a mongrel dog which lives by scavenging. |
| *Puggaree* | Loose turban-like head cover, usually white, and commonly rather scruffy; also spelled *puggree*. |
| *Punkah* | Originally a large piece of woven cloth suspended from the ceiling and moved continuously by a *punkah-wallah* to provide a cooling draught of air. After electricity was introduced the word also referred to a large electric fan in the ceiling. |
| *Punkah-wallah* | The man who operated the cloth type of *punkah*. Typically he sat or lay outside the room in the veranga, and, so it is said, moved the *punkah* with a length of string connected to his big toe. |
| *Sari* | Piece of long coloured cloth worn by Hindu women as an overall garment. |
| Sweeper | A member of the Untouchable caste who was employed to do the lowliest of jobs. |
| *Thug(-gee)* | Member of religious association which once lived by highway murder and robbery; now defunct. |
| Thunderbox | Inside primitive toilet. The contents were removed by a sweeper. |
| *Tonga* | A two-wheeled horse-drawn passenger vehicle in India. |
| Untouchable | See *outcaste*. |
| *Wallah* | Man, person; usually used in conjunction with a descriptive word as in *char-wallah*. |
| Wog | Term which was widely used in the services when referring to Indians or other native peoples with dark skins. It is, I believe, derived from the initials of Worthy Oriental Gentleman. |

# Bibliography

This is not a comprehensive bibliography. It is a list of books most of which I have at one time owned and enjoyed reading, and many of which I still have on my shelves.

**Books referred to in the text**

Barnes, M. (ed.), *Montagne del Monde*, 1955, Garzanti (undated). A summary of the mountain climbs of the previous year; includes an account, without photographs, of my flight to Everest.

Barnes, M. (ed.), *The Mountain World,* Allen and Unwin, 1955. As above.

Bickers, R. T., *The Battle of Britain*, Salamander, 1990. A profusely illustrated and comprehensive account of the Battle of Britain.

Bozman, E. F. (ed.), *Everyman's Encyclopaedia*, Dent, 1958.

Calder, A., *The People's War*, 2nd ed. Panther, 1971. An account of the civilian side of the Second World War as experienced in Britain.

Carr, S. J., *You are not Sparrows*, Ian Allan, 1975. An entertaining and revealing account of life in the RAF between the wars, mainly in the Middle East.

Congdon, P., *Per Ardua ad Astra*, Airlife Publishing, 1987. A factual description of the peacetime RAF forty years after the Second World War. The formalities of the peacetime Officers' Mess make my hair stand on end!

Douglas & Clydesdale, Marquess of, and McIntyre, D. F., *The Pilot's Book of Everest*, William Hodge, 1936. One of the two main accounts of the Westland-Houston flight to Everest in 1933.

Douglas-Hamilton, J., *Roof of the World*, Mainstream, 1983. A more recent account of the Westland-Houston flight to Everest in 1933.

Fellowes, P. F. M., Blacker, L. V. S., Etherton, P. T. and The Marquess of Douglas and Clydesdale, *First Over Everest – The Houston-Mount Everest Expedition*, Bodley Head, 1933. The other of the two main books describing the Westland-Houston flight to Everest in 1933 (see Douglas & Clydesdale above).

Gibbs-Smith, C. H., *The Aircraft Recognition Manual*, British Aviation Publications, 1944. A comprehensive book of aircraft silhouettes for the recognition of aircraft during the Second World War. Most of the drawings of aircraft in the present text were based on these silhouettes.

Hagen, L., *Indian Route March*, Pilot Press, 1946. Life of a soldier drafted to India during the Second World War; the book shows India as it really was.

Hamilton, T., *The Life and Times of Pilot Officer Prune*, HMSO, 1991. A recent resurrection of the mythical Pilot Officer Prune of *Tee Emm*, a journal designed to warn aircrew of the dangers of carelessness.

Hart, E., *Spring Imperial*, Corgi, 1989. A novel of India, a large part being centred on Quetta.

Hastings, M., *Bomber Command*, Pan, 1981. A history of Bomber Command during the Second World War.

Hilton, J., *Lost Horizon*, Macmillan's Cottage Library, 1936. The adventure story from which the name Shangri La came.

Hürlimann, M., *Traveller in the Orient*, Thames and Hudson, 1960. An illustrated account of travels through India and places further east.

Jackson, R., *Thirty Seconds at Quetta*, Evans Brothers, 1960. A well-written description of the devastating earthquake at Quetta in 1935.

Kaye, M. M., *Sun in the Morning*, Viking/Penguin, 1990. An autobiography describing the childhood in India of the novelist M. M. Kaye.

Montgomery, B., *Monty's Grandfather*, pp. 42 & 129, Blandford Press, 1984. A biography of General Montgomery's grandfather, told by his son, mostly of India around the period of the India Mutiny.

Moorhouse, G., *Calcutta*, Penguin, 1974. Contains an absorbing description of Calcutta, warts and all.

Moorhouse, G., *India Britannica*, p. 207. Paladin, 1984. A history of India from the days of the East India Company up to Independence.

Neame, K., 'Alone Over Everest' in *The Mountain World* (ed. Barnes, M.), pp. 133-141, Allen and Unwin, 1955. An account, without illustrations, of my flight to Everest.

Neame, K., 'Flight Over Everest' in *Lilliput*, Oct.-Nov. 1952. An account, without photographs, of my flight to Everest; it was ghost-written.

'Nemisis', 'Flight Over Everest' in *St Mary's Hospital Gazette*, Vol. 58, No. 5, July-Aug 1952, pp. 130-5. An account, with photographs, of my flight to Everest in the Gazette of the medical school where I was a student.

'Nemesis', 'Yet Unconquered' in *St Mary's Hospital Gazette*, Vol 59, No. 2, March 1953, pp. 34-7. A brief account of the problems of climbing Everest as they appeared in 1953.

Norton, E. F., *The Fight for Everest: 1924*, Arnold, 1925. One of the classic books of the earlier expeditions to Everest.

Partridge, E., *A Dictionary of RAF Slang*, Michael Joseph, 1945.

Quill, J., *Spitfire*, Arrow, 1985. Quill was for many years the main test pilot for the Spitfire, and this is his account of those days.

Rébuffat, G., *Du Mont Blanc à l'Himalaya*, Arthaud, 1955. A book of photographs of mountains, including one of mine (Plate 64) looking east over Lhotse (Everest's twin) towards Makalu and Kangchenjunga.

Scott, R. L., *God is My Co-pilot*, Charles Scribner's Sons, 1943. American Air Force Col. Scott's autobiography of his flying days up to 1942.

Shipton, E., *The Mount Everest Reconnaissance Expedition 1951*, Hodder and Stoughton, 1952. An account of the first expedition to Everest from Nepal; the first section includes, anonymously, several of my photos of the mountain.

Sims, E. H., *Fighter Exploits*, Corgi, 1974. A critical history of air fighting.

Smith, C. B., *Evidence in Camera*, David and Charles, 1958. Photographic reconnaissance during the Second World War.

Smith, J., 'Origin of Species - I' in *The Aeroplane*, 20 December 1946. A brief description of the various marks of Spitfire.

Spurling, H., *Paul Scott*, Hutchinson, 1990. A biography of Paul Scott, the author who wrote *The Jewel in the Crown*, a novel about India.

Sutcliffe, R. C., *Meteorology for Aviators*, HMSO, 1940.

Ullman, J. R., *Kingdom of Adventure – Everest*, Collins, 1948. A summary of expeditions to Everest up to 1948.

Unsworth, W., *Everest*, Grafton Publishing, 1991. A summary of expeditions to Everest, including a brief mention of various flights to the mountain.

Woodham-Smith, C., *Florence Nightingale*, Chapter 18, Reprint Society, 1952. A biography of Florence Nightingale which includes details of the appalling health problems of British troops in India in the nineteenth century.

Unknown, *Pilot's Notes for Spitfire XIV & XIX*, 2nd edition. Air Ministry, 1946. The pilot's manual for flying these two marks of Spitfire.

**Books on flying in the RAF, not mentioned above, which are worth reading:**

Clostermann, P., *The Big Show*, Chatto & Windus, 1951. A personal account of the Battle of Britain from the Spitfire pilot's point of view.

Hemingway, K., *Wings over Burma*, Quality Press, 1944. After reading this book in the 1950s I made this note: 'Definitely the best book I have read on the RAF in this war… What makes the book are the little chunks of cross-talk and good-natured banter which are so typical of life on a squadron.'

Hillary, R., *The Last Enemy*, Pan, 1956, as Clostermann above.

Lacey, G., *Fighter Pilot*, Corgi, 1978. A fighter pilot's experiences in the Battle of Britain and in the Far East.

Rawnsley, C. F. and Wright, R., *Night Fighter*, Corgi, 1959. A vivid account of the problems and activity of night fighters over Britain after the installation of radar for detecting bombers at night. Although not related to the text I include this book since it is so absorbing.

**Books on India which I have found enjoyable:**

NON-FICTION

Allen, C. (ed.), *Plain Tales from the Raj*, Andre Deutsch, 1975. Various accounts of the life of the British in India in the hey-day of the British Raj.

Collins, L. and Lapierre, D., *Freedom at Midnight,* Collins, 1975. An interesting description of the events leading up to Indian Independence.

Draper, A., *The Amritsar Massacar*, Buchan and Enright, 1985. A good balanced account of the massacre by Col. Dyer of a large crowd of trapped Indians in Amritsar in 1919.

FICTION

Fitzgerald, V., *Zemindar*, The Bodley Head, 1981. An absorbing novel of the time of the Indian Mutiny and of the Siege of Lucknow. Don't be put off by its size.

# BIBLIOGRAPHY

Forrister, H., *Thursday's Child*, Fontana, 1985. Experiences of the young English wife of an Indian suddenly transported to India to make a life in inadequate Indian accommodation.

Kaye, M. M., *Shadow of the Moon*, Penguin, 1979. A remarkably vivid novel of the escape of some of the British during the Indian Mutiny. Has a more authentic feel of real events in India than the author's better known *The Far Pavilions*.

Masters, J., Numerous well-known and well-written books on life in India between the Wars and in the last century; I particularly recommend *Bowhani Junction* (Penguin, 1960), *The Deceivers* (Penguin, 1955) and *Night-runners of Bengal* (Michael Joseph, 1951).

Mehta, G., *Raj*, Shows through the eyes of an Indian princess how the Courts of the independent Kings of India lived during the time of the British Raj.

Scott, P., *The Jewel in the Crown* (the first volume of *The Raj Quartet*). Panther, 1973. Illustrates the problem of a penurious Indian returning to British India after being educated at a public school in England. I found that although I enjoyed the book at first reading, a second reading plumbed the depths of the subject. The three other volumes of *The Raj Quartet* are pale by comparison.

Scott, P., *Staying On*, Panther, 1978. A vivid, at times amusing, and at times sad, account of the difficulties of an ageing married ex-Army couple who decide to remain in India after Independence.

# Index

Page numbers for Tables, Figures and Plates are included at the front of the book (pages ix to xii).

**AC**1, AC2, 235
Accelerated course, 11-2
Accidents, flying, 19
  burst tyre, 98, 143
  Arthur Chin's, 99
  due to faulty oxygen, 53, 71, 108
  at RAF Wunstorf, 219, 234
  own damage to oleo leg, 98
  problems searching crashed aircraft, 198
  fatal accidents, 234
ACOS, see *Aircrew Officers' School*
ACRC, see *Aircrew Receiving Centre*
Adelphi Hotel, Bombay, 134
Advanced Flying Training School, 29-38, 223, 225, 227, see also *Cranwell*,
  examinations, 36-7
  passing out, 36-7
AFC, see *Airfield controller*
Agra, 106-7, 123, 137-8, 139
  from the air, 123
  Taj Mahal, 106-7, from the air, 123
Agricultural Institute, sortie to, 109, 139-40
Ahmedabad airfield (civilian), 130, 132-4, 137-8
Aircraft, see also under *Anson, Auster, Dakota, De Havilland 82A, Oxford, SG38, Spitfire, Tiger Moth, York, Grunau, Harvard, Hotspur, Master*
  at Celle, 55, 58
  at Palam, 88, 96-155
  flown, 226, 228
  flown in, 229
Aircrew, medical examination, 2, 46, 108, 207-8, 219
  Officers' School, Hereford, 13-28, 223, 225, 235
  Receiving Centre, 235,
  Torquay, 8-11, 26, 223, 225
  selection for, 10-11
  training for accelerated course, 11-2
Airfield Controller, 235
  information pamphlet, 112-3
Airfields, in England, see *Benson, Cranwell, Ouston, Perth*
  in Germany, see *Celle, Wunstorf*
  in India,
  Ahmedabad (civilian), 121, 130, 132-4, 137-8
  Barrackpore (RAF), 121, 129
  Bhopal (RIAF), 119, 121-3, 125-6, 128
  Chakeri (RAF), 121, 123-4
  Chaklala (RAF), 180-1
  Dhingar (deserted), 173, 178
  Drigh Road (RAF), 121, 199, 201-4, 206-7
  Dum Dum (RAF), 121, 129, 148-50, 153-5, 158, 160
  Hakimpet (RAF), 121, 125
  Ibis (deserted), 172-3
  Jodhpur (civilian), 199-203
  Karachi (civilian), 203
  Mauripur (RAF), 74, 79-80, 83-4, 86-7, 89, 121, 180 203-4, 206-7
  Nagpur (RAF), 121
  Palam (RAF), see *Palam*
  Pishin (deserted), 173, 175, 177
  Poona (RAF), 126, 134
  Ranchi (RAF), 129
  Samungli (RAF), 169-71, 173-5, 177-9, 236
  Santa Cruz (civilian), 130, 133-4, 136-8, 207
  Sibi (deserted), 170-3, 177-8
  Spezand (deserted), 173, 177-8
  Yelahanka (RAF), 83, 125-7
  Ahmedabad, 130, 132-4, 137-8
Air-Land Rescue Exercise, 188-98
Airman, 235
Airspeed, 235

# INDEX

Air Traffic Control duty (Wunstorf), 212-4, 216-9
Air Training Corps, 1, 4, 6, 235
Alcohol, effect of, 177, 199
Aldis lamp, 192, 235
Altitude flights, see *Height climbs*
Anson (aircraft), 5, 7, 55, 58, 201
Aptitude tests, 10, 11, 235
Assam, 129
Assessment, Educational and Vocational Training, 205
ATC see *Air Training Corps*
Auchinleck, Field Marshal, 91
Auster (aircraft), 18, 59-61, 219, 235
at Palam, 96, 188-9, 193, 198
Autobahn, 58

**B**abbacombe, 9
Bad Harzburg, 70
BAFO, see *British Air Force of Occupation*
Baksheesh, 84, 186, 207, 245
Baldwin, Warrant Officer, 93, 95, 160
Baluchistan, sortie to, 83, 169-70, 198, 202, 207
Banas river, 120, 138
Bangalore, 83, 125
Banganga river, 119-20
BAOR, see B*ritish Army on the Rhine*
Barrackpore, RAF airfield, 121, 129
Bath, the only one in India, 135
Bath, swimming, 91
Bearer, 245, at Mauripur, 79-80
at Palam, 89, 90, 180
Beauman, Wing Commander, 162, 164
Bed-roll, 245
Benson, RAF airfield, xiii, 40-1, 46-53, 57-8, 71, 96
Betel nut, 78
Betwa river, 122
Bevin Boys, 1, 235
Bhopal, airfield, 119, 121-3, 125-6, 128
Bibby, bibbies, 130, 136, 245
Birds around Palam, 103-4
Biro ballpoint pen, 65
Black, Flying Officer 'Blackie', 93-5, 106, 125, 132, 137, 146, 179, 208
Blister hangar, 18, 236

Blood waggon, 100, 236
BOAC, see *British Overseas Airways Corporation*
Bombay, 77, 108, 130-6, 187, 208
Adelphi Hotel, 134
brothels, 135
'cages', 135
Number 5 Grant Road, 135
RAF Worli, 207-8, 224
Bombing, 33, 55, 68
Bowser, 124, 133, 242
Bradshaw, 170, 202, 236
Bridgnorth, RAF, 11-12
British Air Force of Occupation, 54, 235-6
British Army on the Rhine, 54, 235-6
British Overseas Airways Corporation, 72, 236
Bromide in the tea, 12
Brunswick ruins, 68-9
Built-in wind, see *Wind*
Bull/bullshit, 12, 14, 236
BUMPF (mnemonic), 31
Bundu, 189, 196, 246
Burqa, 77, 246
Burst tyre, 98, 100
Burton, gone for a, 212, 238
Burton Wood, RAF, 211

**C**adet, aircrew, 4, 8, 26, 37
myself as, 27
'Cages', the, Bombay, 135
Call-sign, 110, 203
Camera, 236
my own (Leica), xv, 35, 146, 196
jamming of, 210
RAF oblique, 40-1, 44, 58, 130, 140, 155, 159-60, 167, 236, 241-2
RAF vertical, 40-2, 51, 58, 124, 128, 130, 136, 139, 148, 159, 169, 176, 242, 245
ports for, 97
Camp followers at Palam, 71
Cantonment, 89, 91, 101, 105, 180, 197, 246
Career in medicine, 152, 159
Cawnpore, sortie to, 123-5, 149
Celle, 54
RAF airfield, 54-61, 63-6, 68, 70-1, 93, 212, 217
Chakeri, RAF airfield, 121, 123-4

253

Chaklala, RAF airfield, 180-1
Chambal river, 119-20, 123, 138
Chappal, 83, 246
Chappli, 83, 246
Char, 136, 204, 246
Charpoy, 80-1, 90, 128, 135, 146, 246
Char-wallah, 85, 94, 96, 246-7
Chatti, 90, 246
Chikko, 246
Chin, Arthur, crash and death of, 71, 96
   remains of crash, 99
Chomolhari, Mt, 152
Chota, 246
   Club, 91
   swimming at, 91
Church, Dr J. E., 149, 152-3, 161
Circuit, 236
Circuits and bumps, 236
Civilian flying licence, 152
Civvies, 236
Clamp, 236
Clamped down, 236
Clot, 236
Clottishness, 236
Club, Chota, see *Chota Club*
Cockpit pressurization, 230, 241
College, RAF Cranwell, see *Cranwell*
Colliery, visit to, 7
Combined Operations Exercise, 130
Commission, short service, 1, 12-3, 36
Communications Squadron at Palam, 88, 94, 141, 188, 190-1
Compass, gyro, 43, 110, 115-7, 120, 143, 170, 176, 192, 199, 200 238
   magnetic, 24, 33, 43, 45, 116-7, 170, 192, 240
Computer, Navigational, adapted, 116-7, 128, 218, 233
Connaught Circus, New Delhi, 104, 140
Controller, airfield, see *Airfield controller*
Course, Advanced Flying Training, 29-38, 223, 225, 227,
   Aircrew Officers' School, 13-4, 235
   Elementary Flying Training, 16, 26, 237
   Gliding, 6, 21-2
   Intelligence, 10-11, 65, 205-6
   Spitfire Photo Reconnaissance 40 and see

*Photographic Reconnaissance*
   University Short, 1-4, 8, 13, 15
Cranwell, RAF airfield, 28-39, 143
   RAF College, 37-8
Crash, problems when searching for, 198
Crashes, see *Accidents*
Crate, 236
Credenhill, 13-4
Cuttack, sortie, to, 128
Cwt, 236

**D**acoit, 79, 246
Daily Inspection, 62, 134, 178, 237
Dakota (aircraft), 6, 65, 72, 180-1, 204-5, 212, 237
   at Palam, 88
Daman (Portuguese), 133-4
Darjeeling, 148-50, 158, 160, 180
Dead reckoning, 44-5, 111, 204, 237
Deaths of, Chin, Arthur, 71, 96
   Leheta, Ali, 71, 108
   Strachan, Bill, 40-1, 53, 71,
   see also *Accidents*
Deck, 237
Decompression chamber, 46
De Havilland 82A, see *Tiger Moth*
Delhi, 75-6, 79
   New, 79, 83, 87-9, 101, 107, 143-4, 149, 207
   cinema, 105
   Connaught Circus, 104, 140
   Indra Chauk, 104
   Jai Singh II's observatory, 105
   Jantar Mantar, 105
   shopping in, 104
   transport, 106
   Viceroy's Palace, 104
Demob, 218
Desert, Sind, 76, 202
   Thar, 76, 144, 170, 198-9, 201-2, 207
Deviation, magnetic, 45, 240
Dhingar (deserted airfield), 173, 178
Dhobi, 246
Dhobi-wallah, 79, 246
Dhoti, 77, 246
Dhulia, sortie to, 126
Dispersal, 18, 23, 55, 95, 98, 113, 132, 189, 197, 200, 203, 216, 237

# INDEX

Dope, 16, 237
Drigh Road, RAF airfield, 121, 199, 201-4, 206-7
  ferry of Spitfire to, 201-4, 206-7
Drop-tank, 40, 149-50, 155, 157, 197, 231, 237
  for Everest flight, 159
Dum Dum, RAF airfield, 121, 129, 148-50, 153-5, 158, 160
Durham University Short Course, 3-4, see also *Colliery*
Duty in Flying Control (Wunstorf), 212-4, 216-9

**E**ducation and Vocational Training assessment, 205
Elementary Flying Training School, 16, 26, 237
  examinations, 36-7
  passing out, 36-7
End of European War, 26, 167, 223
  War in Far East, 29, 223
Engines of Spitfires,
  Griffon, 57, 62, 141, 230, 238, 240
  Griffon v. Merlin, 96-8
  Merlin, 57, 230, 240
Entry to University Short Course, requirements, 1-4
Eskimo Nell, 5
Estimated Time of Arrival (ETA), 114, 117, 120, 179, 203, 237
Everest, Mt, xiii-xv, 87, 148-62
  aftermath of my flight to, 162-8
  climber on, L. R. Wager, 4
  flights: directly over the summit, 168
  Indian Air Force flight (1953), 167
  Mosquito flight (1945), 167
  photographic survey (1984), 168
  Spitfire (my flight in 1947), 148-162
  Westland-Houston Expedition (1933), 167
  photographs of, 148-68
  publications resulting from my flight, 162-8
  talk on BBC about my flight to, 166
Examinations,
  Advanced Flying Training, 36-7
  Durham University Short Course, 3-4
  Elementary Flying Training, 16, 26, 237
Exercise, Air-land Rescue, 188-98

Combined Operations, 130

**F**ear syndrome, 215
Ferry of Spitfire to Drigh Road, 201-4, 206-7
Finger trouble, 218, 234, 237
First solo, in Tiger Moth, 26, 226, 228
  in Harvard, 31, 226, 228
  in Spitfire, 39-41
Five Squadron, see *Number 5 Squadron*
Flamingoes, 86
Flight, 237
Flight path, 44, 237, 244
Flights, analysis of my, 255
Flights, maps of,
  from Benson, England, 50, 52
  from Celle, Germany, 56
  from Palam, India, 88
  Air-Land Rescue Exercise, 191
  first three sorties in India, 115
  to Nanda Devi, 145
  to Kangchenjunga and Everest, 151
  sortie to Baluchistan, 171, 173
  sortie to south India, 126
  sorties in India, 109
  from RAF Wunstorf, 213
  table of flights: from RAF Benson, 50
  from RAF Celle, 56
  to south India, 126
Flying accidents, see *Accidents*
Flying at night, see *Night flying*
Flying Control,
  Duty Officer (Wunstorf), 212-4, 216-9
  functions in India, 91, 110, 122, 130, 133-4
Flying licence, civilian, 219
Flying Log Book, xiii, 20, 23, 218, 226, 233
Flying map, Palam area, 88
Flying Officer, promotion to, 54-5
Flying record, my, 226-8
Flying speeds, of Spitfires, 232-3
Flying Training School, Advanced, see *Advanced Flying Training School*
  Elementary, see *Elementary Flying Training School*
Forced landing, 22, 25, 27, 32, 132, 145
Formate, 238
Fray, Squadron Leader Gerry, 89, 93, 98, 141, 180, 219, 220

burst tyre, 98, 100
Free From Infection (VD), 207, 237
Fuel capacity of Spitfires, 231
Fuel consumption of Spitfires, 231
Fyzabad, sortie to, 123-5

**'G'** 238
Ganges river, 117, 123-4, 142-4
Gari Parbat, 143
*Georgic*, m.v., troopship, 208-9
Germany, 54-72, 212-220
Ghari, 105, 182, 190, 192-7, 246
Glacier, Kangshung, 156-7
   Rongbuk, 156-7
   Zemu, 154-5, 160
Gliding, at RAF Wunstorf, 214-5
   Course (Salzgitter), 66-8, 70
Gone for a Burton, 212, 238
Gong, 238
Gogra river, 123
Gorge to Quetta, 169-70, 172-8
Gosport, 17, 20
Grant Road, Number 5, Bombay, 135
Gremlin, 138, 238
Griffon engine, see *Engines*
Groundcrew, 24, 44, 68-9, 76, 94, 97, 124-5, 141, 149, 158-60, 174, 178-9, 190, 192, 200, 238
Groundspeed, 33, 44, 115, 117, 120, 137, 143, 179, 202, 233, 238
Grunau (glider), 66-8, 214-5, 238
Gunnery, 33
Gyro compass, 43, 110, 115-7, 120, 143, 170, 176, 192, 199, 200 238
Gwalior, 122-3

**H**abbaniya RAF airfield, Iraq, 73
Hakimpet, RAF airfield, 121, 125
Harijan, 246-7
Harvard (aircraft), 29-36, 39, 46, 58, 226, 228, 237-9
   at Palam, 95, 108, 136, 188, 197
   used in riot recce, 195
Harz Mountains, 66, 70
Hathi Parbat, 142-3
Heading, 238
Heating of water at Palam, 91

Height climbs, in Harvard, 39
   in Spitfire, 117, 119, 128
   in Tiger Moth, 24
Hereford, 13, 235
High hop, 67-8, 239
Himalaya, 123-4, 148-61, 167
   attempt to photograph, 124, 136, 148
Holiday in India, 83, 180-7, 190
Homer, range of, 51-2, 210, 239
   from Palam, 111, 118, 124, 138, 158, 201, 203
   in Baluchistan, 178-9
   saving me from disaster, 144-7
Hornchurch, RAF Station, 54, 72
Hoshangabad, sortie to, 119-21, 123
Hotspur (glider), 5-6, 8, 239
Houseboat in Kashmir, 184-5
Hyderabad, in Hyderabad State, 125
   in Sind, 202-3

**I**AS, see *Indicated airspeed*
Ibis (deserted airfield), 172-3
Immunizations, 10, 72, 239
INA, see *Indian National Airways*
Independence Day, India, 199, 206, 208
   of India, 78-9, 89, 106, 188
Indicated airspeed, 117, 155, 202, 232-3, 235, 239, 242, 244
India, 73-161, airfields, see *Airfields*
   animals, 103
   birds, 103-4
   countryside, 76-145, 189, 196, 246,
   health, 81-3
   holiday in, 83, 180-7, 190
   Independence Day, 199, 206, 208
   independence of, 78-9, 89, 106, 188
   insects, 102-3
   living conditions, 79-81, 90, 102-3
   mail, loss of, 187
   malaria in, 81, 83, 221
   map-reading in, 114, 143, 150
   maps of, airfields visited, 121
   first three sorties, 115
   flying map of Palam area, 88
   flying map of north India, 74
   flying map of photographic sorties, 109
   flying map south India, 126, see also under

*Flights*
 navigation in, 111-8
 servants, 75-81
 sorties in, 110-1, 119
 preparation for sorties, 110
 the climate, 75-6
 the monsoon, 76, 101, 114, 117, 194, 197-8
 the people, 76-9
 wild life, 103-4
Indian National Airways (INA), 88, 246
 watching landings of, 88
Indore, sortie to, 119-23, 138
Indus river, 170-2, 178, 202
Information pamphlet for Palam, 112-3
Inoculations, see *Immunizations*
Instrument flying, 17, 32, 36, 49, 51-2, 239-40
Intelligence course, 10-11, 65, 205-6
Intercom, 30, 32, 238-40, 244
Irons, 10

**J**abs, see also *Immunization,* 10, 72, 239
Jackals, 103
Jai Singh II's observatory, 105
Jaipur, 105, 132, 201
Jallo, 246
James, Flight Lieutenant 'Jimmy', 40, 53, 93, 95, 190, 199, 208
Jantar Mantar, 105
Jellaba, 210, 246
Jhelum river, 183-4, 184
Jumna river, 107, 122, 143-5, 193, 246
Jodhpur airfield (civilian), 199-203

**K**amet, Mt, 142
 and Wing Commander Beauman, 162, 164
Kangchenjunga, Mt, sortie to, 148-161, 169
Kangshung glacier, 156-7
Karachi, 73, 76-8, 81-7, 130, 135, 174-5, 199, 203-4, 206-7, 211
 airfield (civilian), 203
 Boat Club, 86
 built-in wind, 174
 flamingos at, 86
 salt pans, 86
Kashmir, 180-7, 190, 205
 houseboat in, 184-5
 Kashmir Art Chamber, 186
 sailing in, 185-7

Khaki drill, 83-4, 246
Khoh river, 142-4
Khyber Pass, 182, 204
King's Regulations, 15
Kite, 192, 194, 197, 239
Kite-hawks, 103-4
Knot, 239
Kohala, 183
Kolar Gold Fields, sortie to, 125
Korangi Creek, sortie to, 125
Kukri, 206
Kula Kangri, 152, 154

**L**alitpur, sortie to, 119, 122
Lamp, Aldis, see *Aldis lamp*
Lapse rate, 233, 239
Leheta, Ali, death of, 71, 108
Leica, see *Camera*
Lhotse, 156, 166
Light, Very, see *Very Light*
Line-shoot, 240
Link Trainer, 32-3, 239-40
Liverpool, 210-12, 218, 221
Living quarters in India, 79-81, 90, 102-3
Loose-wallah, 7
Lost! 141-7
Low hop, 67-8, 240
Lower Topa, RAF hill station, 180, 182-3, 187-8
Luqa, RAF Station, Malta, 73
Lyneham, RAF Station, 72-3

**M**addukarai, sortie to, 125
Mag drop, 240
Magnetic compass, 24, 33, 43, 45, 116-7, 170, 192, 240
Magnetic deviation, 45, 240
Magnetic variation, 240
Makalu, Mt, 155, 157, 168
Malir river, 203
Malaria, 81, 83, 221
Map-reading in India, see *Navigation*
Maps, see under *Flights* and *India*
Mason, Claude, 4, 7
Master (aircraft), 30, 45-6, 51-2, 211, 228, 237, 240
Mauripur, RAF airfield, 74, 79-80, 83-4, 86-7, 89, 121, 180 203-4, 206-7

bearers at, 79-80
built-in wind, 87
Medical, examination for aircrew, 2, 46, 108, 135
  records, 224
  School, St Mary's Hospital, 165, 206, 217, 221
Medicine as a career, 205-6
Medmenham, RAF, 40
Merlin engine, see *Engines*
Merta Road, 201
Met., 240
  flight, 40
  wallahs, 149-50, 160
Meteorological flight, see *Met.*
MG car, 52-3, 84
Mile, English, 240
  nautical, 241
Mochi, 85, 246
Monsoon, 76, 101, 194
  flying in, 114, 117, 198
  landscape appearance in, 197
Mosquito net, 83, 126
Motor cycles, b34
Mount Everest, see *Everest*
Mountbatten, Lord Louis, 89, 91
MT, 14, 241
Murree, 80, 180, 182-3
Muzaffarabad, 183
Myself as Cadet, 27

NAAFI, see *Navy Army & Air Force Institute*
Nagin Bagh, sailing on, 185-7
Nagpur, RAF airfield, 121
  sortie to, 109
Nanda Devi, 141-2, 146, 162
Nautical mile, 241
Navigation, as Cadet, 4, 22, 25, 32, 34, 36, 39, 44-5, 51, 60
  in India, 111, 114, 116-9, 123-5, 169-70, 197, 200, 202
Navigational Computer, adapted, 116-7, 128, 218, 233
Navy Army & Air Force Institute, 10, 61, 241
NCO, 14, 241
Neame, Geoffrey, as pilot, 5

Neame, K. D. as Cadet, 27
Nellore, sortie to, 125
New Delhi, see *Delhi*
Night flying, 23
  in the Harvard, 32
  in the Tiger Moth, 26
Nimach, sortie to, 128
North Salsette, sortie to, 130, 134, 136-7, 149, 207
Number 2 Squadron, 54-5, 57-8, 93, 212,
Number 5 Squadron, 204-6
Number 34 Squadron (Palam), see also *Palam*, 93, 95, 110-1, 113, 122, 141, 188, 190, 205, 218-9,
  accidents, 96, 99
  burst tyre, 98, 100
  char-wallah, 96
  Commanding Officer, , see also *Fray,* 93, 219
  disbandment, 206
  Dispersal, 95
  members of, 93, 95, see also *Black, Robinson, James, Rees, Shukla, Turner-Ettlinger*
  photographic surveys, 96
  preparations for sorties, 109-11
  sorties,
  squadron dog (Rocky), 94
  Spitfires, 96-8, 108-10, 119, 128
  working hours, 4, 91, 99
Number 684 Squadron, 167

Oblique camera, 58, 97, 159-60, 167, 241, and see *Camera*
Oblique photography, in Germany, 58-9
  of Kangchenjunga, 155, 158-61
  of North Salsette, 130, 134, 136-7, 149
Observatory of Jai Singh II, 105
Officers' Mess, 12-3
  at Celle, 57
  at Mauripur, 77
  at Palam, 89, 92, 160
Ootacamunde, sortie to, 125, 180
Operational Training Unit, 39, 241
Other Ranks, 241
Ouston, RAF airfield, 5
Outcastes, 76, 247
Oxford (aircraft), 5, 6, 241

# INDEX

Oxygen, 46, 48, 109, 128, 170, 178, 241
  effects of lack of, 34, 108, 143, 166, 205, 241
  on flight to Mt Everest, 150, 156-7, 167
  on Nanda Devi flight, 141-2
  fault in supply, 53, 71, 108

**P**alam, RAF airfield, 88-120, 123-8, 130-9, 141-50, 153, 160, 169-70, 174-8, 180-1, 186-7, 190-206, see also *Number 34 Squadron*
  aircraft, 96-7
  Auster, 96, 188-9, 193, 198
  bearers, 89-90, 180
  birds around, 102-4
  camp followers, 71
  Communications Squadron, 88, 94, 141, 188, 190-1
  Control Tower, 110
  countryside around, 102-7
  Dakotas (aircraft), 88
  Flying Control, 189, 195
  Harvard (aircraft), 95, 108, 136, 188, 197
  heating of water, 91
  Homer, 111, 118, 124, 138, 158, 201, 203
  information pamphlet, 112-3
  Officers' Mess, 89, 92, 160
  preparation for flights, 109-11
  Spitfires, see *Spitfires*
  Transport Squadron, 96
  wildlife around, 102-4
Pancake, 110, 203, 241
Panjnad river, 170-1
Parachutes, 14, 204, 216
Partition of India, 78, 89
Pathan, 80, 169, 247
Peacetime RAF, 2, 12-3, 29, 41, 212, 214
Perforated steel plating, 57, 242
Perth, RAF airfield, 7, 16, 18, 24-7, 29, 31-3, 52, 133
Peshawar, 178, 182, 204
Petrol bowser, 124, 242
Photo recce, see *Photographic reconnaissance*
Photographic Interpretation Unit, 40
Photographic reconnaissance, 35, 39-54, 168-9, 242, see also *Spitfires*

Spitfire XI, 58, 243
Spitfire XIX, 57
  run, 243
  sortie, 243, see also *Sorties*
Spitfire, technique, 40, 46
  surveys in India, 88, 93-100
  technique, 41-2
Photography, RAF, oblique, 40-1, 44, 58, 130, 140, 155, 159-60, 167, 236, 241-2, see also *Oblique*
  vertical, 40-2, 51, 58, 124, 128, 130, 136, 139, 148, 159, 169, 176, 242, 245
  camera ports for, 99
Pi-dog, 247
Piggott, Flight Lieutenant, 94, 96, 188
Pilot Officer, promotion to, 36, 38
Pilot's Flying Log Book, xiii, 20, 23, 218, 226, 233
'Pindi, see *Rawalpindi*
Pinpoint, 6, 45, 111, 114-5, 119-20, 122, 132-4, 136-8, 149, 168, 170-2, 177, 193, 199, 202-3, 242
Pishin airfield (deserted), sortie to, 173, 175, 177
Pitch, variable, see *Variable pitch*
Poona, RAF airfield, 126, 134
Port, camera, aircraft camera, see *Camera*
Port Said, 210
Portuguese territory, 133-4
Prang, 145, 192, 242
Pre-flight procedure, 19-20, 32, 110
Precession, 170, 238, 242
Preparation for sorties in India, 110
Pressurization of Spitfire cockpit, 230, 241
Prickly heat, 83, 94
Procedure, pre-flight, 19-20, 32, 110
Promotion, to Flying Officer, 54-5
  to Pilot Officer, 36, 38
Propeller pitch, 30-1, 245
Propeller swinging, 19-20, 28, 243
Prostitutes in Bombay, 136
Prune, Pilot Officer, 34, 237, 242
Puggaree, 77, 247
Pulgaon, sortie to, 111
Punkah, 75, 135, 247
Punkah-wallah, 75, 247

Quetta, 169-70, 172-8
Qutb Minar, 106

**R**AF College, Cranwell, see *Cranwell*
RAF in peacetime, 2, 12-3, 29, 41, 212, 214
Ramganga river, 123, 142
Ranchi, RAF airfield, 129
Range of Homer, see *Homer*
Range of Spitfires, 232, 242
Rats in bed, 129
Rawalpindi, 180, 182-3, 187
Red Sea, 209-10
Rees, Flight Lieutenant Johnny, 93, 108, 119, 208
Requirements for entry to University Short Course, 1-4
Rescue of crashed aircraft, problems, 190
Revs, 243
Riot reconnaissance, 96, 188-9
River, Banas, 120, 138
  Banganga, 119-20
  Betwa, 122
  Chambal, 119-20, 123, 138
  Ganges, 117, 123-4, 142-4
  Gogra, 123
  Indus, 170-2, 178, 202
  Jhelum, 183-4, 184
  Jumna, 107, 122, 143-5, 193, 246
  Khoh, 142-4
  Malir, 203
  Panjnad, 170-1
  Ramganga, 123, 142
  Sabarmati, 132
  Tapti, 138
Roadhog, 110, 203
Robinson, Flight Lieut. 'Robbie', 93
Roger, 110, 203, 243
Rongbuk glacier, 156-7
Royal Air Force Volunteer Reserve, 2, 242
Rpm, 243
R/T, 243
Ruins of Brunswick, 68-9
Run, photo reconnaissance, 41-3, 118, 120-2, 124, 136, 139, 148, 160, 168, 175-6, 183, 243

**S**abarmati river, 132
Sailing in Kashmir, 185-7
Salzgitter gliding course, 66-8, 70
Salt pans, 86
Samungli, RAF airfield, 169-71, 173-5, 177-9, 236
  built-in wind, 174
Sandal, chappal or chappli, 83, 246
Santa Cruz, civilian airfield, 130, 133-4, 136-8, 207
Sari, 78, 247
SBA, 243
Scone, 16, 20, 25
Scotland, flying training in, 16-25, 51
  visit to, 7
Scramble, 110, 243
Search for crashed aircraft, exercise, 188-98
Selection for, accelerated course, 9-11, 29, 38
Selling, flying over, in a Spitfire, 51
  in an Auster, 219
SG 38 (glider), 66-8, 214-5
Shahjahanpur sortie, 111-8
Ship launch, visit to, 7
Shipton, Eric, 162, 165
Shoot a line, 135, 240, 243
Short Course, RAF University, 1-4, 8, 13, 15
Short service commission, 1, 12-3, 36
Shukla, Flight Lieutenant Johnnie, 93-4, 106, 205, 208
Sibi airfield (deserted), 170-3, 177-8
Sind Desert, 76, 202
Skating, ice, 7-8
Snake in bed, 128-9
Snow Survey of Himalaya, 152, 155, 161
Solo, first, see *First solo*
Somervell, T. H., 158
Songs, bawdy, 5, 27
Sortie, photo reconnaissance, 35, 39-54, 168-9, 242
Sorties, first three in India, map of, 115
  from Celle, 56
  in India, 109
  to Agricultural Institute, 109, 139-40
  to Baluchistan, 83, 169-70, 198, 202, 207
  to Cawnpore, 123-5, 149
  to Cuttack, 128
  to Dhulia, 126

# INDEX

to Fyzabad, 123-5
to Hoshangabad, 119-21, 123
to Indore, 119-23, 138
to Kangchenjunga, 148-161
to Kolar Gold Fields, 125
to Korangi Creek, 125
to Lalitpur, 119, 122
to Maddukarai, 125
to Nagpur, 109
to Nellore, 125
to Nimach, 128
to North Salsette, 130, 134, 136-7, 149, 207
to Ootacamunde, 125, 180
to Pishin airfield (deserted), 173, 175, 177
to Pulgaon, 111
to Shahjahanpur, 111-8
to south India, 125-8
to Spezand airfield (deserted), 173, 177-8
to Sylhet, 129
to Vellore, 125
to Zhob Valley Road, 176-7
South Col, 156-9, 166
Speeds, flying, see *Flying speeds*
Spezand airfield (deserted), sortie to, 173, 177-8
Spinning, 21-3, 32
Spitfire photographic reconnaissance, 57-8, 242-3
  course at RAF Benson 39-53
  members of, 40
  technique of, 41-2
Spitfires, 39-53, 243
  cockpit layout, 16-7, 49
  cockpit pressurization, 230, 241
  drop tank, 40, 149-50, 155, 157, 159, 197, 231, 237
  engines, 230
  ferry to Drigh Road, India, 201-4, 206-7
  first flight in, 39-41
  flying speeds, 232-3
  fuel capacity, 231
  fuel consumption, 231
  range, 233
  technical data, 232
  Mark VII, 40, 48, 52-3, 238
  Mark IX, 47-8, 228
  Mark XI, 40, 48, 52, 58, 96-8, 240
    at Palam, 141, 145, 147
  Mark XIV, 57, 60, 62-4, 232-3
  Mark XVI, 69, 167
  Mark XIX, 55, 58-60, 62, 231-3
    at Palam, 95-9, 109, 132, 141-2. 154, 178, 199, 212, 230
    compared with XI, 96-7, 141-2
  problems in hot climate, 98-9
    starting engine, 97
    take-off in, 99
Sport at Cranwell, 37-8
Squadron, No 2, see *Number 2 Squadron*
  No 5, see *Number 5 Squadron*
  No 34 see *Number 34 Squadron*
Srinagar, holiday in, 180-7, 190
  wood-carving factory, 186
Standard Beam Approach, 243
Starboard, 243
Staying in RAF, 29
Stick, 243
Stracathro, RAF Station, 25
Strachan, Bill, 40-1, 53, 71
Suez Canal, 209-11
Sunday Statesman, 152, 161
Surveys, photographic, in India, 88, 93-100
Sweeper, 247
Swimming in India, at Karachi, 82, 86
    at the Chota Club, 91
Swing, 243
Swinging the propeller, 19-20, 28, 243
Sylhet, sortie to, 129

**T**, 22, 132-3, 244
Taj Mahal, 106-7, 123
Tapti river, 138
Target, photo reconnaissance, 41-5, 51-2, 118-9, 122, 124, 129-30, 137-8, 148, 153, 195
Taxi or Taxy, 244
Technical data of Spitfires, 232
T.-E., see *Turner-Ettlinger*
Tee Emm, 34, 242
Tests, Aptitude and Intelligence, 10-11, 65, 205-6
Thar Desert, 76, 144, 170, 198-9, 201-2, 207
Thirty-four Squadron, see *Number 34 Squadron*

Thug(-gee), 247
Thunder-box, 80, 247
Tibet, 142, 153-7, 159-62, 246
Tiger Moth (aircraft), 16-28, 30-2, 35, 39, 58, 60, 66, 133, 235, 237, 239, 244-5
*Times* newspaper, 163-5
Tit, 33, 192, 244
Toc H, 10, 244
Toilets in India, 80, 90
Tonga, 105, 247
Topa, Lower, see *Lower Topa*
Torquay, 8-11, 26, 223, 225
Track, 34, 43-5, 114, 123, 137-8, 171, 179, 202, 244
Trailing edge, 244
Trainer, Link, see *Link Trainer*
Training, Educational and Vocational, see *Educational and Vocational for aircrew*, see *Aircrew*
Trolley-acc, 244
Troopship, m.v. *Georgic,* 208-9
True airspeed, 244
Turner-Ettlinger, Flight Lieut. Derek ('T.-E.'), 93, 130, 135, 190, 193-4, 200, 204, 212
Two Squadron, see *Number 2 Squadron*
Type, 244

**U**daipur, 132
Undercarriage, 30-1, 49, 58-9, 73, 98-9, 216, 244
University Short Course, see *Durham University Short Course*
Untouchables, 76, 79-80, 94, 247
U/S, 244

**V**ariable pitch, 31, 245
Variation, magnetic, 240
V-E Day, 212, 245
Vellore, sortie to, 125
Vertical camera, 245, and see *Camera*
Very Light, 245
Viceroy of India (Mountbatten), 89, 91
  palace of, 104
Viking (aircraft), 88
V-J Day, 29, 245
Vultures, 103

**W**AAF, 53, 245
Wager, L. R., 4
Wallah, 247
War, end of, see *End of*
Wavell, Field-marshal, 89, 91
Westland-Houston Expedition, 158, 167-8
Whitefield landing ground, 18, 23, 27
Wilco, 110, 203, 245
Wildlife around Palam, 102-4
Wind, built-in, at Karachi (Mauripur), 174
  at Samungli, 174
Wing, 9, 14, 245
Wings, awarding of, 36, 245
Wog, 247
Working hours at Palam, 99
Worli, RAF, Bombay, 207-8, 224
Wunstorf, RAF airfield, 131, 212-9
  accidents at, 234
  flights from, 213

**Y**ard, 245
Yelahanka, RAF airfield, 83, 125-7
York (aircraft), 71-4, 89, 112, 245

**Z**emu glacier, 154-5, 160
Zhob Valley Road, sortie to, 176-7